Individuation in
Light of Notions of Form
and Information

CARY WOLFE, *Series Editor*

Individuation in Light of Notions of Form and Information

GILBERT SIMONDON

Translated by Taylor Adkins

posthumanities 57

UNIVERSITY OF MINNESOTA PRESS

MINNEAPOLIS • LONDON

The University of Minnesota Press gratefully acknowledges the work of Drew Burk, consulting editor, in the completion of this project.

Originally published in French as *L'individuation à la lumière des notions de forme et d'information,* copyright Éditions Jerôme Millon, 2005.

Earlier editions of portions of this work appeared in French as *L'Individu et sa genèse physico-biologique,* Presses Universitaires de France, 1964, and *L'Individuation psychique et collective,* copyright Éditions Aubier, 1989.

The publisher acknowledges the work of Arne De Boever, Gregory Flanders, and Alicia Harrison, as well as the contributions of Rositza Alexandrova and Julia Ng, on a prior translation of portions of this work.

This work received support from the French Ministry of Foreign Affairs and the Cultural Services of the French Embassy in the United States through their publishing assistance program.

Published by the University of Minnesota Press
111 Third Avenue South, Suite 290
Minneapolis, MN 55401-2520
http://www.upress.umn.edu

Printed in the United States of America on acid-free paper

The University of Minnesota is an equal-opportunity educator and employer.

27 26 25 24 23 22 21 20   10 9 8 7 6 5 4 3 2 1

Library of Congress Cataloging-in-Publication Data
Names: Simondon, Gilbert, author. | Adkins, Taylor, translator.
Title: Individuation in light of notions of form and information / Gilbert Simondon ; translated by Taylor Adkins.
Other titles: Individuation à la lumière des notions de forme et d'information. English
Description: Minneapolis : University of Minnesota Press, 2020. | Series: Posthumanities; 57
"Originally published in French as L'individuation à la lumière des notions de forme et d'information, copyright Éditions Jerôme Millon, 2005." | Contents: volume 1. [no title given]—volume 2. Supplemental texts. |
Summary: "A long-awaited translation on the philosophical relation between technology, the individual, and milieu of the living" —Provided by publisher.
Identifiers: LCCN 2020013478 | ISBN 978-0-8166-8001-6 (v. 1 ; hc) | ISBN 978-0-8166-8002-3 (v. 1 ; pb) | ISBN 978-1-5179-0951-2 (v. 2 ; hc) | ISBN 978-1-5179-0952-9 (v. 2 ; pb)
Subjects: LCSH: Haecceity (Philosophy) | Individuation (Philosophy) | Individuality. | Ontogeny. | Hylomorphism.
Classification: LCC BD395.5 .S5613 2020 | DDC 111—dc23
LC record available at https://lccn.loc.gov/2020013478

In memory of
Maurice Merleau-Ponty

Contents

VOLUME I

Publisher's Note   xiii

Foreword: *Introduction to the Problematic of Gilbert Simondon*
JACQUES GARELLI   xv

Introduction   1

PART I. PHYSICAL INDIVIDUATION

1. Form and Matter   21

*Foundations of the Hylomorphic Schema: Technology of
Form-Taking*   21

  • The Conditions of Individuation   21

  • Validity of the Hylomorphic Schema; the Dark Zone of the
    Hylomorphic Schema; Generalization of the Notion of
    Form-Taking; Modeling, Molding, Modulation   29

  • Limits of the Hylomorphic Schema   32

Physical Signification of Technical Form-Taking   37

  • Physical Conditions of Technical Form-Taking   37

  • Qualities and Implicit Physical Forms   41

  • Hylomorphic Ambivalence   43

The Two Aspects of Individuation   47

  • Reality and Relativity of the Foundation of Individuation   47

- The Energetic Foundation of Individuation: Individuation and Milieu   51

2. Form and Energy   55

Structures and Potential Energy   55

- The Potential Energy and the Reality of the System; Equivalence of Potential Energies; Dissymmetry and Energetic Exchanges   55
- Different Orders of Potential Energy; Notions of Phase Changes and of the Stable and Metastable Equilibrium of a State. Tammann's Theory   61

Individuation and System States   68

- Individuation and Crystalline Allotropic Forms; Being and Relation   68
- Individuation as the Genesis of Crystalline Forms Starting from an Amorphous State   77
- Epistemological Consequences: Reality of Relation and the Notion of Substance   88

3. Form and Substance   95

Continuous and Discontinuous   95

- Functional Role of Discontinuity   95
- The Antinomy of the Continuous and the Discontinuous   98
- The Analogical Method   100

Particle and Energy   110

- Substantialism and Energeticism   110
- The Deductive Process   112
- The Inductive Process   122

The Non-substantial Individual: Information and Compatibility   126

- Relativistic Conception and the Notion of Physical Individuation   126
- Quantum Theory; Notion of the Elementary Physical Operation That Integrates the Complementary Aspects of the Continuous and the Discontinuous   135

- The Theory of the Double Solution in Wave Mechanics   149
- Topology, Chronology and Order of Magnitude of Physical Individuation   158

PART II. THE INDIVIDUATION OF LIVING BEINGS

1. Information and Ontogenesis: Vital Individuation   167

Principles toward a Study of the Individuation of the Living Being   167

- Information and Vital Individuation; Levels of Organization; Vital Activity and Psychical Activity   167
- Successive Levels of Individuation: Vital, Psychical, Transindividual   177

Specific Form and Living Substance   180

- Insufficiency of the Notion of Specific Form; Notion of the Pure Individual; Non-univocal Nature of the Notion of the Individual   180
- The Individual as Polarity; Functions of Internal Genesis and of External Genesis   185
- Individuation and Reproduction   188
- Undifferentiation and Dedifferentation as Conditions of Reproductive Individuality   199

Information and Vital Individuation   208

- Individuation and Regimes of Information   208
- Regimes of Information and Rapports between Individuals   215
- Individuation, Information, and the Structure of the Individual   221

Information and Ontogenesis   225

- Notion of an Ontogenetic Problematic   225
- Individuation and Adaptation   231
- Limits of the Individuation of the Living. Central Characteristic of the Being. Nature of the Collective   236
- From Information to Signification   244
- Topology and Ontogenesis   250

2. Psychical Individuation   257

Signification and the Individuation of Perceptive Units   257

- Segregation of Perceptive Units; the Genetic Theory and the Theory of Holistic Grasping; Determinism of Good Form   257

- Psychical Tension and Degrees of Metastability. Good Form and Geometrical Form; the Different Types of Equilibrium   260

- Relation between the Segregation of Perceptive Units and the Other Types of Individuation. Metastability and Information Theory in Technology and Psychology   261

- Introduction of the Notion of Quantum Variation into the Representation of Psychical Individuation   264

- The Perceptive Problematic; Quantity of Information, Quality of Information, Intensity of Information   265

Individuation and Affectivity   272

- Consciousness and Individuation; the Quantum Nature of Consciousness   272

- Signification of Affective Subconsciousness   273

- Affectivity in Communication and Expression   274

- The Transindividual   277

- Anxiety   282

- The Affective Problematic: Affection and Emotion   285

Psychical Individuation and the Problematic of Ontogenesis   291

- Signification as Criterion of Individuation   291

- The Relation to the Milieu   295

- Individuation, Individualization, and Personalization. Bi-substantialism   296

- Insufficiency of the Notion of Adaptation to Explain Psychical Individuation   304

- The Problematic of Reflexivity in Individuation   308

- The Necessity of Psychical Ontogenesis   319

3. Collective Individuation and the Foundations of the Transindividual   327

The Individual and the Social, Group Individuation   327

  • Social Time and Individual Time   327

  • Interiority Groups and Exteriority Groups   328

  • Social Reality as a System of Relations   330

  • Insufficiency of the Notion of the Essence of Man and of
Anthropology   332

  • Notion of Group Individual   334

  • Role of Belief in the Group Individual   335

  • Group Individuation and Vital Individuation   336

  • Pre-individual Reality and Spiritual Reality: The Phases
of Being   341

The Collective as Condition of Signification   344

  • Subjectivity and Signification; the Transindividual
Character of Signification   344

  • Subject and Individual   348

  • The Empirical and the Transcendental. Ontogenesis and
Pre-critical Ontology. The Collective as Signification
That Overcomes a Disparation   349

  • The Central Operational Zone of the Transindividual:
Theory of Emotion   350

Conclusion   356

Notes   381

Bibliography   397

VOLUME II: SUPPLEMENTAL TEXTS

Publisher's Note   xiii

Complementary Note on the Consequences of the Notion of
Individuatio   401

1. Values and the Search for Objectivity   403

  Relative Values and Absolute Values   403

  *The Dark Zone between the Substantialism of the
Individual and Integration into the Group*   405

The Problematic of and Search for Compatibility 407

Conscience and Ethical Individuation 408

Ethics and the Process of Individuation 409

2. Individuation and Invention 412

The Technician as Pure Individual 412

The Technical Operation as a Condition of Individuation.
Invention and Autonomy; Community and Technical
Transindividual Relation 413

Individuation of the Products of Human Effort 418

The Individuating Attitude in the Human Relation to the
Invented Technical Being 423

Allagmatic Nature of the Individuated Technical Object 428

History of the Notion of the Individual 435

SUPPLEMENTS

Analysis of the Criteria of Individuality 655

Allagmatics 663

Form, Information, and Potentials 674

Notes 701

Publisher's Note

This first English-language translation of Gilbert Simondon's magnum opus *Individuation in Light of Notions of Form and Information* follows the comprehensive, authorized edition published in France by Éditions Millon in 2013. Unlike the earlier 1964 Presses Universitaires de France and 1989 Aubier editions, which divided the thesis into two separate works, the text is presented here in its complete and intended order. The complete doctoral thesis appears in its entirety as volume 1 of this two-volume edition. Both those familiar with Simondon as well as newcomers to his work will find that the more recent Millon edition also includes valuable research notes, lectures, drafts, and related texts that provide a unique insight into the author's thinking process; these supplemental texts appear as volume 2 of this edition.

The publisher would like to thank Nathalie Simondon and Dominique Simondon for their guidance and generous cooperation in making this integral work of contemporary thought available to English-language readers.

Foreword

Introduction to the Problematic of Gilbert Simondon

JACQUES GARELLI

THE PHILOSOPHICAL AND SCIENTIFIC HORIZON
OF THE METHOD

If it has been noted that this work is paradoxically situated at the confluence of a meditation inspired by the Ionian physiologists on the notion of *Physis,* Anaximander's thought on the unlimited (ἄπειρον) [ápeiron], Plato's thought on the One and the indefinite dyad of the Large and Small (such as this principle particularly appears in the discussions of books *M* and *N* of Aristotle's *Metaphysics*), the critique of the Aristotelian and substantialistic, atomistic, hylomorphic principle of Leucippus and Democritus and, moreover, the most recent theories of thermodynamics, quantum physics, and information,[1] it has rarely been emphasized that *The Individual and Its Physico-biological Genesis* was dedicated "in memory of Maurice Merleau-Ponty." This is an essential guiding thread, at least if the "memory" implies recognition and is therefore faithful in its recollection. Of what? Of the Merleau-Pontian thought of the pre-individual in its ties to individualizing formations, of its invitation to contemplate the pre-Socratic thought of the "element," of its critique of Gestalt theory, of hylomorphic dualism and symmetrically of the materialist atomism developed by several currents of contemporary psychology, and lastly, of a radical critique of Nothingness and the dialectic, in the sense that this notion and this procedure manifest a sort of reverse positivism of negation that steers philosophy away from the pre-individual dimension of the World.

Furthermore, on the methodological plane there is an attitude shared by Merleau-Pontian phenomenology and the epistemology of microphysics, such as it is stated in Niels Bohr and Werner Heisenberg, according to which we cannot radically separate the scientific "object" discovered at the end of research from the path of the thought and the operative processes that have led to revealing and constructing it. This attitude is developed with an extreme originality and a personal inflection due to the Simondonian conception of transduction and information that we will have to carefully examine. Moreover, it seems difficult to perceive the problematic of Gilbert Simondon which, among other things, poses the question *On the Mode of Existence of Technical Objects*[2] as a renewed form of physicalism. The dedication to Merleau-Ponty would therefore make such a positivist attitude of this style rather unexpected.

On the contrary, what Gilbert Simondon invites us to contemplate and remodel according to a radically new perspective is the strange relation between the pre-Socratic thought of the "Unlimited" and of the "element," on the one hand, and that of the Merleau-Pontian style of pre-individual Being in its processes of individuation, which are linked (and this is the very paradox and barely understood originality of Gilbert Simondon) to the thermodynamic conception of metastable systems that are irreducible to the order of identity, unity, and alterity. Such are the stakes of this work whose force of invention prohibits any attempt seeking to isolate it in a current of thought that would form a school.

If phenomenology can glean something of interest from this meditation, it would be through the questions posed to it, through the course, pathways, bifurcations, and modes of problematization that Simondon's meditation deploys on the horizon of the very questions inherent to the phenomenological enterprise. Furthermore, it is on behalf of the central question of the pre-individual, in its processes of individuations, that we are attempting to grasp the legitimacy of the notions of metastable system, potential, and energetic tensions (of transductivity and information) in a thought of the pre-individuality of being.

REEVALUATION OF CLASSICAL CONCEPTS AND MODES OF THOUGHT: CRITIQUE OF THE PRINCIPLE OF INDIVIDUATION

In a note from February 1960, Merleau-Ponty writes:

> But what is fine is the idea of taking literally the *Erwirken* of thought: it is really *empty*, is of the *invisible*—All the positivist bric-a-brac of "concepts," "judgements," "relations" is eliminated, and the mind wells up as water in the fissure of Being—We must not look for spiritual things, there

are only structures of the void—But I simply wish to plant this void in the visible Being, show that it is its *reverse side*—in particular the reverse side of language.[3]

Gilbert Simondon's critique of the principle of individuation—whose corollaries are those of form, matter, substance, and fixed and stable (autonomous) terms posited as realities-in-themselves that form the structure of the World, relations, and inductive and deductive judgments—proceeds in the same critical style as the one recommended by Merleau-Ponty.[4]

In fact, this mutual appeal of Merleau-Ponty and Gilbert Simondon to the radical recasting of philosophical concepts will be articulated through the conscious apprehension of a tightly conjoined movement of being and of thought, a movement which generates the complex processes of individuations that arise from a transindividual dimension of being.

The striking simplicity of Gilbert Simondon's demonstration—from the very first lines of his doctoral thesis—should not make us forget all the preparatory work that stems from a profound meditation on the Ionian physiologists[5] as well as the thought of Plato and Aristotle. Thus, the conclusion of a long historical meditation followed up by years of teaching and reflection is what leads to the introduction of the present work: what is the crux of the argument?

THE UNQUESTIONED PRESUPPOSITIONS OF THE PRINCIPLE OF INDIVIDUATION

The first presupposition has an ontological characteristic in the sense in which takes for granted that the individual is the essential reality to be explained.[6] This conviction comes from the primacy accorded by Aristotle to the Individual, the σύνολον [súnolon], regarding the question of Being qua Being. As Simondon asks, why should Being in its totality end up integrally in a multiplicity of individualities to be known? Why would the being, as such, not include a pre-individual dimension? Correlatively, why would the individual, such as it appears, not conserve a dimension of pre-individuality in its dimension of being, which would be somewhat associated and irreducible to what can be thought in terms of the "individual"? This is a dimension that would never cease to intervene in the formation and evolution of the individual, which, afterwards, takes on a twofold, relative value: with respect to pre-individual being (from which it proceeds without eliminating) and with respect to itself, insofar as the individual conserves an associated

pre-individual dimension that never stops modeling its future individualizations. If this were the case, the whole quest for the principle of individuation
and the very idea of this principle would have to be reformed.

Indeed, we should recall that Duns Scotus writes his treatise *On the Principle of Individuation* concerning a theological problem, that of "the distinction between angels and persons." This work involves a problematic that
develops within the framework of a metaphysical discussion that is subor-
dinated to Aristotelian logic and guided by hylomorphic dualism and the
theory of four causes. Thus, starting from "Question I" of *Ordinatio* II, distinction 3, part I, which is entitled "Whether material substance is individual or singular of itself, i.e. from its nature," Duns Scotus expresses himself
in the following terms:

> As to the third distinction one must ask about the distinction of persons
> in angels. But to get a view of this distinction in angels one must first
> inquire about the distinction of individuals in material substances; and
> just as different people speak differently about these distinctions, so they
> speak in different ways about the plurality of individuals in the same spe-
> cies of angels.[7]

However, the second question manifests the substantialistic origin of the
discussion in the objection that Aristotle addresses to Plato. It is stated in
these terms:

> For the affirmative: In book VII of the *Metaphysics*, philosophy established
> against Plato that "the substance of each thing belongs to that of which it is
> substance and does not belong to anything else."[8]

The logical and metaphysical processes of the discussion along with the
thought of substance (which is never called into question) need to be critiqued for the problem of individuation to be posed.

The second unquestioned presupposition is that individuation has a principle that would be anterior to it and would allow for the formation of the
singular individual to be explained. The fact that this three-dimensional
hierarchical structure (the individual, individuation, principle of individuation) is polarized by an unquestioned ontological privilege granted to the
individual (which constitutes the ultimate finality of research) is aggravated
by the fact that the quest for the principle of individuation as such derives

from a paralogism that crystallizes into the twofold nature bestowed upon the principle. In this sense, two historical attitudes pursue this false path. The first, which is substantialist, atomist, and monist, discovers in the atom of Leucippus and Democritus the absolute elementary principle that allows for an explanation of the formation of the individual and of the individuated universe. The theory of the clinamen in Epicurus explains the fortuitous formation of more complex individuated structures based on the unitary atom. Despite the caveats of Bohr and Heisenberg, modern atomistic materialisms that continue to conceive of quantum particles as infinitesimal first substances with an autonomous reality qua formation of matter follow the path of this same illusion.[9] The paralogism consists in conferring onto the already individuated atom the status of a principle that is supposed to explain the very formation of the individual as such. In other words, and in a contradictory way, the individual is elevated to an object of research while also being taken as a principle of its own explanation. But the dualistic hylomorphic attitude of the Aristotelian style hardly escapes from the same contradiction, since *the* form and *the* matter, insofar as they are conditions and principles of the formation of the σύνολον [súnolon], are in fact treated as unitary terms, already individuated "causes." However, it is not enough to explain that it is exclusively by abstraction and *a posteriori* that these principles can be extracted from the single concrete reality that the σύνολον [súnolon] is, for, on the one hand, they are elevated to supreme and therefore principal and primary metaphysical causes. But, on the other hand, Gilbert Simondon's novelty is to demonstrate—through concrete examples borrowed from the formation of natural individualities, such as islands in a river, sand dunes under the pressure of the wind, ravines hollowed out by water streams, and the formation of crystals, but also through technological examples, like the fabrication of a brick or the cutting of a tree trunk—that the formation of a natural or technical individual never ends up in the application of *a* form to *a* matter. The hylomorphic schema certainly leaves out the energetic conditions of form-taking—which reside in the already deposited energetic conditions in the structure of matter—that natural conditions due to chance or manpower can unleash, orient, and channel in the formation of an individual. Conversely, at the end of the half-chain of form-taking, there is no structuring form that does not depend on a certain material structure of the form that allows for the potential energy included in the form to structure matter. This is an extremely complex problem that renders the hylomorphic principle of individuation obsolete. However, on the plane of artistic creation, i.e. the formation of material individualities which, through the assemblage of their structure, provoke thought, it can be shown that the formation of a poem (which in its individuality is irreducible to another poem), the formation of a painting, or the formation of a statue never involves a monistic or hylomorphic principle of individuation. But it does involve a process of differentiation that develops from a field of pre-individual tensions and constitutes the metastable horizon of the World of the work. Thus, the quest for the hylomorphic principle of individuation (be it atomistic, substantialistic, or dualistic) is led to the contradiction of seeking—within the individual already formed in atoms or particularized according to the fixed terms of a form and of a matter raised into causes— what would precisely have had to explain the formation of the individual as such. This situation leads Simondon to pose the following questions:

Can individuation be conceived as without-principle, since it is itself a process intrinsic to the formations of individuals, which are never completed, never fixed, never stable, but always accomplishing in their evolution an individuation that structures them, without these individuals fully eliminating the associated charge of pre-individuality that constitutes the horizon of transindividual Being from which they stand out?

METHODOLOGICAL CONSEQUENCES OF THIS DISPUTE

Such is the radical novelty of Gilbert Simondon's problematic, which will allow us to conceive in terms of transduction the processes of differentiations that are deployed starting from a metastable pre-individual system, wrought with tensions, of which the individual is one of the phases of deployment. It's in this context that the notions of potential charge, oriented tensions, supersaturation, and phase-shift, borrowed from thermodynamics, and the notion of the resonance internal to systems, intervene. According to this perspective, instead of reducing ontogenesis to the dimension restricted to and derived from the genesis of the individual, it is a question of conferring onto it the vaster characteristic of the "becoming of being, that through which the being becomes insofar as it is, qua being."[10] The ontological dimension of the problem is reinforced in the care with which Simondon emphasizes the incompetence of the principle of identity and of the excluded middle, formed in a perspective of substantialist and identitarian logic of the individuated being in order to deal with the problematic of pre-individuated being. This is why Gilbert Simondon can declare:

Unity, which is characteristic of the individuated being, and identity, which authorizes the usage of the principle of the excluded middle, do not apply to pre-individual being, which explains why the world cannot be recomposed after the fact with monads, even by adding other principles like sufficient reason in order to organize these monads into a universe.[11]

This reference to Leibniz, as well as references to the pre-Socratic philosophers and to Plato and Aristotle, attest to the philosophical breadth of the debate that is irreducible to a strictly physicalist attitude. Not only does Gilbert Simondon justify the philosophical usage of notions borrowed from thermodynamics as part of a paradigm shift, he deftly accounts for the historical methodological reasons that have boxed the Ancients into alternative trenches, established between being and becoming, movement and rest, substantial stability and chaotic instability.[12]

However, three givens intervene in the comprehension of the metastable equilibrium with which thermodynamics has familiarized us and which Simondon introduces into his problematic in a very original way.

First, we must consider the potential energy of a system.

Second, we must consider the notion of order of magnitude and of different scales within the system.

Third, we must consider the increase of entropy, which corresponds to the energetic degradation of the system and implies the resolution of initial potentialities. Thus, the apprehension of individualizing forms is a correlate of the progressive degradation of potential energy. A so-called completed form, which is a stabilized energy, corresponds to the highest degree of negentropy.

Guided by this paradigm, which is borrowed from thermodynamics and not from the physics of fixed substances that ignores the problems of energy (as the concepts of classical philosophy confirm, particularly with the idea of *res extensa*), Simondon will attempt to think the order of a being's preindividuality in terms of supersaturated potential charges within a metastable system, on the basis of which the degradation of energy sequential to a state of overtension of the system will produce processes of differentiations and individuations. Thus, it is by phase-shifting that a metastable system charged with a supersatured energetic potential individualizes while also simultaneously spouting—from its not-yet-individualized internal tensions—a profusion of individualizing forms, which, afterwards, are capable of being structured into further systems and reforming into new metastable equilibria. Consequently, according to Simondon's expression:

... every operation and every relation within an operation is an individuation that splits and phase-shifts pre-individual being, all while correlating the extreme values and orders of magnitude, which are initially without mediation.[13]

This is a situation that confers onto relations a charge of being that exceeds and overflows the order of strictly logical knowledge and significations. And it allows us to avoid the dualism between the act of abstract intellectual knowledge and the inert objects on which the cognitive act bears.

How is this pitfall avoided?

First, by conferring a dimension of being onto the relations traditionally treated in strictly logical terms, as can be seen at work in the classical theories of deduction and induction.

Second, by treating the operation of transduction in conjunction with that of individualizing form-taking, which manifests the passage from the pre-individual metastable field to individuations in formation. Let's examine the first point. The relations between the fields of extreme tensions of the metastable system charged with potentiality have the status of being, to the extent that the differential values between what can no longer be qualified by preexisting terms are not yet individualized but correspond to the "dimensions" and "scales of tensions" from which the resolving energy of the system emerges. According to this perspective:

> Relation does not spring forth between two terms that would already be individuals; relation is an aspect of the *internal resonance of a system of individuation*; it belongs to a system state. This living being, which is both more and less than unity, conveys *an interior problematic* and *can enter as an element into a problematic that is vaster than its own being*. For the individual, participation is *the fact of being an element in a vaster individuation* through the intermediary of the *charge of pre-individual reality that the individual contains*, i.e. due to the potentials that it harbors.[14] (Simondon's emphasis)

According to the second point, transduction, in strict solidarity with the discharge of the supersaturated potential energy of a metastable system, will appear as a form-taking and, on this basis, in the conjoined, twofold topological and noetic sense, as "in-formation." Since, through the very movement in which a process of transduction—the correlate of the discharge of pre-individual potential energy of a metastable system—topologically "in-forms" a structure, which is given to be witnessed and to be thought, we can see that it noetically "informs" about what it makes appear and according to its associated pre-individual charge, i.e. the horizon of pre-individual being from which it detaches. This is why transduction (in contrast with induction and deduction, which do not have the status of being but are strictly logical relations exterior to the preexisting terms that they link up) manifests as never exterior to the terms that it brings forth, according to a twofold dimension of thought and of being. As an individualizing movement of knowledge, but also a movement of being, transduction is a form-taking in conjunction with the energetic discharge of the metastable system that is revealed as being more than unity and more than identity. On this basis:

> Transduction is therefore not merely the reasoning of the mind; it is also intuition, because it is that through which a structure appears in a domain of a problematic as providing the resolution to the problems posed. But contrary to *deduction,* transduction does not go elsewhere to seek a principle to resolve the problem of a domain: it extracts the resolving structure from the very tensions of this domain, just as the supersaturated solution crystallizes due to its own potentials and according to the chemical nature that it holds, not with the contribution of some foreign form. . . . [T]rans-duction is a discovery of dimensions whose system makes the dimensions of each of the terms communicate, such that the complete reality of each of the terms of the domain can become organized into newly discovered structures without loss or reduction.[15]

Furthermore, the good form is not the stabilized, fixed form that Gestalt theory believed to locate, but the form rich in energetic potential, charged with future transductions. The good form does not stop making us think, and, in this sense, it does not stop generating further individuations, to the extent that it allows us to anticipate future individuations. Therefore, the information borne out of transductive movements is no longer conceived as the transmission of an already coded and established message sent by an emitter and transmitted to a receiver, but as form-taking: this is topological information, which, on the basis of a field wrought with the pre-individual tensions of the very movement in which the form is individualized, informs in the noetic sense the same thing as what appears topologically and from which it detaches. This is a "timeline," a "Worldline," which points toward a pre-individuality of being and which is the source and the origin of the latter. In this sense, information is a "theater of individuations." This involves a situation that cannot be understood except within the framework of the passage of an energetic problematic of metastable states to states in the process of stabilization, which, afterwards, are in a state of resolution, but also of energetic impoverishment, just as volcanic rocks, in the splendor of their individual forms, manifest the energetic death of an anterior lava flow. Furthermore, the pure form—the good form of Gestalt theory—is a stabilized energy that has arrived at the end of all its processes of individuation and transformation. The same can be said of the pure and completed pictorial form, which is outlined in the horizon of the quasi-illegible muddle of anterior sketches, such as the admirable preparatory designs of drafters that allow the quill to run, forming the pre-individual matrix for future beginnings. On this basis, the design is a metastable field wrought with tensions from which progressively emerge the lines in which the individuating forms stabilize. Nonetheless, these forms will be able to again become energetic capacity if they are paired with other forms and if they are integrated into a more complex structure in which they will compose as energetic potential into phases of tensions and a quest for resolution. The act of the painter in direct grips with this field of colored and linear metastability is a theater of individuations.

Such is the situation, for example, of a fragment of a bust photographed in a "collage," which in itself possesses a fixed form of a fragment of stable reality, indexed and defined by a name, but which, once it is integrated into the new "system," takes on a value of a potential charge whose enigmatic dimension is relative to the metastable whole of the composition. However, in this metastable system in a phase of internal resonance, it is the enigmatic characteristic of form-taking introduced by a foreign element that remodels the whole by making questions emerge. This is what indicates that questioning is crossed chiasmically on the meta-unitary structure of the composition, charged with a potential for inexhaustible forms and meanings.[16] Thus, form-taking in the topological sense of the term, through its structural metastability charged with unresolved tensions, reveals topological "information" and noetic "information" tightly interwoven and held in an overlapping chiasmus.[17]

Moreover, Gilbert Simondon's meditation focuses on the non-identitarian World, where individuations always reflect an underlying field of pre-individuality that is most often unapparent or forgotten. And it is precisely this inexhaustible enigma that Simondon attempts to contemplate.

The Crisis of Understanding in the Physical Sciences and Its Consequences in the Philosophical Conception of Beings

Nonetheless, an interrogation remains concerning the usage of theories borrowed from thermodynamics and quantum physics in the philosophical problematic of the pre-individual and the contemporary conception of beings. Without discussing the properly technical aspect of the problem, it is nevertheless necessary to recall the complexity of the debate, and it is important to reflect on the exemplary prudence of Niels Bohr and Werner Heisenberg each time they have tackled the question concerning the philosophical status (but which could also be called the "mode of being") of the quantum particle. This question of ontological consequence was central to the meditations of these physicists. It is also worth recalling the end of the conversation between these two scientists, which concerns the notion of *"Understanding" in Modern Physics.*[18] This is a problem that is also our own, not just as soon as the question of beings is posed, but also as soon as the philosopher—acknowledging that the dominant state of nature is not matter but energy—calls into question the capacity of our mind to "understand" the components of this phenomenon.

Thus, the pressing question formulated by Heisenberg:

> If the inner structure of the atom is as closed to descriptive accounts as you say, if we really lack a language for dealing with it, how can we ever hope to understand atoms?

Bohr hesitated a moment, as Heisenberg reports, then said:

> I think we may yet be able to do so. But in the process we may have to learn what the word "understanding" really means.[19]

It is by having this attitude of circumspection present to the mind that we can attempt to evaluate it, and this attitude is no less prudent in Simondon when he refers to the theory of quanta and to the possible usage of wave mechanics in the clarification of the pre-individual problematic. The crisis of meaning that has shaken the scientific and philosophical problematic of the twentieth century cannot avoid these questions.

Thus, after having contested mechanism and energeticism, which remain theories of identity that cannot on this basis completely account for reality,[20]

Simondon notes the insufficient nature of the theory of fields added to the theory of corpuscles, just like the conception of the interaction between fields and particles, due to the fact that these attitudes remain partially dualistic. Nevertheless, according to Simondon, they allow us to regain our bearings toward a renewed theory of the pre-individual.[21]

Here, we find Simondon returning to the theses that Bohr elaborated regarding the complementarity of the theory of quanta and of wave mechanics and where Simondon, via a new path of exploration, tries to "see the convergence of these two new theories, that of quanta and that of wave mechanics, which to this very day have remained impenetrable to one another."[22]

In fact, it is a question of envisioning these two theories as "*two ways of expressing the pre-individual* through the different manifestations in which it intervenes as pre-individual."[23]

According to this methodological approach, Simondon notes:

> By way of another path, the theory of quanta grasps *this regime of the pre-individual* that surpasses unity: an exchange of energy occurs through elementary quantities, as if there were an individuation of energy in the relation between particles, which can in a sense be considered as physical individuals.[24]

It is in the framework of this hypothesis integrated into what he calls "an analogical philosophy of the 'as if'" that this philosopher proposes to conceive, below the order of the continuous and the discontinuous, "the quantic and the metastable complementary (the more than unity), which is the true pre-individual."[25]

Reflecting on the necessity in which physics is found to correct and pair together basic concepts, Simondon suggests the hypothesis according to which this necessity "perhaps translates the fact that *concepts are adequate only to individuated reality* and not to pre-individual reality."[26] If this is taken into account, no positive physical certainty can give an objective solution to a philosophical problem, such as the one posed by the pre-individual dimension of a primordial "there is," from which will be released, afterwards, a detailed problematic of beings in the phase of individuation, precisely because the act of "understanding" is crossed chiasmically over the physical field and because this conjoined structure of being and knowledge poses a philosophical problem that exceeds through its interlinked structure of "chiasmus" a simple problem of a positive style, whatever the timeframe of the envisioned scientific theory may be.

It is thanks to this framework of thought that the reevaluation of the principle of complementarity stated by Niels Bohr and the signification to be granted to the twofold approach of the physics of corpuscles and wave mechanics—such as Louis de Broglie reformulated it at the end of his life after his simplified presentation to the Solvay Conference in 1927, which had been critiqued by the founders of quantum physics—are presented in a new light. On this basis, Simondon suggests, in addition to the reevaluation of Niels Bohr's principle of complementarity, an original interpretation of Heisenberg's uncertainty principle as well as a reevaluation of the introduction of statistical calculus into the mathematical formulation of this principle.[27] It is in this framework of reform that Simondon presents his conception of transduction as the effort of thinking, in one and the same unity, "the object" of research and the movement of knowledge that drives it.

Afterwards, taking into account this reform of method, the question that immediately arises is knowing whether the distinction posited by Heisenberg between the effective reality of the quantum particle and the knowledge the physicist has of it, does not appear as tainted with a dualism that would be controlled by the methodological privilege granted to the individual unit of the quantum particle initially considered as the "reality" to be explained, whereas it perhaps only appears as a possible process of individuation coming from a pre-individuality that would be in a relation of discontinuity relative to the field of its manifestation.

Such are the philosophical and not just epistemological stakes of Gilbert Simondon's questioning. In fact, this non-identitarian conception of beings, which must be returned to a field of primordial metastability, exceeds the framework of a subatomic physics or a problematic of the technical object and of vital individuation.[28] This conception is established following three different axes of research, (1) through the perception of the thing in the world, (2) through the question of artistic creation in its entirety, (3) through the timeless conception of ontological difference, as long as the question of Being, as Heidegger teaches, remains that of the Being of beings.[29]

However, the non-identitarian dimension of beings, in regard to which ontological difference is marked, prevents us from posing this question according to the terms used by Heidegger in each of his works.[30] For what this philosopher took as an individual reality (with a fixed and stable unitary nature) of "intraworldly" beings is immediately revealed as a non-being, non-*ens*, "no-thing." This is what unexpectedly introduces the problematic of Nothingness at the very heart of the structure of beings, which, afterwards, are no longer beings! This is a paradox that requires surpassing the question of ontological difference such as Heidegger conceived it.[31]

Thus, a whole field of contemporary philosophical research is invited to fundamentally renew the mode of questioning of the thing in its relation to the pre-individuality of the world. Beyond the strictly epistemological character of his undertaking, not the least of Gilbert Simondon's merits was to have drawn philosophical attention to this paradigm shift in thought.

Introduction

There are two paths according to which the reality of being qua individual can be approached: a substantialist path, which considers the being as consisting in its unity, given to itself, founded on itself, not engendered and as resistant to what is not itself; and then there is a hylomorphic path, which considers the individual as generated by the encounter of a form and a matter. The self-centered monism of substantialistic thought is opposed to the bipolarity of the hylomorphic schema. Yet both of these two ways of approaching the reality of the individual have something in common: both suppose that there is a principle of individuation prior to individuation itself that is capable of explaining, producing, and guiding it. We are prompted to revisit the conditions of the individual's existence starting from the constituted and given individual. This manner of posing the problem of individuation based on the acknowledgment of the existence of individuals conceals a presupposition that must be clarified, since it involves an important aspect of the solutions that are proposed and embedded in the search for the principle of individuation: namely the fact that the individual qua constituted individual is the interesting reality, i.e. the reality to be explained. The principle of individuation will be sought as a principle that is capable of accounting for the characteristics of the individual without a necessary relation with the other aspects of the being that could be correlative to the appearance of a real individuated entity. *Such a perspective of research grants an ontological privilege to the constituted individual.* Thus, it runs the risk of not actualizing a veritable ontogenesis that would put the individual back into the system of reality within which individuation takes place. *One of the postulates in the search for the principle of individuation is that individuation has a principle.* In the very notion of this principle, there is a certain characteristic that foreshadows the constituted individuality along with the properties that it will have when it will be constituted; to a certain extent, the notion of a *principle of individuation* emerges from a genesis in reverse, an *inverted* ontogenesis: to account for the genesis of the individual with its definitive characteristics, we must suppose the existence of a first term, the principle, which contains within it the very explanation for what is individual in the individual, thereby accounting for its haecceity. But we would precisely have to show that ontogenesis can have a first term as an initial condition: a term is already an individual or at the very least something that can be individualized and can be a source of haecceity or fabricated into multiple haecceities; everything that can be a support of relation already shares the same mode of being as the individual, whether this be the atom, the eternal and indivisible particle, the first matter, or the form: the atom can enter into a relation with other atoms via the *clinamen,* thereby constituting an individual (be it viable or not) through the infinite void and endless becoming. Matter can receive a form and establish ontogenesis in this matter-form relation. If there were not a certain inherence of the haecceity to the atom, to matter, or even to form, there wouldn't be the possibility of finding a principle of individuation in these invoked realities. *To seek the principle of individuation in a reality that precedes individuation itself is to consider individuation strictly as ontogenesis.* The principle of individuation is then the source of haecceity. Both atomistic substantialism and the hylomorphic doctrine *de facto* avoid the direct description of ontogenesis itself; *atomism* describes the genesis of the composite, like the living body, which merely has a precarious and perishable unity that stems from a random encounter and will dissolve back into its elements when a force greater than the force of cohesion will attack it in its composite unity. The forces of cohesion themselves, which could be considered the composite individual's principle of individuation, are thrust back into the structure of the elementary particles, which exist eternally and are the veritable individuals; in atomism, the principle of individuation is the very existence of the infinity of atoms: it is always already there the moment when thought can become conscious of its nature: individuation is a fact; individuation, for each atom, is the atom's own given existence and, for each composite, the fact that the composite is what it is by virtue of a random encounter. Conversely, according to *the hylomorphic schema,* when we consider the matter and form that will become the σύνολον [súnolon],[1] the individuated being is not already given: we do not observe ontogenesis because we are always situated ahead of this form-taking that ontogenesis is; the principle of individuation therefore is not grasped in the individuation itself as an operation but in what this operation requires in order to exist, namely a matter and a form: the principle is supposed to be contained either in the matter or in the form, since the operation of individuation is not supposed to be capable of *supplying* the principle itself but only of *putting it to work*. The search for the principle of individuation is finished either after individuation or before individuation, depending on whether the model of the individual is physical (for substantialistic atomism) or technological (for the hylomorphic schema). But in both cases, there is *a dark zone* that conceals the operation of individuation. This operation should be considered as something to be explained and not that in which the explanation must be found: hence the notion of the principle of individuation is to be explained, because thought is taken towards the completed individuated being for which it is necessary to account by passing through the stage of individuation so as to end up with the individual after this operation. There is thus a supposition of the existence of a temporal succession: first the principle of individuation exists; then this principle operates in an operation of individuation; and then the constituted individual appears. If, on the contrary, we supposed that individuation doesn't just produce the individual, we would not seek to pass quickly through the stage of individuation to arrive at this ultimate reality that the individual is: we would try to grasp ontogenesis in the whole unfolding of its reality and *to know the individual through individuation rather than individuation starting from the individual.*

We would like to show that it is necessary to reverse the search for the principle of individuation by considering the operation of individuation as primordial, on the basis of which the individual comes to exist and the unfolding regimes and modalities of which the individual reflects in its characteristics. The individual would then be grasped as a relative reality, a certain phase of being which supposes a pre-individual reality prior to it and which, even after individuation, does not fully exist all by itself, for individuation does not exhaust in a single stroke the potentials of pre-individual reality, and, moreover, what individuation manifests is not merely the individual but the individual-milieu coupling.[2] The individual is therefore relative in two senses: because it is not the entire being, and because it results from a state of the being in which it neither existed as individual nor as principle of individuation.

Individuation is thus considered ontogenetic only insofar as it is an operation of the complete being. Individuation must then be considered as a partial and relative resolution that manifests in a system which contains potentials and includes a certain incompatibility with respect to itself, an incompatibility that consists of forces of tension and the impossibility of an interaction between the extreme terms of the dimensions.

The word *ontogenesis* takes on its full meaning if, instead of granting it the restricted and derived sense of the individual's genesis (in opposition to a vaster genesis, for example that of the species), it is made to designate the nature of the being's becoming, that through which the being becomes insofar as it is, qua being. It is possible that the opposition of being and becoming may be valid only within a certain doctrine that supposes that the very model of being is substance. But it is also possible to suppose that becoming is a dimension of the being and corresponds to the being's capacity to phase-shift with respect to itself, to resolve itself by phase-shifting; *pre-individual being is being in which no phase exists*; the being in which an individuation is completed is that in which a resolution appears through the division of the being into phases, i.e. becoming; becoming is not a framework in which the being exists; it is the being's dimension, the mode of resolution of an incompatibility that is rich in potentials.[3] *Individuation corresponds to the appearance of phases in the being that are the phases of the being*; it is not an isolated consequence deposited on the edge of becoming but this very operation as it is undergoing completion; individuation can only be understood on the basis of this initial and homogeneous supersaturation of the being without becoming that afterwards is structured and becomes, making the individual and milieu appear according to becoming, which is a resolution of the initial tensions and a conservation of these tensions as a structure; in a certain sense, it could be said that the sole principle we can be guided is *that of the conservation of being through becoming*; there is conservation of being through becoming all throughout the exchanges between structure and operation, proceeding by way of quantum leaps via successive equilibria. In order to think individuation, we must consider being not as substance or matter or form, but as a tense, supersaturated system above the level of unity, as not merely consisting in itself, and as unable to be thought adequately by means of the principle of the excluded middle; the concrete being or complete being, i.e. pre-individual being, is a being that is more than a unity. Unity, which is characteristic of the individuated being, and identity, which authorizes the usage of the principle of the excluded middle, do not apply to pre-individual being, which explains why the world cannot be recomposed after the fact with monads, even by adding other principles like sufficient reason in order to organize these monads into a universe; unity and identity merely apply to one of the phases of being, posterior to the operation of individuation; these notions cannot help us discover the principle of individuation; they do not apply to ontogenesis understood in the full sense of the term, i.e. to the becoming of the being qua being which splits and phase-shifts while individuating.

Individuation has not been able to be adequately thought and described because only a single form of equilibrium was known, namely stable equilibrium; what was unknown was precisely metastable equilibrium; being was implicitly supposed in a state of stable equilibrium; however, stable equilibrium excludes becoming because it corresponds with the lowest level of potential energy possible; a stable equilibrium is achieved in a system when all possible transformations have occurred and no propulsive force remains; all potentials have been actualized, and systems that have succumbed to their lowest energetic levels cannot transform again. The Ancients only knew stability and instability, rest and movement, but they did not know metastability clearly and objectively. In order to define metastability, it is necessary to establish the notion of the potential energy of a system, the notion of order, and the notion of the increase of entropy;[4] it is therefore possible to define this metastable state of being, which is quite different from stable equilibrium and rest and which the Ancients couldn't establish in their search for the principle of individuation because they lacked a clear physical paradigm that could clarify its utilization.[5] Consequently, we will begin by attempting to present *physical individuation as a case of the resolution of a metastable system* on the basis of a *system state*, like that of supercooling or supersaturation involved in the genesis of crystals. Examples of the process of crystallization have been carefully researched and can certainly serve as paradigms in other domains, but crystallization does not exhaust the reality of physical individuation. Thus, we must consider if we can interpret certain aspects of microphysics by means of this notion of the becoming of being in a metastable state, particularly the nature of the complementarity of the concepts utilized in microphysics as pairs (wave-corpuscle, matter-energy). Perhaps this duality is due to the fact that scientific conceptualism supposes the existence of a real that consists of terms between which there are relations insofar as terms are not modified by relations in their internal structure.[6]

Yet, we can also suppose that reality is initially, in itself, similar to the supersaturated solution (and even more so in the pre-individual regime), *more than unity and more than identity,* and that it is capable of manifesting as wave or corpuscle, matter or energy, because every operation and every relation within an operation is an individuation that splits and phase-shifts pre-individual being, all while correlating the extreme values and orders of magnitude, which are initially without mediation. Complementarity would then be the epistemological reverberation of the initial and original metastability of the real. Because they are theories of identity, neither *mechanism* nor *energeticism* fully account for reality. In addition to the theory of corpuscles, the theory of fields and the theory of the interaction between fields and corpuscles are still partially dualistic but *lean toward a theory of the preindividual*. By way of another path, the theory of quanta grasps *this regime of the pre-individual* that surpasses unity: an exchange of energy occurs through elementary quantities, as if there were an individuation of energy in the relation between particles whereby particles can somewhat be considered as physical individuals. Perhaps it would be in this sense that we could see the convergence of these two new theories, that of quanta and that of wave mechanics, which to this very day have remained impenetrable to one another: they could be envisioned as *two ways of expressing the pre-individual* through the different manifestations in which it intervenes as pre-individual. Below the continuous and the discontinuous, there is the quantic and the metastable complementary (the more than unity), which is the true pre-individual. The necessity of correcting and pairing basic concepts in physics perhaps expresses the fact that *concepts are adequate only to individuated reality* and not to pre-individual reality.

We would then understand the paradigmatic value of the study of the genesis of crystals as processes of individuation: this would allow us to grasp on the macrophysical scale a phenomenon that depends on system states which belong to the microphysical domain and which are molecular and not molar; we would grasp activity that *is at the limit* of the crystal in its formation. Such an individuation is not the encounter of a preliminary form and a preliminary matter existing as previously constituted separate terms, but a resolution emerging within a metastable system rich in potentials: *form, matter, and energy preexist in the system*. Neither form nor matter is sufficient. The veritable principle of individuation is mediation, which generally supposes an original duality of orders of magnitude and an initial absence of interactive communication between them and then a communication between orders of magnitude and stabilization.

While a potential energy (the condition of a *superior* order of magnitude) is actualized, a matter is organized and divided (the condition of an *inferior* order of magnitude) into structured individuals on an *intermediate* order of magnitude that develops through an intermediate process of amplification.

What leads to and founds crystallization it is the energetic regime of the metastable system, but the crystals' form expresses certain molecular or atomic characteristics of the constituting chemical species.

In the domain of the living, the notion of metastability can also be used to characterize individuation; but individuation no longer occurs in a strictly *instantaneous,* quantum, abrupt, and definitive way, as in the physical domain, which leaves in its wake a duality of the milieu and the individual insofar as the milieu has been robbed of the individual (because the former and the latter no longer coincide) and insofar as the individual has lost the dimension of the milieu. Such an individuation also undoubtedly exists for the living being as an absolute origin; but it is doubled by an ongoing individuation, which is life itself, according to the fundamental mode of becoming: *the living being conserves within itself an ongoing activity of individuation*; it is not merely a result of individuation, like the crystal or molecule, but a theater of individuation. Furthermore, unlike that of the physical individual, the whole activity of the living being is not concentrated at its limit; in the living being there is a more complete regime of *internal resonance* that requires ongoing communication and that maintains a metastability, which is a condition of life. This is not the only characteristic of the living being, and the living being cannot be compared to an automaton that would maintain a certain number of equilibria or would seek compatibilities among several requirements based on a formula of a complex equilibrium composed of simpler equilibria; the living being is also a being that results from an initial individuation and amplifies this individuation, which is something that is not done by the technical object to which cybernetic mechanism would want to functionally compare it. In the living being there is *an individuation by the individual* and not merely an operation resulting from an individuation completed in a single stroke, as though it were a fabrication; the living being resolves problems, not just by adapting, i.e. by modifying its relation to the milieu (like a machine is capable of doing),[7] but by modifying itself, by inventing new internal structures, and by completely introducing itself into the axiomatic of vital problems.[8] *The living individual is a system of individuation, an individuating system, and a system that is in the midst of undergoing the process of individuating*; internal resonance and the translation of self-relation into information take place in this system of the living being. In the physical domain, internal resonance characterizes the limit of the individual in the midst of undergoing the process of *individuating*; in the living domain, internal resonance becomes the criterion of the whole individual qua individual there is internal resonance in the system of the individual and not merely in what the individual forms with its milieu; unlike that of the crystal, the organism's internal structure does not merely result from the activity that is accomplished and from the modulation that takes place at the limit between the domain of interiority and the domain of exteriority; perpetually centered outside itself, perpetually peripheral relative to itself and active at the limit of its domain, the physical individual has no veritable interiority; on the contrary, the living individual has a veritable interiority because individuation takes place from within; inside the living individual, the interior is also constitutive, whereas in the physical individual only the limit is constitutive, and what is topologically interior is genetically anterior. The living individual is contemporaneous with itself in all its elements, which is not the case for the physical individual, for the latter includes a past that has radically passed, even when it is still in the process of growing. At the interior of itself, the living being is a node of informative communication; it is a system within a system, involving *within itself* a mediation between two orders of magnitude[9].

Indeed, a hypothesis can be made that is analogous to the hypothesis of quanta in physics and also to the hypothesis of the relativity of levels of potential energy: it can be supposed that individuation does not fully exhaust pre-individual reality and that a regime of metastability is not merely sustained by the individual but carried by it, such that the constituted individual transports along with it a certain associated charge of pre-individual reality that is animated by all the potentials which characterize it; an individuation is relative, like a structural change in a physical system; a certain level of potential remains, and further individuations are still possible. This pre-individual nature, which remains associated with the individual, is a source for future metastable states from whence new individuations will be able to emerge. According to this hypothesis, it would be possible *to consider every veritable relation as having the status of being* and *as developing from within a new individuation*; relation does not spring forth between two terms that would already be individuals; relation is an aspect of the *internal resonance of a system of individuation*; it belongs to a system state. This living being, which is both more and less than unity, conveys *an interior problematic* and *can enter as an element into a problematic that is vaster than its own being.* For the individual, participation is *the fact of being an element in a vaster individuation* through the intermediary of the *charge of pre-individual reality that the individual contains,* i.e. due to the potentials that it harbors.

It then becomes possible to think the relation interior and exterior to the individual as participation without invoking new substances. The psyche and the collective are constituted by individuations that come after vital in-dividuation. *The psyche continues vital individuation in a being that, in order to resolve its own problematic,* is itself forced to intervene as an element of the problem through its action as *subject*; the subject can be conceived as the unity of the being qua individuated living being and qua being that is the representative of its action through the world as an element and dimension of the world; vital problems are not self-enclosed; their open axiomatic can only be saturated by an indefinite sequence of successive individuations that always engage more pre-individual reality and incorporate it in the relation to the milieu; affectivity and perception are integrated in emotion and in science, both of which suppose a recourse to new *dimensions.* However, the psychical being cannot resolve its own problematic in itself; its charge of pre-individual reality, at the same time as it is individuating as a psychical being that surpasses the limits of the individuated being and incorporates the living being in a system of the world and the subject, makes participation possible as a condition of the individuation of the collective; insofar as it is collective, individuation turns the individual into a group individual that is associated with the *group* through the pre-individual reality that the in-dividual bears, a pre-individual reality that, paired with the pre-individual reality of other individuals, *individuates into a collective unit.* Collective and psychical individuations are both reciprocal with respect to one another; they make it possible to define a category of the transindividual, which attempts to account for the systematic unity of interior (psychical) individuation and exterior (collective) individuation. The psycho-social world of the transin-dividual is neither the brute social nor the inter-individual; it supposes a veritable operation of individuation on the basis of a pre-individual reality that is associated with individuals and is able to constitute a new problem-atic which has its own metastability; it expresses a quantum condition that is correlative with a plurality of orders of magnitude. The living being is pre-sented as a *problematic being,* both superior and inferior to unity. To call the living being problematic is to consider becoming as a dimension of the living being: the living being exists according to becoming, which operates a mediation. The living being is an agent and theater of individuation; its becoming is an ongoing individuation, or rather, *a sequence of the manifes-tation of individuation* advancing from metastability to metastability; thus, the individual is neither substance nor a simple part of the collective: the collective intervenes as a resolution of the individual problematic, and this means that the basis of collective reality is already partially contained within the individual as the pre-individual reality that remains associated with the individuated reality; what is generally considered as *relation* due to the improper hypothesis of the substantialization of individual reality is in fact a dimension of individuation through which the individual becomes: relation, to the world and to the collective, is a *dimension of individuation* in which the individual participates based on *pre-individual reality,* which progressively individuates.

Thus, psychology and the theory of the collective are tied together: ontogenesis is that which indicates what participation in the collective is as well as what the psychical operation conceived as the resolution of a problematic is. The individuation that is life is conceived as the discovery in a conflictual situation of a new axiomatic that incorporates and unifies all the elements of this situation into a system that contains the individual. In order to understand what the psychical activity at the heart of the theory of individuation as a resolution of the conflictual nature of a metastable state is, the veritable ways in which metastable systems become established in life must be discovered; in this sense, both the notion of the *individual's adaptive relation to the milieu*[10] and the critical notion of the *knowing subject's relation to the object known* must be modified; knowledge is not constructed abstractly on the basis of sensation but problematically on the basis of *an initial tropistic and taxic unity, which is the coupling of tropism and sensation, an orientation of the living being in a polarized world*; even here it is necessary to detach ourselves from the hylomorphic schema; there is not a sensation that would be a matter constituting an *a posteriori* given for the *a priori* forms of sensibility; *a priori* forms are an initial resolution by the discovery of the axiomatic of tensions resulting from the encounter of *primitive tropistic and taxic unities*; the *a priori* forms of sensibility are neither *a prioris* nor *a posterioris* obtained via abstraction but the structures of an axiomatic that appears in an operation of individuation. In the tropistic and taxic unity, there is already the world and the living being, but the world merely appears there as a *direction,* as the polarity of a gradient that situates the individuated being in an *indefinite dyad,* the median point of which it occupies and which extends out from it. Perception and then science continue to resolve this problematic, not just through the invention of spatiotemporal frameworks, but through the constitution of the notion of the object, which becomes the *source* of the initial gradients and organizes them according to a *world.* The distinction between the *a priori* and the *a posteriori*—a byproduct of the hylomorphic schema in the theory of knowledge—obfuscates in its dark zone the veritable operation of individuation, which is the center of knowledge. The very notion of qualitative or intensive series should be thought according to the theory of phases of being: it is *not relational* and subtended by a preexistence of extreme terms but develops on the basis of an initial intermediate state that localizes the living being and inserts it into the gradient that gives a directionality to the tropistic and taxic unity: the series is an abstract vision of the direction according to which the tropistic unity is oriented. We must start with individuation, with the being grasped in its center according to spatiality and becoming, and not with a substantialized *individual* facing a *world* that is foreign to it.[11]

The same method can be employed to explore affectivity and emotivity, which constitute the resonance of the being with respect to itself and connect the individuated being back to the pre-individual reality that is associated with it, just as tropistic and taxic unity and perception link it to the milieu. The psyche consists of successive individuations that allow for the being to resolve the problematic states corresponding to the ongoing establishment of communication of that which is larger than it and that which is smaller than it.

But the psyche cannot be resolved at the level of the individuated being alone; it is the basis of participation in a vaster individuation, that of the collective; calling itself into question, the individual being alone cannot go beyond the limits of anxiety, which is an operation without action, an ongoing emotion that does not manage to resolve affectivity, an obstacle through which the individuated being explores its dimensions of being without the ability to surpass them. *The notion of the transindividual corresponds to the collective taken as the axiomatic that resolves the psychical problematic.*

Such a set of reforms of notions is supported by the hypothesis that an information is never relative to a single and homogeneous reality but to two orders in a state of *disparation*: information, whether this be at the level of tropistic unity or at the level of the transindividual, is never deposited in a form that is able to be given; it is the tension between two disparate reals, it is *the signification that will emerge when an operation of individuation will discover the dimension according to which two disparate reals can become a system*; information is therefore an initiation of individuation, a *requirement for individuation*, for the passage from the metastable to the stable, it is never a given thing; there is no unity and identity of information, for information is not a *term*; it supposes the tension of a system of being in order for it to be adequately received; it can only be inherent to a problematic; information is *that through which the non-resolved system's incompatibility becomes an organizational dimension in the resolution*; information supposes a *phase change of a system*, for it supposes a first pre-individual state that individuates according to the discovered organization; information is the formula of individuation, a formula that cannot exist before this individuation; we could say that information is always in the present, actual, for it is the direction according to which a system individuates.[12]

This study is founded on the following conception of being: being does not have a unity of identity, which is that of a stable state wherein no transformation is possible; being has a *transductive unity*, i.e. it can phase-shift with respect to itself, it can overflow itself on both sides from *its center*. What is taken as a *relation or duality of principles* is in fact this overflowing expanse of a being, insofar as a being is more than unity and more than identity; becoming is a dimension of a being, not what comes to it according to a succession undergone by an initially given and substantial being. Individuation must be grasped as the being's becoming and not as a model of the being that would exhaust its signification. The individuated being is neither the whole being nor the first being; *instead of grasping individuation on the basis of the individuated being, the individuated being must be grasped on the basis of individuation and individuation on the basis of pre-individual being*, which is distributed according to several orders of magnitude.

The intention of this study is therefore to examine the *forms, modes, and degrees of individuation* in order to put the individual back into being according to the three levels of the physical, the vital, and the psycho-social. Instead of supposing substances so as to account for individuation, we have chosen to take the different regimes of individuation as the basis of various domains, such as matter, life, mind, and society. The separation, layering, and relations of these domains appear as aspects of individuation according to its different modalities; the more fundamental notions of first information, metastability, internal resonance, energetic potential, and orders of magnitude are substituted for the notions of substance, form, and matter.

Yet, in order for this modification of notions to be possible, it is necessary to introduce both a new method and a new notion. The method consists in not trying to compose the essence of a reality via a *conceptual* relation between two preexisting extreme terms, and it also consists in considering every veritable relation as having the status of being. Relation is a modality of being; it is simultaneous with respect to the terms whose existence it guarantees. A relation must be grasped as a relation in being, a relation of being, a manner of being, and not a simple rapport between two terms that could be adequately known via concepts because they would have an effectively prior, separate existence. It is because terms are conceived as substances that relation is a rapport of terms and that being is separated into terms, since being is initially, before any examination of individuation, conceived as substance. Conversely, if substance is no longer the model of being, it is possible to conceive relation as the being's non-identity vis-à-vis itself, the inclusion in the being of a reality which is not merely identical with it, such that being qua being, before any individuation, can be comprehended as more than unity and more than identity.[13] This kind of method supposes an ontological type of postulate: at the level of being grasped before any individuation, the principle of the excluded middle and the principle of identity are no longer applicable; these principles only apply to the already individuated being, and they define an impoverished being that is separated into milieu and individual; consequently, they do not apply to the being's whole, to the ensemble formed later on by the milieu and the individual, but merely to what of pre-individual being has become individual. In this sense, classical logic cannot be used to think individuation, for it forces us to think the operation of individuation with concepts and rapports among concepts that merely apply to the results of the operation of individuation considered partially.

The usage of this method, which considers the principle of identity and the principle of the excluded middle as too narrow, unlocks a notion that has a multitude of aspects and domains of application: that of *transduction*. By transduction we mean a physical, biological, mental, or social operation through which an activity propagates incrementally within a domain by basing this propagation on a structuration of the domain operated from one region to another: each structural region serves as a principle and model, as an initiator for constituting the following region, such that a modification thereby extends progressively throughout this structuring operation. The simplest image of the transductive operation is provided by the crystal, which, starting from a tiny germ, increases and extends following all the directions in its supersaturated mother liquor: each previously constituted molecular layer serves as the structuring basis for the layer in the process of forming; the result is an amplifying reticular structure. The transductive operation is an individuation in progress; within the physical domain, it can be effectuated in the simplest way via progressive iteration; but within more complex domains, like the domains of vital metastability or of the psychical problematic, it can advance with a constantly variable pace and extend into a domain of heterogeneity; there is transduction when there is an activity that starts from a being's structural and functional center and extends in various directions based on its center, as if multiple dimensions of the being appeared around this center; transduction is the correlative appearance of dimensions and structures within a being in a state of pre-individual tension, i.e. in a being which is more than unity and more than identity and which has not yet phase-shifted with respect to itself in multiple dimensions. The extreme terms attained by the transductive operation do not exist before this operation; its dynamism stems from the initial tension of the system of the heterogeneous being that phase-shifts and develops dimensions according to which it will be structured; it does not come from a tension between terms that will be attained and deposited at the extreme limits of transduction.[14] Transduction can be a vital operation; in particular, it expresses the orientation of organic individuation; it can be a psychical operation and an effective logical procedure, although it is not at all limited to logical thought. In the domain of knowledge, it defines the veritable measure of invention, which is neither inductive nor deductive, but transductive, i.e. corresponds to a discovery of the dimensions according to which a problematic can be defined; it is an analogical operation, at least based on what is valid about this kind of operation. This notion can be used to think the different domains of individuation: it applies to all cases wherein an individuation is realized, manifesting the genesis of a web of rapports founded on the being. The possibility of using an analogical transduction to think a domain of reality indicates that this domain is effectively the groundwork of a transductive structuration. Transduction corresponds to this existence of rapports that takes hold when pre-individual being individuates; it expresses individuation and allows for individuation to be thought; it is therefore a notion that is both metaphysical and logical; *it applies to ontogenesis and is ontogenesis itself.* Objectively, it makes it possible to understand the systematic conditions of individuation, internal resonance,[15] and the psychical problematic. Logically, it can be used as the basis of a new type of analogical paradigmatism in order to pass from physical individuation to organic individuation, from organic individuation to psychical individuation, and from psychical individuation to the subjective and objective transindividual, all of which defines the plan of this research.

We could certainly assert that transduction would not be presented as a logical procedure having a proof value; furthermore, we don't mean to say that transduction is a logical procedure in the current sense of the term; it is a mental procedure, and even much more than a procedure, it is the mind's way of discovering. This way of discovering consists in *following the being in its genesis,* in accomplishing the genesis of thought at the same time as the genesis of the object is accomplished. In this research, it is called upon to play a role that dialectics could not play, for the study of the operation of individuation does not seem to correspond to the appearance of the negative as a second stage, but to an immanence of the negative within the initial condition through the ambivalent form of tension *and* incompatibility; this is what is most positive in the state of pre-individual being, namely the existence of potentials, which is also the cause of the incompatibility and non-stability of this state; the negative appears initially as an ontogenetic incompatibility, but it is in actuality merely the other side of a wealth of potentials; therefore, it is not a substantial negative; it is never a stage or phase, and individuation is not a synthesis or return to unity but the phase-shift of the being based on its pre-individual center of potentialized incompatibility. From this ontogenetic perspective, time itself is considered as an expression of the *dimensionality of the being that is individuating.*

Transduction is therefore not merely the reasoning of the mind; it is also intuition, because it is that through which a structure appears in a domain of a problematic as providing the resolution to the problems posed. But contrary to *deduction,* transduction does not go elsewhere to seek a principle to resolve the problem of a domain: it extracts the resolving structure from the very tensions of this domain, just as the supersaturated solution crystallizes due to its own potentials and according to the chemical species that it holds, not with the contribution of some foreign form. It is also not comparable to *induction,* for induction truly conserves the characteristics of the terms of reality included in the studied domain, drawing the structures of the analysis from these terms themselves, but it only conserves what is positive in these terms, i.e. *what is common* to all terms, thereby eliminating what is singular from them; on the contrary, transduction is a discovery of dimensions whose system makes the dimensions of each of the terms communicate, such that the complete reality of each of the terms of the domain can become organized into newly discovered structures without loss or reduction; resolving transduction *operates the inversion of the negative into the positive*: that through which the terms are not identical to one another, that through which they are *disparate* (in the sense that this term assumes within the theory of three-dimensional vision) is integrated into the system of resolution and becomes a condition of signification; there is no impoverishment of information contained in the terms; transduction is characterized by the fact that the result of this operation is a concrete fabric including all the initial terms; the resulting system is made of that which has become concrete and includes the whole concrete; the transductive order conserves the concrete and is characterized by the *conservation of information,* whereas induction requires a loss of information; just like dialectics, transduction conserves and integrates the opposed aspects; unlike dialectics, transduction does not suppose the existence of a preliminary time as the framework in which the genesis unfurls, since time itself is a solution, a dimension of the discovered systematic: *time emerges from the pre-individual just like the other dimensions according to which individuation effectuates itself.*[16]

However, in order to think the transductive operation, which is the basis of individuation in its various levels, the notion of form is insufficient. The notion of hylomorphic form is part of the same system of thought as that of substance, or that of rapport as a relation posterior to the existence of terms: these notions have been elaborated based on the results of individuation; they can only grasp an impoverished real without potentials, and consequently one that is incapable of individuating.

The notion of form must be replaced with that of information, which supposes the existence of a system in a state of metastable equilibrium that can individuate; unlike form, information is never a single term but the signification that emerges from a disparation. The ancient notion of form, such as the hylomorphic schema upholds, is too independent from any notion of system and metastability. The notion of form provided by Gestalt theory on the contrary conveys the notion of system and is defined as the state toward which the system tends when it finds its equilibrium: it is a resolution of tension. Sadly, an overly superficial physical paradigmatism has led Gestalt theory to consider that the only state of equilibrium of a system that can resolve tensions is the state of stable equilibrium: Gestalt theory has ignored metastability. We would like to take up Gestalt theory again and, with the introduction of a quantum condition, show that the problems posed by Gestalt theory cannot be directly resolved via the notion of stable equilibrium but only via the notion of metastable equilibrium; good form is therefore no longer simple form, pregnant geometrical form, but *significative form,* i.e. that which establishes a transductive order within a system of reality bearing potentials. This good form is what maintains the energetic level of the system, conserves its potentials by making them compatible: it is the structure of compatibility and viability, it is the invented dimensionality according to which there is compatibility without degradation.[17] The notion of form consequently deserves to be replaced by that of information. During this replacement, the notion of information must never be reduced to signals or supports or vehicles of information, *as the technological theory of information tends to do when it is siphoned by abstraction from the technology of transmissions.* The pure notion of form must therefore be saved twice from an overly superficial technological paradigmatism: first, relative to ancient culture due to the reductive usage of this notion in the *hylomorphic schema*;

second, relative to the state of the notion of information in modern culture, to save information as signification from the *technological theory* of information conceived by way of the experience of transmissions through a channel. For we actually uncover the same goal at work in the successive theories of hylomorphism, good form, and then information: the goal that seeks to discover the inherence of significations to *being*; and it is precisely this inherence that we would like to discover in the operation of individuation.

Thus, a study of individuation can tend toward a reform of fundamental philosophical notions, for it is possible to consider individuation as what must be known beforehand about being. Even before wondering how it is legitimate or illegitimate to bear judgments on beings, it can be considered that being is said in two senses: in a first, fundamental sense, being is insofar as it is; but in a second sense, always superposed on the first sense in logical theory, being is being insofar as it is individuated. If it were true that logic bears on statements relative to being only after individuation, a theory of being anterior to all logic would have to be established; this theory could serve as the foundation to logic, for nothing proves in advance that being is individuated in a single possible way; if several types of individuation existed, several logics would also have to exist, each corresponding to a definite type of individuation. The classification of ontogeneses would make it possible to *pluralize logic* with a valid foundation of plurality. As for the axiomatization of the knowledge of pre-individual being, it cannot be contained in a preliminary logic, for no norm or system detached from its content can be defined: by being accomplished, only the individuation of thought can accompany the individuation of beings other than thought; we therefore cannot have an immediate knowledge or a mediated knowledge of individuation, but we can have a knowledge that is an operation parallel to the operation known; we cannot *know individuation* in the ordinary sense of the term; we can only individuate, be individuated, and individuate within ourselves; this apprehension is therefore, in the margin of knowledge properly speaking, an analogy between two operations, an analogy that is a certain mode of communication. The individuation of the real, exterior to the subject, is grasped by the subject due to the analogical individuation of knowledge within the subject; but it is *through the individuation of knowledge* and not through knowledge alone that the individuation of non-subject beings is grasped. Beings can be known through the knowledge of the subject, but the individuation of beings can only be grasped through the individuation of the subject's knowledge.

PART I

Physical Individuation

CHAPTER ONE

Form and Matter

I. Foundations of the Hylomorphic Schema: Technology of Form-Taking

1. The Conditions of Individuation

The notions of form and matter cannot help us resolve the problem of individuation unless they are logically first with respect to the position of this problem. Conversely, if we discovered that the hylomorphic system expresses and contains the problem of individuation, it would be necessary (lest we be forced into begging the question) to consider the search for the principle of individuation as logically anterior to the definition of matter and form.

It is difficult to consider the notions of matter and form as innate ideas. However, at the very moment when we would be tempted to assign them a technological origin, we are taken aback by the remarkable capacity for generalization these notions possess. Along with the brick or marble, clay and the statue aren't the only things that can be thought according to the hylomorphic schema, because very many events of formation, genesis, and composition in the living world and the psychical domain can also be thought in the same manner. The logical force of this schema is so great that Aristotle was able to utilize it in order to sustain a universal system of classification applicable to the real both according to the logical path and according to the physical path, thereby guaranteeing the harmony of the logical order and the physical order and making inductive knowledge possible. Even the rapport of the soul and the body can be thought according to the hylomorphic schema.

A basis as narrow as that of the technological operation only seems to be able to sustain a paradigm with a similar force of universality with great difficulty. Thus, in order to examine the foundation of the hylomorphic schema, we need to acknowledge the meaning and the extent of the role played in its genesis by the technical experience.

The technological nature of the origin of a schema does not invalidate this schema, on condition, however, that the operation serving as the basis of formation for the utilized concepts fully passes into and is expressed in the abstract schema without alteration. Conversely, if the abstraction is carried out superficially and unfaithfully by masking one of the fundamental dynamisms of the technical operation, then the schema is false. Instead of having a veritable paradigmatic value, it would be nothing but a comparison, a more or less rigorous approximation according to the case.

However, in the technical operation that gives rise to an object with form and matter (like a brick of clay), the real dynamism of the operation is quite far from being able to be represented by the matter-form pair. The form and the matter of the hylomorphic schema are an abstract form and an abstract matter. The definite being that can be shown (this brick drying on this board) does not result from the combination of an unspecified matter and an unspecified form. If we take fine-grained sand, moisten it, and pack it into a brick mold, then we will get a heap of sand and not a brick after we take it out of the mold. If we take clay and put it through the rolling mill or the spinneret, then we will not get a plate or wire but a pile of broken layers and short cylindrical segments. Clay conceived as the support of an undefined plasticity is the abstract matter. The right-angled parallelepiped conceived as a brick form is an abstract form. The concrete brick does not result from the joining of the clay's plasticity and the parallelepiped. In order for there to be able to be *a* parallelepipedic brick, a really existing individual, an effective technical *operation* must institute a mediation between a determinate mass of clay and this notion of the parallelepiped. However, the technical operation of molding is not enough by itself: moreover, this operation does not institute a direct mediation between a determinate mass of clay and the abstract form of the parallelepiped;[1] the mediation is prepared by two chains of preliminary operations that make a matter and form converge toward a common operation. To give a form to the clay is not to impose the parallelepipedic form onto raw clay: it is to pack the prepared clay into a fabricated mold. If we start from the two ends of the technological chain, the parallelepiped and the clay in the quarry, then we can experience the impression of realizing in the technical operation an encounter between two realities of heterogeneous domains and of instituting a mediation through communication between an inter-elementary, macrophysical order larger than the individual and an intra-elementary, microphysical order smaller than the individual.

In the technical operation, what must be considered is precisely the mediation itself: in the chosen case, it consists in making a prepared block of clay completely fill a mold and drying it afterwards by conserving this defined contour without cracks or disintegration. However, the preparation of the clay and the construction of the mold are already an active mediation between the raw clay and the impossible geometrical form. The mold is constructed so that it can be opened and closed without damaging its contents. Certain forms of geometrically conceivable solids have only become realizable with very complex and subtle devices. Even today, the art of constructing molds is one of the most delicate aspects of the foundry. Furthermore, the mold isn't just constructed; it's also prepared: a certain coating or a dry powdering will prevent the humid clay from sticking to the walls of the mold when it is removed, thus keeping it from forming cracks or disaggregating. In order to produce a form, one must construct a *certain defined* mold, prepared in a *certain* fashion with a *certain* type of matter. Thus, there is an initial pathway that goes from the geometrical form to the concrete material mold, parallel to the clay, a form which exists in the same manner as it and is posited alongside it in the order of magnitude of the manipulable. As for the clay, it is also submitted to a preparation; as a raw matter, it's what the shovel raises to the surface at the edge of the marsh with roots of rush and gravel grains. Dried, crushed, sifted, wetted, shaped, and kneaded at length, it becomes this consistent and homogeneous dough that is plastic enough to be able to embrace the contours of the mold in which it is pressed and firm enough to conserve this contour long enough for this plasticity to disappear. In addition to its purification, the preparation of the clay seeks to obtain homogeneity and the best degree of chosen humidity to reconcile plasticity and consistency. In the raw clay, there is the capacity to become a malleable mass with the dimension of the future brick due to the colloidal properties of aluminum hydrosilicates: these colloidal properties make it possible for the movements of the technical half-chain ending in the prepared clay to be effective; the molecular reality of the clay and of the water it absorbs is organized by the preparation in such a way as to be able to behave during individuation as a homogeneous totality on the level of the brick about to appear. Prepared clay is a clay in which each molecule—despite its place relative to the walls of the mold—will be effectively put into communication with all the pressures exerted by these walls. Each molecule intervenes on the level of the future individual and thereby enters into interactive communication with the order of magnitude superior to the individual. On its side, the other technical half-chain descends toward the future individual; the parallelepipedic form is not just any form; it already contains a certain schematism that can direct the construction of the mold, which is a set of coherent operations contained in the implicit state; the clay is not just passively deformable; it's actively plastic, because it's colloidal; its capacity to receive a form is not distinct from its capacity to keep it, because keeping and receiving amounts to the same thing: to undergo a flawless deformation with a coherence of molecular chains. The preparation of the clay is the constitution of this state of equal distribution of molecules and this arrangement into chains; the shaping has already begun the moment when the craftsman stirs the paste before introducing it into the mold. This is because the form is not just the fact of being parallelepipedic; it is also the fact of being flawless in the parallelepiped, without bubbles of air and without cracks: unblemished cohesion is the result of a formation, and this formation is merely the exploitation of the colloidal characteristics of the clay. Before any elaboration, the clay in the marsh is already in a form, since it is already colloidal. The craftsman's labor uses this elementary form, without which nothing would be possible and which is homogeneous relative to the form of the mold: there is merely a change of scale in the two technical half-chains. In the marsh, the clay indeed has colloidal properties, but these properties exist molecule by molecule or grain by grain in this state; this already involves form and is what will later maintain the homogeneous and well-molded brick. The quality of matter is the form's source, an element of the form whose scale is modified by the technical operation. In the other technical half-chain, the geometrical form becomes concretized and becomes the dimension of the mold, e.g. collected wood, sawdust, or damp wood.[2] The technical operation prepares two half-chains of transformation that encounter one another at a certain point when the two elaborated objects have compatible characteristics and are on the same scale; this putting into relation is not singular and unconditional; it can take place in stages; what we consider to be a single instance of shaping is often just the latest episode in a series of transformations; when the block of clay receives the final deformation that allows it to fill the mold, its molecules are not reorganized completely and in a single stroke; they are displaced slightly relative to one another; their topology is maintained, and what is involved is merely one last total deformation. However, this total deformation is not just a shaping of the clay by its contour. The clay yields a brick because this deformation operates on masses whose molecules are already arranged relative to one another, without air, without grains of sand, and with a good colloidal equilibrium; if the mold didn't guide all of this already constituted prior arrangement into one last deformation, then it would never produce any form; it could be said that the form of the mold only operates on the form of the clay and not on the clay matter. The mold limits and stabilizes rather than imposing a form: it provides the goal of deformation and achieves it by interrupting it according to a definite contour: it *modulates* the ensemble of the already formed sections: the action of the worker who fills the mold and packs the clay continues the prior action of kneading, stretching, and shaping: the mold plays the role of a fixed set of modeling hands, acting like halted kneading hands. We could make a brick with our hands without a mold by prolonging the kneading through a fashioning that would continue it without interruption. Matter is matter because it contains a positive property that allows it to be modeled. To be modeled is not to undergo arbitrary displacements but to organize matter's plasticity according to definite forces that stabilize the deformation. The technical operation is a *mediation* between an inter-elementary ensemble and an intra-elementary ensemble. The pure form already contains actions, and the raw material is the capacity of becoming; the actions contained in the form encounter the becoming of the matter and modulate it. In order for the matter to be able to be modulated in its becoming, it must—like the clay at the moment when the worker packs it into the mold—have a deformable reality, i.e. a reality that does not have a definite form but all forms indefinitely and dynamically, since this reality, while it possesses inertia and consistency, is a depository of force (at least for an instant) and is identical point by point with this force; in order for the clay to fill the mold, it is not enough for it to have plasticity: it must transmit the pressure that the worker impresses on it, and each point of its mass must be a center of forces; the clay is pushed into the mold that it fills; it propagates the energy of the worker within its mass. While the mold is being filled, a potential energy becomes actualized.[3] The energy that pushes the clay must exist potentially in the mold-hand-clay system for the clay to fill all the empty space, and this energy develops in every direction and is halted only by the boundaries of the mold. The walls of the mold then intervene not on the whole as materialized geometrical structures but point by point as fixed places that do not allow the expanding clay to advance and oppose against the pressure developed by the clay an equal force in the opposite direction (principle of reaction) without carrying out any work, since they are not displaced. The walls of the mold relative to an element of the clay play the same role as an element of this clay relative to another nearby element: the pressure of one element relative to another within the mass is almost as strong as that of an element of the wall relative to an element of the mass; the only difference is that the wall is not displaced, whereas the elements of the clay can be displaced relative to the others and relative to the walls.[4] A potential energy that is translated within the clay by the forces of pressure is actualized while the mold is being filled. The matter conveys with it the potential energy being actualized; the form, which is here represented by the mold, plays an informing role by exerting forces without work, forces that limit the actualization of the potential energy momentarily borne by the matter. This energy can be actualized in a given direction with a given rapidity: the form is the limit. The relation between matter and form thus does not take place between inert matter and a form coming from outside: there is a common operation that is on the same level of existence between matter and form; this common level of existence is that of *force,* which arises from an energy momentarily borne by the matter yet drawn from a state of the total higher-dimension, inter-elementary system with a superior dimension that expresses the individuating limitations. The technical operation constitutes two half-chains that verge—starting from the raw matter and the pure form—toward one another and combine. This combination is made possible by the dimensional correspondence of the two ends of the chain; the successive links of the elaboration transfer characteristics without creating new ones: they merely establish changes in orders of magnitude, changes in level, and changes in state (for example, the passage from the molecular state to the molar state, from the dry state to the humid state); what is present at the material end of the half-chain is the capacity for matter to convey a potential energy point by point, which can provoke a movement in an undetermined direction; what is present at the end of the formal half-chain is the capacity for a structure to condition a movement without carrying out work through a play of forces that do not displace their point of application. This affirmation, however, is not rigorously true; in order for the mold to be able to limit the expansion of the modeling clay and statically direct this expansion, the walls of the mold must develop a force of reaction equal to the pressure of the clay; the clay recedes and becomes tightly packed (thereby filling out the empty space) when the reaction of the walls of the mold is slightly more elevated than the forces exerted in the opposite directions within the mass of the clay; conversely, when the mold is completely filled, the internal pressures are equal throughout to the walls' forces of reaction, so that there is no longer any movement taking place. The reaction of the walls is thus the static force that directs the clay during the filling of the mold by preventing expansion in certain directions. However, the forces of reaction can only exist due to a very slight elastic flexing of the walls; from the matter's point of view, it could be said that the formal wall is the limit beginning from which a displacement in a determined direction is only possible at the expense of a very large increase in work; but in order for this condition of increased work to be effective, it must begin to be realized before the equilibrium is disrupted and before the matter takes on other directions in which it is not limited, since the matter is pushed by the energy that it carries with it and that it actualizes by advancing; thus, there must be a little work from the walls of the mold that corresponds to the slight displacement of the point of impact of the forces of reaction. But this work *is not added* to the work that produces the actualization of the energy borne by the clay; it is no longer involved in the work of actualization; it does not interfere with the latter; we can also reduce it as much as we like; a thin wooden mold noticeably becomes deformed under the abrupt pressure of the clay and then progressively returns to its original position; a thick wooden mold displaces less; a cast-iron or flint mold hardly displaces at all. Furthermore, the positive work of the mold returning to its original position largely compensates for the negative work of deformation. The mold can have a certain elasticity; it simply must not have plasticity. Matter and form are brought together as *forces*. The only difference between the regime of these forces for matter and form is the fact that the forces of the matter come from an energy borne by the matter that is readily available, whereas the forces of the form are forces that produce nothing but a small amount of work and intervene as limits of the actualization of the matter's energy. It is not in the infinitely short instant that matter and form are different, but in becoming; the form is not the bearer of potential energy; the matter is only informable matter because it can, point by point, be the bearer of an energy that becomes actualized;[5] the preliminary treatment of the raw matter aims to make the matter the homogeneous support of a definite potential energy; through this potential energy, the matter becomes; the form, however, does not become. In the instantaneous operation, the forces of the matter and the forces that arise from the form are not different; they are homogeneous relative to one another and belong to the same instantaneous physical system; but they do not belong to the same temporal ensemble. The work exerted by the forces of the elastic deformation of the mold no longer exist after the molding; they are nullified or degrade into heat and have not produced anything on the order of magnitude of the mold. Conversely, the potential energy of the matter is actualized on the order of magnitude of the clay mass by producing a distribution of the elementary masses. That is why the preliminary treatment of the clay prepares this actualization: it renders each molecule interdependent with the other molecules and renders the ensemble deformable, so that each portion equally participates in the potential energy whose actualization is the molding; it is essential that all the portions (without discontinuity or privilege) have the same chances to deform in any direction whatsoever; a lump or a stone are domains of non-participation in this potentiality that is actualized by localizing its support; they are parasitic singularities.

The fact that there is a mold, i.e. limits of actualization, creates in the matter a state of reciprocity in the forces that lead to equilibrium; the mold does not act from the outside by imposing a form; its action reverberates within the whole mass through the action of molecule to molecule and portion to portion; the clay at the end of molding is the mass in which all the forces of deformation encounter in every direction forces equal and in opposite directions to those of which their equilibrium consists. *The mold translates its existence into the matter by making it tend towards a condition of equilibrium.* For this equilibrium to exist, there must be a certain quantity of potential energy not yet actualized in the whole system at the end of the operation. It would not be precise to say that the form plays a static role while the matter plays a dynamic role; in fact, in order for there to be a single system of forces, the matter and form both must play a dynamic role; but this dynamic equality is only true for a moment. The form does not evolve and is not modified because it does not contain any potentiality, whereas the matter evolves. The matter is the bearer of potentialities that expand and are distributed uniformly in it; the homogeneity of the matter is the homogeneity of its possible becoming. Each point has as many chances as all the others; the matter about to take form is in a state of complete *internal resonance*; what occurs at one point reverberates within all the others, the becoming of each molecule reverberates within all the others at all points and in all directions; the matter's elements are neither isolated from one another nor heterogeneous relative to one another; all heterogeneity is a condition of the non-transmission of forces and therefore a condition of internal non-resonance. The plasticity of the clay is its capacity to be in a state of internal resonance as soon as it is subjected to a pressure in an enclosure. The mold as a limit is that through which the state of internal resonance is provoked, but the mold is not that through which the internal resonance is realized; the mold is not what uniformly transmits in all directions the pressures and displacements within the malleable clay. It cannot be said that the mold gives form; it is the clay that takes form according to the mold because it communicates with the worker. The *positivity* of this form-taking is that of the clay and the worker; it is this internal resonance, the work of this internal resonance.[6] The mold intervenes as a condition of enclosure, limit, halted expansion, and direction of mediation. The technical operation institutes internal resonance in the matter taking form by means of energetic conditions and topological conditions; the topological conditions can be called form, and the energetic conditions express the entire system. Internal resonance is a *system state* that requires this realization of energetic conditions, topological conditions, and material conditions; resonance is an exchange of energies and movements in a determined enclosure, a communication between a microphysical matter and a macrophysical energy based on a singularity whose dimension is intermediate and topologically defined.

2. Validity of the Hylomorphic Schema; the Dark Zone of the Hylomorphic Schema; Generalization of the Notion of Form-Taking; Modeling, Molding, Modulation

The technical operation of form-taking can therefore serve as a paradigm if we require this operation to indicate the veritable relations it institutes. However, these relations are not established between the raw matter and the pure form but between the prepared matter and the materialized form: the operation of form-taking doesn't just suppose raw matter and form but also energy; the materialized form is a form that can act as a limit, as the topological boundary of a system. The prepared matter is one that can transmit energetic potentials, the technical manipulation of which charges it. In order to play a role in the technical operation, the pure form must become a system of points of impact of the forces of reaction while the raw matter becomes a homogeneous bearer of potential energy. Form-taking is the mutual operation of the form and the matter in a system: the energetic condition is essential, and it is not contributed by the form alone; the whole system is the center of potential energy precisely because form-taking is an in-depth operation within the whole mass, the consequence of which is a state of energetic reciprocity of the matter relative to itself.[7] The distribution of energy is what is what determines in form-taking, and the mutual conformity of the matter and the form is relative to the possibility of the existence and characteristics of this energetic system. The matter is what bears this energy, and the form is what modulates the distribution of this very energy. At the moment of form-taking, the matter-form unity is in the energetic regime.

The hylomorphic schema only retains the extremes of these two half-chains elaborated by the technical operation; the schematism of the operation itself is obscured and ignored. There is a hole in hylomorphic representation that makes the true mediation disappear, i.e. the very operation that attaches the two half-chains to each other by instituting an energetic system, a state that evolves and must effectively exist for an object to appear with its haecceity. The hylomorphic schema corresponds to the knowledge of someone who remains outside the workshop and considers nothing but what goes in and goes out; in order to know the true hylomorphic relation, it's not even enough to enter the workshop and work with the craftsman: we would have to penetrate into the mold itself in order to follow the operation of form-taking on the different scales of magnitude of physical reality.

Grasped in itself, the operation of form-taking can be carried out in several ways and according to modalities that are seemingly very different from one another. The veritable technicity of the operation of form-taking greatly surpasses the conventional limits that separate the fields and domains of labor. Consequently, through the study of the energetic regime of form-taking, it becomes possible to approximate the molding of a brick with the functioning of an electronic relay. In an electronic tube like a triode, the "matter" (bearer of the potential energy actualized) is the cloud of electrons emanating from the cathode in the cathode-anode-effector-generator circuit. The "form" is what limits this actualization of reserve potential in the generator, i.e. the electrical field created by the difference in potential between the control grid and the cathode, which is opposed to the cathode-anode field created by the generator itself; this counter-field is a limit to the actualization of potential energy, just as the walls of the mold are a limit for the actualization of the potential energy of the clay-mold system carried by the clay in its displacement. The difference between the two cases resides in the fact that the operation of form-taking is finite in time for the clay: it tends fairly slowly (in several seconds) toward a state of equilibrium, and then the brick is removed from the mold; the state of equilibrium is utilized in the unmolding when this state is attained. In the electronic tube, we utilize a support of energy (an electron cloud in a field) with a very slight inertia, such that the state of equilibrium (equivalence between the distribution of electrons and the gradient of the electrical field) is obtained in an extremely short time relative to the example of the brick (several milliseconds in a large tube and several tenths of a millisecond in very small tubes). Under these conditions, the potential of the control grid is utilized as a *variable mold*; the distribution of the support of energy in proportion to this mold is so rapid that it is carried out without an appreciable delay for the majority of applications: the variable mold then serves to differentiate in time the actualization of a source's potential energy; we do not stop when equilibrium is attained but continue by modifying the mold, i.e. the tension of the grid; the actualization is almost instantaneous, and there is never a halt for the unmolding, since the circulation of the support of energy is equivalent to a *perpetual unmolding*; a modulator is a *continuous temporal mold*. Here, the "matter" is almost uniquely the support of potential energy; it nevertheless always conserves a definite inertia that prevents the modulator from being infinitely fast. In the case of the clay mold, on the contrary, what is technically utilized is the state of equilibrium that can be conserved by unmolding: a sufficient amount of the clay's viscosity is then accepted in order for the form to be conserved in the course of unmolding, even though this viscosity slows down the form-taking. Conversely, in a modulator the viscosity of the bearer of energy is reduced as much as possible, since we do not seek to conserve the state of equilibrium after the conditions of equilibrium have ended: it is easier to modulate the energy carried by compressed air than by pressurized water, and it is even easier to modulate the energy carried by electrons in transit than by compressed air. The mold and the modulator are the extreme cases, but the essential operation of form-taking is accomplished in the same way for both; it consists in the establishment of an energetic regime, whether or not it persists. To mold is to modulate in a definitive way; to modulate is to mold in a continuously and perpetually variable way.

Many technical operations utilize a form-taking that has intermediate characteristics between molding and modulation; thus, a spinneret and a rolling mill are molds with a continuous regime that create a definitive profile in successive stages (called passes); unmolding is continuous in this case, just like in a modulator. We could conceive a rolling mill that would really modulate matter and fabricate, for example, a crenellated or indented ingot; rolling mills that produce striated sheet metal *modulate* matter, whereas a smooth rolling mill merely *models* it. *Molding* and *modulation* are the two extreme cases of which *modeling* is the intermediate case.

We would like to show that the technological paradigm is not without value and that to a certain extent it allows us to think the genesis of the individuated being, but only on the express condition that we retain as an essential schema the relation of matter and form *through the energetic system* of form-taking. Matter and form must be grasped *during form-taking* at the moment when the unity of the becoming of an energetic system constitutes this relation on the level of the homogeneity of forces between matter and form. What is central and essential is the energetic operation, which supposes energetic potentiality and a limit of actualization. The initiative of the genesis of substance neither boils down to matter as passive nor to form as pure: what generates is the *complete system,* and it generates because it is a system of the actualization of potential energy that combines in an active mediation two realities of two different orders of magnitude within an intermediate order.

In the classical sense of the term, individuation cannot have its principle in matter or in form; neither form nor matter are enough for form-taking. The veritable principle of individuation is genesis itself in the course of being carried out, i.e. the system in the course of becoming while energy is actualized. The veritable principle of individuation cannot be sought in what exists before individuation occurs or in what remains after individuation is completed; what is individuating is the energetic system, to the extent that it realizes within it this internal resonance of the matter about to take form and a mediation between orders of magnitude. The principle of individuation is the singular manner in which the internal resonance of *this* matter about to take *this* form is established. What makes it such that a being is itself, different from all others, is neither its matter nor its form but the operation through which its matter has taken form in a certain system of internal resonance. The principle of individuation of the brick is neither the clay nor the mold: other bricks than this will emerge from this pile of clay and this mold, and they will each have their own haecceity, but the principle of individuation is this operation through which the clay, at a given moment in an energetic system that consisted of the smallest details of the mold as well as the smallest pilings of this humid earth, has taken form under a certain pressure, distributed in a certain way, diffused in a certain way, and actualized in a certain way: there has been a moment when the energy of the pressure has been transmitted in all directions from each molecule to all the others, from the clay to the walls and from the walls to the clay: the principle of individuation is the operation that realizes an energetic exchange between the form and the matter up to the point that the ensemble ends in a state of equilibrium. It could be said that the principle of individuation is *the allagmatic operation common to matter and form through the actualization of potential energy.* This energy is the energy of a system; it can produce effects in all the points of the system equally, is available, and can be communicated. This operation depends on the singularity or singularities of the concrete *here and now*; it envelops them and amplifies them.[8]

3. Limits of the Hylomorphic Schema

Nevertheless, the technological paradigm cannot be extended in a purely analogical way to the genesis of all beings. The technical operation is completed in a limited time; after actualization, it leaves behind a partially individuated, more or less stable being that inherits its haecceity from this operation of individuation that has constituted its genesis in a very short time; at the end of several years or several thousand years, the brick turns back into dust. The individuation is completed in a single stroke; the individuated being is never more perfectly individuated than when it leaves the hands of the craftsman. Thus, there is a certain exteriority of the operation of individuation relative to its result. Conversely, in the living being the individuation is not produced by a single operation that is limited in time; the living being is to itself partially its own principle of individuation; it continues its individuation, and, instead of merely being a result that progressively degrades, the result of an initial operation of individuation becomes the principle of a further individuation. The individuating operation and the individuated being are not in the same relation within the product of the technical effort. Instead of a becoming after individuation, the becoming of the living being is always a becoming between two individuations; the individuating and the individuated are in a prolonged allagmatic relation in the living being. In the technical object, this allagmatic relation only exists for a moment when the two half-chains are connected to one another, i.e. when the matter takes form: in this moment, the individuated and the individuating coincide; when this operation is finished, they become separate; the brick does not bring its mold along with it,[9] and it becomes detached from the worker who or the machine that has pressed it. After its initiation, the living being continues individuating itself; it is simultaneously the individuating system and the partial result of individuation. A new regime of internal resonance is established in the living being, the paradigm of which technology does not provide: a resonance through time created by the recurrence of the result going back toward the principle and becoming principle in turn. Just like in the technical individuation, an ongoing internal resonance constitutes the organismic unit. But, in addition, a resonance of the successive, a temporal allagmatics, is superimposed onto this resonance of the simultaneous. The living being's principle of individuation is always an operation, just like form-taking, but this operation has two dimensions, that of simultaneity and that of succession through ontogenesis maintained by memory and instinct.

It can then be asked if the veritable principle of individuation is not better indicated by the living being than by the technical operation, and if the technical operation could be known as individuating without the implicit paradigm of life that exists in us, since we are the ones who know the technical operation and practice it with our bodily schema, our habits, and our memory. This question has a large philosophical scope, since it leads us to ask if a true individuation can exist outside life. In order to know it, what should be studied is not the technical, anthropomorphic, and consequently zoomorphic operation, but the processes of the natural formation of the elementary units that nature presents outside the realm defined as living.

Thus, the hylomorphic schema outside technology is insufficient in its commonplace types because it ignores the very center of the technical operation of form-taking and leads in this sense to ignoring the role played by the energetic conditions in form-taking. Furthermore, even if it is reestablished and completed as a matter-form-energy triad, the hylomorphic schema runs the risk of improperly objectifying a contribution of the living in the technical operation; the intention of the fabricator is what constitutes the system due to which energetic exchange is established between matter and energy in form-taking; this system is not part of the individuated object; however, the individuated object is thought by the human being as having an individuality as a fabricated object relative to the fabrication. The haecceity of this brick as a brick is not an absolute haecceity and is not the haecceity of this preexisting object because it is a brick. It is the haecceity of the object as a brick: it brings with it a reference to the intention of its usage and, through it, a reference to the fabricating intention and therefore to the human activity that has constituted the two half-chains joined into a system for the operation of form-taking.[10] In this sense, the hylomorphic schema is perhaps only seemingly technological: it is the reflection of vital processes in an abstractly known operation that derives its consistency from what is made by a living being for other living beings. This is how the great paradigmatic capacity of the hylomorphic schema is explained: coming from life, it returns to life and is applied to life, but it has a deficiency that stems from the fact that the apprehension of consciousness that made it explicit has grasped it through the improperly simplified case of technical form-taking; it grasps types more so than individuals and examples of a model more so than realities. The matter-form duality, which grasps merely the extreme terms of what is larger and smaller than the individual, leaves in obscurity the reality that is of the same order of magnitude as the produced individual and without which the extreme terms would remain separate, i.e. an allagmatic operation that is deployed on the basis of a singularity.

Nevertheless, it is not enough to critique the hylomorphic schema and to reproduce a more exact relation in the unfolding of technical form-taking in order to discover the veritable principle of individuation. It is also not enough to suppose in the knowledge gained from the technical operation a primarily biological paradigm: even if the matter-form relation in technical

form-taking is easily (adequately or inadequately) known due to the fact
that we are living beings, a reference to the technical domain still remains
necessary for us to clarify, specify, and objectify this implicit notion that the
subject brings with him. If an experience of the vital is the condition for a
representation of the technical, the representation of the technical in turn
becomes one of the conditions for the knowledge of the vital. Thus, we are
sent back from one order to the other, such that the hylomorphic schema
seems to owe its own universality mainly to the fact that it establishes a certain reciprocity between the vital domain and the technical domain. This
schema is also not the only example of a similar correlation: automatism in its
various forms has been used with more or less success in order to penetrate
the functions of the living being by means of representations that originate
with technology, from Descartes to contemporary cybernetics. Nevertheless,
an important difficulty emerges in the utilization of the hylomorphic schema:
it does not indicate what is the principle of individuation of the living being,
precisely because it grants to the two terms an existence prior to the relation
that joins them, or at the very least because it cannot allow us to think this
relation clearly; it can only represent the mixture or the piecemeal combination; *the manner in which the form informs the matter is not sufficiently
specified by the hylomorphic schema.* To utilize the hylomorphic schema is
to suppose that the principle of individuation is in the form or even in the
matter, but not in the relation of the two. The dualism of substances (soul
and body) is rooted in the hylomorphic schema, and we should consider
whether this dualism has in fact originated with the technical sphere.

In order to delve deeper into this examination, we need to consider all
the conditions that surround a notional awareness. If there were nothing but
the living individual being and the technical operation, then the hylomorphic schema perhaps could not be constituted. In fact, it indeed seems that
the middle term between the living domain and the technical domain, at the
origin of the hylomorphic schema, was social life. What the hylomorphic
schema primarily reflects is a socialized representation of labor and an
equally socialized representation of the individual living being; the coincidence between these two representations is the mutual foundation of the
extension of the schema from one domain to the other and the guarantee of
its validity in a determined culture. The technical operation that *imposes a
form on a passive and undetermined matter* isn't just an operation considered
abstractly by the spectator who sees what goes in and out of the workshop
without knowing the elaboration properly speaking. This is essentially the
operation controlled by the free man and executed by the slave; the free man

chooses the matter—which is undetermined because it suffices to designate it generically by the name substance—without seeing it, without manipulating it, and without preparing it: the object will be made of wood or iron or clay. The veritable passivity of the matter is its abstract availability behind the given order other men will execute. This passivity is the passivity of the human mediation that will procure the matter. The form corresponds to what the man who commands has thought by himself and what he must express positively when he gives his orders: the form is therefore *of the order of the expressible*; it is prominently active because it is what is imposed on those who manipulate the matter; it is the very content of the order, that through which he governs. The active characteristic of the form and the passive characteristic of the matter correspond to the conditions of the transmission of the order, which supposes social hierarchy: it is in the content of the order that the indication of the matter is an indetermination, whereas the form is determination, i.e. expressible and logical. It is also through social conditioning that the soul is opposed to the body; it is not through the body that the individual is a citizen, participates in collective judgments and shared beliefs, and lives on in the memory of his fellow citizens: the soul is distinguished from the body just as the citizen is distinguished from the living human being. The distinction between matter and form, between the soul and the body, reflects a city that contains citizens in opposition to slaves. It should indeed be noted however that the two schemas, the technological and the civic, if they coincide with one another in their distinction of the two terms, do not assign them the same role in the two pairs: the soul is not pure activity, full determination, while the body would be passivity and indetermination. The citizen is individuated as a body, but he is also individuated as a soul.

The vicissitudes of the hylomorphic schema originate from the fact that it is neither directly technological nor directly vital: it stems from the technological operation and from the vital reality mediated by the social, i.e. by the already given conditions (in inter-individual communication) of an effective reception of information, with the order of fabrication as a case in point. This communication between two social realities, this operation of reception which is the condition of the technical operation, obscures in the technical operation what allows the two extreme terms (form and matter) to enter into interactive communication: information, the singularity of the "here *and now*" of the operation, a pure event in the dimension of the individual about to appear.

II. Physical Signification of Technical Form-Taking

1. Physical Conditions of Technical Form-Taking

Nevertheless, if the psycho-social conditioning of thought can explain the vicissitudes of the hylomorphic schema, the former can hardly explain the permanence of the latter and its universality in reflection. This permanence throughout successive aspects and this universality that infinitely spans various domains seem to require a less easily modifiable foundation than social life. The discovery of this unconditional foundation requires the physical analysis of the conditions of possibility of form-taking. Form-taking itself requires matter, form and energy, and singularity. But, for a raw matter and a pure form to be able to divide two technical half-chains that will be rejoined by the grasping of singular information, it is necessary that raw matter already contain, before any elaboration, something that can forge a system leading to the terminal point of the half-chain whose origin is pure form. This condition must be sought *in the natural world* before any sort of human elaboration. Matter must be structured in a certain way for it to already have the properties that are the condition of form-taking. In a certain sense, we could say that matter contains the coherence of form before form-taking; yet this coherence is already a configuration with the function of form. Technical form-taking utilizes prior natural form-takings that have created what could be called a haecceity of raw matter. A tree trunk in the timber yard consists of abstract raw matter insofar as it is considered a volume of wood to be used; only the essence to which it belongs approximates the concrete by indicating that a certain behavior of matter will be encountered at the moment of form-taking: a pine tree trunk is not a fir tree trunk. But this aforementioned tree, this trunk, has a haecceity in its totality and in each of its parts, right up to a definite level of smallness; there is a haecceity in its totality in the sense in which the tree trunk is straight or curved, almost cylindrical or regularly conical, sectioned off more or less roundly or in a strictly flattened manner. This haecceity of the ensemble is truly how this trunk is distinguished from all others; it is not merely how the tree can be recognized perceptively but what is technically a principle of choice when the tree is utilized in its totality, for example in order to make a beam; this trunk is more suitable than another depending on the situation due to its particular features, which are already features of form, specifically a form worthy of the carpenter's technique, even though this form is presented by raw and natural matter. A tree in the forest can be recognized by looking for the trunk best suited to a certain precise usage: the carpenter merely needs to go into the forest. Secondly, the existence of implicit forms becomes manifest the moment when the craftsman works on the raw matter: a second level of haecceity manifests therein. A trunk quartered or stripped by a circular saw leaves behind two regular beams, but these are less solid than those from the same trunk broken into wedges; however, the four blocks of wood are seemingly equal, despite the quartering procedure utilized. But the difference consists in how the mechanical saw cuts the wood *abstractly* along a geometrical plane, without respecting the slack undulations of the fibers or their expansively spiral winding: the saw cuts the fibers, whereas the wedge separates them merely into two halves: the crack proceeds by respecting the continuity of the fibers, curving around a knot, following the heart of the tree, and guided by the implicit form that the force of the wedge reveals.[11] Similarly, a lathed tree fragment acquires a revolving geometrical form from this operation: but the lathing cuts a certain amount of the fibers, such that the figure's geometrical envelopment acquired through revolution cannot coincide with the sectioning of the fibers; the true implicit forms are not geometrical but topological; the technical labor must respect these topological forms that constitute a parceled haecceity, a possible information without anything lacking. The extreme fragility of unrolled wood, which prevents their usage in a single non-laminated layer, results from the fact that this procedure, which combines linear sawing and lathing, veritably yields a sheet of wood but without respecting the orientation of the fibers above a sufficient length: in this case, the explicit form produced by the technical operation does not respect the implicit form. Knowing how to use a tool is not merely to have acquired the practice of the necessary gestures; it is also knowing how to recognize, by means of the signals that come to man through the tool, the implicit form of the matter being worked upon at the precise spot that the tool attacks. The plane is not merely what cuts out a more or less thick chip; it is also what makes it possible to feel if the chip is cut out finely without splinters, or even if it begins to be uneven, which signifies that the orientation of the lines of the wood is opposed by the movement of the hand. What makes certain simple tools simpler, like the drawknife, which does excellent work, is that, due to their non-automaticity and the non-geometrical nature of their movement, which is entirely supported by the hand and not by an external system of reference (like the lathe), these tools allow for us to grasp continuous and precise signals that invite us to follow the implicit forms of workable matter.[12] The mechanical saw and the lathe violate the wood and misrecognize it: this feature of the technical operation (what could be called the conflict of levels of forms) reduces the possible number of raw materials that can be used to produce an object; all wood can be worked with a drawknife; some types of wood are already difficult to polish; but very few types of wood are suitable for the lathe, a machine which chips away along an orientation that ignores the wood's implicit form, the particular haecceity of each part; some types of wood that would be excellent for cutting tools, which can be oriented and modified during the labor process, become unusable for the lathe, which irregularly attacks them and gives them a rough, spongy surface by detaching bundles of fibers. The only types of wood suitable for the lathe are fine-grained or almost homogeneously grained with a system of fibers mirrored by a system of transversal or oblique bonds between bundles; however, these types of wood, which have a non-oriented structure, are not necessarily the ones that offer the greatest resistance and greatest elasticity to bending forces. Wood treated by the lathe loses the benefits of its implicit information; it presents no advantage over a homogeneous matter, like a malleable mold matter; on the contrary, its implicit form runs the risk of conflicting with the explicit form one wants to give it, thereby frustrating the agent of the technical operation. Finally, at the third degree, there is an elementary haecceity of workable matter that intervenes absolutely in the elaboration by imposing implicit forms, which are limits that cannot be surpassed; this is not matter as an inert reality but matter that harbors implicit forms imposing preliminary limits to the technical operation. In wood, this elementary limit is the cell or sometimes the differentiated mass of cells, if the differentiation is fairly extensive; thus, a vesicle, which is the result of a cellular differentiation, is a formal limit that cannot be surpassed: a wooden object cannot be constructed if the wood's details would have an order of magnitude inferior to that of the cells or the masses of differentiated cells when they exist. For example, if we wanted to construct a filter made of a thin laminate of wood pierced with holes, we could not make holes smaller than the grooves already found in the wood naturally formed; the only forms that can be imposed by the technical operation are those of an order of magnitude superior to the elementary implicit forms of the matter utilized.[13] The discontinuity of matter intervenes as form, and what happens at the level of the element happens at the level of the haecceity of the ensembles: the carpenter looks in the forest for a tree with the desired form because he cannot significantly straighten or curve a tree, and he must guide himself toward spontaneous forms. Similarly, the chemist or bacteriologist who would like a filter of wood or earth will be unable to pierce a slab of wood or clay: he will choose a fragment of wood or slab of clay whose natural pores have the dimension he desires; the elementary haecceity intervenes in this choice; no two porous slabs of wood are exactly alike because each pore exists in itself; one cannot be certain of the caliber of a filter except after trying it out because the pores are the results of a form-taking elaborated before the technical operation; the technical operation, which is an operation of modeling, molding, and sawing, functionally adapts the support of these elementary implicit forms but does not create the elementary implicit forms: one must cut wood perpendicularly to the fiber in order to have porous wood, whereas one must cut it longitudinally (parallel to the fibers) in order to have elastic and resistant wood. These exact implicit forms, i.e. the fibers, can be utilized either as pores (by transversal section) or as resistant elastic structures (by longitudinal section).

It could be said that the technical examples are still plagued by a certain zoomorphic relativism when the implicit forms are solely distinguished with respect to the use that can be made of them. Yet it should be noted that scientific instrumentation appeals to implicit forms in a completely similar way. The discovery that crystals can diffract X-rays and also gamma rays has objectively founded the existence of the implicit forms of raw matter wherein sensory intuition could grasp nothing but a homogeneous continuum. Molecular lattices act like a network that has been traced by hand on a slab of metal: but this natural network has an even greater elementary lattice that is much smaller than the finest networks that can be fabricated, even with micro-tools; thus, at the extremity of the scale of magnitudes, the physicist acts like the carpenter who goes out to look for a suitable tree in the forest: the physicist chooses to analyze the X-rays of a certain wavelength of the crystal that forms a network with an elementary lattice of the same order of magnitude as this wavelength; and the crystal will be cut according to a certain axis so that one can best use this natural network it forms, or it will be assaulted by the bundle of rays according to the best direction. Science and technics are no longer distinguished at the level of the utilization of implicit forms; these forms are objective and can be studied by science, just as they can be used by technics; furthermore, the only means that science has to study them inductively is to implicate them in an operation that reveals them; given an unknown crystal, we can discover its elementary lattice by sending out bundles of X-rays or gamma rays with a known wavelength onto it in order to be able to observe the figures of diffraction. The technical operation and the scientific operation are joined together in the operative mode they instigate.

2. Qualities and Implicit Physical Forms

The hylomorphic schema is insufficient to the extent that it does not account for implicit forms, since it distinguishes between the pure form (which is called form) and the implicit form, which is conflated with other features of matter under the name quality. In fact, quite a large number of qualities attributed to matter are in fact implicit forms; and this conflation does not merely imply an imprecise classification; it also conceals an error: veritable qualities do not possess a haecceity, whereas implicit forms contain a haecceity to the highest extent.[14] Porosity is merely a global quality that a piece of earth or wood could lose or gain without a relation of inherence to the matter that constitutes it; porosity is the aspect under which the functionality of all these elementary implicit forms, which include the pores of wood such as they in fact exist, present themselves to the order of magnitude of human manipulation; pores become dilated or condensed, obstructed or cleared. Implicit form is real and exists objectively; quality often results from the choice that the technical elaboration makes concerning implicit forms; the same wood will be permeable or impermeable according to the manner in which it has been cut, whether perpendicular or parallel to the fibers.

When it is used to describe or characterize a type of matter, quality just ends up as an approximate, somewhat statistical knowledge; the essential porosity of a tree is the greater or lesser chance one has to encounter a certain number of non-obstructed vesicles per square centimeter. Quite a few qualities—particularly those relative to superficial states, like smoothness, granulation, polish, coarseness, and softness—designate statistically predictable implicit forms: this qualification is merely a global evaluation linked to the magnitude of a certain implicit form generally presented by a certain matter. Descartes put a lot of effort into reducing qualities to elementary structures because he did not dissociate matter and form and because he considered matter as capable of essentially conveying forms to all levels of magnitudes, not only to the level of the extreme smallness of the corpuscles of subtle matter but also to the level of the primordial vortices from which our galaxies emerged. The vortices of subtle matter, which constitute light or transmit magnetic forces, are on the small scale what cosmic vortices are on the large scale. The form is not attached to a determinate order of magnitude, like the technical elaboration would lead us to believe, insofar as it reduces to qualities of matter all the forms that constitute this matter as an already structured being before any elaboration.

It can thus be asserted that the technical operation reveals and utilizes already existing material forms and moreover constitutes them from other forms on a scale larger than implicit natural forms work upon; the technical operation integrates implicit forms rather than imposing a totally new and foreign form on a matter that would remain passive vis-à-vis this form; technical form-taking is not an absolute genesis of haecceity; the haecceity of the technical object is preceded and supported by several layers of natural haecceity that it systematizes, reveals, and clarifies and that comodulate the operation of form-taking. This is why it can be supposed that the first types of matter elaborated by humans were not absolutely raw matter but matter already structured on the scale of human tools and human hands: plant and animal products, already structured and specialized by their vital functions—like skin, bone, bark, the supple wood of the branch, and flexible vines—were certainly used rather than absolutely raw matter; these seemingly first matters are the vestiges of a living haecceity, and this is why they are already present themselves to the technical operation as elaborated, and whereby all that remains for the operation is to accommodate them. The Roman water skin is a goatskin sewn at the extremities of the legs and neck but still conserves the aspect of the animal's body; this also applies for the tortoise shell of the lyre or the skull of the bull still bearing horns, which is used to support the bar to which the strings of the primitive musical instrument are fastened. The tree could be modeled while it was still alive, while it would grow by developing according to a direction given to it; this can be seen with the bed of Ulysses, which is made from an olive tree whose branches Ulysses bends to the ground while the tree was still young; having become large, the tree dies, and Ulysses, without uprooting it, makes it into the frame for his bed, constructing the room around the place where the tree had grown. Here, the technical operation accommodates the living form and partially diverts the latter for its own benefit by leaving the care of completing the positive work of growth to the spontaneity of life. Furthermore, the distinction between form and matter certainly does not result from pastoral or agricultural techniques, but instead from certain limited artisanal operations, like those of ceramics and the fabrication of bricks from clay. Metallurgy does not fully allow us to think by means of the hylomorphic schema, since the raw material, which is rarely in the pure natural state, must pass through a series of intermediary states before receiving the form properly speaking; after it has received a definite contour, it is still submitted to series of transformations that add qualities to it (tempering, for example). In this case, the form-taking is not visibly carried out in a single instant but in several successive operations; we cannot strictly distinguish form-taking from qualitative transformation; the forging and tempering of a steel ingot are anterior for the former and posterior for the latter to what could be called form-taking properly speaking; forging and tempering are nevertheless constitutions of objects. Only the dominance of techniques applied to types of matter made plastic through preparation can guarantee the hylomorphic schema a semblance of explanatory universality, since this plasticity suspends the action of the historical singularities carried by the matter. But this involves a borderline case that conceals the singular action of information in the genesis of the individual.

3. Hylomorphic Ambivalence

Under these conditions, we can pose the question concerning what the attribution of the principle of individuation to matter rather than to form depends on. In the hylomorphic schema, individuation through matter corresponds to this characteristic of an obstacle or a limit, which is matter in its technical operation; what makes one object different from another is the set of particular limits—varying from one case to another—that guarantee that this object possesses its haecceity; the experience of the recommencement of the construction of objects coming out of the technical operation is what gives the impression of attributing to matter the differences that guarantee that one object is individually distinct from another. Matter is what is conserved in an object; what makes it such that the object is itself is the fact that the state of its matter at any moment summarizes all the events that this object has undergone; form, which is merely a fabricating intention, a voluntary arrangement, can neither age nor become; it is always the same, from one fabrication to another; it is at least the same qua intention for the consciousness of the one who thinks and gives the order of fabrication; it is the same abstractly for the one who controls the fabrication of a thousand bricks: he wants them all to be identical, of the same dimension, and according to the same geometrical figure. Whence results the fact that, when the one who thinks is not the one who works, there is in reality nothing in his thought except a single form for all the objects of the same collection: the form is generic not logically or physically but socially: a single order is given for all the bricks of the same type; this order consequently cannot differentiate the bricks effectively molded after fabrication into distinct individuals. The same does not apply when one thinks the operation from the point of view of the one who carries it out: a specific brick is different from another specific brick not just according to the matter required to make it (if the matter has been suitably prepared, it can be homogeneous enough not to spontaneously introduce notable differences between successive moldings), but also and above all according to the unique nature of the unfolding of the molding operation: the worker's gestures are never exactly the same; the schema is perhaps a single schema, from the start of the labor until the end, but each molding is directed by a set of particular psychical, perceptive, and somatic events; the veritable form (the one that directs the arrangement of the mold), the paste, and the regime of successive gestures change from one copy to the other like so many possible variations on the same theme; fatigue as well as the overall state of perception and of representation intervene in this particular operation, which is equivalent to a singular existence of a particular form for each act of fabrication, thereby translating into the reality of the object; the singularity, the principle of individuation, would then be in the information.[15] One could say that in a civilization that divides humans into two groups (those who give orders and those who carry them out), the principle of individuation, in line with the technological example, is necessarily attributed either to the form or the matter but never to both together. The one who gives orders to be carried out but does not accomplish them and only controls the result is one who has a tendency to find the principle of individuation in the matter— the source of quantity and plurality—because this person does not experience the rebirth of a new and particular form in each fabricating operation; thus, Plato considers that when the weaver has broken a shuttle, he fabricates a new shuttle not by fixing the eyes of the body on the pieces of the broken shuttle but by contemplating with the mind's eye the form of the ideal shuttle that he already finds within himself. Archetypes are unique for each type of beings; there is a single ideal shuttle for all sensible shuttles, past, present, and future. On the contrary, the one who carries out the labor does not see in the matter a sufficient principle of individuation, because for him matter is prepared matter (whereas it is raw matter for the one who gives orders without working, since he does not prepare it himself); however, the prepared matter is precisely what is by definition homogeneous since it must be capable of taking form. Therefore, the necessity of renewing the effort of labor in each new unit is what introduces a difference between successively prepared objects for the man who works; in the temporal series of the day's efforts, each unit is inscribed as its own instant: the brick is the fruit of this effort, of this trembling or resolute, hasty or weary action; the brick carries with it the imprint of a moment of the man's existence, it solidifies this activity exerted upon homogeneous, passive matter waiting to be worked; it emerges from this singularity.

Yet there is a considerable amount of subjectivity in the point of view of the master as well as in that of the artisan; the haecceity of the object defined in this way gets at nothing but the partial aspects; what the master perceives gets at the fact that objects are multiple; their number is proportionate to the quantity of matter employed; the number results from the fact that this very mass of matter has become this very object, this other mass of matter, this other object; the master rediscovers the matter in the object, like the tyrant who, with the help of Archimedes, uncovered the fraud of the goldsmith who mixed a certain mass of silver with the gold that would have been reserved to make a golden crown: for the tyrant, the crown is a crown made of this gold, of this particular gold; its haecceity is foreseen and awaited even before the action of fabrication, since the artisan, for the one who commands without laboring, is the man who possesses the techniques to transform the matter without modifying it, without changing the substance. For the tyrant, what individualizes the crown is not the form that the goldsmith gives it but the matter already having a quiddity before its transformation: this very gold, and not any metal whatsoever or even any gold whatsoever. Even today, the search for the haecceity in matter practically exists in the man who commands the artisan. For a landowner of the forest, the act of giving wood to a sawmill to chop up supposes that the wood will not be exchanged against that of another landowner, and that the products of the sawing operation will be made from the wood provided. However, this substitution of matter would not be a fraud, like in the case of the goldsmith who mixed silver with gold in order to be able to conserve a certain quantity of fine gold. But the attachment of the landowner to the conservation of his matter depends on irrational motives, one of which no doubt is the fact that the haecceity does not simply recover an objective characteristic detached from the subject but has the value of a belonging and of an origin. Only a commercially abstract thought could fail to attach a price to the haecceity of the matter and fail to seek a principle of individuation in it. The man who gives the matter to be elaborated places value on what he knows, what is attached to him, what he has surveyed and seen grow; for him, the initial concrete is the matter insofar as it is his, belongs to him, and this matter must be extended into objects; due to its quantity, this matter is a principle of the number of objects that will result from form-taking. This tree will become this or that plank; all the trees taken individually one-by-one will become this heap of planks; there is a passage from the haecceity of the trees to the haecceity of the planks. What this passage expresses is the permanence of what the subject recognizes of himself in the objects; the expression of the self here is the concrete relation of property, the bond of belonging. By placing the haecceity in information, the artisan does no act otherwise; but

since he is not the landowner of the matter on which he works, he does not
know this matter as a singular thing; it is foreign to him, it is not linked to
his individual history, to his effort qua matter; it is merely that on which he
works; he ignores the origin of the matter and elaborates it in a preparatory
way until it no longer reflects its origin, until it is homogeneous, ready to take
form, just like any other matter suitable for the same labor; the artisanal operation to a certain extent denies the historicity of the matter concerning what
is human and subjective about it; conversely, this historicity is known to the
one who has supplied the matter and valued it because it is deposited with
something subjective, because it expresses human existence. The haecceity
sought in the matter depends on a lived attachment to a specific matter that
has been associated with human effort and has become the reflection of this
effort. The haecceity of the matter is not purely material; it is also a haecceity
with respect to the subject. Conversely, the artisan expresses himself through
his effort, and the workable matter is nothing but the support and occasion
of this effort; it could be said that from the artisan's point of view the object's
haecceity only begins to exist through the effort of shaping; since this effort
of shaping temporally coincides with the beginning of the haecceity, it is natural that the artisan attributes the foundation of the haecceity to information, although form-taking is perhaps nothing but an event concurrent with
the advent of the haecceity of the object, the veritable principle of which is
the singularity of the *here and now* of the complete operation. Likewise, the
haecceity begins to exist for the proprietor of the matter with the purchase or
act of planting a tree. The fact that later this tree will be matter for a technical operation does not yet exist; this tree has a haecceity not as future matter but as an object or aim of an operation. Later, this tree will conserve the
haecceity for the proprietor but not for the artisan, since he has not planted
the tree and has not bought it as a tree. The artisan who signs and dates his
work attaches to the haecceity of this work the meaning of his definite effort;
for him, the historicity of this effort is the source of this haecceity; it is the
initial origin and the principle of individuation of this object. The form has
been a source of information through the work.

    On the other hand, if the question of the foundation of individuation can
be legitimately posed, and if this principle is sought somewhat in the form
and somewhat in the matter according to the type of individuation taken as
a model of intelligibility, it is probable that the technological cases of individuation in which form and matter have a meaning are still very particular
cases, and nothing proves that the notions of form and matter are generalizable. By contrast, what brings forth the critique of the hylomorphic schema,

the existence of a middle and intermediate zone between form and matter (the zone of the singularities that are the initiators of the individual in the operation of individuation), certainly must be considered an essential feature of the operation of individuation. It is at the level of these singularities that matter and form encounter one another in technical individuation, and it is at this level that the principle of individuation is the initiator of the operation of individuation: it can therefore be wondered if individuation in general couldn't be understood starting from the technical paradigm obtained through a recasting of the hylomorphic schema, leaving a central place to the singularity that plays a role of active information between form and matter.

III. THE TWO ASPECTS OF INDIVIDUATION

1. Reality and Relativity of the Foundation of Individuation

[The individuation of objects is not entirely independent from the existence of man; the individuated object is an individuated object for man: in man there is a need to individuate objects, which is one of the aspects of the need to recognize oneself and to rediscover oneself in things, and also to rediscover oneself in things as a being who has a definite identity stabilized by a role and an activity. The individuation of objects is not absolute; it is an expression of man's psycho-social existence. However, it cannot be arbitrary; there must be a support that justifies and receives it. Despite the relativity of the principle of individuation such as it is invoked, individuation is not arbitrary; it is indissociable from an aspect of the object that it considers, perhaps wrongly, as the only one possessing a signification: but this aspect nevertheless is truly recognized as having a signification; what does not conform to the real is the exclusion of the other points of view within which one could be placed to find other aspects of individuation. This is the unique and exclusive attribution of the principle of individuation to a given type of reality, which is subjective. But the very notion of individuation and the search for individuation, taken in itself as expressing a need, are not devoid of signification. The subjectivity of individuation for man and the tendency to individuate objects should not lead to the conclusion that individuation does not exist and does not correspond to anything. A critique of individuation should not necessarily lead to the disappearance of the notion of individuation but instead should prompt an epistemological analysis that should lead to a veritable apprehension of individuation.][16]

Critique and epistemological analysis cannot be restricted to indicating a possible relativity of the search for the principle of individuation, and they cannot be restricted to indicating its subjective, psycho-social signification. It is furthermore necessary to study the content of the notion of individuation in order to see if it expresses something subjective and if the duality between the conditions of the attribution of this principle to form or to matter is rediscovered in the very content of the notion. Without researching the principle of individuation, the following question can be posed: what is individuation? Yet here an important divergence appears between two groups of notions. It can be asked why an individual is what it is. It can also be asked why an individual is different from all other individuals and cannot be confused with them. Nothing proves that the two aspects of individuation are identical. To confuse these two aspects is to suppose that an individual is what it is (at the interior of itself, in itself, relative to itself) because it involves a definite relation with other individuals and not with another specific individual, but with all other individuals. In the first sense, individuation is a set of intrinsic characteristics; in the second sense, individuation is a set of extrinsic characteristics, i.e. relations. But how can these two series of characteristics accommodate one another? In what sense do the intrinsic and the extrinsic form a unity? Should intrinsic and extrinsic characteristics really be separated and considered as effectively intrinsic and extrinsic, or instead should they be considered as indicating a deeper, more essential mode of existence that is expressed in the two aspects of individuation? But then, can it still be said that the basic principle is indeed the principle of individuation with its usual content, i.e. supposing that there is reciprocity between the fact that a being is what it is and the fact that it is different from other beings? It seems that the veritable principle must be discovered at the level of the compatibility between the positive aspect and the negative aspect of the notion of individuation. Perhaps then the representation of the individual will have to be modified, just like the hylomorphic schema in its incorporation of information.

How can what is proper to an individual be bound to what this individual would be if it did not possess what it possesses on its own? We should question if an individual's singularity or singularities play a real role in individuation, or instead if these are secondary aspects of individuation that are added to it but do not play a positive role.

To place the principle of individuation in form or in matter is to suppose that the individual can be individuated by something that preexists its genesis and contains individuation in embryo. The principle of individuation precedes the genesis of the individual. When we search for a principle of individuation that exists before the individual, we are forced to place it in matter or in form, since only form and matter preexist; because they are separated from one another and because their union is contingent, the principle of individuation cannot be made to reside in the system of form and matter qua system, since the latter is only constituted the moment when matter takes form. Any theory that wants to make the principle of individuation preexist individuation must necessarily attribute it to form or to matter and exclusively to one or the other. In this case, the individual is merely the union of a form and a matter, and it is a complete reality. And yet the examination of the operation of form-taking as incomplete as that realized by the technical operation shows us that, even if implicit forms already preexist, form-taking can only be effectuated if matter and form are joined in a single system by an energetic condition of metastability. We have called this condition the system's internal resonance, which establishes an allagmatic relation during the actualization of potential energy. In this case, the principle of individuation is the state of the individuating system, this state of allagmatic relation within an energetic complex that includes all the singularities; the veritable individual exists for a mere instant during the technical operation: it lasts as long as the form-taking.[17] After this operation, what remains is a result that will begin to degrade and not a veritable individual; this is an individuated being rather than a real individual, i.e. an individuating individual, an individual undergoing individuation. The veritable individual is one that conserves its system of individuation with it, thereby amplifying singularities. The principle of individuation is in this energetic system of internal resonance; form is only the individual's form if it is form for the individual, i.e. if it is suitable for the singularity of this constituting system; matter is the individual's matter only if it is matter for the individual, i.e. if it is implicated in this system, if it enters into this system as the vehicle of energy and is distributed in accordance with the distribution of energy. However, the appearance of this reality of the energetic system no longer allows us to say that there is an extrinsic aspect and an intrinsic aspect of individuation; it is at the same time and through the same characteristics that the energetic system is what it is and is distinguished from other systems. Form and matter, which are realities anterior to the individual and separate from one another, can be defined without considering their relation to the rest of the world, since these are not realities that have any reference to energy. But the energetic system in which an individual is constituted is neither more intrinsic nor extrinsic to this individual: it is associated with this individual, it is this individual's associated milieu. Through its energetic conditions of existence, the individual does not merely exist within its own limits; it emerges from a singularity. For the individual, relation has the value of being; the extrinsic cannot be distinguished from the intrinsic; what is truly and essentially the individual is the active relation, the exchange between the extrinsic and the intrinsic; there is extrinsic and intrinsic relative to what is first. What is first is this system of internal singular resonance, this system of the allagmatic relation between two orders of magnitude.[18] In terms of this relation, there is the intrinsic and the extrinsic, but the individual is truly this relation and not the intrinsic, which is merely one of the concomitant terms: the intrinsic, the interiority of the individual, would not exist without the ongoing relational operation that the ongoing individuation is. The individual is the reality of a constituting relation, not the interiority of a constituted term. It is only when the result of a completed (or supposed completed) individuation is considered that the individual can be defined as a being with an interiority relative to which an exteriority exists. The individual individuates and is individuated before any possible distinction of the extrinsic and the intrinsic. The third reality, which we call milieu or constituting energetic system, should not be conceived as a new term that would be added onto matter: the milieu is the very activity of relation, the reality of the relation between two orders that communicate across a singularity.

The hylomorphic schema is not merely inadequate for the knowledge of the principle of individuation; it also leads to a representation of individual reality that is incorrect: it turns the individual into the possible term of a relation, whereas the individual, on the contrary, is a theater and agent of a relation; the individual can only be a term in an ancillary way because it is essentially a theater or agent of an interactive communication. To want to characterize the individual in itself or relative to other realities is to turn it into a relational term, i.e. into a relation with itself or a relation with another reality; first, one must find the point of view from which the individual can be grasped as an activity of relation, not as a term of this relation; properly speaking, the individual is in relation neither with itself nor with other realities; it is the being *of* relation and not a being *in* relation, for relation is an intense operation, an active center.

Consequently, the act of researching if the principle of individuation is what makes it such that the individual is positively itself, or if it is what makes it such that the individual isn't other individuals, does not correspond to individual reality. The principle of the individual is the individual itself in its activity, which is relational in itself as a center and singular mediation.

2. The Energetic Foundation of Individuation:
Individuation and Milieu

We would like to show that the principle of individuation is not an isolated reality, that it is not localized within itself, and that it does not preexist the individual like an already individualized embryo of the individual; that the principle of individuation, in the strict sense of the term, is the complete system in which the genesis of the individual takes place; that, moreover, this system outlasts itself within the living individual as a milieu associated with the individual in which individuation continues to take place; and that life is therefore an ongoing individuation, an individuation continued through time, extending a singularity. What the hylomorphic schema lacks is the indication of the condition of communication and of metastable equilibrium, i.e. the condition of internal resonance in a determined milieu, which can be designated by the physical term of system. The notion of system is necessary to define the energetic condition, for potential energy only exists relative to the possible transformations in a defined system. The limits of this system are not arbitrarily selected by the knowledge that the subject gains from them; these limits exist relative to the system itself.

According to this path of research, the constituted individual wouldn't be able to seem like an entirely detached, absolute being in conformity with the model of substance, like the pure σύνολον [súnolon]. Individuation would be nothing but one of the possible becomings of a system and would be able, moreover, to exist on several levels and more or less completely; the individual as a definite, isolated, consistent being would be merely one of the two parts of the complete reality; instead of the σύνολον [súnolon], the individual would be the result of a certain organizational event occurring within the σύνολον and dividing it into two complementary realities: the individual and the associated milieu after individuation; the associated milieu is the complement of the individual relative to the original whole. *The individual alone is therefore not exactly a type of being; for this reason, it cannot maintain a relation qua term with another symmetrical term.* The separate individual is an incomplete, partial being that can only be adequately known if it is put back into the σύνολον from whence it originates. The model of being is either the σύνολον before the genesis of the individual or the individual-associated milieu coupling after the genesis of the individual. Instead of conceiving individuation as a synthesis of form and matter or of body and mind, we shall represent it as a splitting, a resolution, a non-symmetrical distribution occurring in a totality based on a singularity. For this reason, the individual is not a concrete being, a complete being, to the extent that it is merely a part of the being after the resolving individuation. The individual cannot account for itself on the basis of itself, because it is not the being's whole to the extent that it is the expression of a resolution. It is simply the complementary symbol of another real, i.e. the associated milieu (here, as in Plato, the word symbol is taken in the original sense with respect to the usage of relations of hospitality: a stone broken into two halves produces a pair of symbols; each fragment, conserved by the descendants of those who have bound together relations of hospitality, can be brought together with its complementary piece in a way so as to reconstitute the initial unity of the broken stone; each half is a symbol relative to the other; it is the complementary of the other relative to the initial whole. The symbol is not what each half is relative to the people who produced it, but each half relative to the other half with which it reconstitutes the whole. The possibility of the reconstitution of a whole is not a part of hospitality but an expression of hospitality: it is a sign). Individuation will thus be presented as one of the possibilities of the being's becoming that responds to certain definite conditions. The method employed consists in not being given beforehand the realized individual that must be explained but in grasping the complete reality before individuation. Indeed, if the individual is grasped after individuation, then we wind up with the hylomorphic schema because nothing would remain in the individuated individual except these two visible aspects of form and matter; yet the individuated individual is not a complete reality, and individuation is not explainable by means of the mere elements that the analysis of the individual after individuation can discover. The role of the energetic condition (the condition of the state of the constituting system) cannot be grasped in the constituted individual. This is why it has been ignored even to this day; in fact, the different studies of individuation have wanted to grasp in the constituted individual an element capable of explaining the individuation of this individual: this would only be possible if the individual were and had always been a complete system unto itself. But individuation cannot be inducted on the basis of the individuated: the genesis of the individual in a system can only be followed step by step; at a certain point, every regressive step seeking to lead back to individuation—starting from individuated realities—discovers another reality, a supplementary reality that can be variously interpreted according to the presuppositions of the system of thought in which the research is carried out (for example, by resorting to the schema of creation in order to put matter and form into relation, or instead, in the doctrines that want to avoid creationism, by resorting to the clinamen of atoms and the force of nature that pushes them to encounter one another with an implicit effort: *conata est nequiquam*,[19] which is what Lucretius says about Nature).

The essential difference between the classical study of individuation and what we are presenting here is the following: individuation will not be considered solely from the perspective of the explanation of the individuated individual; it will be grasped, or at the very least we will say that it should be grasped, before and during the genesis of the separate individual; individuation is an event and an operation within a reality that is richer than the individual that results from it.[20] Furthermore, the separation initiated by the individuation within the system cannot lead to the individual's isolation; individuation, then, is the structuration of a system without a separation of the individual and its complementary, such that individuation introduces a new regime of the system but does not break the system. In this case, the individual must be known, not abstractly, but by going back to individuation, i.e. by going back to the state starting from which it is possible to genetically grasp the entire reality of which the individual and its complement of being is composed. The principle of the method we are proposing consists in supposing that there is a conservation of being and that thinking cannot occur except based on a complete reality. This is why it is necessary to consider the transformation of a complete domain of being, all the way from the state that precedes individuation up to the state that follows or extends it.

This method does not seek to diminish the consistency of the individual being but merely to grasp it in the system of concrete being in which its genesis takes place. If the individual is not grasped in this complete systematic ensemble of being, it is treated according to equally improper and divergent paths: either it becomes an absolute and is conflated with the σύνολον [súnolon], or it is reduced to the being in its totality so much that it loses its consistency and is treated as an illusion. Indeed, the individual is not a complete reality; nor does the individual continue to have the entirety of nature as its complementary, in front of which it would become an inferior reality; the individual's complementary is a reality on the same order as its own, like the being of a pair relative to the other being with which it is paired; at the very least, it is through the intermediary of this associated milieu that the being is connected back to what is larger than it and to what is smaller than it.

[In a certain sense, there is a complete opposition between Leibniz's monad and Spinoza's individual, because Leibniz's world is composed of individuals, whereas Spinoza's world includes, properly speaking, only a single individual, nature; but this opposition in fact arises from the individual's lack of relativity with respect to a complementary reality of the same order as its own; Leibniz fragments individuation down to the extreme limits of smallness, thereby according even individuality to the smallest elements of a living body; conversely, Spinoza expands individuation all the way to including the limits of the whole—that through which God is naturing nature—that is, individuation itself. There is no mention in either the work of Spinoza or Leibniz regarding a relation of the individual to an associated milieu, no mention of a system on the same order of magnitude within which the individual can receive a genesis. The individual is mistaken for the being and is considered as coextensive with the being. Under these conditions, the individual considered as coextensive with the being cannot be situated: all reality is simultaneously too small and too large to receive the status of individual. Everything can be individual, and nothing can be fully individual.][21] On the contrary, if the individual is grasped, not as the term of a relation but as the result of an operation and as the theater of a relational activity perpetuated in it, it is defined with respect to the ensemble it constitutes with its complement, which is of the same order of magnitude as it and on the same level as it after individuation. Nature in its entirety is not composed of individuals and is not itself an individual: it is composed of domains of being that can or cannot harbor individuation. In nature, there are two modes of reality that are not those of the individual: domains that have not been the theater of an individuation, and what remains of a concrete domain after individuation when the individual is subtracted. These two types of reality cannot be conflated, for the first designates a complete reality, whereas the second designates an incomplete reality that can only be explained by genesis, i.e. based on the system from which it emerges.

If we propose to know the individual relative to the systematic ensemble in which its genesis occurs, we discover that there is a function of the individual with respect to the concrete system envisioned according to its becoming; individuation expresses a phase change of the being of this system, thereby avoiding its degradation, incorporating the energetic potentials of this system as structures, making antagonisms compatible, and resolving the internal conflict of the system. Individuation perpetuates the system through a topological and energetic change; the veritable identity is not the identity of the individual relative to itself but the identity of the system's concrete permanence throughout its phases. The true haecceity is a functional haecceity, and the origin of finality lies in this underpinning of the haecceity that it translates into an oriented functionality, into an amplifying mediation between orders of magnitude initially without communication.

Thus, in terms of providing an adequate knowledge of the conditions and process of physical individuation, the insufficiency of the matter-form relation leads us to analyze the role played by potential energy in the operation of individuation insofar as this energy is the condition of metastability.

CHAPTER TWO

Form and Energy

I. Structures and Potential Energy

1. The Potential Energy and the Reality of the System; Equivalence of Potential Energies; Dissymmetry and Energetic Exchanges

The notion of potential energy in physics is not absolutely clear and does not correspond to a rigorously defined extension; thus, it would be difficult to specify if the thermal energy stored in a heated body should be considered as potential energy; its potential nature is bound to a possibility of the system's transformation through the modification of its energetic state. A body whose every molecule would possess the same quantity of energy in the form of thermal agitation would not possess any quantity of thermal potential energy; indeed, the body would thus have attained *its most stable state.* Conversely, a body that would possess the same total quantity of heat—but in such a manner that this quantity would be in one region of molecules at a higher temperature and in another region of molecules at a lower temperature— would possess a certain quantity of thermal potential energy. Furthermore, this quantity of potential energy cannot be considered as eventually added to the non-potential energy contained in the body; this quantity is *a fraction of the total energy of the body that can give rise to a transformation, whether reversible or not;* this relativity of potential that characterizes energy becomes manifest clearly if it is supposed, for example, that a body heated homogeneously (and thus not possessing any thermal potential energy if it is the sole body constituting a system) can manage to make a potential energy appear if it is put into contact with another body of a different temperature. The capacity for an energy to be potential is strictly linked to the presence of a heterogeneity, i.e. of dissymmetry relative to another energetic support; by taking up example again, we can indeed consider a particularly demonstrative borderline case: if a body were heated in such a way that it contains certain molecules at a higher temperature and others at a lower temperature, and if these molecules are not grouped in two separate regions but mixed together randomly, for a microphysical observer the body would still contain the same quantity of potential energy when the molecules are grouped in a hot region as in a cold region, because the sum of potential energies presented by all the couplings formed by a hot molecule and a cold molecule would be numerically equal to the potential energy presented by the system formed by the group of all the hot molecules and the group of all the cold molecules; nevertheless, this sum of potential energies of the molecular pairs would not correspond to any physical reality, to any potential energy of the overall system; for this to happen, it would be necessary to organize the disorder by separating the hot molecules from the cold molecules; this is what the hypothesis of Maxwell's demon shows extremely well, which is taken back up and discussed by Norbert Wiener in his *Cybernetics*. The attentive consideration of the type of reality represented by potential energy is quite instructive for the determination of a method adapted to the discovery of individuation. Indeed, reflecting on potential energy teaches us that there is an order of reality that we can grasp neither through the consideration of a quantity nor through the consideration of a quality, nor by resorting to a simple formalism; potential energy is not a simple way of seeing, an arbitrary consideration of the mind; it instead corresponds to a capacity of *real* transformations in a system, and the very nature of the system is more than an arbitrary grouping of beings operated by thought because, for an object, the fact of belonging to a system defines for this object the possibility of mutual actions relative to the other objects that constitute the system, a possibility which ensures that the belonging to a system is defined by a virtual reciprocity of actions between the terms of the system. But the reality of potential energy is not that of an object or a substance consisting in itself and "having no need of anything else in order to exist"; indeed, it requires a system, i.e. at least another term. No doubt, we must struggle against the habit that leads us to grant the highest degree of being to substance conceived as absolute reality, i.e. reality without relation. Relation is not a pure epiphenomenon; it is *convertible into substantial terms,* and this conversion is reversible, like that of potential energy into actual energy.[1]

If a distinction of terms is useful for determining the results of the analysis of significations, relation can be called the arrangement of the elements of a system that has a scope surpassing a simple arbitrary view of the mind, and we can reserve the term of rapport for an arbitrary, fortuitous relation

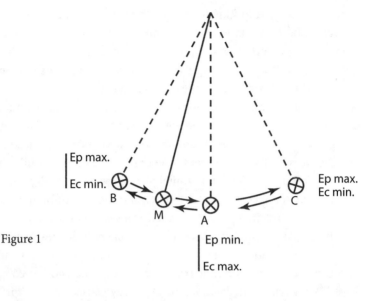

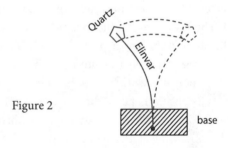

Figure 1

Figure 2

that is not convertible into substantial terms; relation would be a rapport just as real and important as the terms themselves; consequently, it could be said that a veritable relation between two terms is in fact equivalent to a rapport among three terms.

We shall begin with this postulate: *individuation requires a true relation,* a relation that can only be given in a system state that envelops a potential. The consideration of potential energy is not merely useful insofar as it teaches us to think the reality of relation; it also offers us a possibility of measure through the method of reciprocal convertibility; for example, let's consider a series of increasingly complicated pendulums, and let's attempt to note the transformations of energy of which they are the source during a period of oscillation: we shall see that we can confirm not only the convertibility of potential energy into kinetic energy, then into potential energy, which is converted back into kinetic energy, but also the equivalence of two different forms of potential energy converted into one another through a determinate quantity of kinetic energy. First, take for example a simple pendulum labeled OM that oscillates in the earth's gravitational field (Figure 1); if A is the point of the trajectory closest to the center of the earth, and if B and C are the extreme symmetrical positions relative to the axis OA, the potential energy is at a minimum in A, and the kinetic energy is at a maximum; conversely, in B and C, the potential energy is maximum, while the kinetic energy is minimum. If the horizontal plane passing through point A is taken as an equipotential surface of reference and the axes of mobile coordinates with respect to point O are considered as a system of reference for measuring the displacement of the axes of immobile coordinates, it could be said that potential energy is null in A and kinetic energy null in B and C: these two forms of energy are thus transformed into one another completely, at least if we neglect the degradation of energy caused by friction. Now let's take the case of a pendulum like the one constructed by Holweck and Lejay that enabled the establishment of the gravimetric network in France (Figure 2). The lower part of this pendulum is made of an elastic wire of encased Elinvar, and the upper portion involves a chunk of quartz. The connected pieces are placed in a vacuum tube in order to reduce damping. The operative principle at work here is the following: when the pendulum is distanced from its position of equilibrium, the momentums of the elastic forces and of the forces of gravity act in opposite directions, and, through a suitable adjustment, we can bring these two momentums to being only slightly different; since the period is determined by the difference of these momentums, it can be said that what has been created is a system allowing for the conversion of one form of potential energy into another form of potential energy via a certain quantity of kinetic energy equivalent to the quantitative difference between these two potential energies; if the two potential energies (that which is expressed through the momentum of elastic forces and that which is expressed through the momentum of gravitational forces) were rigorously equal, the pendulum would have a period of infinite oscillation, i.e. would be in a state of indifferent equilibrium. Everything occurs as if the potential energy that is effectively converted into kinetic energy and then reconverted into potential energy during an oscillation were an energy resulting from the difference between two other potential energies. The same pendulum, brought back to 180°, would on the contrary bring about an addition of two potential energies in the form of kinetic energy at the lowest point of the trajectory traversed by the chunk of quartz.

Ultimately, we could constitute a more complex system of pendulums coupled together without damping (weighted pendulums or torsion pendulums) (Figures 3 and 4). In this case, we would witness beats on each pendulum, and these beats would be more spaced out according to how weak the coupling would be. These beats themselves occur in a manner of quadrature,

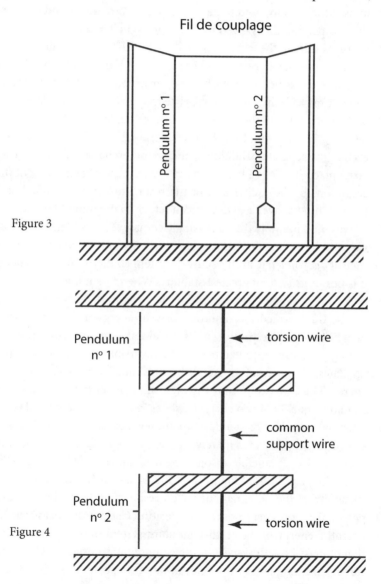

Fil de couplage

Pendulum n° 1

Pendulum n° 2

Figure 3

Pendulum n° 1

torsion wire

common support wire

Pendulum n° 2

torsion wire

Figure 4

i.e. because each of the pendulums seems to stop when the other reaches its maximum amplitude; the energy of the oscillations is transferred alternatively from one of the pendulums to the other. In a similar experiment, can we still estimate that the period of the resulting oscillation (of the transfer of energy) corresponds to a determinate potential energy? Yes, because if K designates the coefficient of the coupling between the oscillators that the two pendulums constitute, and ω designates the pulsation of these two pendulums, which is supposed to be the same for both, the period of the beats on the two pendulums is given by the expression $T = 2\pi \,/\, K\omega$. Here, potential energy resides in the fact that initially one of the two pendulums is animated by a movement, whereas the other pendulum is immobile; this dissymmetry is what causes the passage of energy from one pendulum to the other. If pendulums with the same appropriate frequency (animated by synchronous oscillation and with the same phase) were coupled together, the appropriate resulting period would not be the same as the period of the oscillation of each of the separate pendulums, and yet no exchange of energy would have taken place. There is a beat in the case where the dissymmetry of the initial conditions of the exciter and of the resonator can be nullified and transformed into its inverse and then can return to the initial state.

We could multiply the increasingly complex cases of energetic exchanges; we would find that potential energy always seems to be *bound to a system's state of dissymmetry*; in this sense, a system contains potential energy when it is not in its state of greatest stability. When this initial dissymmetry produces an exchange of energy within the system, the modification produced can be transformed into another form of energy; in this case, the system does not immediately return to its initial state: for it to return there, the preceding transformation will need to be reversible; in such a case, the system oscillates. This oscillation establishes the equality of two forms of potential energy. Thus, we can already distinguish the identity of two energetic states from the equality of two energetic states in the case of potential energy: two potential energies are identical when they correspond to the same physical state of the system, with merely a difference of measurements that could be suppressed by a suitable displacement of the axes of reference; therefore, when the pendulum of Figure 1 oscillates, it establishes the reciprocal convertibility of the potential energy corresponding to position B and of the potential energy corresponding to position C; since the measurement of the potential energy of the earth-pendulum system only depends on the position of mass M with respect to the equipotential surfaces (which are in this case horizontal planes), the determination of position B or position C only depends on the direction chosen for the measurement of elongation; the inversion of this direction makes it possible to identify the physical states corresponding to states B and C for the measurement of potential energy.

By contrast, let's consider the example of the Holweck-Lejay pendulum; it is no longer possible to identify (through a simple displacement of the conventions of measurement) the states of potential energy corresponding to the couplings of the forces of gravity and those corresponding to the elastic forces that come from the bending of the Elinvar wire. The oscillation, however, establishes the reciprocal convertibility of these two forms of energy, and this leads us to consider them as equal when the pendulum's state of indifferent equilibrium is found to be realized: potential energy defines the real formal conditions of the state of a system.[2]

2. Different Orders of Potential Energy; Notions of Phase Changes and of the Stable and Metastable Equilibrium of a State. Tammann's Theory

The potential energies of the three physical systems we have contemplated can be said to belong to the same order, not merely because they are mutually convertible during one of the system's periods of oscillation, but also because this conversion occurs continuously; it is this very continuity of conversion that permits the latter to be an oscillation in the proper sense of the term, i.e. to be effectuated according to a sinusoidal law in terms of time. It is indeed necessary to rigorously distinguish between a veritable oscillation—during which there is a conversion of one form of energy into another form of energy (which defines a period depending on the potentials in question and on the system's inertia)—and a mere recurrent phenomenon, during which a phenomenon that is non-recurrent by itself, like the discharge of a capacitor through a resistance, unleashes in its occurrence another phenomenon that brings the system back to its initial state. The latter case is that of phenomena of relaxation, which are called, perhaps misleadingly, oscillations of relaxation, the most contemporary examples of which are found in electronics in "oscillator" assemblages utilizing thyratrons, or in multivibrators, or even in naturally occurring geysers.

Nevertheless, if the existence of veritable oscillations in physical systems can allow us to define those energies that can be submitted to reversible transformations and therefore can be equal by their quantity as potential energies that are equivalent in terms of their form, there are also systems in which an irreversibility of transformations manifests a difference of order between potential energies. The most well-known irreversibility is the one illustrated by the research of thermodynamics and what the second principle of this

science (Carnot's principle) states concerning the successive transformations of a closed system. According to this principle, the entropy of a system
increases in the course of successive transformations.[3] The theory of the
theoretical maximum efficiency of heat engines conforms to this principle
and verifies it, to the extent that a theory can be validated by the fruitfulness
of the consequences that can be drawn from it. But this irreversibility of
the transformations of mechanical energy into caloric energy is perhaps not
the only irreversibility that exists. Furthermore, the apparently hierarchical
aspect implied in this rapport of a noble form to a degraded form of energy
runs the risk of obscuring the very nature of this irreversibility. Here, we are
dealing with a change in the order of magnitude and the number of systems
in which this energy exists; in fact, energy may not change in nature, yet its
order may change; this is what happens when the kinetic energy of a body in
movement is transformed into heat, as in the example often cited in physics
of a lead bullet colliding with an undeformable plane and transforming all of
its energy into heat: the quantity of kinetic energy remains the same, but what
the bullet's energy was in its entirety, considered with respect to the axes of
reference for which the undeformable plane is immobile, becomes the energy
of each traveling molecule relative to the other molecules within the bullet.
What has changed is the structure of the physical system; if this structure
could be transformed in the inverse direction, the transformation of energy
would also become reversible. Here, irreversibility stems from the passage of
a unified macroscopic structure to a fragmented and disorganized microscopic structure;[4] the notion of disorder further expresses microphysical
fragmentation itself; if molecular displacements were truly organized, the
system would in fact be unified; the macroscopic system formed by the bullet in movement relative to an undeformable plane and by this plane can be
considered as an organized set of molecules animated by parallel movements;
an organized microscopic system in fact has a macroscopic structure.

Yet, if we consider the exchanges of energy implicated in state changes
(like melting, vaporization, and crystallization), we will notice the appearance of particular cases of irreversibility bound to the changes of the system's
structure. When looking closely at a crystalline structure, for example, we
can clearly see how the ancient notion of the *elements* has to give way to a
theory that is both structural and energetic: the continuity of liquid and
gaseous states allows us to unify these two states in the shared domain of
fluid in the homogeneous state; by contrast, this domain of the homogeneous state is clearly separate (due to the frontier constituted by the curve of
saturation) from non-homogeneous states.

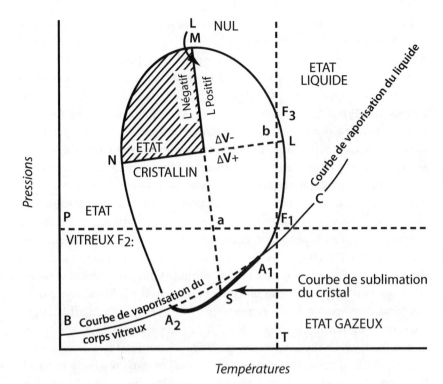

Figure 5

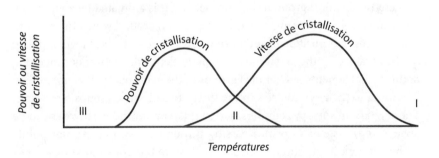

Figure 6

Between the crystalline and amorphous states, there is an evident discontinuity that we can liken to what exists between an energy of the macroscopic
order and an equal energy in absolute value but of the microscopic order,
like the thermal energy in which the aforementioned example has been able
to degrade during an irreversible transformation. Indeed, according to Tammann's hypothesis, the crystalline state would be characterized by the existence of privileged directions in crystallized substances. The properties of
these substances present different values following the direction in question;
such are the properties clarified by the study of the geometrical form of crystals and the various manifestations of crystalline anisotropy; the amorphous
state, on the contrary, which includes gaseous, liquid, or (vitreous) amorphous solid states, is characterized by the absence of privileged directions;
the properties of amorphous substances present values that do not depend on
the considered direction. A body in the amorphous state does not possess a
determined geometrical form and is isotropic. Only an external action—
such as a non-uniform pressure, a pulling, a twisting or the existence of an
electrical or magnetic field—can render a body amorphous, particularly a
vitreous, temporarily anisotropic body. If an amorphous body is represented
as a body in which the constitutive particles are arranged in a disorganized
way, we could suppose that the crystal, on the contrary, is a body in which
the elementary particles, atoms, or groups of atoms are arranged according
to organized distributions called crystalline networks. Bravais acknowledges
a distribution of the various elements or chemical groups of a crystal in terms
of a system in which each point represents the center of gravity of these various elements or chemical groups. (This simplified expression supposes the
element or chemical group to be immobile; if it is animated by a vibration,
the regular point represents the average position around which the element
vibrates; this is its position of equilibrium). All these systems of regular points
can be obtained by the juxtaposition of parallelepipedic networks containing
nothing but elements or chemical groups of the same nature that are ranked
according to their symmetries in the thirty-two classical groups of crystals.
The crystal's anisotropy is understood in this way, for these networks can be
divided into systems of planes passing through the various regular points
of the network in question, insofar as each system is constituted by a set of
planes that are parallel with and equidistant to one another: these systems
of planes correspond to privileged directions along which the crystals' lim-
itative surfaces can be arranged. Accepting Bravais's theory, Tammann completes this representation of the differences between the states of matter by
assimilating the amorphous solids with liquids that are endowed with a large

amount of viscosity and rigidity; this reveals that there is a veritable continuity between the solid and liquid states of a vitreous body; for example, at the normal temperature of its usage, glass presents an exceptional rigidity; when the glass blower raises the temperature, both the rigidity and the viscosity of the glass progressively diminishes until, at a very high temperature, what remains is a veritable liquid. The milky melting characteristic of amorphous solids never shows two distinct phases. Thus, Tammann considers the amorphous solid as a liquid whose rigidity and viscosity have been sufficiently reduced due to extremely high temperatures. The theoretical consequences of Tamman's hypothesis are quite important: a liquid that experiences a reduction of temperature without passing to the crystalline state is continually transformed into a vitreous body. It is therefore in a state of supercooling. Experiments on piperine, $C_{17}H_9O_3N$, and betol, $C_{10}H_7CO_2C_6H_4OH$, which are substances that melt at 128°C and 95°C respectively and easily remain in supercooling, have confirmed this hypothesis. But the mere consideration of the structures corresponding to the various states is incomplete and leaves behind an indetermination; this consideration must be completed by the study of the *different energetic levels* linked to each state and of the exchanges of energy that are produced during the state changes. Tammann's theory has an exemplary value because it leads to a study of the correlation between structural changes and energetic exchanges. In fact, it allows us to determine the conditions and the limits of the stability of crystalline and amorphous states. There are many bodies that can be present in the crystalline state or the amorphous state; yet, depending on temperature and pressure conditions, sometimes the crystalline state is stable while the amorphous state is metastable, and sometimes vice versa. The passage from the metastable state to the stable state gives rise to a determinate thermal effect and to a determinate volumetric effect. This important consequence of Tammann's theory can be represented by Figure 5. If we begin with a liquid substance in the state of stable equilibrium under a pressure P, and if we progressively lower the temperature by maintaining this constant pressure, the representative points will be displaced from right to left on F_1P parallel to the axis of temperatures. If the representative point enters into the domain of stability of the crystalline state, the liquid in question will be in the metastable state. In this state, the supercooled liquid can pass to the crystalline state, and this passage depends on two factors: the power of spontaneous crystallization that this liquid presents (defined by the number of crystalline germs that spontaneously appear in a set time within a given volume of liquid), and, on the other hand, the speed of crystallization, i.e. the speed at which a crystalline germ develops. The state of supercooling is easy to bring about if the maxima of these two factors (depending on the temperature) are sufficiently distant from one another such that one of the factors corresponds to a practically null value of the other factor; at this point, since these two factors both tend toward zero when the temperature continues to decrease, it is possible to cross quite rapidly through region II, which corresponds to a small but non-null probability of crystallization, and to arrive at region III, for which the chances of crystallization are practically null (Figure 6). While the liquid is in the metastable state, we can initiate crystallization, which is brought about with an emission of heat. This crystallization makes it possible to measure a latent heat of crystallization, which is the difference between the caloric capacity of the mass considered in the amorphous state and that of the same mass considered in the crystallized state, multiplied by the variation of temperature: $dL = (C_a - C_c)dt$. However, since the specific heat of a substance held in the crystalline state is inferior to the specific heat of this same substance held in the liquid or amorphous state, the latent heat of crystallization varies in the same direction as the temperature. It diminishes when the temperature lowers; thus, for a sufficient lowering of temperature, what will happen is that the latent heat of crystallization is nullified and then changes sign. The line MS of Figure 5 represents the location of the representative points for which the latent heat of crystallization is null depending on the various values that the pressure (which is constant for the same experiment) can take. Now let's consider the same liquid substance in the stable state at temperature T, which is in the domain of stability of the liquid state; if the pressure increases, we enter the domain of stability of the crystalline state. Since the liquid is then in the metastable state, the possible crystallization will correspond, for each pressure considered, with a variation ΔV of the volume that accompanies this transformation. If V_c and V_a are the respective volumes of the considered mass of the substance, whether in the crystallized state or in the amorphous state, then we get the formula: $d\Delta V = dV_a - dV_c$. If the variation of volume is affected in the direction of a contraction of the + sign, it will be found that, as in the case of the latent heat of melting, ΔV diminishes when the pressure increases, because a substance held in the amorphous state is more compressible than in the crystallized state. For a sufficient increase of pressure, ΔV can be nullified and then change sign. The curve LN of Figure 5 is the set of points for which the variation of volume is null. Below this curve, ΔV is positive (contraction); above this curve, ΔV is negative (dilatation). From the limits of the variation of the latent heat of crystallization and of the variation of volume, we can deduce the form of the crystallization-melting curve: along this curve, there are two triple points, A_1 and A_2, for which the crystal, the amorphous body, and the gas could coexist in mutual equilibrium. In A, the crystallization-melting curve encounters both the crystal's curve of sublimation A_2SA_1 and the vitreous body's curve of vaporization A_1B; this curve of vaporization extends the liquid's curve of vaporization A_1C. Furthermore, for each pressure, there would correspond two points of crystallization-melting in which the crystal could coexist either with the liquid or with the vitreous body (for pressure P, for example, these two points would be F_1 and F_2). At temperatures lower than this second point of crystallization, the representative point of the substance would again enter the domain of stability of the amorphous state. At this point, the vitreous state would be a stable state, and the crystalline state would be a metastable state with respect to the vitreous body. Undoubtedly, at these low temperatures, the speeds of transformation would be so low that they would be practically null; but this theoretical reversibility of stable and metastable states nevertheless keeps all of its importance; it has not been possible to further provide evidence experimentally for point L of the maximum of the melting temperature or point M of the maximum of the melting pressure, but the experiment has shown that all the melting curves have their concavity turned toward the decreasing temperatures, and that for water and several other substances this concavity is found, starting from the triple point A_1, in the portion of the ascending melting curve in the direction of the decreasing temperatures.

The interest of Tammann's hypothesis for the study of individuation is to establish the existence of conditions of indifferent equilibrium between two physical states, one of which is amorphous and the other of which is crystalline, i.e. states that are opposite in terms of their structures, the first of which is non-organized and the second of which is organized. The relation between two structural states thus takes on an energetic sense: indeed, the existence and the position of the triple points are determined based on considerations relative to the latent heat of crystallization and to the variation of volume according to pressure, i.e. to thermodynamic work. The limits of a structural type of domain of stability are determined by energetic considerations. This is why, in order to broach the study of physical individuation properly speaking, we wanted to define the energetic aspect of the relation between two physical structures. An energetic characteristic is linked to every structure, but, inversely, a modification of the structural characteristic of this system can correspond to any modification of the energetic conditions of this system.

For a physical system, the fact of having a given structure involves the possession of an energetic determination. This energetic determination can be assimilated to a potential energy, for it only becomes manifest in a transformation of the system. But, unlike the potential energies studied above, which are capable of partial and progressive transformations according to an ongoing process, the potential energies linked to a structure can only be transformed and unleashed by a modification of the conditions of stability of the system that contains them; thus, they are linked to the very existence of the system's structure; this is why we shall say that potential energies corresponding to two different structures are of different orders. The only point at which they are continuous with respect to one another is the point at which they are nullified, as in points A_1 and A_2 and F_1 and F_2 of Figure 5. In the case of a pendulum, on the contrary, where two potential energies bring about a mutual ongoing conversion, as in the Holweck-Lejay pendulum (Figure 2), the sum of these two energies and of the kinetic energy remains constant during the course of a transformation. The same thing even applies in the more complex case that Figure 3 represents. Conversely, the state changes undergone by the system forces us to consider a certain energy linked to the structure, an energy which is indeed a potential energy, but which is not capable of an ongoing transformation; for this reason, it cannot be considered suitable for the case of identity or of equality defined above. This energy can only be measured in a state change of the system; while the state remains, it is conflated with the very conditions of stability of this state. This is why we will choose to name those energies that express the limits of stability of a structural state as structural potential energies. These potential energies constitute the real source of the formal conditions of possible geneses.

II. Individuation and System States

1. Individuation and Crystalline Allotropic Forms; Being and Relation

We are attempting to show the validity of the notion of structural potential energy by using it as an instrument for the study of cases in which the notion of physical individuation requires a very delicate usage, and this is because these cases constitute quite a remarkable prefatory example: that of crystalline allotropic forms of the same substance. It will indeed be possible in a similar case to grasp individuation not only at the most primitive level but also at the level most exempt from any inessential logical inference. If it is possible to determine the characteristics of individuation at this level, these characteristics will be anterior to any idea of substance (since it is a question of the same body), of quality, and of quiddity. And yet, if we take up, for example, the study of the crystallization of sulfur, we shall see that it can exist in the solid state in several allotropic forms, the main two of which are sulfur crystallized in the orthorhombic system (octahedral sulfur) and sulfur crystallized in the monoclinic system (prismatic sulfur). At room temperature, octahedral sulfur is in a stable state; octahedral crystals of natural sulfur can be found in certain Tertiary terrains; the crystals that we prepare remain clear indefinitely. Conversely, the prismatic form is metastable with respect to the octahedral form; a crystal of this form, albeit clear when it has been recently prepared, becomes opaque when it is left to itself; the crystal maintains its external form, but a microscopic examination reveals that fragments into a mosaic of juxtaposed octahedral crystals,[5] which is where the observed opacity comes from. The metastable state of prismatic sulfur is called crystalline supercooling. This relation between crystalline prismatic and octahedral states exists for temperatures below 95.4°C, but reverses starting from 95.4°C up to 115°C, which is the melting temperature. In this interval, prismatic sulfur is in stable equilibrium, and octahedral sulfur is in metastable equilibrium. Under atmospheric pressure, 95.4°C is the temperature of equilibrium between these two crystalline varieties.

With this in mind, it can be asked: what does the individuality of each of these two forms consist in? What ensures the stability of these forms, what makes it so that they can both exist at a determined temperature? When either of these two forms is found in a state of metastability, a crystalline germ is required, i.e. a point of departure for crystallization, so as to help it transform into the other stable form. Everything happens as if metastable equilibrium could only be disrupted by the local deposit of a singularity contained in a crystalline germ that can disrupt this metastable equilibrium; once it has been initiated, the transformation propagates, for the action that is exerted at the start between the crystalline germ and the metastable body is then exerted gradually between the transformed parts and the parts that are not yet transformed.[6] Physicists ordinarily use a word borrowed from the vocabulary of biology to designate the action of depositing a germ: they say that the substance is inseminated with a crystalline germ. A particularly demonstrative experiment consists in placing supercooled sulfur into a U-tube, then inseminating each of the branches of the U-tube with a crystalline germ that is octahedral on one side and prismatic on the other; the sulfur contained in each branch of the tube then crystallizes according to the crystalline system that is determined by the deposited germ; the two allotropic forms of crystallized sulfur are thus in perfect contact in the middle part of the tube. If the temperature is lower than 95.4°C, the sulfur remains transparent, and the branch containing the octahedral sulfur becomes opaque starting with the line of contact between the two crystalline varieties. Opacity begins to manifest at the contact of these two allotropic varieties, and it gradually propagates to the point of taking over the whole branch containing the prismatic sulfur. Conversely, if the temperature is maintained between 95.4°C and 115°C, the direction of the transformation is inverted: the branch containing prismatic sulfur remains transparent, and the branch containing octahedral sulfur becomes opaque starting with the line of contact between the two crystalline varieties. Lastly, at a temperature of 95.4°C, the speed of propagation of these transformations is null. There is thus a temperature at which equilibrium is attained between these two crystalline varieties. From a certain perspective, this experiment entails the creation of a sort of competition for a finite quantity of substance between two systems. For all temperatures other than the temperature of equilibrium (and lower than the melting temperature of octahedral sulfur), one of the forms occupies the whole crystallizable substance, and the other completely disappears.[7]

And here, we begin to grasp one of the primary and fundamental aspects of physical individuation. Individuation as an operation is not linked to the identity of a matter but to a state modification. Sulfur conserves its crystalline system only if a singularity is not presented to make the less stable form disappear. A substance conserves its individuality when it is in the most stable state proportionate to its own energetic conditions. This state's stability becomes manifest due to the fact that, if the energetic conditions remain the same, this state cannot be modified by the introduction of a germ presenting an initiation of a different structure; relative to substances that are in a different state, this substance can on the contrary provide germs capable of involving a modification of the state of these substances. A stable individuality is thus formed when two conditions are met: a certain structure must correspond to a certain energetic state of the system. But this structure is not directly produced by the energetic state alone, for it is distinct from the latter; the initiation of structuration is critical; most often in crystallization germs are deposited from the exterior. Thus, there is a historical aspect to the manifestation of a structure in a substance, insofar as the structural germ must appear. Pure energetic determinism does not suffice for a substance to attain its state of stability. The beginning of structuring individuation is an event for the system in a metastable state. Thus, in general, even in the simplest process of individuation, a relation takes place between the body under consideration and the temporal existence of beings external to it that intervene as the evental conditions of its structuration. The constituted individual holds within it the synthesis of energetic and material conditions and of an informational condition, which is generally not immanent. If the encounter between these three conditions has not taken place, the substance has not attained its stable state; it then remains in a metastable state. However, let's note that this genetic definition of individuation through the encounter of the three necessary conditions leads to the notion of the hierarchical relativity of states of individuation. Indeed, when there is a very large hiatus between the energetic state of a substance[8] and its structural state (for example, sulfur in the state of supercooling), if a structural germ is presented, it can involve a change of the substance's structural state without however leading it to its state of absolute stability. If at a temperature of 90°C supercooled sulfur receives a prismatic germ, its structural state changes, and it becomes crystallized sulfur in the prismatic system. It has passed from an initial metastable state to a second metastable state; the second is more stable than the first. But if a second structural germ intervenes, i.e. a crystal of octahedral sulfur, the structural state still changes, and the whole mass becomes octahedral sulfur. In this sense, we understand why crystalline supercooling constitutes a less precarious state than liquid supercooling; a structural germ has already been encountered, but it has deposited a structure that is incapable of absorbing into the structuration all the potential energy represented by the state of supercooling. Complete individuation is the individuation that corresponds to a full deployment of the energy contained in the system before structuration; it leads to a stable state; conversely, incomplete individuation is that which corresponds to a structuration that has not absorbed all the potential energy of the initial non-structured state; it leads to a state that is still metastable. For the same substance, there are as many possible types of structures as there are hierarchical levels of metastability; for example, in phosphorous, we encounter three levels of metastability. Furthermore, it is important to note that the levels of individuation are perfectly discontinuous with respect to one another; the existence of energetic conditions of equilibrium between two levels immediately following one another in the hierarchical scale can neither obscure the structural discontinuity of these two levels, nor their energetic discontinuity; thus, going back to the example of sulfur, when octahedral sulfur is brought to 95.4°C under atmospheric pressure, it is necessary to provide 2.5 calories per gram in order for it to transform into prismatic sulfur; consequently, there is a specific latent heat of transformation of octahedral sulfur into prismatic sulfur. This energetic discontinuity is also discovered by the fact that the melting point of the metastable variety is always lower than that of the more stable variety for all chemical types.

Therefore, it would seem that it is possible for there to be several levels of individuation underway throughout the ongoing changes of the allotropic forms of an element; only one of them corresponds to a complete individuation; there are a finite number of these states, and they are discontinuous with respect to one another both due to their energetic conditions and their structural conditions. The effective existence of an individualized state results from the fact that two independent conditions are achieved simultaneously: an energetic and material condition resulting from an actual state of the system, and an evental condition, which most often involves a relation to a series of events that arise from other systems. In this sense, the individuation of an allotropic form begins with a historical type of singularity. Two flows of volcanic lava of the same chemical composition can each be at different points of crystallization; these are local singularities of the eruption that are translated—through the particular genesis of this crystallization—into the individuation of the allotropic form involved. In light of this, all the characteristics for a substance that result from this double (energetic and historical) conditioning are part of its individuality. Due to the studies of physical chemistry, the geologist knows based on the history of rocks how to interpret the relative size of the crystals that constitute them. A paste that seems amorphous but is finely crystallized indicates a rapid cooling of the substance; large crystals, of which only the external form remains and whose entire matter is divided into microscopic crystals of another system, indicate that there have been successive crystallizations, the first form having become metastable with respect to the second. From the simple point of view of allotropic forms, an examination of metamorphic rocks is also fruitful for learning about the historical and energetic conditions of geological phenomena, like that of magma, whose source is eruptive: calcschist, quartzite, schist, gneiss, and mica schist correspond fragment by fragment to a certain particular modality of endometamorphism or exometamorphism for a determined pressure, temperature, and degree of humidity. Thus, we see that the consideration of the energetic conditions and of the singularities in the genesis of a physical individual does not in any way lead to recognizing mere types instead of individuals; on the contrary, it explains within the limits of a domain how the infinity of the particular values assumed by the magnitudes that express these conditions can lead to an infinity of different results (for example, the dimension of crystals) for the same structural type. Without borrowing anything from the domain of biology and without accepting the notions of common genus and specific difference, which would be too metaphorical here, it is possible based on the discontinuities of conditions to define types that correspond to domains of stability or metastability; then, within these types, it is possible to define particular beings that differ from one another based on that which (within the limits of the type) is capable of a finer, sometimes continuous variation, like the speed of cooling. In this sense, the individuality of a particular being rigorously includes the type as well as the characteristics capable of varying within a type. We should never consider a certain particular being as belonging to a type. The type is what belongs to the particular being just as much as the details that singularize it the most, since the existence of the type in this particular being results from the same conditions as those at the origin of the details that singularize the being. There are types because these conditions vary discontinuously by delimiting domains of stability; but because within these domains of stability certain parameters, which are part of the conditions, vary more finely, each particular being is different from a certain number of others. The original particularity of a being is not different in nature from its typological reality. The particular being does not *possess* its most singular characteristics any more so than its typological characteristics. Both the former and the latter are *individual* because they result from the encounter of energetic conditions and singularities, the latter of which are historical and local. If, within the interior of the same domain of stability, conditions that are still variable are not capable of an infinity of values but merely a finite number of values, it will have to be acknowledged that the number of effectively different beings able to appear is finite. In a certain quantity of substance, there could then be several identical beings that seem indiscernible. Certainly, on the macrophysical level we hardly ever encounter several indiscernible individuals, even in crystallization; furthermore, a substance in crystalline supercooling ends up transforming into the stable form relative to which it is metastable; but we should not forget that if we find ourselves in the presence of a large quantity of elements, nothing can guarantee the absolute purity of an allotropic form. A certain number of germs of the stable allotropic form can exist within a substance that appears to have a single form. Particular local conditions can be equivalent to this structural germ (for example, a trace of chemical impurity). Ultimately, to consider simple substance, we must therefore take the microscopic point of view. At this level, it seems that there can be veritable indiscernibles.

At the level where individuality seems to be the least accentuated (in the allotropic forms of the same element), it is not merely linked to the identity of a substance, the singularity of a form, or the action of a force. A pure substantialism, a pure theory of form, or a pure dynamism would be equally

powerless facing the necessity of accounting for physicochemical individuation. To seek the principle of individuation in matter, form, or force is to
be condemned to only explaining individuation in these seemingly simple
particulars, like, for example, that of the molecule or the atom. Instead of
constituting the individual's genesis, this would be to suppose this genesis
as already formed in the formal, material, or energetic elements and, due to
these elements already harboring individuation, to generate through composition an individuation that is in fact simpler. This is why we have not wanted
to undertake the study of the individual by beginning with the elementary
particle so as to mistake such a complex case as being simple. We have chosen
the most precarious aspect of individuation as the first term of the examination. And from the very beginning, it has seemed to us that this individuation
was an operation resulting from the encounter and compatibility between a
singularity and energetic and material conditions. The name allagmatic could
be given to such a genetic method that seeks to grasp individuated beings
as the development of a singularity that unifies (on an intermediate order of
magnitude) the overall energetic conditions and material conditions; in fact,
we should note that this method does not involve a pure causal determinism
through which a being would be explained when its genesis in the past
would have to be accounted for. In fact, the being extends in time the meeting of the two groups of conditions that it expresses; it is not just the result
but also the agent, both the milieu of this meeting and the extension of this
realized compatibility. In terms of time, the individual is not in the past but
in the present, for it only continues to conserve its individuality to the extent
that this constitutive combination of conditions persists in and is extended
by the individual itself. The individual exists such that the mixture of matter
and energy that constitutes it is in the present.[9] This is what could be called
the active consistency of the individual. This is why every individual can be
a condition of becoming: a stable crystal can be the germ for a metastable
substance in a state of crystalline or liquid supercooling. Dynamism alone
cannot account for individuation, because dynamism wants to explain the
individual through a single fundamental dynamism; yet the individual doesn't
just harbor a hylomorphic encounter; it stems from a process of amplification
unleashed in a hylomorphic situation by a singularity, and it extends this
singularity. We can indeed just as legitimately call a hylomorphic situation
that in which there is a certain quantity of matter grouped into subsets of
a system isolated with respect to one another, or a certain quantity of matter in which the energetic conditions and spatial distribution are such that
the system is in a metastable state. The state containing forces of tension

(a potential energy) can be called the system's form, insofar as its dimensions, its topology, and its internal isolations are what maintain these forces of tension; form is the system insofar as it is macrophysical and insofar as it is a reality that envelops a possible individuation; matter is the system envisioned at the microphysical, molecular level.

A hylomorphic situation is a situation in which there is nothing but form and matter and therefore two levels of reality without communication. The establishment of this communication between levels (with energetic transformations) is the initiation of individuation; it supposes the appearance of a singularity, which could be called information and which either comes from the outside or is subjacent.

[However,[10] the individual conceals two fundamental dynamisms, one of which is energetic and the other of which is structural. The individual's stability is the stability of their association. Right away, the following question can then be posed concerning the degree of reality such an investigation could lay claim to: should we consider such an investigation to be capable of attaining and grasping a real? Or is this sort of investigation not, on the contrary, subjected to this relativity of knowledge that seems to characterize the experimental sciences? In order to respond to this need for examination, it is necessary to distinguish the knowledge of phenomena from the knowledge of the relations between states. Relativistic phenomenalism is perfectly valid to the extent that it indicates our incapacity to absolutely know a physical being, at least without recreating its genesis and relative to the manner in which we know or believe to know the subject in the isolation of self-consciousness. But what remains at the basis of the critique of knowledge is this postulate that being is fundamentally substance, i.e. in-itself and for-itself. The critique of pure reason is essentially addressed to the substantialism of Leibniz and Wolff; through the latter, this postulate affects all substantialisms and those of Descartes and Spinoza in particular. The Kantian noumenon is not unrelated to the substance of rationalist and realist theories. But if we refuse to admit that being is fundamentally substance, the analysis of the phenomenon can no longer lead to the same relativism; the conditions of sensory experience indeed prevent a knowledge of physical reality through intuition alone. But we cannot deduce as definitively as Kant a relativism of the existence of *a priori* forms of sensibility. If noumena are indeed not pure substance but also consist of *relations* (like exchanges of energy or passages of structures from one domain of reality to another domain of reality), and *if relation has the same status of reality as the terms themselves,* as we have tried to show in the preceding examples—insofar as relation is not an *accident* relative to a substance but a *constitutive, energetic and structural condition that is extended in the existence of constituted beings*—then the *a priori* forms of sensibility that allow us to grasp relations because they are a power of organizing according to *succession* or according to *simultaneity* do not create an irremediable relativity of knowledge. If relation effectively has the value of truth, then both the relation within the *subject* and the relation between the *subject* and the *object* can have the value of reality. True knowledge is a relation, not a simple formal rapport comparable to the rapport of two figures between them. True knowledge is knowledge that corresponds to the greatest possible stability in the given conditions of the *subject-object relation*. There can be different levels of knowledge, just as there can be different degrees of stability of a relation. There can be a type of knowledge that is the most stable possible for a certain subjective condition and a certain objective condition; if a later modification of subjective conditions (for example, the discovery of new mathematical relations) or objective conditions turns up, the old type of knowledge can become metastable with respect to a new type of knowledge. The rapport of the inadequate to the adequate is in fact that of the metastable relative to the stable. Truth and error are not opposed as two substances but are opposed as a relation enveloped in a *stable* state to a relation enveloped in a *metastable* state. Knowledge is not a rapport between an object substance and a subject substance, but a *relation between two relations*, one of which is in the domain of the object and the other of which is in the domain of the subject.

The epistemological postulate of this study is that the relation between two relations is itself a relation. Here we take the word relation in the sense defined above, which, opposing relation to the simple rapport, gives it the value of *being,* for relation persists in beings as a condition of stability and defines their individuality as resulting from an operation of individuation. If this postulate of the method of the study of constitutive relations is accepted, it then becomes possible to understand the existence and validity of an approximate knowledge. Approximate knowledge is not completely different from exact knowledge; it is merely less stable. Every scientific doctrine at any moment can become metastable with respect to a doctrine that has become possible due to a change in the conditions of knowledge. This however does not mean that the preceding doctrine should be considered false; it is also not *logically negated* by this new doctrine; its domain is merely submitted to a new structuration that leads it to stability. This doctrine is neither a form of *pragmatism* nor a new *logical empiricism,* for it does not suppose the usage of any criterion external to this relation that knowledge is, like intellectual utility or vital motivation: no commodity is required to validate knowledge. It is neither *nominalist* nor *realist,* for nominalism or realism can only be understood in doctrines that suppose that the absolute is the highest form of being and in doctrines that attempt to conform all knowledge to the knowledge of the substantial absolute. This postulate that being is the absolute underpins the dispute over universals conceived as a critique of knowledge. However, Abelard has fully perceived the possibility of separating the knowledge of terms from the knowledge of relation; despite the unintelligent jokes to which he has been submitted, he has brought forth with this distinction an extremely fruitful principle that takes on its full meaning with the development of the experimental sciences: *nominalism* for the knowledge of terms, *realism* for the knowledge of relation: this is the method that we can gain from Abelard's teaching in order to apply it by universalizing it. This realism of relation can thus be grasped as the postulate of research. If this postulate is valid, it is legitimate to ask the analysis of a particular point of the experimental sciences to reveal to us what physical individuation is. The knowledge that these sciences give us is in fact valid as knowledge of relation and can only give to philosophical analysis a being consisting in relations. But if the individual is precisely such a being, this analysis can reveal it to us. One could object that we are seeking a particular case and that this reciprocity between the *epistemological postulate* and the *known object* prevents legitimizing this arbitrary choice from outside, but we specifically believe that every thought, precisely to the extent that it is real, is a *relation,* i.e. includes a historical aspect in its genesis. A real thought is *self-justifying* but not justified before being structured: it includes an individuation and is individuated, thereby possessing its own degree of stability. In order for a thought to exist, it requires not just a logical condition but also a relational postulate that allows for its genesis to be accomplished. If we can resolve other problems in other domains with the paradigm that the notion of physical individuation constitutes, we could consider this notion as stable; if not, it will merely be metastable, and we will define this metastability with respect to the more stable forms we could have discovered: it will then conserve the prominent value of an *elementary paradigm.*]

2. Individuation as the Genesis of Crystalline Forms Starting from an Amorphous State

Is this manner of envisioning individuality still valid for defining the difference of crystalline forms relative to the amorphous state? If energetic conditions were the only ones to be considered, the answer would be immediately positive, for the passage from the amorphous state to the crystalline state is always accompanied by an energy exchange; at constant pressure and temperature, the passage from the crystalline state to the liquid state is always accompanied by an absorption of heat; there is presumably a latent heat of melting for the crystalline substance that is always positive. If, on the other hand, structural conditions alone were required, no new difficulty would be presented: the genesis of the crystalline form closest to the amorphous state could be assimilated to any passage whatsoever from one allotropic crystalline form to another. However, when we consider the difference between a substance in the amorphous state and the same substance in the crystalline state, it seems that the preceding definition of physical individuation is applicable only with a certain number of transformations or specifications. These modifications or specifications stem from the fact that the amorphous state cannot be treated as individual and that the absolute genesis of the individuated state is more difficult to define than its relative genesis through the passage from a metastable form to a stable form. The previously studied case then becomes a particular case vis-à-vis this more general case.

The passage to the crystalline state from an amorphous state can be formed in different ways: a solution that evaporates until saturation, vapors that condense on a cold wall (sublimation), or the slow cooling of a melted substance can lead to the formation of crystals. Can it be claimed that the discontinuity between the amorphous state and the crystalline state is sufficient for determining the individuated nature of this state? This would be to suppose that there is a certain symmetry and equivalence between the amorphous state and the crystalline state, which is not proven. In fact, we indeed observe a stage in the variation of physical conditions (temperature change, for example) while the crystals are forming, indicating that an energetic exchange occurs. But it is important to note that this discontinuity can be fragmented and not given *en masse* in certain cases, like those of organic substances with complex molecules, for example para-azoxyanisole; according to G. Friedel, these bodies (which are called liquid crystals by the physicist Lehmann who discovered them) present mesomorphic states that are intermediate between the amorphous state and the pure crystalline state. In their mesomorphic states, these substances are liquid but present properties of anisotropy, for example optical anisotropy, as M. Mauguin has shown. On the other hand, it is possible to obtain the same type of crystals starting from a concentrated solution of a melted liquid that is left to cool down or starting from a sublimation. It is therefore not with respect to the amorphous substance that the crystal consequently individualizes. The veritable genesis of a crystal as an individual is instead to be sought in the dynamism of the relations between the hylomorphic situation and a singularity. For example, let's consider the property that is characteristic of the crystalline state: anisotropy. The crystal possesses two types of completely different anisotropy. The first is continuous anisotropy: certain vectoral properties of crystals vary continuously with direction; this is the case of electrical, magnetic, and elastic properties and properties related to thermal dilation, caloric conductibility, and the speed of the propagation of light. But alongside these properties, we note other properties that vary discontinuously with direction: they are expressed by the existence of linear directions or planar directions with particular properties, whereas the neighboring directions do not possess them to any degree. Thus, the crystal can only be limited externally by certain linear and planar directions, according to the law stated by Romé de l'Isle in 1783: the dihedral angles that make up the natural facets of a crystal are constant for the same type. Similarly, the cohesion, such as it is revealed by the planes of cleavages or the appearances of parting, manifests a discontinuous anisotropy. Ultimately, the most beautiful example of discontinuous anisotropy is the diffraction of X-rays. A bundle of X-rays that strikes a crystal is reflected in a limited number of planes with well-determined orientations. However, these properties of discontinuous anisotropy arise from the genesis of the crystal as an individual and not as exemplary of a type; each individual is structured in this way. In an aggregate of crystals assembled without any order, each crystal has defined its facets, its dihedral angles, and its corners according to a *direction* of the ensemble that is explained by *external* circumstances, whether mechanical or chemical, and yet according to rigorously determined *internal* rapports starting from the singular genesis. For the crystal, the fact of being an individual consists in the fact that it has *developed* in this way relative *to itself.* There is ultimately at the end of the genesis a crystal individual, because an organized ensemble has developed around a crystalline germ that incorporates an initially amorphous matter that is rich in potentials by structuring it according to a proper arrangement of all the parts with respect to one another. Here, there is a veritable interiority of the crystal that consists in the fact that the order of the elementary particles is universal within a determined crystal; the unicity of this structure for all the elements of the same individual designates the initial existence of a germ that not only has initiated the crystallization as a change of state but also has been the unique principle of the structuration of the crystal in its particularity. This structural germ has been the origin of an active orientation that is progressively imposed onto all the elements included in the crystal as its growth continues; an internal historicity, which extends throughout the genesis starting from the microphysical germ all the way up to the ultimate limits of the macrophysical edifice, creates a completely particular homogeneity: the germ's initial structure cannot positively involve the crystallization of an amorphous body if the latter is not in a metastable equilibrium: a certain energy is required in the amorphous substance that receives the crystalline germ; but from the moment the germ is present, it possesses the value of a principle: its structure and its orientation take control of this energy of the metastable state; the crystalline germ, containing nothing more than an extremely small amount of energy, is nevertheless capable of guiding the structuration of a mass of matter several million times greater than its own. Undoubtedly, this modulation is possible because the crystal's successive stages during its development serve as relays for this initial structuring singularity. But it nevertheless remains true that the passage from the initial germ to the crystal resulting from the structuration of a single layer of molecules around this germ has indicated the capacity of the amplification of the ensemble constituted by the germ and the amorphous milieu. The phenomenon of growth is consequently automatic and indefinite, since all the successive layers of the crystal have the capacity to structure the amorphous milieu that surrounds them while this milieu remains metastable; in this sense, a crystal is endowed with an indefinite power of growth; a crystal can have its growth stopped, but it can never be considered complete, and it can always continue to grow if it is put back into a metastable milieu that it can structure. It is important to note quite particularly that the nature of the exteriority or interiority of the conditions is modified by the genesis itself. At the moment when the crystal is not yet constituted, the energetic conditions can be considered as exterior to the crystalline germ, whereas the structural conditions are carried by this germ itself. Conversely, when the crystal has grown, it has at least partially incorporated certain amounts of substance that constituted the support of the potential energy of the metastable state while they were amorphous. Thus, we cannot speak of energy external to the crystal, for this energy is carried by a substance that is incorporated within the crystal in its own growth. This energy is only provisionally exterior.[11] Furthermore, the interiority of the crystalline germ's structure is not absolute and does not autonomously regulate the structuration of the amorphous mass; in order for this modulating action to be able to be carried out, the structural germ must bring with it a structure corresponding to the crystalline system in which the amorphous substance can crystallize; the crystalline germ does not have to have the same chemical

nature as the amorphous crystallizable substance, but there must be an identity between the two crystalline systems in order for the apprehension of the
potential energy contained in the amorphous substance to be carried out.
The difference between the germ and the amorphous crystallizable milieu is
therefore not constituted by the absolute presence or absence of a structure
but by the state of actuality or virtuality of this structure. The individuation
of a system essentially results from the meeting of a mainly structural condition and a mainly energetic condition. But this meeting is not necessarily
fruitful. In order for it to have constitutive value, it is also necessary that the
energy can be actualized by the structure in accordance with local material
conditions. This possibility neither depends on the structural condition alone
nor on the energetic condition alone but on the compatibility of the germ's
crystalline systems and the substance that constitutes the milieu of this germ.
Thus, a third condition is manifested that we have not been able to note in
the preceding case because it was necessarily fulfilled, since the structural
germ and the metastable substance were of the same chemical nature. Here
it is no longer a question of the scalar quantity of potential energy nor of
the pure vectoral properties of the structure carried by the germ, but a question of a third type of rapport (which can be called analogical) between the
latent structures of the still amorphous substance and the germ's actual structure. This condition is required for there to be a veritable amplifying relation
between this structure of the germ and this potential energy carried by an
amorphous substance. This relation is neither purely quantitative nor purely
qualitative; it is different than a rapport of qualities or a rapport of quantities; it defines the mutual *interiority* of a structure and of a potential energy
within a singularity. This interiority is not spatial, for we are witnessing here
the action of a structural germ on its environment; it is not an equivalence
of terms, since the terms, statically and dynamically, are dissymmetrical. We
use the word analogy to designate this relation, because the content of Platonic thought relative to paradigmatism in its ontological foundations seems
to us more fruitful in this sense for consecrating the introduction of a relation
that includes energetic quantity and structural quality. This relation is information: the germ's singularity is effective when it arrives in a tensed hylomorphic situation. A precise analysis of the relation between a structural germ
and the milieu that it structures shows that this relation requires the possibility of a polarization of the amorphous substance by the crystalline germ.
The active range of this polarization can be very minuscule: from the moment
that a first layer of amorphous substance has become a crystal around the
germ, it plays the role of a germ for another layer, and the crystal can at that

point develop bit by bit. The relation of a structural germ to the potential energy of a metastable state is established in this polarization of amorphous matter. We must therefore seek the foundation of a genesis constituting the individual here. From the very beginning and from a macrophysical point of view, the individual always appears as the *bearer* of polarization; indeed, it is worth noting that polarization is a transitive property: it is simultaneously a consequence and a cause; a body constituted by a process of polarization exerts a series of polarizing functions, merely one of which is the crystal's capacity to grow.[12] Perhaps it would be possible to generalize the physical consequences of Pierre Curie's 1894 studies on symmetry. Curie's laws can be stated in two forms; the first utilizes current concepts: a phenomenon possesses all the elements of symmetry of the causes that produce it, and the dissymmetry of a phenomenon is found again in the causes. Furthermore, the produced effects can be more symmetrical than the causes, which means that the reciprocal of the first law is not true. This amounts to stating that if a phenomenon presents a dissymmetry, this dissymmetry should be found again in the causes; this dissymmetry is what creates the phenomenon. But, above all, the particular interest of Curie's laws resides in their precise state-ment: a phenomenon can exist in a milieu that possesses its characteristic symmetry or that of one of the subgroups of this symmetry. It will not be manifested in a more symmetrical milieu. The characteristic symmetry of a phenomenon is the maximum symmetry compatible with the existence of this phenomenon. This characteristic symmetry must be defined for each phenomenon, like the electrical field, the magnetic field, and the electro-magnetic field characteristic of the propagation of a light wave. However, it is acknowledged that the number of symmetry groups presenting one or several axes of isotropy is limited, and crystallographers have determined the possibility of only seven groups: (1) the symmetry of the sphere; (2) the direct symmetry of the sphere (that of a sphere filled with a liquid endowed with a rotatory power); (3) the symmetry of the cylinder of revolution (which is that of an isotropic body compressed in one direction, that of the cylinder's axis); (4) the direct symmetry of the cylinder, i.e. that of a cylinder filled with a liquid endowed with a rotatory power; (5) the symmetry of the cone's frustum; (6) the symmetry of a cylinder turning on its axis; (7) the symme-try of the rotating frustum of the cone. The first two systems present more of an axis of isotropy, and the last five present a single axis. Due to these systems, it is acknowledged that the symmetry characteristic of the electri-cal field is that of a cone's frustum, while the symmetry characteristic of the magnetic field is that of the rotating cylinder. It can then be understood under what conditions a physical individual, whose genesis has been determined by a polarization corresponding to a structure characterized by a certain type of symmetry, can produce a phenomenon that presents a determined polarization.

Thus, a phenomenon noted by Novalis and celebrated in the poetic invocation of the "tire-cendres" crystal (tourmaline) can be understood based on the system of the symmetry of the cone's frustum. The symmetry of the tourmaline is that of a triangular pyramid. A crystal of heated tourmaline reveals an electrical polarity in the direction of its ternary axis. The tourmaline is already polarized at ordinary temperatures, but a slow displacement of electrical charges compensates this polarization; the heating only modifies the state of polarization in a manner such that the compensation no longer takes place given a certain time; but the crystal's structure has not been modified. Similarly, magnetic rotatory polarization is linked to the symmetry characteristic of the magnetic field, that of the rotating cylinder. Ultimately, the interpretation becomes particularly interesting in the case of the phenomenon of piezoelectricity discovered by Jacques and Pierre Curie. It consists in the appearance of electrical charges through the compression or mechanical dilation of certain crystals; since the phenomenon consists in the appearance of an electrical field, the symmetry of the system that produces this field (the crystal and forces of compression) must be at best that of the frustum of the cone. Hence the fact that pyroelectric crystals can be piezoelectric; by compressing a crystal of tourmaline along the ternary pyroelectric axis, the appearance of electrical charges of the opposite sign are established. By contrast, crystals like those of quartz, which only have a ternary symmetry (the extremities of the binary axes are not equivalent), are not pyroelectric but piezoelectric, because, when a pressure is exerted along a binary axis, the only element of symmetry common to the crystal and the compression is this binary axis; this symmetry, a subgroup of the symmetry of the frustum of the cone, is compatible with the appearance of an electrical field along this axis. In such a crystal, the electrical polarization can also be determined by a compression perpendicular to the facets of the prism; the only element of symmetry common to the crystal's symmetry and to the cylindrical symmetry of compression is the binary axis perpendicular to the direction of the force of compression. The result is that crystals with no center of symmetry can be piezoelectric. This is the case of Rochelle salt (potassium sodium tartrate), which is orthorhombic and has an enantiomorphic hemihedry and whose chemical composition is indicated by the formula $CO_2K—CHOH—CHOH—CO2Na$.

The habit that compels us to think according to common genera, specific differences, and distinctive features is so strong that we cannot avoid using terms that imply an implicit natural classification; with this reservation in mind, if we consent to subtract from the word property the meaning that it takes in a natural classification, we shall say that, according to the preceding analysis, the properties of a crystalline individual express and actualize the polarity or bundle of polarities that have presided over its genesis by prolonging this polarity. A crystal, which is a structured matter, can become a structuring being; it is both the consequence and the cause of this polarization of matter, without which it would not exist. Its structure is a received structure, since it has required a germ; but the germ is not substantially distinct from the crystal; it remains included in the crystal, which becomes like a more extensive germ. Here the *soma* is coextensive with the *germen,* and the *germen* is coextensive with the *soma.* The *germen* becomes *soma*; its function is coextensive with the *limit* of the crystal that develops. This power of structuring an amorphous milieu is in some sense a property of the crystal's limit;[13] it requires dissymmetry between the interior state of the crystal and the state of its milieu. The genetic properties of a crystal are prominently manifested on its surface; these are the limit's properties. Thus, if we want to be rigorous we cannot say the "properties of the crystal"; they are instead modalities of the relation between the crystal and the amorphous body. It is because the crystal is perpetually unfinished, in a maintained state of suspended genesis, that it possesses what can be uniquely called "properties"; these properties are in fact the ongoing disequilibrium manifested by the relations with the polarized fields or by the creation (at the limit of the crystal and around it) of a field that has a polarity determined by the crystal's structure. By generalizing Curie's laws, we would find that a purely amorphous substance would not create polarized fields if it weren't rendered anisotropic by particular polarizing conditions, like a compression according to a determined direction, or a magnetic field.[14] A singularity is polarized. The veritable properties of the individual are at the level of its genesis and, for this very reason, at the level of its relation with other beings, since, if the individual is the being that is always capable of continuing its genesis, this genetic dynamism resides in its relation to other beings. The ontogenetic operation of the crystal's individuation is accomplished on its surface. The interior layers represent a past activity, but the superficial layers are the deposits of this power of growing insofar as they are in relation with a structurable substance. The individual's limit is what is in the present; it is the limit that manifests the individual's dynamism and that makes this relation exist between the structure and the hylomorphic situation. A being totally symmetrical in itself and symmetrical with respect to the beings that would limit it would be neutral and without properties. *Properties are not substantial but relational*; they only exist through the interruption of a becoming. Temporality, insofar as it expresses or constitutes the most perfect model of asymmetry (the present is not symmetrical with the past, because the flow of time is irreversible), is necessary to the individual's existence. Perhaps there is also a perfect reversibility between temporality and individuation, since time is always the time of a relation, which can only exist at the limit of an individual. According to this doctrine, it could be said that time is relation and that there is no veritable relation that is not asymmetrical. Physical time exists as a relation between an amorphous term and a structured term, the first being the carrier of potential energy and the second that of an asymmetrical structure. What also results from seeing things this way is that every structure is simultaneously structuring and structured; each structure can be grasped in its twofold aspect when it is manifested in the present of the relation between an amorphous potentialized state and a substance structured in the past. From that point, the relation between the future and the past would be the very thing that we witness between the amorphous milieu and the crystal; the present, the relation between the past and the future, is like the polarizing asymmetrical limit between the crystal and the amorphous milieu. This limit can neither be grasped as a potential nor as a structure; it is not interior to the crystal, but it no longer belongs to the amorphous milieu. However, in another sense, it is an integral part of both terms, since it is provided with all of their properties. The two preceding aspects (including the belonging and non-belonging of the limit to the limited terms), which are opposed like the thesis and the antithesis of a dialectical triad, would remain artificially distinguished and opposed without the characteristic of their constitutive principle: this dissymmetrical relation is indeed the principle of the genesis of the crystal, and the dissymmetry continues throughout the genesis; whence results the nature of the indefiniteness of the crystal's growth; *becoming is not opposed to being; it is the constitutive relation of being qua individual.* Consequently, we can say that the physicochemical individual constituted by a crystal is in becoming, qua individual. And it is indeed on this intermediate level (between the ensemble and the molecule) that the veritable physical individual exists. It can certainly be said in a derivative sense that a certain amount of sulfur is individualized by the fact that it is presented in a determined allotropic form. But this determined state of the overall ensemble does nothing but express on the macroscopic level the underlying and most fundamental reality of existence in the mass of real individuals that have a community of origin. The individualized characteristic of the ensemble is merely the statistical expression of the existence of a certain number of real individuals. If an ensemble envelops many physical individuals from various origins and different structures, it is a mixture and remains poorly individualized. The veritable support of physical individuality is effectively the operation of elementary individuation, even if it only appears indirectly at the level of observation.

[The[15] quite remarkable meditation that Plato delivers in the *Parmenides* on the rapport of being and becoming, resuming or announcing the meditation of the *Philebus,* cannot lead to the discovery of a mixture of being and becoming; the dialectic remains antithetical, and the content of the τρίτον τι [tríton ti][16] cannot seem to be anything but an unsatisfying postulation. This is because Plato cannot find in Greek science the notion of a suspended becoming that is asymmetrical and immutable. The alternative between static being and the inconsistent emanation of γένεσις [genesis] and φθορά [phthorá][17] could not be avoided by the introduction of any mixture. Participation among ideas and even among the number-ideas, such as we find it in the *Eponymous* or as we reconstruct it based on books M and N of Aristotle's *Metaphysics* with the theory of the μέτριον [métrion],[18] still conserves the notion of the superiority of the one and the immobile over the multiple and the moving. Becoming remains conceived as movement, and movement remains conceived as imperfection. Nevertheless, through this infinite dawn that is Plato's thought in the decline of his life, we can sense the search for a real mixture of being and becoming, which is intuited rather than defined in the direction of ethics: *to be immortalized in the sensible,* and thus also in becoming. If the *Timaeus* were written at this moment, perhaps we would have had since the fourth century a doctrine of the mixture of being and becoming. After this effort remained fruitless, seemingly due to the esoteric nature of Plato's teaching, the philosophical meditation inspired by Plato with Speusippus and Xenocrates returns to the dualism founded by Parmenides, this father of the thought upon which Plato authorized himself to bear a sacrilegious hand in order to say in some way and in some relation that being is not and that non-being is. The accepted separation between physics and reflexive thought has become an avowed philosophical attitude starting with Socrates, who, disappointed by the physics of Anaxagoras, wanted to bring philosophy back "from the sky to the earth." Aristotle's work certainly marks a vast encyclopedic effort, and physics is reintroduced. But *this* physics, deprived of mathematical formulation after the repudiation of archetype-structures and preoccupied with classification more than measures, is not what can provide paradigms for a reflection. The synthesis of being and becoming, failed at the level of inert being, could not be solidly carried out at the level of the living being, since it would have been necessary to know the genesis of the living being, which still to this day is an object of research. Furthermore, the Western philosophical tradition is almost entirely substantialistic. It has ignored the knowledge of the real individual because it could not grasp the latter in its genesis. Whether conceived as indivisible and eternal molecule or as richly organized living being, the individual was grasped as a given reality, useful for explaining the composition of beings or for discovering the finality of the cosmos, but not as a knowable reality itself.

We want to show through this work that the individual can now be an object of science and that the opposition declared by Socrates between physics and reflexive and normative thought must finally be done away with. This turning point implies that the relativity of scientific knowledge *[savoir]* is no longer conceived within an empiricist doctrine. And we should note that empiricism involves the theory of induction, for which the concrete is the sensible and the real is identical to the concrete. The theory of knowledge *[connaissance]* must be modified down to its roots, i.e. the theory of perception and sensation. Sensation must appear as the relation of a living individual with the milieu in which it is found. However, even if the content of this relation does not initially constitute a science, it already possesses a value insofar as it is relation. The fragility of sensation stems above all from that fact that it is asked to reveal substances, something it cannot do because of its fundamental function. If there is a certain number of discontinuities between sensation and science, this is not a discontinuity like the one that exists or is supposed to exist between genera and species but like the one that exists between different hierarchized metastable states. The presumption of empiricism, which is relative to the chosen point of departure, is only valid in a substantialistic doctrine. Since this epistemology of relation can only be expounded upon by supposing the individual being as defined, it was impossible for us to indicate it before utilizing it; this is why we began our study by way of a paradigm borrowed from physics: only later on did we *derive* the reflexive consequences resulting from this point of departure. This method can seem quite primitive: it is in fact similar to that of the Ionian "Physiologists"; but it is presented here as a postulate, for it seeks to found an epistemology that would be anterior to any logic.]

3. Epistemological Consequences: Reality of
Relation and the Notion of Substance

What modification have we had to contribute to the conception of physical individuation by passing from the individuation of allotropic forms to the more fundamental individuation of the crystal with respect to the amorphous substance? The idea that individuation consists in an operation has remained unmodified, but we have been able to specify that the relation that this operation[19] establishes can sometimes be currently operative and sometimes in suspense, thereby assuming all the apparent characteristics of substantial stability. Here, relation is observable as an active limit, and its type of reality is that of a limit. In this sense, we can define the individual as a *limited* being, but only on condition of thereby understanding that a limited being is a polarizing being that possesses an indefinite dynamism of growth with respect to an amorphous milieu. The individual is not substance, for substance is not limited by anything other than itself (which is what leads Spinoza to conceive substance as infinite and unique). Every rigorous substantialism excludes the notion of the individual, as we can see in Descartes, who could not explain to Princess Elizabeth in what the union of the substances in Man consists, and even more so in Spinoza, who considers the individual as a semblance. The *finite* being is the exact contrary of the *limited* being, for *the finite being is self-limiting,* since it does not possess a sufficient quantity of being to grow endlessly; on the contrary, in this indefinite being that the individual is, the dynamism of growing does not stop, since the successive stages of growing are like a number of relays due to which increasingly large quantities of potential energy are captured in order to organize and incorporate increasingly considerable amounts of amorphous matter. Thus, relative to the initial germ, crystals visible to the naked eye are already considerable edifices: a cubic micrometer of diamond contains more than 177,000,000,000 atoms of carbon. It can therefore be thought that the crystalline germ has enlarged enormously when it attains the size of a crystal that is visible at the limit of the separative power of optical microscopes. But it is also known that it is possible to "nourish" an artificial crystal in a supersaturated solution quite carefully maintained in conditions of slow growth so as to obtain a crystalline individual weighing several kilograms. In this case, even if it were supposed that the crystalline germ is already an edifice of large dimensions relative to the atoms of which it is composed, we would find that a volume of a cubic decimeter has a mass one quadrillion times superior to that of a supposed crystalline germ at 1 cubic micrometer of volume. Crystals of an ordinary size—which almost constitute the totality of the terrestrial surface, like those of quartz, feldspar, and mica, which make up the composition of granite— have a mass equal to several million times that of their germ. Thus, it is completely necessary to suppose the existence of a feedback mechanism that allows for the extremely small amount of energy contained in the germ's limit to structure a rather considerable mass of amorphous substance. In fact, the limit of the crystal is the germ during growth, and this limit is displaced to the degree that the crystal grows; it is composed of atoms that are always new, but it remains dynamically identical to itself and grows on the surface by conserving the same local characteristics of growth. This primordial role of the limit is particularly highlighted by phenomena such as figures of corrosion and especially of epitaxy, which constitute a remarkable counterproof. Figures of corrosion, which are obtained in the assault of a crystal by a reagent, manifest tiny depressions with regular contours that could be called negative crystals. However, these negative crystals have a different form depending on the facet of the crystal on which they appear; fluorine can be attacked by sulfuric acid; yet fluorine crystallizes in the form of cubes which, when struck, yield facets parallel to those of the regular octahedron. Through corrosion, quadrangular pyramids can be seen to appear on the facet of the cube, while little triangular pyramids appear on the facet of the octahedron. All the figures that appear on the same facet have the same orientation. Epitaxy is a phenomenon that occurs when a crystal is taken as the support of a substance during crystallization. Nascent crystals are oriented by the crystalline facet (of a different chemical substance) on which they are placed. The crystal's symmetry or dissymmetry appears in these two phenomena. Thus, when calcite and dolomite (CO_3Ca and $(CO_3)^2CaMg$) are attacked by diluted nitric acid, calcite presents symmetrical figures of corrosion on a facet of cleavage, while dolomite presents dissymmetrical figures. These examples show that the characteristics of the limit of the physical individual can appear in each point of this individual, thereby again becoming a limit (for example, here, through cleavage). The individual can therefore play a role of information and end up, even locally, as an active singularity, capable of polarizing.

Nevertheless, we can wonder whether these properties (particularly the property of homogeneity, as we shall note) can still exist on the very small scale: is there an inferior limit of this crystalline individuation? In 1784, Haüy formulated the reticular theory of crystals, and this was confirmed in 1912 by Laue due to the discovery of the diffraction of X-rays by crystals, which behave as a network. Haüy studied calcite, which presents itself in extremely various forms; he discovered that all the crystals of calcite through cleavage can yield the same rhombohedron, which is a parallelepiped whose six facets are equal diamond shapes and form together an angle of 105° 5′. Through the phenomenon of parting, we can make these rhombohedrons increasingly small and visible only through a microscope. But the form does not change. Haüy supposed a limit to these successive divisions, and he imagined the crystals of calcite as stacks of these elementary rhombohedrons. With Laue's method, it became possible to measure with X-rays the dimensions of this elementary rhombohedron, whose height is equal to 3.029×10^{-8} cm. Halite, which has three rectangular cleavages, consists of indivisible elementary cubes whose ultimate measure is 5.628×10^{-8} cm. We can therefore consider a halite crystal as constituted by material particles (molecules of sodium chloride) arranged in the nodes of a crystalline network constituted by three sets of reticular planes intersecting at a right angle. The elementary cube is called a crystalline lattice. Calcite will be constituted by three systems of reticular planes, which together form an angle of 105 5′ and are each separated by the constant interval of 3.029×10^{-8} cm. Each crystal can be considered as constituted by a network of parallelepipeds. This reticular structure not only accounts for the stratification parallel to the cleaves, but even more so for the various modes of stratification. Thus, in the cubic network, which explains the structure of halite, we can observe a stratification parallel to the diagonals of the cube. This stratification appears in zinc sulfide. The nodes of the cubic network can be arranged in reticular planes parallel to the facets of the regular octahedron: above we have seen the cleavage of fluorite, which corresponds to such a stratification. We ought to contemplate this notion of multiple stratification particularly, for it gives both an intelligible and a real content to the idea of limit. The limit is constitutive when it is no longer the material boundary of a being but is its structure, constituted by the ensemble of points, which are analogous to any other point of the crystalline milieu. The crystalline milieu is a periodic milieu. To know the crystalline milieu completely, all we need to know is the content of the crystalline elementary lattice, i.e. the position of the different atoms; by submitting the latter to translations according to the three axes of coordinates, we will find all the analogous points that correspond to them in the milieu. The crystalline milieu is a triply periodic milieu whose period is defined by the lattice parameters. According to Jean Wyart, "we can compose an image, at least in the plane, of the crystal's periodicity by comparing it to the indefinitely repeated *motif* of a wallpaper.[20]" Wyart also adds: "We also find this motif in all the nodes of a network of parallelograms; just like the crystal's *elementary lattice*, the sides of the elementary parallelogram do not have any existence." Thus, the limit is not predetermined; it consists in structuration; the moment that an arbitrary point is chosen in this triply periodic milieu, both the elementary lattice and a set of spatial limits are determined. In fact, the shared source of the limit and the structuration is the milieu's periodicity. Here, with a more rational content, we rediscover the already indicated notion of the indefinite possibility of growth; the crystal can grow while conserving all its characteristics because it possesses a periodic structure; the growth is therefore always identical to itself; a crystal has no center that allows us to measure the distance of one point of its exterior contour with respect to its center; relative to the crystal's structure, its limit is no more distant from the center than the other points; the crystal's limit is in virtually every point, and it can really appear in each point through a cleavage. The words interiority and exteriority cannot be applied with their usual meaning to this reality that the crystal is. On the contrary, let's consider an amorphous substance: it must be bounded by a membrane, and its surface can have properties that belong exclusively to the surface. Thus, a drop of water produced by a water dropper takes on during its formation a certain number of successive aspects that can be studied by mechanics; these aspects depend on the diameter of the tube, the force of attraction due to gravity, and the superficial tension of the liquid; here, the phenomenon is extremely variable according to the order of magnitude adopted, since the envelope acts as an envelope and not as a limit. Furthermore, let us indeed remark that amorphous bodies can in certain cases take on regular forms, like that of mist formed by drops of water; but we cannot speak of the individuation of a water drop like we speak of the individuation of the crystal, because the former does not possess a periodic structure, at least not rigorously and in the totality of its mass. A drop of water with large dimensions is not exactly identical for all its properties to a drop of water with small dimensions.[21]

The individuation that we will characterize through the example of the crystal cannot exist without an elementary discontinuity on a more restricted scale; it takes an edifice of atoms to constitute a crystalline lattice, and this structuration would be very difficult to conceive without an elementary discontinuity. It's true that when Descartes wanted to explain all physical effects through "figure and movement" he sought to found the existence of forms on something other than elementary discontinuity, which was inconceivable in a system where an the absolute vacuum is excluded, insofar as extension is substantialized and becomes *res extensa*; thus, Descartes also considered crystals quite carefully, and he even attentively observed the genesis of artificial crystals in a supersaturated solution of sea salt by attempting to explain it through figure and movement. But Descartes experiences great difficulty in discovering the foundation of structures; at the beginning of *Meteors,* he strives to show a genesis of spatial boundaries starting from the opposition of the direction of the rotation of two neighboring vortices; movement is what primordially individuates regions of space; in a mechanics without live forces, movement indeed can seem to be a purely geometrical determination. But movement by itself in a matter-space continuum cannot easily constitute an anisotropy of physical properties; that Descartes's attempt made to explain the magnetic field through figure and movement, starting from spirals generated by the poles of the magnet and pivoting around themselves, remains unfruitful: we can indeed use this hypothesis to explain how two poles of the same name repel one another, or how two poles of contrary names attract one another. But we cannot explain the coexistence of these two properties, because this coexistence requires an anisotropy, whereas Descartes's space-matter is isotropic. Substantialism can only explain phenomena of isotropy. Polarization, the most elementary condition of relation, remains incomprehensible in a rigorous substantialism. Thus, Descartes also strives to explain all the phenomena in which a field manifests vectorial magnitudes via the mechanism of subtle matter. He devoted a lot of attention to crystals because they presented him with a clear illustration of the reality of figures; they are substantialized geometrical forms; but, since his system excludes the vacuum, Descartes's system made it impossible to recognize what is fundamental in the crystalline state, namely the genetic individuation of periodic (and therefore discontinuous) structure, which is opposed to the continuous or to the disorder of the amorphous state.

However, to be fully rigorous, we should not claim that if the crystalline state is discontinuous, then the amorphous state is continuous; in fact, the same substance can present itself in the amorphous state or in the crystalline state without a modification of its elementary particles. But, even if it is composed of discontinuous elements like molecules, a substance can behave as continuous from the moment that enough elementary particles are implicated in the production of the phenomenon. Indeed, a multitude of disorganized actions, i.e. those that obey neither a polarization nor a periodic distribution in time, have average sums that are distributed in an isotropic field. These include, for example, the pressures in a compressed gas. The example of Brownian motion, which sheds light on the thermal agitation of large molecules, also illustrates this condition of isotropic milieus; if, in order to observe this movement, we consider increasingly large visible particles, the movements of these particles end up becoming imperceptible; this is because the instantaneous sum of the energies received on each facet of the portion of molecules in a state of agitation is increasingly low with respect to the mass of the observable particle; the more voluminous the particle, the more elevated the number of collisions on each facet per unit of time; since the distribution of these collisions occurs at random, the forces per unit of surface are more constant in time as the surfaces considered are increasingly large, and an observable particle that is voluminous enough remains practically at rest. For sufficient durations and orders of dimensions, the disorganized discontinuous is equivalent to the continuous; it is functionally continuous. The discontinuous can therefore manifest sometimes as continuous and sometimes as discontinuous according to whether it is organized or disorganized. But the continuous cannot functionally present itself as discontinuous, since it is isotropic.

Continuing down this path, we shall find that the aspect of continuity can present itself as a particular case of discontinuous reality, whereas the reciprocal of this proposition is not true. The discontinuous is first with respect to the continuous. This is why the study of individuation, which grasps the discontinuous qua discontinuous, has a very profound ontological and epistemological value: it invites us to ask how ontogenesis is accomplished based on a system bearing energetic potentials and structural germs; there is individuation not of a *substance* but of a system, and this individuation is what generates what we call substance starting from an initial singularity.

Nevertheless, to arrive at an ontological primacy of the individual from these remarks would be to lose sight of the full nature of the fruitfulness of relation. The physical individual that is the crystal is a periodic-structured being that results from a genesis in which a structural condition and a hylomorphic condition containing matter and energy encounter one another in a relation of compatibility. However, in order for the possibility of energy to be captured by a structure, it would have to be given in a potential form, i.e. distributed in an initially *non-polarized* milieu behaving as a continuum. The genesis of the individual requires the discontinuous of the structural germ and the functional continuum of the preliminary amorphous milieu. A potential energy, which is measurable by a scalar magnitude, can be captured by a structure, a bundle of polarities that can be represented vectorially. The genesis of the individual is effectuated by the relation of these vectoral magnitudes and these scalar magnitudes. It is therefore unnecessary to replace substantialism with a monism of the constituted individual. A monadological pluralism would still be a substantialism. However, every substantialism is a monism, whether unified or diversified, in the sense that it merely retains one of the two aspects of being: terms without operative relation. The physical individual integrates in its genesis the mutual operation of the continuous and the discontinuous, and its existence is the becoming of this ongoing genesis, prolonged in activity, or in waiting.

This supposes that individuation exists on an intermediate level between the order of magnitude of the particulate elements and that of the molar ensemble of the complete system; on this intermediate level, individuation is an operation of amplifying structuration that makes the active properties of initially microphysical discontinuity pass to the macrophysical level; individuation is initiated on the level at which the discontinuous of the singular molecule is capable (in a milieu in a "hylomorphic situation" of metastability) of modulating an energy whose support is already a part of the continuum in the population of randomly arranged molecules, i.e. in a superior order of magnitude relative to the molar system. The polarizing singularity initiates in the amorphous milieu a cumulative structuration that spans the initially separated orders of magnitude: the singularity, or information, is that in which there is communication between orders of magnitude; as the initiator of the individual, it is conserved in the latter.

CHAPTER THREE

Form and Substance[1]

I. Continuous and Discontinuous

1. Functional Role of Discontinuity

The Socratic injunction whereby reflexive thought was asked to return to heed the call of ethics instead of physics has not been accepted in all philosophical traditions. According to Plato's expression, the "sons of the Earth" have remained stubborn in their search through the knowledge of physical nature to find the unique solid principles for individual ethics. Leucippus and Democritus had already shown the way. Epicurus establishes his moral doctrine on the basis of a physics, and this same approach can already be seen at work in Lucretius's magnificent didactic and epic poem. But it is worth noting that one of the primary characteristics in the relation between philosophy and physics for the Ancients is that the ethical conclusion is already presupposed in the physical principle. Physics is already ethics. The atomists necessarily define their ethics within their physics when they turn the atom into a substantial and limited being that passes through different combinations without changing. The composite has a level of reality inferior to the simple, and this composite that man is will be wise if he knows and accepts his own temporal, spatial, and energetic limitation. It has been said that the atomists minted Eleatic being: and in fact, as Parmenides reveals in his poem, which is a narrative of his initiation into Being, the rounded and coined Σφαῖρος [Sphairos],[2] happy in its circular plenitude, fragments *ad infinitum* into the atoms: but it is always immutable matter, whether one or multiple, that confines being. The relation between the atoms of being, made possible due to the introduction of the void, which is substituted for the negativity of Parmenidean becoming, has no veritable interiority. Lawlessly emerging from countless dice throws, relation conserves throughout its existence the

essential precariousness of its constitutive conditions. For the atomists, relation depends on being, and nothing substantially grounds it in being. Emerging from a "clinamen" without finality, relation remains pure accident, and
only the infinite number of encounters in the infinity of elapsed time has been
able to lead to many viable forms. Consequently, there is no case in which
the human composite can attain substantiality; but he can avoid relations,
which, due to their groundlessness, are necessarily destructive and snatch
from him the little time he has to exist by bringing him to think on death,
which has no substantial reality. The state of *ataraxia* is a state in which the
human composite concentrates on himself as much as possible and leads him
to the closest state of substantiality he can possibly attain. The "*templa ser-
ena philosophiae*"[3] make it possible to construct not a veritable individuality
but the state of the composite conceivably closest to the simple.

There is a symmetrical postulate in Stoic doctrine. There, man is no longer
a true individual. The only true individual is unique and universal: it is the
cosmos. Only the cosmos is substantial, one, perfectly bound by the internal
tension of the πῦρ τεχνικὸν ὁ διέχει πάντα [pūr technikòn ho diéxei pánta].[4]
This creative fire (also called "seminal fire," πῦρ σπερματικόν [pūr sperma-
tikón]) is the principle of the immense pulsation that animates the world.
Man, an organ of this great body, can only find a truly individual life in harmony with the rhythm of the whole. This harmony, which is conceived as
the resonance that harp makers create through the equality of tension of
two chords of equal weight and length, is a participation of the activity of
the part in the activity of the whole. Although rejected by the atomists, finality plays an essential role in the system of the Stoics. This is because relation
is essential for the Stoics, since it elevates the part that is man all the way
up to the whole that is the cosmos-individual; conversely, for the atomists,
relation can only distance man from the individual (i.e. the element) by en-
gaging him in a participation that is in fact disproportionate with the individual's dimensions.

In this sense, the ethical intention needed to turn to physics in two opposite directions. For the atomists, the veritable individual is infinitely below
man's order of magnitude; for the Stoics, it is infinitely above. The individual is not sought in the order of magnitude of the human being but at the
extremities of the scale of conceivable magnitudes. In both cases the physical individual is sought with a rigor and a force that indicate how much man
feels his life engaged in this search. And it is perhaps this very intention that
led the Epicureans and the Stoics to not want to take up a common and
everyday being as the model for the individual. The atom and the cosmos

are absolute in their consistency because they are the extreme limits of what man can conceive. The atom is absolute as non-relative to the degree attained by the process of division; the cosmos is absolute as non-relative to the process of addition and the search for definition through inclusion, since it is the term that includes all others. The only difference, which is quite important due to its consequences, is that the absolute of the whole envelops relation, whereas the absolute of the indivisible excludes it.

Perhaps we need to see in this search for an absolute individual outside the human order a desire to seek that does not submit to the prejudices that arise with the integration of man into the social group; the walled city is repudiated in these two discoveries of the absolute physical individual: through a self-folding in Epicureanism, through surpassing and universalization in the Stoicism of cosmic citizenship. This is precisely why neither of the two doctrines manages to think relation in its general form. The relation between atoms is precarious and amounts to the instability of the composite; the relation of part to whole absorbs the part in the whole. Thus, the relation of man to man is approximately similar in the two doctrines; the Stoic sage remains αὐτάρκης καὶ ἀπαθής [autárkes kaì apathés].[5] He considers his relations with others as part of the τὰ οὐκ ἐφ᾽ ἡμῖν [tà ouk eph hemin].[6] The *Enchiridion* of Epictetus compares familial relations to the occasional gathering of a hyacinth bulb that a mariner encounters while taking a short stroll on an island; if the boatswain shouts that it is time to leave, there's no time to lose; the mariner would risk being pitilessly abandoned on the island, for the captain does not wait. Book IV of Lucretius's *On the Nature of Things* similarly treats the human passions based on yearnings, and it partially reduces their meaning to a rapport of possession. In Epicureanism, the only veritable relation is that of man with himself, and in Stoicism, the only veritable relation is that of man with the cosmos.

Thus, the search for the fundamental physical individual remained fruitless for the Ancients because it was too often diverted for ethical motives toward the discovery of a substantial absolute. In this sense, the moral thought of Christianity no doubt has indirectly and sufficiently done some good for the research of the individual in physics; by having given a non-physical foundation to ethics, it has freed the research of the individual in physics from its moral principle, thereby liberating it.

Since the end of the eighteenth century, a functional role has been given to a discontinuity of matter: Haüy's hypothesis on the reticular constitution of crystals is a case in point. Furthermore, in chemistry the molecule becomes the center of relations and no longer merely a depository of materiality. The nineteenth century didn't invent the elementary particle, but it continued to enrich it with relations to the extent that it robbed the particle of substance. This path has led to the consideration of the particle as bound to a field. The final step of this research was taken when it was possible to measure, in terms of the variation of energetic levels, a change of the structure of the edifice constituted by particles in mutual relation. The variation of mass linked to a liberation or an absorption of energy, and thus to a change of structure, profoundly solidifies what relation is as equivalent to being. Such an exchange, which allows us to state the rapport that measures the equivalence of a quantity of matter and a quantity of energy and thus the equivalence of a change in structure, demolishes any doctrine that connects the modifications of substance back to substance as pure contingent accidents, without which substance remains unmodified. In the physical individual, substance and modes are on the same level of being. Substance consists in the stability of the modes, and the modes consist in the changes in level of the energy of substance.

Relation was raised to the status of being the moment the notion of discontinuous quantity was associated with the notion of the particle; a discontinuity of matter that would merely consist in a granular structure would still fail to deal with the majority of problems raised by the conception of the physical individual in Antiquity.

The notion of discontinuity must become essential to the representation of phenomena in order for a theory of relation to be possible: it must not only apply to masses but also to charges, to the positions of stability particles can occupy, and to the quantities of energy absorbed or expended in a change of structure. The quantum of action is the correlative of a structure that changes via abrupt leaps without intermediary states.

2. The Antinomy of the Continuous and the Discontinuous

It could nevertheless be objected that the advent of a quantum physics would be unable to nullify the need to maintain a wave associated with each corpuscle, which is only understood in a hypothesis of the continuity of propagation and in a hypothesis of the continuity of the energy exchanges implicated in the phenomenon. It seems that the photoelectric effect alone summarizes this antinomy of the necessity of discontinuous quantities and the equal necessity of a continuous distribution of energy: there is a threshold for the frequency of "photons," as if each photon had to convey a quantity of energy at least equal to the energy of the escape of an electron from metal. But, moreover, there is no threshold for intensity, as if each photon could be considered as a wave covering a surface of indeterminate dimension and could neverthe-less put all its energy into a perfectly localized point.

Perhaps this antinomy would appear less accentuated if the results from the previous analyses could be retained in order to apply them to this even more general case. Here, unlike the case of the crystal, we no longer have the distinction between a discontinuous, structured, periodic region and an amorphous continuous region supporting scalar magnitudes. But, syn-thesized in the same being and borne by the same support, we still have a structured parameter and an amorphous parameter that is pure potential. The discontinuous is in the mode of relation, which is effectuated by abrupt leaps, like the leap between a periodic milieu and an amorphous milieu or between two milieus with a periodic structure; here, the structure is the sim-plest, that of the particle's unicity. A particle is a particle not insofar as it occupies a certain place spatially, but insofar as it only exchanges its energy with other supports of energy in a quantum manner. Discontinuity is a modal-ity of *relation*. Here, it is possible to grasp what is called the "two comple-mentary representations of the real," and these representations are perhaps not merely complementary but really one. This necessity of unifying two complementary notions perhaps stems from the fact that these two aspects of individuated being have been separated by substantialism, and because we have to make an intellectual effort to unify them due to a certain imagi-native habit. For a particle, what is the associated field that we must join with it in order to account for phenomena? For the particle, it is the possibility of being in a structural and energetic relation with other particles, even if these particles behave as a continuum. When a plate of alkaline metal is illuminated by a beam of light, there is a relation between the free electrons contained in the metal and the luminous energy; here, the free electrons behave as beings equivalent to the continuum insofar as they are distributed at random in the plate, as long as they do not receive enough energy to be able to escape from the plate; this energy corresponds to the escape potential and varies with the chemical composition of the metal utilized. Here, elec-trons intervene as supports of a continuous scalar magnitude and do not correspond to a polarized field. They are like the molecules of an amorphous body in a state of thermal agitation. Supposing that they were localizable, their place would not have any importance. The same thing applies for the particles of the light source: their position at the instant when the luminous energy has been emitted doesn't matter. Photoelectric effects can be pro-duced by the light of a star that no longer exists. On the contrary, electrons behave as structured beings insofar as they are susceptible to escape from the plate. A quantity of energy measurable by a certain number of quanta corresponds to this change in their relation with the other particles that constitute the metallic milieu. Similarly, the state changes of each particle that constitutes the source of light intervene in the relation by means of the photon's frequency. The individuality of the structural changes that have taken place in the source is conserved as the energy of the "photon," i.e. as the capacity of luminous energy to carry out a structural change requiring a determinate quantity of energy in a precise point. It is indeed known that the threshold of the frequency of the photoelectric effect corresponds to the necessity for each electron to receive a quantity of energy at least equal to its energy of escape. We are led to posit the notion of "photon" to explain not only this rule of the threshold of frequency, but also the very important fact of the distribution or rather the availability of luminous energy in each of the points of the illuminated plate: there is no threshold of intensity; however, if the electron behaves as a particle in the sense that each electron requires the supply of a determinate quantity of energy to escape from the plate, we might think that it will behave as a particle also in the sense that it will receive a quantity of luminous energy proportionate to the opening of the angle under which it is seen from the light source (according to Gauss's law). This is however what the experiment contradicts; when the quantity of light received by the plate on each unit of surface decreases, there should come a moment when the quantity of light would be too small for each electron to receive a quantity of light equivalent to its escape energy. Yet this moment never arrives; only the number of electrons extracted per unit of time diminishes proportionate to the quantity of light. All the energy received by the alkaline metal plate acts on this particle that is 50,000 times smaller than the hydrogen atom. This is why we are led to consider that all the energy conveyed by the light wave is concentrated in one point, as if there were a corpuscle of light.

3. The Analogical Method

However, should the value of reality be granted to the notion of the photon? It is no doubt fully valid in a *physics of the as if,* but we should ask whether it constitutes a real physical individual. This is required by the manner in which the relation between electrons and luminous energy is effectuated, i.e. ultimately between the state changes of the particles of the light source and the state changes of the particles of the alkaline metal. In fact, perhaps it is risky to consider luminous energy without considering the source from which it originates. Conversely, if we merely want to describe the relation between the light source and the free electrons of the alkaline metal, we will see that it is not absolutely necessary to involve individuals of light and that it is even less necessary to resort to a "probability wave" to account for the distribution of the luminous energy conveyed by these photons onto the surface of the metal plate. It even seems that the hypothesis of the photon is difficult to conserve in cases where an extremely small quantity of light arrives on a large enough surface of alkaline metal. The escape of electrons is then sensibly discontinuous, which can be translated into a "background noise" or shot noise characterized when the currents produced in a circuit by electrons escaping from the metal are amplified and transformed into sound waves as they are collected on an anode due to the difference of potential created between this anode and the plate of photo-emitting metal, which becomes a cathode. If the intensity of the luminous flux is reduced further while the surface of the alkaline metal plate is increased, the number of electrons escaping per unit of time remains constant when the two variations are compensated, i.e. when the product of the surface illuminated by the intensity of light remains constant. However, the probability of an encounter between a photon and a free electron diminishes when the surface of the plate increases and the intensity of the light decreases. Indeed, by acknowledging that the number of free electrons per unit of surface remains constant for every surface, we find that the number of photons diminishes when the surface increases and when the total quantity of light received per unit of time on the whole surface remains constant. We are therefore led to consider the photon as being able to be present everywhere at each instant on the surface of the alkaline metal plate, since the effect only depends on the number of photons received per unit of time and not on the concentration or diffusion of light on a larger or smaller surface. The photon encounters an electron *as if* it had a surface of several square centimeters but exchanges energy with the electron *as if* it were a corpuscle on the electron's order of magnitude, i.e. 50,000 times smaller than the hydrogen atom. And the photon can do all of this while remaining capable of appearing in another effect happening at the same time and under the same conditions as linked to a transmission of energy in a wave form: some bands of interference on the cathode of the photoelectric cell can be obtained without disrupting the photoelectric phenomenon. It would then perhaps be preferable to account for the contradictory aspects of the photoelectric effect through another method. Indeed, if the phenomenon is considered from the aspect of temporal discontinuity it presents when the quantity of energy received per unit of surface is extremely low, we will observe that the escape of electrons occurs when the illumination of the photo-emitting plate has lasted a certain length of time: everything happens here as if a certain amount of luminous energy were summated in the plate. Consequently, it could be supposed that luminous energy transforms in the plate into a potential energy that makes possible the modification of the state of relation of an electron with the particles that constitute the metal. This would make it possible to understand that the place of free electrons does not intervene in the determination of the phenomenon, no more so than the density of "photons" per unit of surface of the metallic plate. We will then be referred back to the case of the relation between a structure and an amorphous substance, which manifests as a continuum even if it is not continuous in its composition. Here, the electrons manifest as a continuous substance because they submit to a distribution that conforms with the law of large numbers in the metal plate. This ensemble constituted by the electrons and the metallic plate in which they are randomly distributed can be structured by the addition of a sufficient quantity of energy that will allow the electrons to escape from the plate. The disorganized ensemble will have been organized. Nevertheless, this hastily presented thesis should be critiqued. There are in fact other ways of increasing the metallic plate's potential energy, for example by heating it; then, starting at temperatures between 700°C and 1250°C, we witness a phenomenon called the thermionic effect taking place, and it is more appropriate to call it the thermoelectric effect: electrons spontaneously escape from a piece of heated metal. When this metal is covered with crystallized oxides, the phenomenon takes place at a lower temperature. Here, the change in distribution occurs without the intervention of any condition besides the elevation of temperature, at least in appearance. However, the energetic condition, namely the temperature of the metal that constitutes a "hot cathode," is not fully sufficient by itself; the structure of the metal surface is also involved: in this sense, we presume that a cathode can be "activated" by the addition of metal traces, for example those of strontium or barium; thus, even in the thermoelectric effect, there are structural conditions for the emission of electrons. However, as in the case of an amorphous substance that passes to the crystalline state through the spontaneous (and even today unexplained) appearance of crystalline germs in its mass, the structural conditions of the thermoelectric effect are always present in ordinary conditions when these conditions are energetic. They are present at least on a large scale for a "hot cathode" with enough emitting surface; but they are present in a much more discontinuous manner on a small scale. If, by means of a focusing apparatus (an electrostatic or electromagnetic lens), we project onto a fluorescent screen electrons emitted at the same instant by the different points of a hot cathode so as to obtain an enlarged optical image of the cathode, what we will see is that the emission of electrons by each point is extremely variable according to the successive instants. The emission takes shape like successive craters of intense activity, and these craters are highly unstable: if an anode is set up in proximity to the cathode in an empty enclosure, with enough difference of potential to collect all the emitted electrons (saturation current) between the anode and cathode, the total current gathered shows fluctuations that arise from these intense local variations of the intensity of the thermoelectric phenomenon. The larger the cathode's surface, the weaker these local variations are with respect to the total intensity; this phenomenon is perceptible in an electronic tube with a very small cathode. It has been sufficiently studied recently under the name of scintillation or "flicker." However, all the points of a cathode are under the same thermal energetic conditions in approximation with very small differences as a result of the metals' elevated thermal conductivity. Even if we supposed slight differences of temperature between the different points of the surface of a cathode, we could not thereby explain the abrupt and important changes of intensity of the emission of electrons between two neighboring points. This is why the thermoelectric effect depends at least on another condition besides the energetic condition, which is always present. The bright and fleeting craters observed in the electrical optic apparatus described above correspond to the appearance or disappearance of this condition of activity on the cathode's surface in a certain determinate point. The study of this phenomenon is not sufficiently advanced for us to specify the nature of these *germs of activity*. But it is important to note that they are functionally comparable to the crystalline germs that appear in a supersaturated amorphous solution. The nature of these germs is still mysterious; but their existence is certain. Nevertheless, we should ask if, in the photoelectric effect, light merely acts by increasing the energy of the electrons. It is interesting to note that electrons escape perpendicularly to the surface of the alkaline metal plate. It is rather regrettable that the elevated temperatures necessary to obtain the thermoelectric effect are not compatible with the conservation of zinc, cesium, or cadmium cathodes; for temperatures barely lower than those in which the thermoelectric effect begins to manifest, we could attempt to see if the minimum frequency of light producing the photoelectric effect would be lowered, which would show that the escape energy had lessened. If this were the case, it could be concluded from this that there are two terms in the electron's escape energy: a structural term and in fact a term representing a potential. However, even in the absence of more precise experiments,

it is possible to glean from this example a certain number of provisional conclusions relative to the study of physical individuation. Indeed, we see a very
remarkable type of relation in the photoelectric effect: from an energetic
point of view, all the free electrons in the illuminated metal plate are *like a
single substance*. Otherwise, we would be unable to understand how there
could be an effect of the accumulation of luminous energy arriving on the
plate up to the quantity of energy necessary for the escape of an electron to
be received. There are cases where the phenomenon cannot be considered as
instantaneous; thus, in this case the luminous energy must have been stored
in reserve beforehand; on the other hand, this energy supposes a communication between all the free electrons, for it can be conceived with great difficulty that the energy has been supplied by a photon that would have taken
longer to act on the electron than the speed of light would allow us to calculate. If the relation between light and an electron occurs more slowly than
the speed of light allows, this is because there is no direct relation between
light and the electron but a relation through the intermediary of a third term.
If the interaction between the "photon" and light is direct, it must be short
enough for the photon, between the beginning and the end of the interaction, to still be practically in the same place. Here, for the displacement of
the photon, we are limited to rehashing the reasoning that has led to the adoption of the idea that the photon can manifest in any illuminated point. But if it
is acknowledged that the photon can manifest its presence everywhere at the
same instant on a plane perpendicular to the direction of displacement, it cannot be acknowledged that the photon can stay in the same place during the
entire duration of a transformation. If, for example, a transformation lasts
1/100,000th of a second, the photon would have had enough time to travel
3,000 meters between the beginning and the end of this transformation. This
difficulty is avoided if we suppose that, between the light and the electron,
energy is summated in the milieu in which the electrons are. This summation
could occur, for example, as an increase in the amplitude of an oscillation or in
the frequency of a rotation. In the latter case, for example, the frequency of
light would intervene directly as a frequency and not as a scalar quantity. If a
direct role of frequency is admitted, we no longer have to represent a photon
whose energy would be represented by the measure of a frequency: frequency
is the structural condition without which the phenomenon of structuration
cannot take place. But the energy intervenes as a scalar quantity in the number of electrons extracted per unit of time. According to this representation,
it would be necessary to consider an electromagnetic field as possessing a
structural element and a purely energetic element: frequency represents this

structural element, while the intensity of the field represents its energetic element. We are saying that frequency *represents* the structural element, but not that it constitutes the latter, for in other circumstances this element will intervene as a wavelength during a propagation in a determined milieu or in a vacuum. A diffraction by the crystalline network involves this structure as a wavelength relative to the geometrical length of the crystalline lattice.

The interest in a representation of structure linked to frequency is not merely that of a greater realism but also that of a much broader universality that avoids creating arbitrary categories of electromagnetic fields (something that seemingly ends in quite a paralyzing substantialism). The continuity between the different manifestations of electromagnetic fields of varied frequencies is established not just in theory but also by scientific and technical experimentation. If, as Louis de Broglie does in *Ondes, corpuscules, mécanique ondulatoire* in figure I (between pages 16 and 17), we inscribe via a logarithmic scale of frequencies the different discoveries and experiments that have made the measurement of an electromagnetic frequency possible, we see that there is a fully established continuity between the six domains initially considered to be distinct: Hertzian waves, infrared, the visible spectrum, ultraviolet, X-rays, and gamma rays. As technicians were going lower in frequency with the domain of waves theoretically discovered by Maxwell and effectively produced by Hertz in 1886 with a decimetric oscillator, Righi, an Italian physicist from Bologne, establishes the existence of waves measuring 2.5 cm. In a work published in 1897, he showed that these waves are intermediary between visible light and Hertzian waves; they possess all the characteristics of visible light. The title of this work, *Optique des oscillations électriques,* is quite important, for it shows an attempt to unify two domains that were at that time experimentally separate, although they had been conceptually joined together in Maxwell's remarkable electromagnetic theory of light: optics and electricity. Following the path opened up by Righi, Bose and Lebedev endeavored, with the aid of the apparatus Bose constructed in 1897, to repeat Hertz's experiments on the refraction, diffraction, and polarization of electromagnetic waves; these two researchers manage to produce electromagnetic waves 6 millimeters long. In 1923, Nickols manages to produce waves 0.29 millimeters long. One year later, Glagoleva-Arkadeva attains 0.124 millimeters. And yet, through optical methods, Rubens and Bayer in 1913 had already been able to isolate and measure a radiation of 0.343-millimeter wavelengths in infrared radiations. Surpassing the simple analogy of the properties of propagation, the two forms of energy previously isolated as two *genera* or at least two *species* would partially overlap in extension (from 0.343

to 0.124 millimeters of wavelength) and would be identical in comprehension, as much for the genesis as for the study of "properties," thus showing the fragility of the thought that proceeds via common genus and specific difference. Common genus and specific differences here are on the same level of being: they both consist as frequencies. Extension and comprehension also overlap, for the statement of the limits of extension utilizes the same characteristics as definition through comprehension. The intellectual course that the progressive discovery of the continuity between Hertzian waves and the visible spectrum manifests is neither inductive nor deductive: it is *transductive*; indeed, visible light and Hertzian waves are not two species of a common genus that would be a genus of *electromagnetic waves*. No specific difference can be indicated to allow us to pass from the definition of electromagnetic waves to that of Hertzian waves or visible light; there is nothing additional in the definition of Hertzian waves or of light than in that of electromagnetic waves. Extension and comprehension do not vary in the inverse direction, as in induction. Furthermore, it can no longer be said that this thought proceeds like deduction through a "transfer of evidence": the properties of luminous electromagnetic radiations are not deduced from the properties of Hertzian electromagnetic waves. They are constituted based on the very measure that allows for both a distinction and a continuity to be established: that of frequency. It's because their only distinction is between the frequency and its inverse wavelength that these two physical realities are neither *identical* nor *heterogeneous* but *contiguous*: this method of *transduction* allows for the establishment of a *topology* of physical beings that neither studies genera nor species. The criterion that allows us to establish limits for each domain also allows us to define in inductive language what the sub-species would become without the addition of any *new* distinctive characteristics and simply through a specification given to the universal nature of comprehension; thus, in the previous example, if we want to account for the differences that exist between centimetric electromagnetic waves and decametric electromagnetic waves, we will have to resort to this characteristic that will also allow us to say why the separative power of an optical microscope is greater in violet light than in red light: it will be revealed that the reflection, refraction, and diffraction of an electromagnetic wave depends on the rapport between the order of magnitude of the wavelength and that of the elements of the matter constituting the mirror, diopter, or network. If we take the example of reflection, for instance, the condition for this phenomenon to occur is that the mirror irregularities must be smaller compared to the wavelength of the electromagnetic emission to be reflected. The "optical luster" of silver or mercury is necessary for reflecting the violet light of short wavelengths. On the other hand, red light is already suitably reflected by a less highly polished metallic surface; infrared radiations can be reflected by a plate of lightly oxidized copper; centimetric radar waves reflect off a non-polished metallic surface. Decimetric radar waves reflect off a finely netted metallic lattice. Metric waves reflect off a trellis of metallic bars. A trellis with broad links made of cables suspended from pylons, or even a row of pylons, suffices for the reflection of decametric or hectometric waves. Similarly, it takes the minuscule structure of a crystalline network to diffract X-rays, whereas a network made of lines delicately hand carved on a plate of metal is enough to guarantee the diffraction of visible light. The metric waves of television diffract off the crenelated peaks of the Sierra Mountains, which is a natural network of very large cells. More complex properties, like the rapport between the quantity of energy reflected and the quantity of energy refracted for each wavelength that encounters a semi-conductive obstacle, like the complexly structured Kennely-Heaviside layer, can be interpreted using a similar method that is neither inductive nor deductive. The word analogy seems to have taken on a pejorative meaning in epistemological thought. However, veritable analogical reasoning should not be confused with the completely sophistical method that consists in inferring identity from the properties of two beings that have any characteristic in common whatsoever. The veritable analogical method is rational to the extent that the method of *resemblance* can be confused and untrustworthy. According to the definition of Bruno de Solages, veritable analogy is an identity of rapports and not a rapport of identity. The transductive progress of thought effectively consists in establishing the identities of rapports. These identities of rapports strictly are not at all based on resemblances but are instead based on differences, and their goal is to explain the latter: they tend toward logical differentiation and do not at all tend toward assimilation or identification; thus, the properties of light seem quite different from those of Hertzian waves, even in a limited and specific case like that of reflection on a mirror; a trellis does not reflect light and reflects Hertzian waves, whereas a small, perfectly polished mirror reflects light and almost does not reflect a metric or decametric Hertzian wave at all, and certainly not a hectometric wave. To account for these resemblances or differences is to resort to the existing identity of rapports between all the phenomena of reflection; the quantity of energy is large when an obstacle, constituted by a substance whose singularities are small with respect to the wavelength of electromagnetic energy, is interposed into the trajectory of the electromagnetic wave. There is identity of rapport between, on the one hand, the light wavelength and the dimension of irregularities of the mirror surface and, on the other hand, the Hertzian wavelength and the length of the elementary lattice of the trellis off which it reflects. The transductive method is therefore the application of veritable analogical reasoning; it excludes the notions of genus and species. Conversely, an illegitimate use of reasoning through resemblances is noticeable in the attempts to *assimilate* the propagation of light to that of sound based on several resemblances, like their reflection on the same mirrors (a watch is placed in the middle of a parabolic mirror; a second, similar mirror would allow us to obtain an auditory "image" of the watch in the middle of the second mirror). It took Fresnel's strength of mind to stop this improper identification by demonstrating that there is a stark difference between the propagation of sound and the propagation of light: light's elongations are always transversal, whereas those of sound propagating in a gas are always longitudinal; the differences between sound and light in phenomena of polarization were misunderstood due to an identification founded on the most external but also most striking resemblances. This facility that brings us to reason through identification according to resemblances comes from substantialistic habits that lead us to discover not yet known common genera through a random transference of properties. Thus, the notion of ether, which was invented to further perfect the resemblance between the propagation of sound and that of electromagnetic waves, survived well after the experiment of Michelson and Morlay and the quite illogical synthesis of the physical properties it conveyed. It was preferable to suppose the existence of a weightless fluid without viscosity with even more elasticity than steel to be able to conserve the identity of light and sound. Scientific thought is not a pure induction achieved by a classification founded on differences; but it is also not an identification at all costs; it is instead the *distribution* of the real according to a measure, a mutual criterion of extension and comprehension.

It would be easy to complete this analysis by showing how the same application of transductive reasoning allowed us to unify the entire domain of electromagnetic radiations by establishing experimental continuities between the other domains following a complete concatenation. Schumann, Lyman, and then Millikan established the continuity between the visible spectrum and X-rays (from 0.4 to 0.0438 thousandths of a millimeter, or from 4,000 to 438 angstroms). In this manner, we began to understand the intermediate X-rays, since they are too long to be diffracted by natural networks like crystals, whose elementary lattice normally measures only several angstroms. And finally, the domains of X-rays and gamma rays were found in a state of continuity and a quite important overlap, since polonium gamma rays have a wavelength of 2.5 angstroms, which identifies them with ordinary weak X-rays. They constitute the same physical reality, and, if a particular name is kept for them, this is only to relay their mode of production. But they could just as correctly be called X-rays. The general chart of electromagnetic radiations, such as the one created by Louis de Broglie, extends from 10^{-3} angstroms to 3×10^{14} angstroms, i.e. from 10^{-10} millimeters to around 30,000 meters. Without any solution of continuity, it is possible to pass from the most penetrating gamma rays to the longest waves of wireless telegraphy. The knowledge of the unity and diversity of this phenomenon, which is thoroughly spread out on a numerical scale, is one of the most noteworthy successes of this transductive method, which is the foundation for progress in physics. Moreover, this immense monument of logic is also strictly coincident with the real, including in the most refined techniques: MIT's electromagnetic thermometer, which receives, like a radioelectric receiver of extremely short waves, electromagnetic perturbations emitted by the stars, has made it possible to measure the temperatures of the Sun (10,000°K), of the moon (292°K) and of outer space (less than 10°K). The radioelectric theodolite allows us to map out the position of the Sun under cloudy conditions. Radar, which is ten to twenty times more sensitive than the eye, can detect the passage of invisible meteorites with the instruments of optics.

Nevertheless, we should ask if this intellectual edifice, as a condition of stability, does not require an absolute transductivity of all properties and all terms. Without this perfect coherence, the notion of genus would reappear in all its latent obscurity. A notion cannot be created to account for one phenomenon, for example, relative to a determined frequency, and then abandoned for other frequencies. Within a domain of transductivity, there must be a continuity between all properties with variations relative only to the variation of the physical parameters that make the organization of transductivity possible. In the case of the domain of electromagnetic radiations, the reality of the photon cannot be accepted for a determined band of frequency and then abandoned for other frequencies. However, the notion of the photon, this quantum of energy that propagates at the speed of light, is remarkably useful when the photoelectric effect must be interpreted. But it is no longer as interesting when it is a question of infrared or Hertzian waves. It should nevertheless be usable in this domain of large wavelengths.

II. Particle and Energy

1. Substantialism and Energeticism

This impossibility of directly and exclusively positing the corpuscular nature of light was admirably posited by Louis de Broglie in the theory of wave mechanics, a theory which was eventually completed by Bohr with the notion of complementarity between the wave aspect and the corpuscle aspect. We would like to show that this manner of conceiving the physical individual can be integrated quite well into the general theory of the individual as a being that is genetically constituted by a relation between an energetic condition and a structural condition that extend their existence in the individual, which can at any moment behave as a germ of structuration or as an energetic continuum; its relation is different depending on whether it enters into relation with a milieu that is equivalent to a continuum or whether it enters into relation with an already structured milieu. The principle of complementarity, which indicates that the physical individual sometimes behaves as a wave and sometimes as a corpuscle but not in both ways simultaneously in the same phenomenon, would be interpreted, in the doctrine we are presenting, as the result of the asymmetry of every relation: the individual can sometimes play one role and sometimes the other of two possible roles in relation, but not both at the same time. We shall therefore suppose that when a physical individual behaves as a corpuscle, the being with which it is in relation behaves as a wave, and when it behaves as a wave, the being with which it is in relation behaves as a corpuscle. More generally, in every relation there would always be a continuous term and a discontinuous term. This requires that each being integrate a continuous condition and a discontinuous condition into itself.

The substantialism of the particle and the energeticism of the wave developed quite independently from one another during the nineteenth century, because in the beginning they corresponded to domains of research distant enough from one another to authorize the theoretical independence of the principles of explanation. The historical conditions for the discovery of wave mechanics are extremely important for an *allagmatic* epistemology whose goal is to study the modalities of transductive thought as truly adequate for the knowledge of the development of a scientific thought that wants to know the individuation of the real it studies. This epistemological study of the formation of wave mechanics and Bohr's complementarity would like to show (to the extent that it is a question of thinking the problem of the physical individual) that pure deductive thought and pure inductive thought have been rendered ineffective, and that, from the introduction of the quantum of action up to Bohr's principle of complementarity, only a transductive logic has made the development of the physical sciences possible.

In this sense, we are going to show that the "synthesis" of the complementary notions of wave and corpuscle is not in fact a pure logical synthesis but the epistemological encounter of a notion obtained through induction and a notion obtained through deduction; the two notions are not truly synthesized, like those of thesis and antithesis at the end of a dialectical movement, but instead are put into *relation* due to a transductive movement of thought; they conserve their own functional characteristic in this relation. In order for them to be able to be synthesized, they would need to be symmetrical and homogeneous. In dialectics with a ternary rhythm, the synthesis more or less *envelops* the thesis and antithesis by *overcoming* contradiction; the synthesis is therefore *hierarchically, logically, and ontologically* superior to the terms it joins together. Conversely, the relation obtained at the end of a rigorous transduction maintains the characteristic asymmetry of the terms. This is due to the fact that scientific thought relative to the (at first physical, then biological) individual, as we are attempting to show, cannot proceed according to the ternary rhythm of dialectics where the synthesis is the thesis of a higher triad: scientific thought advances not through the elevation of successive planes according to a ternary rhythm but through the extension of transductivity. Due to the principle of complementarity, *relation,* having become functionally symmetrical, cannot with respect to another term present an asymmetry that can be the motor for a further dialectical progression. In terms of reflexive thought, after the exercise of transductive thought, contradiction has become internal to the result of synthesis (since it is relation to the extent that it is asymmetrical). There cannot be a new contradiction between the result of this synthesis and another term that would be its antithesis. In transductive thought, *there is no result of synthesis but merely a complementary synthetic relation*; synthesis is not effectuated; it is never achieved; there is no synthetic rhythm because, insofar as the operation of synthesis is never effectuated, it cannot become a new thesis.

According to the epistemological thesis we are defending, the relation between the different domains of thought is horizontal. It allows for transduction, i.e. not identification or hierarchization but a continuous distribution according to an indefinite scale.

The principles we are going to try to elicit from epistemological examination will therefore have to be considered valid if they are transductible to other domains, like that of technical objects and living beings. Ethics itself will have to seem like a study of relation proper to living beings (here we are using the expression "proper to living beings," whereas in reality there is no rigorous direct relation to living beings: to be more precise, it would be better to say: "commensurate with living beings" in order to indicate that these characteristics, without them being proper to living beings, appear much more significantly in the latter than in any other being, given that they correspond to variables whose values or systems of values pass through a maximum for these beings). Certainly, in a perfect doctrine the problems relative to the frontiers between the "kingdoms" of Nature, and therefore between species, are much less important than in a theory that uses the notions of genus and species. Indeed, sometimes we can conceive of a continuous transition between two domains that could only be separated by the sufficiently arbitrary choice of average parameters, and sometimes we can conceive of thresholds (like the threshold of frequency of the photoelectric effect) that manifest not a distinction between two species but simply a quantum condition of the production of a determined effect. The limit is no longer endowed with singular and mysterious properties; it is quantifiable and merely constitutes a critical point whose determination remains perfectly immanent to the phenomenon studied and to the group of beings analyzed.

2. The Deductive Process

This is the thesis we are going to try to demonstrate or at least illustrate through the analysis of the conditions under which physical science has been led to define the physical individual as a complementary association of the wave and the corpuscle.

The notion of waves seems to have appeared at the end of a remarkable deductive effort, particularly concerning the elucidation of energetic problems, to which it contributes a remarkably rational means of calculation. It extends and renews the tradition of a deductive physics, one that since Descartes has resorted to the classical representations of analytical geometry. Furthermore, it is linked at least historically to the study of macroscopic phenomena. Finally, it has an eminent *theoretical* role that allows us to think (under common principles) extremely vast sets of facts that were previously separated into distinct categories. Conversely, the notion of corpuscle presents the opposite characteristics.

The notion of waves has approximately played identical roles in the interpretation of luminous phenomena and phenomena relative to the displacements of electrified particles (or electric charges); the latter is what allowed Maxwell to hatch the electromagnetic theory of light. The first work solidified around the studies of Fresnel. The second solidified around Maxwell's discovery, which was later experimentally verified by Hertz. Beginning his study of phenomena of diffraction in 1814, Fresnel inherited at least two centuries of experimental and theoretical research. Huyghens had already studied the phenomenon of the double refraction of spar discovered by Bartholin, and he also knew that quartz possesses the same property of birefringence or birefraction. Huyghens had already expounded rational methods and a theory accompanied by geometrical constructions that have remained in esteem; he had observed phenomena of polarization. This thinker of astronomy and geometry brought a theoretician's mind to the problems of physics, which is particularly apparent in his *Cosmotheoros* and his *Dioptrique*. He put forth the idea that light is constituted not by corpuscles in movement but by waves propagating through space. However, this theory was not as satisfying for Huyghens as the solution he gave to the problem of the catenary curve or the Tautochrone curve: it could not explain the phenomenon of the propagation of light rays in a straight line. The problem posed by nature was more difficult to solve than those proposed by Galileo and Leibniz. Descartes's work in its statement of the laws of propagation always manifested the interest of a corpuscular optics in the explanation of the propagation of light rays in a straight line. However, Huyghens's theory could not be abandoned, for Newton himself, even though he was partisan to the corpuscular theory after having discovered a new phenomenon (interferences), was forced to complete the corpuscular theory with a theory of *access*: light corpuscles would pass periodically when they cross material milieus through the access of unimpeded reflection and unimpeded transmission, which would allow for the explanation of colored rings. Let us furthermore note that the hypothesis according to which light would convey periodic elements, even if it were corpuscular in nature, was already explained in Descartes's work: the *Dioptrique* explains that the prism disperses white (polychromatic) light, because each corpuscle of light increasingly deviates as its movement of rotation around itself becomes less rapid. This idea of the rotation of light corpuscles, which stems from the cosmological hypothesis of primordial vortices, leads Descartes into an error, for it forces him to attribute to the vortices of subtle matter constitutive of red light a frequency of rotation higher than that of violet light corpuscles; according to Descartes, this would be due to the fact that the corpuscles of which red light is composed would be vortices of subtle matter that have a diameter less than that of the corpuscles of which violet light is composed. Despite the error relative to the compared frequencies of red and violet, Descartes had the merit of unifying two asymmetrical notions in a very fruitful association. Moreover, it would be false to suppose that Descartes represented light exactly as composed of corpuscles; there is no vacuum in his system, and consequently there is neither atoms nor corpuscles, properly speaking; there are only vortices of *res extensa* in movement. Faced with this confrontation of two traditions, Fresnel steered his researches in such a way as to extend the field of application of a theory that since Huyghens had served merely to explain a handful of phenomena, namely wave theory. Double refraction was known only for two crystalline species: Fresnel examined if this property was encountered in other crystals; after creating experimental apparatuses for shedding light on double refraction in all the crystals in which it could exist, he observed that it existed in almost all crystals, and he explained it by the unequal composition their linear elements should present taken in various directions, which conforms with Haüy's theory about crystalline networks. Afterwards, Fresnel extended this theoretical explanation to cases where an amorphous body is polarized by an external cause: he discovered that a glass prism becomes birefringent when it is compressed. This extension of the scientific object, i.e. of a theory's domain of validity, perfectly illustrates what can be called the transductive method. Moreover, in collaboration with Arago, Fresnel studied the polarization of light. Arago discovered chromatic polarization; Fresnel completed this discovery with the discovery of circular polarization, which is produced by means of a suitably cut birefringent crystal. However, it would be impossible to explain this phenomenon of polarization if we invoked a representation that assimilates the light wave to a sound wave propagating in a gas; Fresnel supposed that vibrations in light waves are transversal, i.e. occur perpendicularly to the direction of propagation. Polarization and double refraction are both explained with this insight. Fresnel had already demonstrated that the hypothesis of waves, just as much as the theory of corpuscles, allows us to explain the phenomenon of the rectilinear propagation of light rays. The results of the works of Malus and Arago managed to confirm this theory. Malus discovered that reflected light is always partially polarized and that simple refraction through glass also partially polarized light. This discovery can be found in a treatise entitled *Sur une propriété de la lumière réfléchie par les corps diaphanes*. Fresnel's theory was verified, and its experimental bases received confirmation when they were expanded upon through the works of Arago, who constructed a photometer allowing for experimental confirmation of the principle deductively discovered by Fresnel (complementarity of reflected light and refracted light). After constructing the polariscope, Arago was able to control all the characteristics of chromatic polarization in a very precise fashion. And hence we see how Huyghens's thought becomes largely justified in his treatise on light, *Traité de la lumière,* from 1690: "In true philosophy, the cause of all natural effects are conceived via reasons of mechanics. This is what must be done in my opinion, or we must give up all hope of ever understanding anything in physics."[7]

Furthermore, Maxwell secured a new step for deductive rationalism founded on the hypothesis of the continuous and corresponding to an energetic preoccupation. To be able to explain the principle of the conservation of energy in the unitary system formed by the unification of the different laws that were discovered separately in the domains of electricity, Maxwell formed the notion of "displacement currents," which is perhaps poorly named but which is the forerunner of the current notion of electromagnetic waves and is extensively unifying for the physical reality called light.

Before the communication of Maxwell's great treatise on electromagnetic theory, four laws gathered together all the previous discoveries relative to "static" and "dynamic" electricity, magnetism, and the relation between fields and currents. Maxwell substituted the following system for the four laws that would express these results:

If we take:

$\vec{B}$ = magnetic induction
$\vec{b}$ = electric induction
H = magnetic field
h = electric field
i = current density
ρ = charge density

Then we can write:

I) $\dfrac{-1}{c}\dfrac{\delta B}{\vec{\delta t}} = \overrightarrow{\text{roth}}$ —Faraday's law of induction

II) $\nabla B = 0$ —Inexistence of the isolated magnetic poles

III) $\dfrac{1}{c}\dfrac{\vec{\delta}_b}{\delta t} = \text{rot } \vec{H} - \dfrac{4\pi\vec{1}}{c}$ —Ampère's theorem on the relations between magnetics fields and currents

IV) $\vec{b} = 4\ \pi\rho$ —Law of electrostatic actions (Gauss's theorem)

The third equation expresses Ampère's theorem on the relations between currents and magnetic fields; but, to be able to write that there is conservation of energy (here, conservation of electricity), Maxwell completed this theorem with the introduction of the displacement current, which is represented by the expression $\dfrac{1\delta_b^-}{c\delta t}$ and which is added to the conduction current i. Then, we can deduce from these equations $\dfrac{\delta\rho}{\delta t} + \nabla \underset{1}{\rightarrow} = 0$, which expresses the conservation of electricity.

This expression of conservation would be impossible without the term in $\delta b / \delta t$. Another extremely important theoretical consequence of this equation system is that, when magnetic induction can be conflated with the magnetic field and electrical induction can be conflated with the electrical field (which is the case of the vacuum), the electromagnetic fields always propagate at the speed of light (speed c); this expression (which measures the rapport of the electromagnetic charge unit to the electrostatic charge unit of the electric charge when magnetic fields and inductions are expressed in electromagnetic units, whereas electrical fields and inductions, charges, and currents are expressed in electrostatic units) has a finite value: it allows for the theoretical calculation of the speed of light in vacuum. This propagation can be analyzed as resulting from the propagation of a set of flat monochromatic waves.

This is when the second stage of the transductive method's fruitful application appeared: Maxwell in fact noted the real analogy, i.e. the identity of rapports, between the propagation of light in a vacuum and the propagation of electromagnetic fields; he then supposed that light is constituted by perturbations of an electromagnetic nature and corresponds only to a certain interval of wavelengths (that of the visible spectrum) of electromagnetic vibrations. The constant c, which was discovered based on considerations contemplating the conservation of energy in electricity, is *transductible* into the measure of the speed of light in vacuum, just as the speed of light in vacuum is transductible into the constant c. This affirmation of a transductivity goes quite further than the discovery of a simple equality between two measures, an equality that could arise from an arbitrary choice of units: *it supposes the physical identity of the measured phenomenon,* an identity that can be obscured by the difference of the aspects according to the particular values chosen in the vast known range. Let us indeed note that here we are not dealing with a generalization or a subsumption: visible light is not a particular "species" of electromagnetic perturbations since the "specific difference" that we could attempt to invoke to distinguish this species from its nearest genus—namely the wavelength of its propagation in a vacuum or more precisely the superior and inferior limits of the measure of this wavelength—involves the definition of the nearest genus itself; an electromagnetic field that would have no wavelength of propagation in a vacuum is inconceivable. As an electromagnetic field, it is already "specified" and can only exist and be thought as gamma ray, X-ray, ultraviolet ray, visible light, infrared ray, and Hertzian wave. The number of species or subspecies that could be discovered in a domain of transductivity like electromagnetic waves has the *power of the continuous*. From long Hertzian waves to the most penetrating gamma rays, there is an infinity of electromagnetic fields of different wavelengths, each of whose properties vary with these wavelengths; between red visible light and violet visible light, there is still an infinity of wavelengths; we can differentiate violet light as much as we like; then the criteria of subspecies are homogeneous with respect to the criteria of the species, and the criterion of a species is contained in the comprehension of the nearest genus; discontinuities, the limits of pseudospecies, can only be introduced due to vital or technical usages; we can talk about red and violet and we can even talk about visible light; but this is because we introduce the consideration of a living being that perceives; the apparent discontinuity does not stem from the known scale of electromagnetic wavelengths but from the rapport between the physiological functions of the living being and these wavelengths: an eye without a crystalline lens perceives an ultraviolet more remote than what the normal eye perceives as the glimpse of a gray glimmer: the bee perceives ultraviolet. The Greeks and Romans did not divide up the visible spectrum like we do, and it seems that human perception has been modified towards the extremity of the spectrum situated on the side of short wavelengths, as the usage of the adjective ἁλιπόρφυρος [halipórphuros][8] in the Homeric writings reveals; we distinguish among several colors where the companions of Ulysses saw only one, something that persists today in certain peoples of the Far East. Several technical necessities have led to dividing up Hertzian waves into bands of 9000 Hz (called channels), because these bandwidths correspond to a useful compromise between the necessities of a transmission that is suitably faithful in its modulation of amplification and the total number of transmitters distinct in functioning that are simultaneously able to be received with a sufficient selectivity. If we can distinguish between long, medium, small, short, and very short waves, this is due to the noticeably important differences between the apparatuses capable of producing them or capable of receiving them and the conditions of propagation that characterize them; thus, all things considered, this distinction is made in accordance with the characteristics belonging not to these electromagnetic fields taken in themselves but in accordance with the limits within which their rapports vary with the technical conditions of production or the atmospheric and stratospheric conditions of propagation. In this sense, waves that range from 20,000 meters to 800 meters will be called long Hertzian waves because they always reflect off one of the Kennely-Heaviside layers, which present for them an index of negative refraction, something that makes it so that they undergo a veritable metallic reflection off the first ionized layer they encounter, a phenomenon highlighted by ionospheric sounding discovered by Sir Edward Appleton. Waves will be called medium when they range from 800 to 80 meters and when they penetrate more deeply into the Kennely-Heaviside layer, thus reflecting well by night but partially absorbed by day due to variations in the ionized layer, whose altitude and degree of ionization is relative to the variable altitude and activity of the sun. These differences therefore arise from a rapport between Hertzian waves and something other than themselves, for example the ionized layer of the upper atmosphere or the practical means of producing or conveying them, either via simple electronic tubes or velocity modulation tubes, a coaxial line, or a waveguide. These distinctions are never founded on the very nature of the phenomenon considered; they do not exist properly speaking according to physical science but only according to technics. This is why there seems to be a dependence of all these technical distinctions with respect to each type of technology: the constructors of electronic apparatuses separate waves whose length is greater than ten meters from those that are shorter, because below ten meters the extreme brevity of time to transmit electrons between a cathode and an anode forces the constructors to predict special assemblages in the internal architecture of an electronic tube; furthermore, the *Service de prévision ionosphérique,*[9] whose goal is to ensure the best performance for transmissions, does not establish the same distinctions. Finally, a certain number of *industrial* concepts have been created, since they arose from a more or less precarious concordance among the "special domains" of all the types of technologies organized in the same industry. These industrial concepts end up becoming *commercial* and *administrative,* increasingly losing their scientific nature, since they are relative to a *usage* and no longer have anything but a *pragmatic sense;* here a *complete specificity* is constituted via the encounter (which has become habitual and collective, i.e. recognized by law or by an administrative regulation) of the limits of the specialty of numerous types of technology, and this specificity is deprived of *scientific signification* and yet possesses an essentially qualitative, emotive, and institutional *psycho-social value.* In this sense, the domain of television is *specific*; it only corresponds to a concrete being through its psycho-social existence. This institution has its technicians (who are animated by an *esprit de corps*), its artists, its budget, its friends, and its enemies; *in the same way,* it has its band of frequencies. Yet there is a mutual contamination of their own different characteristics following a delimitation that results from a competition with other institutions. The determination of television's wavelengths is the result of an expulsion outside the domain already occupied by radio broadcasting and the telecommunications of a technology that is new and quite cumbersome due to the bandwidth necessary for the richness of the quantity of information to be transmitted per unit of time. Constrained to a very high frequency range, the transmission of television is reduced to an initial domain of specialty relative to the properties of the ionospheric layers; the propagation of television waves is straightforward in a direct line from the transmitting antenna to the receiving antenna because there will be no reflection off the Kennely-Heaviside layer. This means that the transmitter and the receiver will have to belong to the same national spirit, i.e. to a dense and homogeneous conglomeration; since it can't be required to convey a veritable information very far, television arrives in a population center already saturated with information and artistic spectacles; it can therefore merely become a means of distraction. Furthermore, this constraint and limitation of the parameters of television broadcast to extremely high frequencies—which frees up the field for a large bandwidth of transmission and is met with the quality of a capital's urban provincialism, its first consequence—forces the transmitted image down a path of research for a perfection oriented toward technical quality, i.e. toward the adoption of a high definition. Favored by the initial circumstances, this adoption of a certain *code of values* creates a normativity that reinforces the conditions that have contributed to it and that legitimizes them after the fact: high definition will make the correct transmission at a great distance even more haphazard. Broadcasting in high definition will lead to the production of expensive apparatuses, and those who build them will have to be that much more careful in how they produce and sell this technology. High-definition technology resides at the extreme limit of what can be commercialized and requires an enormous amount of direct advertising to a specific public wealthy enough to afford living in an urban area rather than a rural one. This then leads to a psycho-social morphology and dynamic that summarize and stabilize the *concept* and *institution* of television; from the capital toward the large populated centers, guided bundles (modulated by frequency and on decimetric waves) are sent forth that transmit programs of distraction over the countryside and towns of a secondary order, which are powerless to participate in this star-shaped network radiating from Paris. The veritable limits of the *concept* of television are thus psycho-social; they are defined by the *closure* of a cycle of *recurrent causalities* that create a type of psycho-social interior milieu endowed with homeostasis due to a certain internal regulation by the assimilation and disassimilation of technologies, procedures, and artists who are recruited through commandeering and bound together by a mechanism of self-defense comparable to that of various closed societies. Particular self-justifying myths are put forth: the research of the sharpness of the image is proclaimed to be more valuable than the research of color attempted by other nations, and in order for this research to justify itself, the distinctive traits of the French people are invoked, who are enamored with clarity and precision and detest the poor taste of color prints, considered only to be suitable for primitives or children. Logical contradiction is accepted here, for this thought is guided by affective and emotive themes; the superiority of sharpness over color is therefore invoked in the name of technical perfection, whereas a simple calculation of the quantity of information required to transmit a colored image and a colorless image and an examination of the degree of complication of the apparatuses used in both cases lead to the inverse result. Thus, the television wave can be thought in two absolutely different ways; if we accept a mode of thought founded on the validity of the species-genus schema, the television wave becomes a *species* of the electromagnetic wave genus whose specific difference is not its wavelength but its *belonging* to the institution that is television; what will create this attribution and found this link of participation will then be an administrative decree (Hague Conference). On the contrary, according to a transductive thought, the wavelengths of television will end up being inserted between numerical limits that do not correspond to clear physical characteristics; they will not be a *species* but a section, a greater or lesser band of a domain of transductivity, that of electromagnetic waves. An important consequence (one that is perhaps paramount for epistemology) of this difference between a transductive thought and a thought that proceeds through genera, species, and relations of inclusion is that generic characteristics are not transductible. In this sense, there are currently two bands in France exploited by television (one toward 46 MHz and the other toward 180 MHz): between these two bands, aviation and police have particular or shared bands; we cannot infer from a property characterizing television waves in the "low" band the existence of the same property in the "high" band; the common link of subsumption does not create any veritable mutual physical property. The only link is this domain's administrative property. That is why this relation of participation creates a certain regime of property (with possible cessions and resumptions), as if it were a matter of a terrain that does not bear its proprietor's imprint but creates a bond of obligation or fealty in the eventual developer: French Television, which is currently unable to exploit the full width of its "low band", has provided a certain extension of this band (toward 47.2 MHz) to the Scouts de France, who use it for telephone and telegraph transmissions. This sub-band has the characteristics of an object with a precarious entitlement, since it can be immediately retracted without advance warning; due to its physical characteristics, it has properties transductible into those of bands with wavelengths that are immediately superior or inferior.

Thus, we have the appearance of a type of physical reality that can be called the domain or field of transductivity, that is distinct from every psycho-social being, that is knowable through concepts, and can justify the usage of thought that employs notions of genus and species through their application on the relation of participation, which may or may not solidify into a relation of property or kinship. Veritable transductive thought utilizes reasoning through *analogy* but never reasoning through *resemblance,* i.e. affective and emotive partial identity. It would be dangerous or misleading to use the same word domain here, for the relation of possession seems to lead back to thought through participation; it would be necessary to say: "a track or path of transductivity" divided up into "bands" and "sub-bands" of transductivity (instead of species and sub-species). Transductive thought establishes a topology of the real, and this typology is not identical to a hierarchization into genera and species.

To determine the criteria of the physical individual, it therefore does not require us to resort to an examination of the relations between genus and species, and then between the species and the individual. The play of transductive thought, whose fruitfulness we have witnessed in the discovery of an immense domain of transductivity, prohibits the usage of this method.

However, if the transductive method is necessary, nothing guarantees that it is sufficient and allows for the apprehension of the physical individual. It could be that the physical individual can only be grasped at the point of encounter and compatibility of two opposite and complementary methods, both of which are incapable of grasping this reality on their own. An electromagnetic wave cannot be considered as a physical individual, since it has no consistency or limit of its own to characterize it; the pure continuum of the transductive domain does not allow us to conceive the individual; obtained at the end of a deductive process based on energetic considerations, the pure continuous of the transductive domain is perfectly rational and can be fully compenetrated by the geometrical intellection of figure and movement. But it does not provide a criterion for isolating this continuous virtuality; it cannot provide the concrete of complete existence. It alone cannot lead to the grasping of the physical individual. Nevertheless, if the physical individual can only be grasped by two complementary types of knowledge, the critical question will be that of the validity of the *relation* between these two types of knowledge and that of its ontological foundation in the individual itself.

3. The Inductive Process

The second path of research that led to the position of wave mechanics and to the principle of complementarity is that which, at the end of an inductive process, has asserted the *discontinuous* nature of physical reality. It provides us with a very different definition of the physical individual from one that could be derived from deductive research in terms of waves.

What type of necessity is encountered at the origin of the corpuscular or discontinuist conceptions of the same physical realities as those we will examine, namely light and electricity? It is essentially the necessity of a structural representation that can provide the foundation for an inductive research.

The notion of a discontinuous structure of electricity appeared in 1833 when Faraday, while studying electrolysis, discovered that, despite which hydrogen compound was used, during the process of breaking it down, for example, the production of a given quantity of hydrogen to the cathode was always linked to the passage of a given quantity of electricity in the solution. Moreover, the quantity of electricity necessary for releasing one gram of hydrogen always deposited 107.1 grams of silver. In this sense, the condition for the discovery of the discontinuity of electricity is its *participation* in discontinuous *actions*; it *plays a role* in the domain of the discontinuous, and particularly in the structural changes of matter. If the validity of the atomic conception of matter is accepted, we will have to accept that electricity itself, which participates in the discontinuous actions that characterize the atomic properties of matter, has a discontinuous structure. Indeed, Faraday discovers that all the chemists' univalent atoms, i.e. those that combine with an atom of hydrogen, seem to be *associated* with the same quantity of electricity; furthermore, all bivalent atoms and trivalent atoms are associated with a quantity that is respectively double and triple that of the univalent atoms. Thus, we hit upon the conclusion that electricity (whether positive or negative) decomposes into elementary particles that behave like veritable electrical atoms. This is the conclusion Helmholtz will come to in 1881. The word "electron," which was first used by G. J. Stoney, designates the natural unit of electricity, i.e. the quantity of electricity that must travel through an electrolytic solution in order to deposit an atom of a univalent element in one of the electrodes. Electricity is grasped in its discontinuity due to its association with the atom, and the charge of the electron has also been calculated based on this association. Indeed, if we know that a determined quantity of electricity is necessary for the electrolysis of a mole (or gram-molecule) of a determined body, and if we also know how many atoms this mole contains (according to Avogadro's number), we will be able to calculate the charge associated with each atom by taking into account the valence of the elements.

This initial inductive discovery was followed by a second discovery that reveals the same method and ends in the same result. After 1895, which is the date of the discovery of X-rays, it will be shown that these rays can make gases conductive by creating a conductibility identical to electrolytic conductibility in which electrical charges are transported by ions, this time not based on the decomposition of a molecule but on that of the atoms themselves, since these ions exist even in a monoatomic gas like argon or neon. This decomposition allows for induction to progress one step further in the research of structures: Stoney's electron remained a quantity of electricity associated with an indivisible physical particle; it now becomes more substantial, because the ionization of gases requires a structural representation in which the negative electrical charge is freed from this heavy support of the electrolytic ion. Ultimately, the discovery of structures was able to reach a new stage two years later. If we are restricted to measuring quantities of electricity that pass through a column of ionized gas, we can conceive the independence of the electron with respect to any heavy material particle. But this independence remains abstract; the experimental principle is what allows us to safeguard the phenomena. If, on the contrary, we push the experimental research further by attempting to physically analyze the content of the discharge tube when the pressure of the gas reduces, we obtain the Crookes dark space that pervades the whole tube when the pressure falls to 1/100th of a millimeter of mercury; this space, which develops very progressively from the cathode while pressure decreases, in some sense makes palpable the physical analysis of the initially continuous ensemble that was the ionized gas in which free electrons could not be discerned from the other electrical charges (namely the positive charges) carried by the ions. At that point, we were able to suppose that the Crookes dark space contained free electrons in transit. The experiments on "cathodic rays" were considered experiments on free electrons. It could certainly be said that in this latter experiment the discontinuity of electrons disappears at the same time as their association with a phenomenon, such as the ionization of a liquid or a gas in which they appear as charges of a determinate magnitude associated with the particles. All the experiments conducted at this time on cathodic rays were macro-physical and revealed the existence of electrical charges in transit in the tube without indicating a discontinuous microphysical structure; the experiment cannot be conducted on a single electron; the luminescence of the glass tube, the perpendicularity of the rays with respect to the cathode, their rec-tilinear propagation, their chemical and caloric effects, the fact that they transfer negative electric charges, and their deviation under the influence of an electrical field and a magnetic field are just a few of the macrophysical effects with a continuous appearance. However, due to the inductive path at the end of which this discovery was obtained, it was necessary to suppose that these cathodic rays were composed of discontinuous particles of elec-tricity because in this way the structure of the experiment was taken into account: the electrons of ionized yet still undifferentiated gas in the disrup-tive discharge, according to the experiment's structure, are *identical* to those occupying the Crookes dark space; the latter are *identical* to the electrons of which the cathodic rays consist. The electrons of the ionization of a gas at the moment of disruptive or non-disruptive discharge are identical to those transmitted by the negative ions in the electrolysis of a body.

Can we consider the inductive method followed in these three interpreta-tions of the experiment as transductive? It is not identical to what appears in the formation of the notion of waves. Indeed, the notion of waves was devel-oped to allow for the introduction of a deductive thought into an increas-ingly broad domain through an expansion of the object; it corresponds to a primacy of theoretical representation; it allows for the synthesis of several results that were separate beforehand: on the contrary, the notion of corpus-cles of electricity was introduced to allow for the *representation* of an exper-imentally observed phenomenon by means of an intelligible structure; at the start, it does not surpass the numerically formulable law but gives it a *representative substructure* due to which an intelligible schema can be paired with the phenomenon. When we move from one experiment to the other, for example from electrolysis to the ionization of a monoatomic gas, we transfer the *same schema*; we discover a new case for the application of the previously discovered schema; but the case is only new *experimentally* and not due to an extension of the object; the electron is always the same, and it is because the electron is the same that induction is possible. On the con-trary, when the continuity between visible light and Hertzian waves is estab-lished, it cannot be said that light is made of Hertzian waves; instead, we define the limit that separates and joins these two bands of the domain of transductivity we explore.

The thought that led from Faraday's laws to the calculation of the mass and charge of the electron carried out a *transfer of identity*. The thought that led from the laws of electricity and from Fresnel's formulas to Maxwell's electromagnetic theory carried out the *development of a domain* that opens up into a continuous infinity of values. Now we are able to distinguish much more clearly in Maxwell's effort between what was merely deductive from what was really transductive; Maxwell did deductive work when he wrote the formula of the displacement current in order to be able to account for the conservation of electricity and join together in a single system of equations the four laws that summarize the whole science of electrical phenomena. But he needed a veritable transduction when he joined the theory of displacement currents with that of the wave propagation of light. The necessity of the continuous is a direct consequence of the application of the deductive method. Yet since a deductive invention is necessary for a transductive progression to be realized, we in fact have in the examination of the birth of wave theory a mixture of the deductive method and the transductive method, rather than an absolutely pure example of the transductive method. Likewise, it is possible to find several traces of the transductive method in the development of the notion of electrified corpuscles: the discovery of rays formed by negative corpuscles of electricity has also led to the search for rays formed by positive particles or positively charged material particles: with a cathodic ray tube that has a cathode pierced with holes, we have obtained not positive electrons but positive rays formed by ions originating from the gas contained in the tube; this is what forms the basis of the study of isotopes with Aston's mass spectrograph. This research leads to a veritable discovery of a vast domain of transductivity when, remarkably, the interpretation of isotopy managed to confirm and complete the periodic classification of elements established by Mendeleev in 1869. This classification itself was the result of a vast induction founded on the consideration of atomic weights and the result of an effort of transductivity oriented toward the periodicity of the properties of known elements ranked by order of increasing atomic weights. But we should note that there is a difference between a domain of transductivity obtained at the end of an essentially deductive process and a domain of transductivity obtained at the end of an essentially inductive process: the first is open on both ends; it is composed of a continuous spectrum of various classified and organized values; the second on the contrary is self-enclosed, and its scope has a periodic structure. It comprises a finite number of values.

III. The Non-substantial Individual:
Information and Compatibility

1. Relativistic Conception and the Notion of Physical Individuation

One of the most difficult problems of reflexive thought is the problem of the relation that can be established between these two results of transductivity. If transductivity conducted based on deduction led to the same results as one conducted based on induction, reflection could be reduced to a search for the compatibility between these two types of results, which are acknowledged as legitimately homogeneous. If on the contrary a hiatus remains between these two types of results, reflection faces this hiatus as a problem, for it is neither possible to classify it in a continuous transductivity nor localize it in a periodic transductivity. The invention of a reflexive transductivity will then be necessary.

The fourth stage of inductive research relative to the corpuscle of negative electricity presents the same characteristic as the previous three; but, in a certain sense, it introduces the elementary quantity of electricity in the individual state, not in its visible corpuscular reality but through the discontinuous effect that it produces when it is combined with a very fine material particle. Here still, we see the discontinuity of electricity manifested by a situation where variations of the charge of material particles occur. The electron is not grasped directly in itself as an individualized particle. In fact, Millikan's experiment consists in introducing between the plateaus of a condenser very tiny drops of a non-volatile liquid (oil, mercury). These drops are electrified by their passage into the atomizer that produces them. In the absence of a field between the condenser's electrodes, they fall slowly. When a field exists, the movement will accelerate or slow down, and the variation of speed can be measured. Yet, by ionizing the air included between the plateaus, we observe that the speed of a given drop undergoes abrupt variations from one moment to the next. These variations are interpreted by admitting that the charge of the drop varies when it encounters one of the gas's ions. The measurements show that the captured charges are simple multiples of an elementary charge, equivalent to 4.802×10^{-10} electrostatic units. This experiment is complemented by those in which the electron intervenes through the discontinuity of its charge.

Let us nevertheless note that this discovery of the corpuscular nature of electricity allows a mystery to remain: the dissymmetry between positive electricity and negative electricity, which cannot by any means be predicted inductively in the corpuscular theory: positive electricity would never be present in the free state, whereas negative electricity is. Indeed, there is no structural reason for a corpuscle to be positive or negative. A qualification of the corpuscle cannot be easily conceived; quality appears in the different modes of the possible combinations of elementary corpuscles, but it cannot be easily conceived at the level of this simple structural element that the corpuscle is. Here we come up against one of the limits of inductive thought; its need for simple representative structures leads it to consider quality as something irrational. Quality resists inductive identification. However, since the eighteenth century experimentation has indicated the qualitative differences of "vitreous" electricity and "resinous" electricity. In order to reduce the element of irrationality, it would be necessary to be able to transform the specific qualitative difference into a clear structural difference. But also, since induction tends toward the simple element, it also tends toward the identification of all the elements with respect to one another: after the discovery of the fact that negative electricity is a universal constituent of matter, we have been able to believe that all matter is made of electricity. In this sense, induction through identification would have consummated science; chemistry and physics would have become a generalized electronics. But reduction to absolute identity has been impossible because it could not remove the dissymmetry between two forms or "species" of electricity. It has indeed been possible to consider that a charge of positive electricity is nothing but a "hole of potential" created by the departure of an electron. But, on the one hand, we then are surpassing the limits of induction seeking the simple structural element, and, on the other hand, we are supposing the reality of a material support made of a substance other than negative electricity. For if all matter were constituted by negative electricity, the departure of an electron could never create a "hole of potential" that would manifest as a positive charge equal in absolute value to the electron but with a contrary sign. The veritable limit of induction is plurality in its simplest and most difficult form to cross: *heterogeneity.* As soon as inductive thought is faced with this heterogeneity that it must resort to transductive thought. But then it encounters the results of deductive thought, whose limits it also finds at a certain point. Inductive thought is found lacking when a representation of the pure discontinuous is insufficient. Deductive thought is found lacking when a representation of the pure continuous is also found lacking. This is why neither of these two modes of thought can lead to a complete representation of the physical individual: consequently, the physical individual has called for the invention of different *systems of compatibility* for the methods or the results. But such epistemological conditions involve a necessary critique of knowledge destined to determine which degree of reality can be apprehended through the invention of a system of compatibility.

We find this beginning of a discovery of compatibility between the inductive method and the deductive method, between the representation of the continuous and that of the discontinuous, in the introduction of relativist mechanics into the domain of the free electron.

Other means of producing free electrons have been discovered: the cathodic ray tube was accompanied by the so-called "thermionic" effect and then the beta decay of radioactive bodies. It was known how to determine the trajectories of electrons in space by noting their points of impact on fluorescent screens or photographic plates capable of being affected by this impact. Wilson's cloud chamber, of which it has been said that it constituted the "most beautiful experiment of the century," makes it possible to follow the trajectory of an electrified particle. At the end of the studies carried out by Perrin, Villard, and Lénard, the electron could be represented as a corpuscle, i.e. a very small object that can be localized in space and that obeys the laws of dynamics of the material point.[10] In an electrical field, the electron, which has a negative charge, is submitted to an electrical force. In a magnetic field, when it is in movement the electron behaves as a small element of a conduction current and is submitted to an electrodynamic type of Laplace force simultaneously perpendicular to the direction of the magnetic field and to the instantaneous direction of movement, and it is numerically equal to the vectorial product of the electron's speed through the magnetic field multiplied by the charge. Under the action of this force, $f = \frac{e}{c} [\vec{v} \times \vec{H}]$, the electron's movement occurs like the movement of a material point with a mass of 0.9×10^{-29} g. Rowland's experiment in 1876 established that a displacement of electrical charges produces a magnetic field, as if it were a question of a conduction current produced by a generator in a fixed conductor.

The inductive value of this discontinuous conception of electricity was particularly revealing in the sense that it made it possible to bring the study of the movement of electrons back to the mechanics of the material point, a theory which has been considered classical for quite a while.

The new mechanics remained theoretical when it was applied to bodies studied by macrophysics; relativist mechanics is indeed valid for all material bodies; it had already successfully explained the "three phenomena in 10^{-8}" that classical mechanics had failed to explain: the theory of relativity gained a lot of momentum when it explained the perihelion of the planet Mercury, which had been noted much earlier. The deviation of sunlight observed during an eclipse confirmed the principle of special relativity. Color changes for moving sources of light led to the same confirmation. However, this theory of relativity, which is a mechanics of extremely rapid movements, could still be contested in the domains of macrophysics. Speaking about the theory of relativity, Le Châtelier declared in his work *L'Industrie, la science et l'organisation au XXe siècle*: "Similar speculations can interest the philosopher but shouldn't captivate men of action who claim to shape nature and guide its transformations". Further on, he adds: "Today the probability of seeing the laws of Newton and Lavoisier disproved is not even one in a billion. It is therefore madness to be preoccupied with similar eventualities or to speak of them and be distracted by them for one instant." Le Châtelier focused his argumentation on the fact that relativist theory only gives results different from those of classical mechanics for bodies animated by speeds above 10,000 kilometers per second. "However, on Earth, we do not know how to produce speeds above 1 kilometer per second, which is the speed of the projectiles of the famous Big Bertha. There is hardly anything save the planet Mercury that possesses a sufficient speed to warrant relativistic speculations. Even in this case, the predicted perturbations are so weak that we are still not in agreement on their magnitude." The second argument is that: "concerning the transformation of radium into helium, all the scientists who have worked on this problem still have not managed to produce altogether 10 milligrams of this gas. However, considering the millions of tons of material that the industry transforms every day, an exception to Lavoisier's law has never been able to be verified." From a macroscopic and pragmatic point of view, Le Châtelier was perhaps correct; he could seemingly accuse the partisans of relativity of corrupting, through their "skepticism" regarding Newton's law of gravitation and Lavoisier's law of the conservation of elements, the students who were overly inclined to follow the snobs and philosophers declaring that these two fundamental laws of science are nothing but the vestiges of an obsolete past, just as Aristophanes already accused Socrates of "καινολογία"[11] in *The Clouds* facing the Athenian public who were anxious about the spread of new ideas. Nevertheless, both on earth and in simple assemblages made possible with the physical apparatuses of an established instruction at the time when Le Châtelier rose up against "the negation of all good sense" for "dotting the i's and clear explanation," there were already bodies animated by speeds above 10,000 kilometers per second, namely electrons in transit in cathodic ray tubes; these corpuscles belong to microphysics due to their dimension, but, in a tube that is several dozen centimeters long and with the energy that can be accumulated at the limits of the secondary winding of a

Ruhmkorff coil, it is possible to transmit to them a speed above that of the fastest celestial bodies: here there is a discovery of magnitudes that in the usual classification of phenomena were not of the same *species*. A corpuscle 1,836 times lighter than the hydrogen atom behaves like a planet during an experiment that is on the order of magnitude of the human body and that requires a force comparable to the force of our muscles.

The mechanics of relativity profoundly modifies the notion of the individual existence of the physical particle; the electron cannot be conceived like an atom was formerly conceived because it rapidly changes place. Ever since the ancient atomists, the atom was a substantial being. The quantity of matter it constituted was fixed. Mass invariance was an aspect of this substantial invariance of the atom. The atom is the corpuscle unmodified by the relation in which it is engaged. The compound results entirely from the atoms that constitute it, but these first elements, the *primordia rerum,* are not modified by the compound they constitute. The relation remains fragile and precarious: it has no power over the terms; *it results from the terms, which are not modes of the relation in any way.*

With the electron envisioned by the theory of relativity, the mass of the corpuscle is variable according to speed, formulated by Lorentz's law as, $m = \dfrac{m_0}{\sqrt{1-\dfrac{v^2}{c^2}}}$ where m_o is the mass of the electron at rest, i.e. 0.9×10^{-27} g, and c is the speed of light in vacuum, and v the speed of the corpuscle under consideration. The dynamics of relativity therefore presents us with a corpuscle which cannot be characterized by a rigorously fixed mass representing the substantiality of an unchangeable matter, a support unmodified by accidental relations, but which also cannot even receive an upper limit for a possible increase of mass and consequently for the energy conveyed and the transformations able to be produced in other bodies by this particle. The whole set of principles of atomist thought that seeks the inductive clarity of corpuscular structures is called into question by Lorentz's law. Indeed, from the point of view in which we are situated to consider each particle in itself, it has already produced a profound change because the fundamental characteristics like mass and the quantity of transported energy must be conceived as *not having an upper limit*: mass tends toward infinity when the speed v tends toward the limit c, which measures the speed of light in vacuum. The individual no longer has this essential characteristic of the atom of the ancients, which is that of being *strictly limited* by its dimension, its mass, and its form and which is consequently endowed with a *rigorous identity* through time, an identity that makes it eternal. But the theoretical consequence of this change in the conception of the physical individual is truly even more important if the mutual relation between particles is considered; if under certain conditions a particle can acquire an energy that tends toward infinity, there is no longer a limit to the possible action of a particle on another particle or a group of other particles, however large that group may be. The discontinuity of particles no longer imposes the *finite* characteristic of possible modifications. The smallest element of a totality can receive as much energy as all the other parts combined. The essentially egalitarian nature of atomism cannot be conserved. The very relation of part to whole is transformed because the relation of part to part is completely modified the moment when one part can exert on the other parts an action stronger than all the other elements of the whole taken together: since each physical individual is *potentially unlimited,* no individual at any moment can be conceived as safe from the possible action of another individual. This mutual isolation of atoms, which for ancient atomists was a guarantee of substantiality, cannot be considered absolute; the *vacuum,* an invaluable condition of energetic isolation and structural independence, which was for Lucretius the very guarantee and condition of the individuality of atoms and their eternity, can no longer ensure this function because distance is only a condition of independence if action through contact alone is effective. In this substantialist atomism, shock can modify the state of an atom's movement or rest but not its own characteristics, like mass; however, if mass varies with speed, a shock can modify the mass of a particle by modifying its speed; *the accidental, totally fortuitous encounter affects substance.* Passivity and activity are merely two symmetrical aspects of energy exchanges; the actual or potential passivity of substance is as essential as its potential or actual activity. Becoming is integrated into being. Relation, which contains the energy exchange between two particles, includes the possibility of a veritable exchange of being. Relation has the value of being because it is *allagmatic;* if the operation remained distinct from the structure that would be its unmodifiable support, the substantialism of the particle could attempt to account for energy exchanges by a modification of the mutual rapport of particles, thus leaving the respective characteristics of each particle unmodified. But since every modification of the *relation* of one particle to the others is also a modification of its internal characteristics, there is no *substantial interiority* of the particle. Here still, the veritable physical individual, as in the case of the crystal, is not *concentric with a limit of interiority that constitutes the substantial domain of the individual* but is on the very limit of the being. This limit is actual or potential relation. An immediate belief in the interiority of beings qua individual no doubt comes from the intuition of the body proper, which seems, in the situation of a man reflecting, to be separate from the world by a material sheath that offers a certain consistency and delimits a closed domain. In reality, a suitably deep psycho-biological analysis would reveal that the relation to the external milieu for a living being is not merely spread out on the external surface of itself. Through the mediation it constitutes between the exterior milieu and the being, the notion of interior milieu, which was formulated by Claude Bernard for the necessities of biological investigation, indicates on its own that the substantiality of the being cannot be confused with its interiority, even in the case of the biological individual. The conception of a physical interiority of the elementary particle reveals a subtle and tenacious biologism apparent even in the most theoretically rigorous mechanism of the ancient atomists. With the appearance of the theory of relativity on the plane of the current physical experiment, this biologism gives way to a more rigorously physical conception of individuation. Let us note however that if the possibility for an increase in the mass of a corpuscle had a limit, we could return to a substantialist atomism simply modified by a logical dynamism. Leibniz's monad is still essentially an atom because its stages of development and involution are regulated by a rigorous internal determinism of the *concrete individual notion*; it doesn't matter that the monad possesses within itself a recapitulation of the modifications of the monads of the whole universe as a microcosm in the form of little perceptions. In fact, from the point of view of the causality of modifications, the monad only draws its modifications from itself and remains absolutely isolated in becoming; the limits of its successive determinations are rigorously fixed by the system of universal compossibility. On the contrary, the physical individual, which is thought according to relativity, has no limits of its own defined once and for all due to its essence: *it is unbounded.* Because of this, the physical individual cannot be determined by a principle of individuation comparable to what Leibnizian dynamics assigns it. The limit and consequently the relation of the individual is never a boundary; it is part of the being itself.

This affirmation cannot be taken as a recourse to pragmatism. For the physical individual, when we say that relation is of the being, we do not take this as meaning that relation *expresses* the being but that it constitutes the being. Pragmatism is still too dualist and substantialist; it just wants to rely on the manifestations of activity as a criterion of the being; this is to suppose that there is a being distinct from operation, an interiority that the exteriorization of action authenticates and expresses by manifesting it. In pragmatism, action is the crossing of a limit. However, according to the doctrine we are presenting here, this limit can neither conceal a reality nor be crossed by action because it does not separate two domains, that of interiority and that of exteriority. This relativistic doctrine cannot lead to a subtler form of pragmatism, like Poincaré's "commodism," which ends up as a scientific nominalism. It is realist without being substantialist and postulates that scientific knowledge is a relation to being; however, in a similar doctrine, relation has the status of being. But the realism of knowledge must not be conceived as a substantialization of the concept; realism is the direction of this knowledge as relation; here, with the theory of relativity, we see it go from the rational to the real; in other cases, it follows the inverse direction, and then what consecrates the vitality of the subject-object relation is the encounter and compatibility of these two epistemological directions. The realism of knowledge is in the progressive growth of the density of the rapport that links the subject term and the object term. It can only be discovered if we seek out the meaning of this derivation.

In inductive research, this is the first step toward the discovery of transductivity through which the corpuscle receives a non-substantialist definition of its individuality. Nevertheless, in the application of the theory of relativity to the electron, there remains an element that constitutes a *substantial bond* between the different successive moments when the mass of the electron varies, even if it always increases by tending toward infinity when the speed tends toward the speed of light in vacuum, i.e. the *continuity* between the different successive measures of mass and energy. Relation is not entirely on the same level as being when substantial magnitudes (mass and energy) are posited as capable of continuous variations.

Here, an important doctrinal point remains to be presented and specified before mentioning the epistemological characteristics of quantum theory. Quantum theory indeed supposes that energetic exchanges between wave and corpuscle or between corpuscle and corpuscle always take place in finite quantities, the multiples of an elementary quantity, i.e. the *quantum,* which is the smallest quantity of energy that can be exchanged. Thus, there is a lower limit to the quantity of energy that can be exchanged. But we should ask in what sense Lorentz's formula can be affected *a priori* by the introduction of a quantum theory and how we should consider the possibility of the indefinite increase of a corpuscle's mass when its speed tends toward the speed of light. If we start from a very small initial speed that progressively increases, at the beginning, we will see that when mass can be conflated with mass at rest, the increase of kinetic energy equivalent to a quantum corresponds to a notable increase in speed: thus, speed can be represented as increasing through abrupt leaps; conversely, when the speed is close to that of light, the increase of kinetic energy corresponding to the addition of a quantum translates into a minuscule increase of speed. When the speed tends toward the speed of light, the addition of a quantum of energy translates into an increase of speed that tends toward zero: the leaps of successive additions of quanta are increasingly minimal: the mode of variation of speed *tends toward a continuous regime.*

The importance of quantum discontinuities is therefore variable with the speed of the particle. This deductive result is important, for it shows that a particle like an electron tends toward a regime of continuity when its speed tends toward the speed of light; it is then functionally macroscopic. But it must be asked if this conclusion is fully valid. What is the veritable sense of this limit, i.e. the speed of light? What is absolutely important is not the exact measure of this speed, but instead the existence of a limit that cannot be attained. However, what would happen if an electron attained a speed very close to that of light? Would there not be a threshold beyond which the phenomenon's aspect would completely change? Physics has already presented at least a very important example of the existence of a limit that could not be predicted by simple extrapolation: we can trace the curves that represent the resistivities of metals according to temperature, and these curves are regular enough in an interval of several hundred degrees. Theory shows that close to absolute zero, the resistivity of a metal should tend toward zero. However, experiments show that for certain bodies, instead of decreasing little by little, the resistivity abruptly falls below any measurable value; this is superconductivity. This phenomenon is produced for lead at 7.2°K, at 3.78°K for tin, and at 1.14° K for aluminum (according to the experiments by Heike Kamerlingh Onnes). Modern particle accelerators make it possible to launch electrons at speeds very close to the speed of light. The energy can then become quite considerable, as in Schenectady's betatron of 100 million electron volts, without the predictions that conform to the theory of relativity being disproven in any way; however, it can be supposed that there is a threshold not yet reached beyond which the phenomenon would change if we could reach it. Consequently, there is currently an empirical limit to the application of the electron's relativity; it is hard to conceive that this limit can be overcome because an infinite energy cannot be transmitted to an electron. Furthermore, there seems to be certain theoretical necessities for conceiving an upper limit to the characteristic physical parameters of the electron, like that of the electrical field that regulates the electron radius (in classical representation); however, if we seek the temperature of a dark body whose density of radiation energy would be due to the propagation of this maximum field, then we find a temperature above the order of 10^{12}°K. This temperature is what seems to be at the center of certain white dwarf stars. Higher temperatures and more intense electromagnetic fields are not known.[12]

We cannot therefore found a reflexive approach around the possibility of the indefinite *theoretical* and *absolute* increase of the mass or energy of a particle like the electron, because for reflexive thought there always remains a distinction between a very broad empiricism and a universal empiricism; an infinite margin of the unexplored will forever remain between the very high levels of attained energies and that of an infinite energy. This is why it is difficult to speak about what an electron would be if it were approaching the speed of light in vacuum; it even seems difficult to specify if we should conceive the possibility of the existence of a superior threshold of speed beyond which the electron might no longer be considered an electron. This margin of imprecision in knowledge cannot be reduced by the adoption of quantum theory, since the increase of mass and energy makes the dynamic regime of the corpuscle tend toward the continuous when its speed tends toward the speed of light. If there were a superior threshold of speed and energy, it could not be determined by quantum considerations.

Here we encounter a domain of epistemological opacity that can cast its shadow on a reflexive theory of physical individuation and mark the existence of an epistemological boundary to transductivity. The agnostic consequence resulting from this would itself be relativized by the boundary marking the beginning of its domain of application, the structure of which could not be internally known. If it is itself a relation, this topology of transductivity can be transductible to another type of individuality.

2. Quantum Theory: Notion of the Elementary Physical Operation That Integrates the Complementary Aspects of the Continuous and the Discontinuous

We will begin by attempting to express to what extent the adoption of a quantum principle modifies this conception of corpuscular individuation and extends the conversion of the notion of the individual initiated in relativist thought. Even if there is actually no rigorous epistemological anteriority of one of the conceptions over the other (in terms of physical theories), a logical anteriority for the conception of individuation reveals itself. Indeed, the individual can be conceived as having a variable mass according to its relation with the other elements of the system in which it is included; to conceive these variations as continuous or discontinuous constitutes a supplementary specification contributed to the theory of relativity. However, this point of view is still too formal; the discontinuous quantification of possible degrees of mass and levels of energy indeed contributes a new type of relation between the same type of individuals. Due to quantification, a new condition of stability is brought into change itself; the existence of successive levels that correspond to increasingly large energies for the corpuscle is the veritable synthesis of continuity and discontinuity; furthermore, here we are presented with a possibility of distinguishing, at a given time, among individuals that belong to a system due to the actual differences of the quantum states that exist between them, which is something that Pauli's principle contributes to and which is the key to a new logic of the individual. Pauli's principle states: "electrons, postulated as identical to the point that they could no longer be distinguished in a system, however cannot have (in an atom or a gas) their four quantum numbers be respectively equal; in other words, when an electron is in one of these quadruply quantified states, this excludes (for every other electron) the possibility of being in the same state (whence its name as the principle of exclusion)."[13] In some sense, when it is completed by such a principle, quantum theory recreates a principle of individuation and stability of discernible states the theory of relativity would lose by destroying the unchangeable substantiality of mass, which is a classical foundation for the identity of beings in a corpuscular theory. A new path for grasping the reality of the individual opens up with quantum theory, whose power of transductivity is so great that it allows for the establishment of a viable relation between an inductive physics of the discontinuous and a deductive energetic theory of the continuous.

Planck introduced the idea of the quantum of action in 1900 due to his work on black-body radiation, i.e. radiation emitted by the surface of a body that perfectly absorbs light when it is maintained at a certain temperature. Black-body radiation can be decomposed by a classical type of analysis (following Fourier) into a sum of monochromatic radiations. If we want to know the energy that corresponds to an interval of frequency $v \to v + \Delta v$ in black-body radiation, we must determine the spectral density or function $\rho(v,T)$ such that $\rho(v,T)\Delta v$ gives the quantity of energy that is contained in the unit of volume and that corresponds to the spectral interval δv, if T designates the temperature of the surfaces of an enclosed chamber whose surfaces, including all the material bodies that it can contain, are maintained at a certain uniform absolute temperature. Here we are at the point of the encounter between an energetic theory (thermodynamics) and a structural research; indeed, the theory of thermodynamics is what allowed Kirchoff to show that this thermal equilibrium radiation in no way depends on the nature of the walls of the chamber or of the bodies included there, but only on a temperature T. Other thermodynamic understandings allow us to demonstrate that the quantity of energy contained in the unit of volume of black-body radiation must increase by four powers to that of the absolute temperature T: this experimentally verified law is called Stefan's law.[14] Ultimately, thermodynamics is also what allowed Wien to demonstrate that $\rho(v,T) = v^3 F\frac{v}{T}$, where F is a function of the variable $\frac{v}{T}$, which the thermodynamic approach is unable to determine.

Thus, thermodynamic research here gave the indication of its own limits and invited scientific thought to go further through an analysis of *the energetic relations* between matter and radiation within the confines of an enclosure at a fixed temperature. This was indeed a necessary encounter between the theory of corpuscles and the theory of electromagnetic radiation defined by Maxwell, between the culmination of research related to the theory of the discontinuous and that of research related to the theory of the continuous. Here is how Louis de Broglie in the cited work presents the epistemological situation at this moment: "Besides, this analysis seemed quite easy, for the theory of electrons then provided a very well-defined schema for the phenomena of the emission and absorption of radiation by matter: it was sufficient to suppose that the sides of the enclosure contained electrons in order to study how these electrons absorbed, on the one hand, a part of the energy of the surrounding black radiation and gave back to it, on the other hand, a certain quantity of energy through the processes of radiation, and then to ultimately explain that the processes of absorption and emission statistically compensated one another in such a way that the spectral composition of the radiation at equilibrium remained at a constant average."[15] Lord Rayleigh and Planck made the initial calculation, which was later confirmed by Jeans and Henri Poincaré. It necessarily led to the following conclusion: the function $\rho(v,T)$ must be expressed $\rho(v,T) = \frac{8\pi k}{c^3} v^2 T$, where k is a certain constant that intervenes in the statistical theories of physics and whose numerical value is well known. (This is the Boltzmann constant, which is $k = 1.37 \times 10^{-16}$ in units of c). This theoretical law, which is known as the Rayleigh-Jeans law, shows an increase of ρ as a function of v, represented by a parabola that increases indefinitely without a maximum; this law leads to the conclusion that the total energy of black radiation would be infinite. This law is only in agreement with experiments for small values of v for a given temperature. These experiments allow us to trace a bell curve representing the variations of ρ according to v for a given temperature. In terms of this new curve, the total quantity of energy $\int_0^{\infty} (\rho(v,T)\delta v)$ contained in the black radiation has a finite value that is given by the area included between the × axis and the bell curve, according to the following empirical formula introduced by Wien: $\rho(v,T) = Av^3 e^{\frac{-Bv}{T}}$.

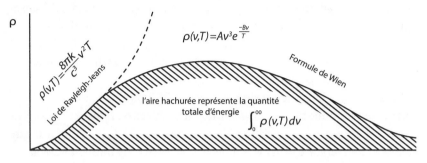

Figure 7

    The theoretical justification for Wien's formula remained to be discovered. Classical corpuscular theory is articulated by classical energetic theory in the following manner, marking a privilege of continuity over discontinuity: an electron animated by a periodic movement of frequency v can continuously emit and absorb the electromagnetic radiation of frequency v. However, this conception would be valid if it were supposed that the *relation* which constitutes the energy exchange between the corpuscle and the electromagnetic wave remained *independent* of the corpuscular individual. But, if relation is conceived as having the value of being, then it seems to extend the wave's energy into the states of the corpuscle and to translate the corpuscle's individual reality into the wave's levels of energy. The fact that this relation is asymmetrical, i.e. creates a rapport between an electromagnetic field (thinkable according to the continuous) and a corpuscle (thinkable according to the discontinuous), necessarily requires relation to simultaneously express discontinuity in energetic terms and continuity in structural terms. Under this condition, *it is not a simple rapport, but a relation that has the value of being.* The quantum characteristic of *relation* defines a mode of reality different from *structure* and continuous energy; this characteristic is that of *operation,* which integrates within it the complementary characteristics of the continuous and the discontinuous: the characteristic of continuity in the operation becomes an *order* of quantum states, which are able to be hierarchized in an increasing series based on an absolute inferior quantity; the characteristic of structuration and individual consistency in the operation becomes the complementary aspect of this hierarchy, i.e. the characteristic of the quantification of exchange. Operation appears as a real relation or real mutual transduction between a continuous term and a discontinuous term, between a structure and an energy.

A substantialist theory of the particle led to a continuous representation of the energetic exchanges between radiation and the particle. Planck supposed on the contrary that it was necessary to admit that an electron animated by a periodic movement of frequency ν can only emit or absorb radiant energy in *finite quantities* of value hν, where h is a constant. According to this hypothesis, the function ρ(ν,T) must have the form: $\rho(\nu,T)=\dfrac{8h\nu^3}{c^3}\dfrac{1}{e^{\frac{h\nu}{kt}}-1}$,

with k always being the same constant as in Rayleigh's law and h being the newly introduced constant. For small values of $\frac{\nu}{T}$, Planck's equation is conflated with Rayleigh's equation, whereas for large values of this quotient it leads to Wien's empirical formula. This formula is also in agreement with the laws of thermodynamics, since it gives, for the radiation's total energy, a finite quantity proportional to T, just as Stéfan's law desires; and this quantity is that of the formula $\rho(\nu,T) = \nu'F\frac{\nu}{T}$, just as Wien's law requires. The constant h (Planck's constant) has the dimensions of the product of an energy by a time, or rather of a quantity of movement by a length; it therefore has the dimensions of the physical quantity called action in mechanics; it plays the role of a unit of action. "The constant h plays the role of a sort of a unit of action, the role, it could be said, of an atom of action. Planck has shown through considerations which I will not develop that this is indeed the profound meaning of the h constant. Whence the name of the 'quantum of action' that he has attributed to it."[16]

Here, we see the intervention of an important element valid both for the history of ideas as well as for the research of the physical individual being itself; the introduction of the quantum of action into physics was indeed considered by Louis de Broglie in 1923–1924 as needing to be incorporated into the fusion of the notions of waves and corpuscles that he brought about within the framework of the classical conceptions on spatiotemporal representations and causality. This conception, which Louis de Broglie called the "theory of the double solution," was described in the May 1927 issue of the *Journal de Physique*. Furthermore, alongside the normally envisioned continuous solutions of the equations of wave mechanics that were considered as having a statistical signification, this theory envisions other solutions that involve a singularity and that allow us to define in space the position of a corpuscle, which then takes on a much better defined individual sense due to this very singularity. The sense of these solutions is no longer statistical like the first ones. Counter to this theory stood the likes of Born, Bohr, Heisenberg, Pauli, and Dirac, who rejected the determinism of classical physics and proposed a purely probabilistic interpretation of wave physics wherein the laws of probability had a primary characteristic and did not result from a hidden determinism; these authors dedicated themselves to the discovery of the "uncertainty relations" proposed by Heisenberg and to Bohr's ideas concerning "complementarity." In October 1927, the Solvay Conference of Physics marked the conflict between deterministic and indeterministic representations; here, Louis de Broglie exposited his doctrine in the form (which he qualified in 1953 as "softened") of the pilot wave; at that time he said, "facing the almost unanimous disapproval attributed to my exposition, I have become discouraged and have returned to the probabilistic interpretation of Born, Bohr and Heisenberg, to which I have remained faithful for twenty-five years." Nevertheless, in 1953, Louis de Broglie questioned if this faithfulness were fully justified; indeed, he observes that David Bohm, an American physicist, had taken back up "his old ideas in the shortened and barely defensible form of the pilot wave." He also observes that J. P. Vigier pointed out a profound analogy between the theory of waves with singularities and Einstein's attempts to represent material particles as field singularities in the framework of general relativity. Material corpuscles as well as photons are represented as singularities within the spatiotemporal field with wave characteristics, the structure of which requires Planck's quantum of action. This is how Einstein's conception of particles and those proposed by Louis de Broglie could be joined in the theory of the double solution: a "grandiose synthesis" of quanta and relativity would be realized in this way.

For the study of individuation in physics, this doctrine presents quite a particular interest, for it seems to indicate that the physical individual, the corpuscle, can be represented as associated with a field without which it would never exist and that this field is not a pure expression of the probability for the corpuscle to be in a particular point at a particular instant ("probability wave"), but that the field is a veritable physical quantity associated with other quantities that characterize the corpuscle; the field, without absolutely belonging to the individual, would be centered around it and would therefore express a fundamental property of the individual, i.e. polarity, which would be there in its simplest form because a field is precisely composed of polarized quantities generally representable by systems of vectors. According to this manner of seeing physical reality, the wave-corpuscle duality would not at all be the apprehension of two "complementary facets of reality" in the sense that Bohr gives this expression, but instead the apprehension of two realities equally and simultaneously given in the object. The wave would no longer necessarily be a continuous wave. This is how the singular atomicity of action, which is the foundation of the theory of quanta, would be understood. The fundamental problem that wave mechanics poses for a theory of the physical individual is in fact the following: in the wave-corpuscle complex, how is the wave linked to the corpuscle? Does this wave belong to the corpuscle in some way? For the wave-corpuscle duality is also a wave-corpuscle pair.

If we begin with the study of waves, the quantum aspect of the emission or absorption of radiation also involves the idea that the energy of radiation during its propagation is concentrated into quanta of hv; consequently, the radiant energy itself is concentrated into grains, and thus we arrive at a first manner of conceiving an association of the wave and the corpuscle when the corpuscle is nothing but a quantum. If radiation is quantified, the radiant energy is concentrated into grains in quanta of the value hv. This conception is necessary to interpret not only the photo-electric effect and the Compton effect, but also the existence of a clear limit on the side of the large frequencies in the continuous spectrum of X-rays emitted by an anticathode submitted to a bombardment of electrons in the Crookes or Coolidge tube (which is what allows for the experimental calculation of the constant h); it provides a basis for the construction of a satisfying theory of the atom and of spectral lines, according to Rutherford's representation, to which Bohr has applied a theory of radiation derived from the theory of quanta. The quantified Rutherford-Bohr atom then had a discontinuous series of possible quantified states, the quantified state being a stable or stationary state of the electron: according to Bohr, in quantified states, the electron does not radiate; the emission of spectral lines then occurs due to the passage from one stationary state to another. However, this doctrine forces us to consider electrons as corpuscles that can only take certain quantified movements. Einstein proposed in 1905 the interpretation of the frequency threshold of the photo-electric effect and of the law that yields the kinetic energy of photoelectrons, $T = K(v-v_0)$, where v is the incident frequency and v_0 the threshold frequency, after returning to the old corpuscular theory of light in a new form by supposing in a monochromatic luminous wave of frequency v that energy is rolled up in the form of a corpuscle of energy hv (h being the Planck constant). Thus, according to this theory, there are grains of energy equal to hv in radiation. The frequency threshold of the photo-electric effect is then given by the equation of the frequency threshold $v_0 = \dfrac{W_0}{h}$, in which w_0 is the electron's work function.

The K constant of the experimental law cited above must be equal to the Planck constant, since the electron will escape with a kinetic energy equal to $T = h\nu - w_0 = h(\nu - \nu_0)$, an equality that verifies that experimental study of visible light, X-rays and gamma rays, as revealed particularly by Millikan's experiments (with a surface of lithium and then of sodium receiving the light emitted by a mercury-arc valve), the experiments of Maurice de Broglie for X-rays, and finally the experiments of Thibaud and Ellis for gamma rays.

In the theory of photons, the photon's individuality is not purely that of a corpuscle, for its energy, given by the expression $E = h\nu$, requires a frequency ν, and every frequency presupposes the existence of a periodicity that is not at all implicated in the definition of a corpuscle consisting in a certain quantity of matter enclosed in its spatial limits. The photons' quantity of movement is guided in the direction of their propagation and is equal to $\frac{h\nu}{c}$. Relative to the upper limit of the continuous spectrum of X-rays emitted by an anticathode, the Duane-Hunt law measures this maximum frequency by the expression $\nu_m = \frac{T}{h} = \frac{eV}{h}$. However, this law can be interpreted directly by admitting that, after the slowing down of the electron incident on the matter of the anticathode, X-rays are emitted by the photons. The largest frequency that can be emitted is the one that corresponds with the case where an electron loses the totality of its kinetic energy in a single stroke: $T = eV$, and the maximum frequency of the spectrum is given by $\nu_m = \frac{T}{h} = \frac{eV}{h}$ in conformance with the Duane-Hunt law.

Ultimately the theory of the photon was corroborated by the discovery of the Raman Effect and the Compton Effect. In 1928, Raman showed that illuminating a substance like benzene with a visible monochromatic radiation of frequency ν yields a diffused light that contains, beyond the frequency ν itself, other frequencies of the form $\nu - \nu_{ik}$, where ν_{ik} are infrared frequencies that can be emitted by the molecules of the diffusing bodies, as well as frequencies in the form of $\nu + \nu_{ik}$ with a much lower intensity. The explanation is clear concerning the theory of photons: if the molecules of the diffusing body are capable of emitting a radiation of frequency $\nu_{ik} = \frac{-E_i - E_k}{h}$ because they are capable of two quantified states of energy E_i and $E_k < E_i$, the body illuminated by the photons of energy $h\nu$ will emit diffused photons after the encounter between the photons and the molecules; the exchange of energy between the molecule and the photon of energy $h\nu$ will be translated by an increase in frequency if the photon has gained energy and by a decrease if it has lost energy. If a molecule gives to a photon the energy $E_i - E_k$ by passing from the quantified state E_i to the quantified state E_k, the energy of the photon after the encounter will be $h\nu + E_i - E_k = h(\nu + \nu_{ik})$. In the inverse case, the diffused photon's energy will be $h\nu-(E_i-E_k) = h(\nu-\nu_{ik})$. In the first case, the photon's frequency will be $\nu + \nu_{ik}$, and in the second case it will be $\nu-\nu_{ik}$.

The Compton effect, which is produced with X-rays and gamma rays, consists in a diffusion of radiation by matter, but in the Compton effect the changes of frequency that correspond to this diffusion do not depend on the nature of the diffusing body and only depend on the direction in which the diffusion is observed. This effect is interpreted by saying that the X-ray and gamma photons encounter in the diffusing body the free or approximately free electrons that are at rest or almost at rest. The variation of the photon's wavelength is due to an energy exchange with an electron; the trajectories of the photon and of the electron can be slowed down after this energy exchange, which is a veritable shock by means of the Wilson chamber, when the photon still produces, after having struck the electron, the birth of a photoelectron, since it has encountered a gas molecule; the electron's trajectory is directly visible in the Wilson chamber due to the ionization it produces (this is Compton's and Simon's experiment).

To clarify this relation of the wave and the corpuscle, Louis de Broglie has resorted to a critique of the concept of corpuscles such as it is used by physicists, and he opposes two conceptions of the corpuscle. The first is one that conceives the corpuscle as "a small, well-localized object that depicts in space through time a sensibly linear trajectory upon which at each moment it occupies a well-defined position and is animated by a well determined speed." But there is a second conception according to which it can be said "that a corpuscle is a physical unit characterized by certain constants (mass, charge, etc.) and capable of producing localized effects in which it intervenes totally and never just in part," like, for example, the photon in the Compton effect or the photo-electric effect. Yet, according to Louis de Broglie, the second definition is a consequence of the first, but the inverse is not true: "one can indeed imagine that there are physical units capable of producing local effects but which cannot be constantly identified with small objects depicting linear trajectories in space."[17] However, we must choose between the ways of defining the relation of the wave and the corpuscle based on this moment. Which term is more real? Are they just as real as each other? Is the wave merely a sort of probability field, which is, for the corpuscle, the probability of locally manifesting its presence by an observable action in such or such point? Louis de Broglie shows that three interpretations are logically possible. This author has wanted to accept what would allow for the broadest synthesis of the notions of waves and corpuscles; starting, as we have tried to indicate, from the two cases where the necessity of this bond was apparent, that of the photon and that of the quantified movements of corpuscles, he has wanted to make this bond possible for electrons and other elements of matter or of light by linking, through formulas wherein the Planck constant h would necessarily figure, the aspects of the wave and the corpuscle indissociably tied to one another.

The first type of relation between waves and corpuscles comes from the work of Arthur Schrödinger, which consists in denying the reality of the corpuscle. Only waves would have a physical signification, analogous to those of the waves of classical theories. In certain cases, the propagation of waves would give rise to corpuscular appearances, but these would be nothing but appearances. "At the start, to clarify this idea, Mr. Schrödinger wanted to assimilate the corpuscle to a small packet of waves, but this interpretation could not be sustained, given the fact that a packet of waves always has a tendency to rapidly and incessantly stretch out in space and would soon not be representing a corpuscle endowed with a prolonged stability."[18]

Louis de Broglie does not accept this negation of the corpuscle's reality; he declares that he wants to accept the wave-corpuscle duality "as a physical fact."

The second interpretation concedes the reality of the wave-corpuscle duality and wants to give it a concrete signification conforming to the traditional ideas of physics, and it considers the corpuscle as a singularity within a wave phenomenon of which it would be the center. But, Louis de Broglie says, the difficulty is knowing why wave mechanics successfully utilizes continuous waves without singularities of the type found in the continuous waves of the classical theory of light.

Lastly, the third interpretation consists in only considering the ideas of the corpuscle and of the continuous wave and in regarding them as complementary facets of reality, in the sense that Bohr gives this expression; this interpretation is qualified by Louis de Broglie as "orthodox."

The second interpretation was at first that of Louis de Broglie in 1924 following the defense of his thesis: he considered the corpuscle as a singularity within an extended wave phenomenon, the whole of which forms nothing but a single physical reality. "Since the movement of the singularity is tied to the evolution of the wave phenomenon and forms its center, it would depend on all the circumstances that this wave phenomenon would encounter in its propagation in space. This is why the corpuscle's movement would not follow the laws of classical mechanics, which is a purely punctual mechanics in which the corpuscle is merely subject to the actions of the forces exerted upon it along its trajectory without undergoing any repercussion from the existence of the obstacles that can be found farther along its trajectory: in my conception, on the contrary, the movement of the singularity would be subject to the influence of all the obstacles that would influence the propagation of the wave phenomenon with which it is interdependent, thus explaining the existence of interferences and diffraction."[19]

However, as Louis de Broglie says, wave mechanics has developed by only contemplating continuous solutions without singularities for equations of propagation (these solutions are customarily designated by the Greek letter Ψ). If the propagation of a wave (a flat and monochromatic Ψ wave) is associated with a uniform and rectilinear movement, then a difficulty is presented: the phase of the wave that allows us to define the frequency and wavelength associated with the corpuscle indeed seems to have a direct physical sense, whereas the wave's constant amplitude seems to be able to be just a statistical representation of the possible positions of the corpuscle. As Louis de Broglie affirms in the same annual conference presentation, "thus there would be a mixture of the individual and of the statistical that would be mysterious and would seem to have to be clarified." This is why de Broglie will postulate in a May article of *Journal de Physique*[20] that all continuous solutions for the equations of wave mechanics are somewhat doubled by a solution with a singularity u that carries a singularity that is mobile in general (the corpuscle) and that has the same phase as the solution Ψ. Between the solution u and the solution Ψ, which both have a wave form, there is no phase difference (since the phase is the same function of x, y, z, t), yet there is a considerable difference of amplitude because solution u conveys a singularity, whereas that of Ψ is continuous. If the equation of propagation is supposedly the same for u and for Ψ, then a fundamental theorem can be demonstrated: the mobile singularity of u must eventually describe a trajectory such that in each point the speed is proportionate to the phase gradient. "It could be said that this is how the reaction of the propagation of the wave phenomenon on the singularity that forms its center would be translated. I am also demonstrating that this reaction could be expressed by considering the corpuscle-singularity as being subject to a 'quantum potential' that was precisely the mathematical expression of the reaction of the wave on it." Thus, the diffraction of light by the edge of a screen can be interpreted by saying that the corpuscle of light is subject to an action of the screen's edge and is thereby diverted from its rectilinear route, just as the partisans of the old corpuscular theory of light proclaim, but by considering that the action of the screen's edge on the corpuscle takes place through the intermediary of this "quantum potential" which is the mathematical expression of the wave on the corpuscle; the wave would therefore serve as a means of energy exchange between the corpuscle and the screen's edge. In this interpretation, the u wave with its mobile singularity therefore simultaneously constitutes the corpuscle and the wave phenomenon that surrounds it, which is a single physical reality. What describes physical reality is the u wave and not the Ψ wave, which has no real physical signification; since the Ψ wave is deemed to have the same phase as the u wave, and the corpuscle-singularity is always displaced by following the phase gradient, the possible trajectories of the corpuscle would coincide with the curves orthogonal to the surfaces equal to the phase of Ψ; this would lead to considering the probability of finding the corpuscle in a point as equal to the square of the amplitude or intensity of the Ψ wave. This principle was already accepted for quite a while in wave mechanics, since it was necessary for establishing the theory of the diffraction of electrons. In 1905, Einstein had already shown that the probability for a photon to be present in a point of space is proportionate to the square of the amplitude of the light wave associated with it; here we rediscover one of the essential principles of the wave theory of light: the density of radiant energy is given by the square of the amplitude of the luminous wave; in this case, the Ψ wave seems like a purely fictive wave, a simple representation of probabilities. But it is worth mentioning that this formal and somewhat nominal characteristic of the Ψ wave was only just so, because, in phase concordance with it, there was a u wave phase with a singularity that really described the central corpuscle of an extended wave phenomenon; and this is how Louis de Broglie concludes his retrospective exposition in 1953: "If we could have the impression that the Ψ wave fully sufficed to describe the behavior of the corpuscle such that we could observe it experimentally, this would be due to the coincidence of phases that formed the cornerstone of my theory."[21] In order to be received at that time, this theory required that we rework the theory of the phenomena of interference, for example that of Young's slits, by only utilizing the u wave with singularities. It would be just as necessary to interpret, with the help of the u wave, the wave mechanics of systems of corpuscles developed in the framework of Schrödinger's configuration space. But in 1953, Louis de Broglie proposes a modification of the u wave: "In 1927, I considered it as a solution with a singularity of the linear equations accepted by wave mechanics for the Ψ wave. Various considerations, particularly the assimilation with the theory of generalized relativity of which I will speak later, have made me think that the veritable equation of u wave propagation could be non-linear like the ones we encounter in Einstein's theory of gravitation, which is a non-linear equation that would admit, as an approximate form, the equation of wave mechanics when the values of u would be weak. If this point of view were exact, we could even admit that the u wave does not behave like a mobile singularity in the strict sense of the word singularity, but merely as a very small, mobile singular region (with dimensions on the order of 10^{-13} cm) within which the values of u would be large enough for the linear approximation to no longer be valid, although it would be fully valid in the space outside this very small region. Unfortunately, this change in our point of view does not facilitate the resolution of the mathematical problems posed, because if the study of the solutions of linear equations with singularities is often difficult, that of the solutions of non-linear equations is even more so."[22] Louis de Broglie attempted to simplify his theory for the Solvay Conference in 1927 by introducing the notion of the "pilot wave," which was essentially the Ψ wave considered as guiding the corpuscle following the formula: "speed proportionate to the phase gradient." Since the corpuscle's movement is defined by the phase gradient that belongs to the solutions u and Ψ, everything seemingly happens as if the corpuscle were guided by the continuous Ψ wave. The corpuscle would then become an independent reality. This representation was not well received by the Solvay Conference, and Louis de Broglie regretted having simplified his theory in the direction of a certain formalism that eventually resulted in a nominalism: "the theory of the pilot wave leads to this unacceptable result of determining the movement of the corpuscle by a physical quantity, the continuous Ψ wave, which has no real physical signification, depends on the state of knowledge of the one who utilizes it, and must vary abruptly when information happens to modify this knowledge. If the conceptions that I have announced in 1927 one day rose again from their embers, this would only occur in the subtle form of the double solution and not in the truncated and unacceptable form of the pilot wave."[23] Louis de Broglie considers that the first form of his theory, which conveys the u wave and the Ψ wave, albeit difficult to justify mathematically, is quite superior to that of the pilot wave, since it is capable (in successful cases) of offering an extremely profound view of the constitution of matter and of the duality of waves and corpuscles and is even perhaps capable of allowing for a rapprochement of quantum conceptions and relativistic conceptions. Nevertheless, this rapprochement is something Louis de Broglie ardently desires, considering it to be "grandiose."

This is why Louis de Broglie once again considers the theory of the double solution (u wave and Ψ wave) as needing to be studied based on the moment he witnesses Bohm and Vigier resume this point of view. Following Bohm's attempt, Vigier establishes a rapprochement between the double solution and a theorem demonstrated by Einstein. After developing the great

lines of generalized relativity, Einstein was preoccupied with the way in which
the atomic structure of matter could be represented by the singularities of the
gravitational field. Nevertheless, in generalized relativity we accept that the
movement of a body is represented in the space-time curve by a geodesics of
this space-time; this postulate allowed Einstein to newly discover the movement of the planets around the Sun and to further interpret by the same
token the centennial displacement of Mercury's perihelion. Since then, if we
want to define the elementary particles of matter by the existence of singularities in the gravitational field, it would have to be possible to demonstrate,
solely on the basis of the equations of the gravitational field, that the movement of singularities occurs following the geodesics of space-time without
having to introduce this result as an independent postulate. Einstein demonstrated this in 1927 while working in collaboration with Grommer, and then
the demonstration was repeated and extended in various ways by Einstein
and his collaborators Infeld and Hoffman. The demonstration of Einstein's
theory presents, as Louis de Broglie claimed in 1953, a certain analogy with
what he had himself presented in 1927 to prove that a corpuscle must always
have its speed guided along the phase gradient of the u wave of which it
constitutes a singularity. "Mr. Vigier fervently pursued attempts to clarify
this analogy by seeking to introduce the functions of the u wave into the
definition of the metrics of space-time. Although these attempts have still
not fully ripened, it is certain that the path he has trekked is quite interesting, for it could lead to a unification of the ideas of general relativity and
wave mechanics."[24] Since material corpuscles and photons are considered to
be singular regions in the metrics of space-time surrounded by a wave field to
which they belong and whose definition would introduce the Planck constant,
it would become possible, according to Louis de Broglie, to unify Einstein's
conceptions on particles and those of the double solution theory. This "grandiose synthesis" of relativity and of quanta would have, among many other
advantages, the advantage of avoiding "subjectivism," which is related, as
Louis de Broglie says, to idealism in the philosophical sense, which tends to
deny the independent physical existence of the observer. "Nevertheless, the
physicist instinctively remains, as Meyerson has strongly emphasized long
ago, a realist," and he has several good reasons for this: "subjectivist interpretations will always give him a feeling of unease, and I ultimately believe
that he would be happy to break away from this."[25] But this synthesis, which
is able to re-establish a much more profound and realist signification of the
double solution theory, would also have another advantage: the singular
zones of various corpuscles can in fact encroach upon one another starting

at a certain scale; this encroachment is not significant and important enough at the atomic scale (10^{-8} to 10^{-11} cm) to constrict the "orthodox" interpretation, but this does not necessarily apply at the nuclear scale (10^{-13} cm). At this scale, it could be that the singular zones of corpuscles encroach upon one another and that these corpuscles can no longer be considered isolated. Thus, we witness the appearance of a new mode of calculation of the relation between physical individuals that would force a consideration of density and of individual characteristics, which are defined as the singularity of the u wave. The theory of nuclear phenomena, and particularly the theory of the forces that maintain the stability of the nucleus, could begin through this new path. Physics could define a structure of particles (which is not possible with the Ψ wave) that excludes any structural representation of particles due to its statistical characteristic. The new types of mesons that have been discovered could thus be provided with a structural image due to this return to spatio-temporal images. The statistical Ψ wave could then no longer be considered a complete representation of reality; and the indeterminism that accompanies these conceptions, in the same way that the impossibility of representing the realities of the atomic scale precisely in the framework of space and time through variables that would be hidden to us, would have to be considered incompatible with this new representation of physical reality.

3. The Theory of the Double Solution in Wave Mechanics

However, it is important to note that if we begin by acknowledging that the physical individual should not be considered as a reality limited to itself and defined by its spatial limits but rather as the singularity of a wave, i.e. as a reality that can be defined by the inherence to its properties but which is also defined by the interaction it has with other physical realities at a distance, the consequence of this initial breadth in the definition of the individual is that this notion remains affected by a coefficient of realism. Conversely, if we begin by upholding the opposite notion of the individual as being defined *stricto sensu* as a particle limited by its dimensions, then this physical being loses its reality, and probabilistic formalism replaces the realism of the preceding theory. It is specifically in probabilistic theories (which accept the classical notion of the individual from the start) that this notion is lacking due to progress in the theory of the probability wave; according to Bohr's expression cited by Louis de Broglie, corpuscles become "unsharply defined individuals within finite space-time limits."[26] The wave also loses all realist physical signification; according to the expression of Destouches, it is nothing more than a representation of probability that depends on the knowledge acquired by the one who utilizes it. "It is personal and subjective like the assessments of probability and, like them, it is abruptly modified when the user acquires new information: this is what Heisenberg has called the 'reduction of the packet of waves by measurement,' a reduction that would alone suffice to demonstrate the non-physical characteristic of the Ψ wave."[27] This probability does not result from an ignorance; it results from pure contingency; such is "pure probability," which does not result from a definite hidden determinism calculable according to hidden parameters; the hidden parameters would not exist.

The physical individual, the corpuscle, becomes in the theories of Bohr and Heisenberg a set of potentialities affected by probabilities; it is nothing more than a being that appears fleetingly, sometimes under one aspect and sometimes under another, in conformity with the notion of complementarity that belongs to Bohr's theory and according to the relations of Heisenberg's uncertainty principle, which are the foundation of an indeterministic and probabilistic theory. In general, neither a well-determined position, a speed, nor a trajectory can be attributed to the corpuscle: it can only be revealed as having a certain speed or position the moment when its measurement or observation is made. At each instant, so to speak, it possesses a whole series of possible positions or states of movement, since these various potentialities can be actualized at the moment of the measurement with certain probabilities. The associated Ψ wave is a representation of the set of the corpuscle's potentialities with their respective probabilities. The extension of the Ψ wave in space represents the indetermination of the corpuscle's positions, which can be revealed to be present in any point whatsoever of the region occupied by the wave with a probability proportionate to the square of the wave's amplitude in this point. The same applies for the states of movement: the Ψ wave has a spectral decomposition in a Fourier series or integral, and this decomposition represents all the possible states of a measurement of the quantity of movement, the possibility of each possible result of such a measurement given by the square of the corresponding coefficient of the Fourier decomposition. This theory has the fortune of finding in front of it, and ready to serve as its means of expression, a perfectly adequate mathematical expression: the theory of functions and proper values, developments in a series of proper functions, matrices, and Hilbert space; thus, all the resources of linear analysis are immediately usable. The double solution theory is not as well served by the current state of development of mathematical formalism; it seems that a certain irregularity in the development of mathematical thought according to various paths has led to a much greater facility of expression for the indeterministic and probabilistic theory than for the double solution theory; but the privilege thus given by a certain state of mathematical development to one of the interpretations of the wave-corpuscle relation should not be considered an index of the superiority of the easily formulable doctrine in terms of what concerns the value of the representation that it gives of physical reality. It is necessary to dissociate formal perfection from fidelity to the real. This fidelity to the real is translated by a certain capacity of discovery and fruitfulness in research. However, the indeterministic and probabilistic theory of the relation between waves and corpuscles seems to have lost this power of discovery and is closed within an increasingly remarkable self-constructive formalism (S matrices, minimum length, non-localized fields) that nevertheless does not allow for the resolution, for example, of problems relative to the stability of the nucleus.

Louis de Broglie considers this opposition between the two conceptions of the wave-corpuscle relation as essentially residing in the deterministic or indeterminisitc postulate. We could also consider that what is in question is the representation of the physical individual, at first in an elementary sense, but then on all levels. Probabilistic theory can only be probabilistic because it considers that the physical individual is what it seems relative to the measuring subject; there is something of a recurrence of probabilities installed in the very being of the physical individual despite the contingency of the relation through which the event of measure intervenes. On the contrary, at the basis of the double solution theory, there is the idea that relation has the value of being and really belongs to being. A particular wave belongs to this individual, and this individual is its center and singularity; the individual is what contains the instrument through which relation is established, since this relation is that of a measurement or some other event that conveys an energy exchange. Relation has the value of being; it is an individuating operation. In the indeterministic and probabilistic theory, a certain static substantialism of the physical individual remains in the subject; the individual can indeed be one of the terms of the relation, but the relation is independent of the terms; in the end, we could say that relation is nothing, it is only a probability for the relation to occur here or there. Relation is not of the same nature as the terms; it is a purely formal thing, something artificial in the profound sense of the term when there is a measurement, i.e. a relation of subject and object. This formalism and this artificiality, which come from an overly narrow definition of physical individuation, then reflects back onto the usual definition of the individual, which is practically defined only by the relation: it then becomes this "unsharply defined individual". Yet the individual precisely cannot be "sharply defined" at the start, before any relation, because it carries its possibility of relation around it and is this possibility of relation. Individuation and relation are inseparable; the capacity of relation belongs to the being and enters into its definition and into the determination of its limits: there is no limit between the individual and its activity of relation; relation is contemporaneous with being; it belongs to being energetically and spatially. Relation and being simultaneously exist as a field, and the potential that relation defines is veritable, not formal. Just because an energy is in a potential form does not mean that it does not exist. The response will be that we cannot define the potential outside of a system; this is true, but it is possible that we need to postulate that the individual is a being which cannot exist as an individual except in relation with a non-individuated real. In the probabilistic conception, it is postulated that the individual can exist alone and afterwards is found to be incapable of incorporating relation, which seems accidental and undetermined. Relation should neither be conceived as immanent to the being nor as external and accidental to it; these two theories unite in their mutual opposition in the sense that they suppose that the individual could be alone by right. If, on the contrary, we posit that the individual forms part of *at least* one system, relation becomes as real as the individual qua being, which could abstractly be conceived as isolated. The individual is *being and relation*; it is a center of activity, but this activity is transductive; it is exerted across and through a field of forces that modifies the whole system in terms of the individual and the individual in terms of the whole system. Relation always exists as potential, but it may or may not be at a certain moment in the process of correlatively modifying the individual and system. Quantum laws seem to indicate that this relation only operates step by step and not continuously, something that guarantees stable states for both the system and the individual despite the conservation of potentials. Formalism supposes that the individual is conceived before relation, which then remains purely calculable without being subjected to the conditions of the individual's energetic states; the individual's state and its state changes are not conceived as the principle and origin of relation; in formalism, relation is not conflated with its energetic modality. On the contrary, in realism, relation is always an energetic exchange that implies an operation on the part of the individual; the structure and operation of the individual are tied together; every relation modifies the structure, and every change of structure modifies the relation, or rather *is* relation, for every change of the individual's structure modifies its energetic level and consequently implies an energy exchange with other individuals constituting the system in which the individual has received its genesis.

Louis de Broglie argues that this realism requires a return to the Cartesian representations of space and time where everything is formed by "figure and movement." Several reservations should be made about this point; Descartes indeed refuses to consider action at a distance to be possible, and he only acknowledges action through contact; an individual must be present in a point in order for it to act there; the Cartesian representation of individuation precisely identifies the individual with its geometrical limits characterized by its figure. On the contrary, it seems that the conception which considers the individual as the singularity of a wave and which consequently requires a field does not accept the Cartesian representation of individuation, even if it accepts its conception of determinism. To recall Bachelard's expression, there is a non-Cartesian epistemology, not in the sense of determinism or indeterminism, but in the sense of what concerns the mode of action of one individual on another, whether through contact or the intermediary of a field (what Bachelard calls "electrism"). However, it would actually be because probabilistic physics begins by way of an initial Cartesian definition of individuation that it culminates in indeterminism. And this initial definition of individuation forms the basic postulate of every physical theory. For Descartes, relation is not considered as part of the individual, does not express the individual, and does not transform the individual; relation is accidental with respect to substance. The indeterministic theory conserves this definition of the individual at least implicitly because this theory calculates the probabilities of presence at a specific point without accounting for the individual that must be present there; this same theory of indeterminism is nothing but a determinism that postulates that hidden parameters do not exist; but what is precisely identical in this determinism and indeterminism is determination, which is always an event for the individual and not a relational operation. For both, determination is a rapport and not a relation, a veritable relational act. This is why we are better off not affirming too much the possibility of a return to the Cartesian conceptions of space and time. As Louis de Broglie has said many times, Einstein's system is much better suited to this conception of individuation than any other, including that of Descartes; a corpuscle that can be represented as the singularity of a field is not conceivable in Cartesian geometrism, insofar as a singularity cannot be introduced into this space qua *res extensa* (extended substance) without excessively modifying Cartesian geometry and mechanics.

In the end, we could ask ourselves whether or not, instead of being capable of entering into the framework of an indeterministic physics or that of deterministic physics, we should consider the theory of singularities as the foundation for a new representation of the real that encompasses these two as particular cases and that should be called the theory of transductive time or the theory of the phases of being.

This definition of a new manner of thinking becoming, which calls for determinism and indeterminism as borderline cases, applies to other domains of reality than that of elementary corpuscles; this is why we have been able to obtain the diffraction of bundles of molecules by crystalline surfaces (Stern, in 1932, obtained the diffraction of molecular rays of hydrogen and helium by verifying Louis de Broglie's relation between the speed and the wavelength, $\lambda = h / mv$, within a margin of 1 percent).

However, it seems difficult to generalize this method by applying it to all orders of magnitude without carrying out a recasting of what could be called the topology and chronology of the physical axiomatic, i.e. without rethinking each time the problem of the individuation of the ensemble in which the phenomenon develops; in this sense, two questions can be posed: what are the limits of the usage of the notion of the photon as a physical individual? What can we consider as the real source of light in the cases where the continuous wave characteristic of light is involved in producing a phenomenon? In these two cases, it seems that the physical system must be considered in its totality.

Let's suppose that a magnetic field, for example, exists and is constant. We can speak of the field's existence and measure its intensity at a determined point, just as we can define its direction. Let's now suppose that what produced this field, for example a current in a solenoid, stops. The field will also stop, not abruptly and simultaneously in all points, but according to a perturbation that extends starting from the field's origin, the solenoid, with the speed of an electromagnetic wave. Can we consider this propagating perturbation as a photon, or at the very least as a grain of energy? If it were a question of an alternating magnetic field, this point of view would be normal, and it would be possible to define a frequency and a wavelength characterizing the presence of this alternating magnetic field. Would it not then be necessary to characterize the presence of the magnetic field, which is continuous in each point, as a potential that is a relation between the solenoid and the bodies capable of transforming these variations of the magnetic field in a current, for example? But it could be supposed that the solenoid would disappear the moment when the current that upholds the continuous magnetic field is cut; this perturbation will not propagate any less, as though the solenoid still existed, and it will be able to produce the same effects of induction in other bodies; here this will no longer be a relation between physical individuals, since one of them will have disappeared the moment when the perturbation will arrive in a determined point far from its origin.

In the same way, it seems quite difficult to give the individuality of the photon to the modifications of an unspecified electromagnetic field. From 10-kilometer radioelectric waves (international and submarine telegraphy) to the most penetrating gamma rays, a formulaic analogy and a veritable continuity in both the modes of production and the physical properties tie together all electromagnetic relations. However, the granular nature of these radiations is quite apparent for short wavelengths, but it becomes extremely unclear for large wavelengths, and, if we wanted, this could tend toward an infinite wavelength corresponding to a null frequency without thereby nullifying the reality of the electrical field and the magnetic field. A perturbation that would occur in these fields would propagate at the speed of light; but if no perturbation took place, then nothing would propagate, and yet the fields continue to exist since they can be measured as continuous fields. Should the continuous field be distinguished from the perturbation that could propagate if it appears? The continuity of the field in each point can also be interpreted as an information indicating that the source still existed at a determined instant. Since the field is real, it would be necessary to suppose as real an infinite wavelength that would correspond to this null frequency. But then the individuality of the grain of energy loses its signification outside the physical beings that radiate or receive this energy. Therefore, it still seems that a definition of physical individuality is to be specified. Perhaps we shouldn't speak of the individuality of the particle of energy like the individuality of the particle of matter; there is a source of the photon and of the electromagnetic perturbation. The conception of space would be contested; it is doubtful that the Cartesian conception can be suitable without being completed. Let us ultimately note that a quantitative formalism is not enough to resolve this difficulty of relation between space and time: the cessation of a magnetic field is not identical to the establishment of the magnetic field; even if the effects of induction that the two variations of flux can provoke in a circuit (both at the end and at the start) are equal in the circuit down to the most refined and exact measurement of the current in every sense, the presence of the constant magnetic field corresponds to a possibility of energy exchange between, for example, the solenoid that creates it and a circuit that is made to turn at a certain distance in such a way as to penetrate one of its sides with a constantly variable flux. When the field no longer exists, this possibility of energetic coupling no longer exists; the regime of possible energy exchanges in the system has changed; it can be said that the system's topology has changed due to the disappearance of a constant field that nevertheless did not transport energy when no flux variation took place. Thus appears the reality of relations other than those of events between individuals (such as a theory of probabilities can make them seem).

Finally, it would be quite important to know whether the new path down which Louis de Broglie wants to see wave mechanics tread suppresses or conserves the indiscernibility of individuals with the same characteristics, for example electrons. Still using probabilistic methods, according to Kahan and Kawal,[28] we must postulate that the probability of finding two electrons in two defined states when they are in interaction is independent from their numbering; this indiscernibility of identical particles disrupts the exchange in the problem that seeks their respective energy levels. We could also wonder if Pauli's principle of exclusion is still valid.

A similar difficulty relative to the individuation of physical systems appears in the phenomenon of interferences: whenever we consider an experiment of interferences in a non-localized field, we theorize this experiment (Young's slits contemplated as a means of producing not a diffraction but two synchronous oscillators, Fresnel's mirror, Billet's lens) by saying that the light waves are emitted by two synchronous sources (which are synchronous because they receive their light from a single source) and that they are themselves nothing but secondary sources arranged at equal distances from a primary source. Yet, if we carefully consider the structure and activity of this primary source, we realize that it is possible to obtain a very clear phenomenon of interference (with extinction practically complete in the dark bands), even if a primary source containing a very large number of atoms is utilized; a source, for example, constituted by a segment of Tungsten filament .5 mm long and .2 mm in diameter necessarily contains several tens of thousands of atoms. Furthermore, we can take an extremely voluminous source, like a carbon arc lamp in which light emanates from a gap and from a point whose active surface (from which the column of luminous vapor stems) is about a square centimeter for a strong intensity. However, since it has passed through a minuscule diaphragm that serves as the primary source, the light that emanates from this strong luminous area is capable of producing the phenomenon of interference as if it were produced by a very small segment of incandescent filament. Then is there a real synchronization between the molecules and the atoms of these large luminous surfaces? Every moment a very large number of non-synchronized oscillators emit light; it would seem normal to consider the phenomenon as a result that conforms with the laws of statistics; we would then have to suppose that the phenomenon of interference will be all the more unclear because there will be a greater number of non-synchronized oscillators (we mean by this not oscillators of different frequencies but relative to an unspecified phase) in order to constitute the primary source; and it does not seem that experimentation verifies this prediction. Yet, given the order of magnitude of the sources utilized, even the smallest sources already contain a large number of elementary oscillators that do not seem to be able to be in phase. These oscillators cannot be in phase when they have different frequencies; however, the phenomenon always occurs even though only the central bands are distinct, since the bands relative to each frequency are less superposed the farther they are from the central band. What is the phase synchronization that can exist between waves emitted by oscillators of the same frequency? Does this synchronization come from the unity of the system that contains them? Is there a coupling that takes place between these oscillators placed at a short distance from one another? But if a primary source is constituted by means of an optical apparatus that unifies the rays emitted by two distinct sources, would this phase synchronization remain? Or instead, is the phenomenon independent of any phase synchronization? It is perhaps noteworthy to link the study of light to that of the source which produces it. The photon's individuality cannot be considered absolutely independent from the oscillator that produces it or from the system to which this oscillator possibly belongs. Thus, all the oscillators included in the same energetic system would have a certain linkage between them that could make synchronization possible, and not only would there be a frequency synchronization but a phase synchronization between these oscillators in such a way that the individuality of the photons is affected and somehow marked by this original systematic community. Finally, let's note that the light originating from a star can still give rise to a phenomenon of interference, as if the source were actually that of an extremely small, real diameter; it nevertheless seems impossible to consider a star as a single oscillator, even if it presents itself with an apparent diameter smaller than any assignable magnitude; the extreme smallness of this apparent diameter cannot in principle change the phase rapport of the different photons picked up by the interferometer; photons that originate from parts quite distant from one another (relative to wavelength) on the star taken as their source can be picked up by this interferometer. Then where does this synchronization come from? It no doubt comes from the apparatus in which the interferences occur; but the latter is not itself a veritable source. Or instead it is necessary to suppose that each photon is divided into two quantities of energy that would be like semi-photons, and that each half of the photon would manage to interfere with the other half on the screen in which the phenomenon is produced; this supposition hardly appears acceptable precisely due to the individual nature of the photon. For all these reasons, it seems that we cannot bestow physical individuality upon the photon in the sense of a material corpuscle; the photon's individuality would merely be proportionate to its frequency, i.e. to the quantity of energy (hv) it transports, without this individuality ever being able to be complete, since it would then require this frequency to be infinite, and no oscillator can produce an infinite frequency. A photon that would have an infinite frequency could be assimilated to a veritable particle of matter. We should still note that there perhaps exists a threshold beyond which it could be said that the photon's frequency corresponds to a veritable individuality: this frequency would be that for which the photon's energy is or would be equal to the energy of a material particle whose transformation into energy would precisely give the quantity of energy which would be the energy of this very high-frequency photon. This photon would then be functionally equivalent to a piece of matter.

4. Topology, Chronology, and Order of Magnitude of Physical Individuation

Furthermore, if we contemplate microphysical reality directly, an interpretation of individuation based on the phenomena of structural change would aim to consider becoming as essentially linked to the operations of individuation carried out in successive transformations; determinism would remain applicable as a borderline case when the system considered is not the theater of any individuation, i.e. when no exchange takes place between energy and structure (which would modify the system's structures), thus leaving it topologically identical to what it was in its previous states; on the contrary, indeterminism would seem like a borderline case when a complete structural change manifests in a system with the transition from one order of magnitude to another; this is the case, for example, of the modifications brought to a system by the fission of an atomic nucleus: intranuclear energies, which up to that point belong to the internal system of this nucleus, are unleashed by fission and can act as a gamma photon or a neutron on the bodies that belong to a system situated on a scale larger than that of the atomic nucleus. Nothing in a macroscopic system allows us to predict at which moment of macroscopic time there will be a fission unleashing an energy that will nevertheless be effective on the macroscopic level. Indeterminism is not merely linked to measurement; it also stems from the fact that physical reality involves topologically interlocking scales of magnitude, each of which has their own becoming and their own particular chronology. Indeterminism would exist in a pure state if there were no correlation between the topology and chronology of physical systems. This absence of correlation is never absolutely complete; this can only be said abstractly of an absolute indeterminism (realizable by a complete internal resonance) or of an absolute determinism (realizable by a complete independence between chronology and topology). The general case is that of a certain level of correlation between a system's chronology and topology, a level which is moreover variable due to the vicissitudes of its own becoming; a system reacts on itself not only in the sense of the principle of entropy through the general law of its internal energetic transformations but also by modifying its own structure through time. The becoming of a system is the manner in which it individuates, i.e. essentially the manner in which it is conditioned according to the different structures and successive operations through which it reverberates within itself and phase-shifts relative to its initial state. Determinism and indeterminism are merely borderline cases because there is a becoming of systems: this becoming is the becoming of their individuation; there is a reactivity of systems with respect to themselves. The evolution of a system would be determined if there were no internal resonance of the system, i.e. no exchange between the different scales that it encompasses and that constitute it; no quantum structural change would be possible, and we could know the becoming of this system in a theory of the continuous or according to the law of large numbers (as thermodynamics does). Pure indeterminism would correspond to such an elevated internal resonance that any modification occurring on a determined scale would immediately reverberate throughout all levels as a structural change. In fact, the general case is that of quantum thresholds of resonance: in order for a modification occurring on one of the levels to reach the other levels, it must be above a certain value; internal resonance only develops discontinuously and with a certain delay from one scale to another; the individuated physical being is not totally simultaneous relative to itself. Its topology and chronology are separated by a certain gap that is variable according to the becoming of the individuated whole; substance would be a physical individual totally resonant with respect to itself and consequently totally identical to itself, perfectly coherent with itself and singular. The physical being must be considered, on the contrary, as more than unity and more than identity, rich in potentials; the individual is undergoing individuation based on a pre-individual reality that sustains it; the perfect individual (totally

individuated, substantial, deprived and emptied of its potentials) is an abstraction; the individual is undergoing ontogenetic becoming, it has with
respect to itself a relative coherence, a relative unity, and a relative identity.
The physical individual must be thought as a chrono-topological whole
whose complex becoming involves successive crises of individuation; the
being's becoming consists in this non-coincidence of chronology and topology. The individuation of a physical ensemble would then be constituted by
the interlinking of the successive regimes of this ensemble.

Such a conception would therefore consider energetic regimes and structural states as convertible with one another through an ensemble's becoming;
due to the notion of orders of magnitude and the notion of thresholds in
exchanges, it would assert that individuation exists between the pure continuous and the pure discontinuous; the notion of thresholds and of quantum
exchange is indeed a mediation between the pure continuous and the pure
discontinuous. It would bring in the notion of information as a fundamental characteristic of individuation conceived according to dimensions both
chronological and topological. We could then speak of a more or less elevated level of individuation: an ensemble would possess a more elevated
level of individuation in proportion to the greater amount of pre-individual
reality it would envelop and compatibilize in its chronological and topological
systematics, or in proportion to the difference between orders of magnitude.

Such a hypothesis supposes that there is no elementary individual, no first
individual anterior to every genesis; there is individuation in an ensemble;
the first reality is pre-individual and is richer than the individual understood
as the result of individuation; the pre-individual is the source of chronological and topological dimensionality. The oppositions between continuous
and discontinuous, particle and energy, would thus express not so much the
complementary aspects of the real as the dimensions that emerge in the real
when it becomes individuated; complementarity on the level of individuated reality would be the translation of the fact that individuation appears,
on the one hand, as ontogenesis and, on the other hand, as an operation of a
pre-individual reality that not only produces the individual, the model of
substance, but also produces the energy or the field associated with the individual; only the associated field-individual pairing accounts for the level of
pre-individual reality.

This supposition of the first pre-individual nature of reality is moreover
what allows us to consider the physical individual veritably as an ensemble;
the individual corresponds to a certain dimensionality of the real, i.e. to an
associated topology and chronology; the individual is an edifice in its most

current form, i.e. in the form in which it appears to us, whether crystal or molecule. As such, it is not an absolute but a reality that corresponds to a certain state of (generally metastable) equilibrium and is founded on a regime of exchanges between the different orders of magnitude that can be modified either by internal becoming or by an external event that brings a certain new condition to the internal regime (for example, an energetic condition when the neutron originating from the fission of a nucleus provokes the fission of another nucleus). Thus, there is a certain consistency of the individual but not an absolute antitypy, an impenetrability in a substantial sense. The consistency of the individual edifice is still founded on quantum conditions; it depends on thresholds.

The limits of the physical individual are also themselves metastable; an ensemble of fissile nuclei isn't really an individuated ensemble if the number of nuclei, taking into account the average radioactivity of the nuclei, is small enough for the fission of a nucleus to have little chance of provoking the fission of another nucleus;[29] everything happens as if each nucleus were isolated from the others; each has its own chronology, and the fission occurs for each nucleus as if it were alone; on the contrary, if a large quantity of fissile material is gathered together, the probability for the results of the fission of a nucleus to provoke the fission of another nucleus increases: when this probability reaches unity, the internal chronology of each nucleus abruptly changes: instead of consisting in itself, it forms a network of internal resonance with the resonance of all the other nuclei capable of fission: the physical individual is then the entire mass of fissile material and no longer each nucleus; the notion of critical mass gives the example of what can be called a relative threshold of individuation: the chronology of the ensemble becomes abruptly coextensive with the topology of the ensemble;[30] there is individuation because there is exchange between the microphysical level and the macrophysical level; the capacity for the ensemble's reception of information abruptly increases. By modifying topological conditions, we can utilize nuclear energy either for abrupt effects (through the gathering of several masses, each inferior to critical mass) or for continuous moderate effects (by controlling the exchange between fissile nuclei by means of a controllable apparatus that maintains the ensemble below the unitary coefficient of amplification, for example through the greater or lesser absorption of radiation). Consequently, it can be said that the degree of individuation of an ensemble depends on the correlation between the system's chronology and topology; this degree of individuation can also be called the level of interactive communication, since it defines the degree of the internal resonance of the ensemble.

From this point of view, it seems possible to understand why the antago- nistic representations of the continuous and the discontinuous, of matter and energy, of structure and operation, are not usable except as complemen- tary pairs; this is because these notions define opposite and extreme aspects of the orders of reality between which individuation is established; but the operation of individuation is the active center of this relation; it is the latter that is the unity of this center that splits into aspects which are complementary for us, albeit in the real they are paired by the continuous and transductive unity of intermediary being, what we call here internal resonance; the com- plementary aspects of the real are extreme aspects that define the dimension- ality of the real. Since we can only grasp reality through its manifestations, i.e. when it changes, we only perceive extreme complementary aspects; but, rather than the real, what we perceive are dimensions of the real; we grasp its chronology and topology of individuation without being able to grasp the pre-individual real that subtends this transformation.

Information, understood as the arrival of a singularity that creates a com- munication between orders of reality, is what we can think most easily, at least in several particular cases like (free or limited) chain reactions. This intervention of a notion of information does not however allow us to resolve the problem of the rapport of different levels of individuation. A crystal is composed of molecules; it requires the unity of energetic conditions (meta- stability) and structural conditions (a crystalline germ) for us to have a crys- tallized supersaturated solution; can an individuated being such as a mole- cule, which is already an edifice, intervene as a structural germ of this larger edifice, i.e. a crystal? Or instead, does it take a structural germ that is already of an order of magnitude superior to that of a molecule for the crystal to be able to begin? In the current state of knowledge, it is difficult to come up with a generalizable answer to this question. It can merely be said that the problem of the rapports of inert matter and life would be clearer if it could be shown that the living being is characterized by the fact that it discovers in its field of reality structural conditions that allow it to resolve its own incom- patibilities, the distance between the orders of magnitude of its reality, whereas inert matter does not have this capacity of the autogenesis of structures; a singularity is required in order for the supersaturated solution to crystallize; does this mean that inert matter does not increase its capital of singularities, whereas living matter increases this capital, since this increase is precisely the ontogenesis of the living being and is capable of adaptation and inven- tion? This distinction can only be given as a methodological hypothesis; it does not seem that we can oppose a living matter and a non-living matter, but instead that we can oppose a primary individuation in inert systems and a secondary individuation in living systems, specifically according to the different modalities of the regimes of communication during these individuations; between the inert and the living, there would then be a quantum difference of the capacity for the reception of information rather than a substantial difference: if it exists, the continuity between the inert and the living would have to be sought on the level that is situated between microphysical reality and macrophysical reality, i.e. on the level of the individuation of systems like the large molecules of organic chemistry, which are complex enough for variable regimes of the reception of information to be able to exist in them and restricted enough in their dimensions for microphysical forces to intervene in them as bearers of energetic and structural conditions.

According to this conception, it could be said that the bifurcation between the living and the non-living is situated on a certain dimensional level, that of macromolecules; phenomena on an inferior order of magnitude, which are called microphysical phenomena, would in fact neither be physical nor vital but pre-physical and pre-vital; the pure non-living physical would only begin on the supra-molecular scale; it is at this level that individuation puts forth the crystal or the mass of protoplasmic matter.

In the macrophysical forms of individuation, we indeed distinguish the living from the non-living; while an organism assimilates by diversifying, the crystal grows through the iteration of an addition of indefinitely ordered layers. But at the level of macromolecules, it can hardly be said whether viruses are living or non-living. To adopt the notion of information reception as an essential expression of the operation of individuation would be to assert that individuation is carried out on a certain dimensional (topological and chronological) scale; below this scale, reality is pre-physical and pre-vital, since it is pre-individual. Above this scale, there is *physical* individuation when the system is capable of receiving information a single time, then develops and amplifies this initial singularity by individuating in a non-self-limited way. If the system is capable of successively receiving several inputs of information (of compatibilizing several singularities instead of iterating the single and initial singularity cumulatively and through transductive amplification) then individuation is vital, self-limited, and organized.

It is customary to see in vital processes a greater complexity than in non-vital physicochemical processes. However, to be faithful (even in the most hypothetical conjectures) to the intention that animates this research, we will suppose that vital individuation does not come *after* physicochemical individuation but during this individuation and before its fulfillment, by suspending it at the moment when it has not reached its stable equilibrium and by making it capable of expanding and propagating before the iteration of the perfect structure merely able to repeat itself, which would conserve in the living individual a bit of pre-individual tension, of active communication, as internal resonance between extreme orders of magnitude.

According to this way of viewing things, vital individuation would come to be inserted in physical individuation by suspending its course, by slowing it down, and by making it capable of propagating in the inchoate state. The living individual would be, in some sense and on its most initial levels, a crystal in the nascent state amplified without stabilizing.

To relate this schema of interpretation to the most current notions, we can appeal to the idea of neoteny and generalize these types of rapports between classes of individuals by supposing a slew of possible neotenic developments in the category of living beings. In a certain sense, animal individuation can be considered more complex than vegetal individuation. However, the animal can also be considered an inchoate plant that develops and becomes organized while conserving the motive, receptive, and reactional possibilities that appear in the reproduction of plants. If it is supposed that vital individuation retains and expands the most precocious phase of physical individuation (such that the vital would be the physical in suspense, slowed down in its process, and indefinitely expanded), it can also be supposed that animal individuation is nourished by the most primitive phase of vegetal individuation, which retains within it something prior to its development as an adult plant and, more specifically, maintains a capacity for receiving information over a much longer period of time.

Thus, it would be understood why these categories of increasingly complex but also increasingly unfinished and decreasingly stable and self-sufficient individuals require more complete and more stable layers of individuals as an associated milieu. Living beings require physicochemical individuals to live; animals requires plants, which are for them, in the proper sense of the term, Nature, in the same way that chemical compounds are for plants.

PART II

The Individuation of
Living Beings

Information and Ontogenesis: Vital Individuation

I. PRINCIPLES TOWARD A STUDY OF THE INDIVIDUATION OF THE LIVING BEING

1. Information and Vital Individuation; Levels of Organization; Vital Activity and Psychical Activity

Physiology poses the difficult problem of levels of individuality depending on the species and according to each being's moments of existence; the same being can in fact exist on different levels; the embryo is not individualized in the same sense as the adult being; furthermore, in fairly related species, there are behaviors that correspond to a more or less individualized life depending on the species, without these differences necessarily seeming to be linked to a superiority or inferiority of vital organization.

To shed some light on this, it would be helpful to define a measure for levels of individuation; however, if the degree of individuality is submitted to variations in the same species depending on the circumstances, it is difficult to measure this individuality absolutely. It would then be necessary to define the type of reality in which individuation takes place, by saying with which dynamic regime it is exchangeable when the level of organization does not vary throughout the whole system that contains the vital unit. Then we would obtain a possibility of measuring the degree of individuality.[1] According to the methodological postulate we just defined, it would be helpful to resort to the study of integration in systems of organization. In fact, organization can occur either in each being or through the organic relation that exists between different beings. In the latter case, the internal organization in the being is duplicated by an external integration; the group is integrative. The only concrete reality is the vital unit, which can in certain cases be reduced to a single being and which in other cases corresponds to an extremely differentiated group of multiple beings.[2]

Furthermore, the fact that an individual is mortal and not divisible by fission or regenerable through protoplasmic exchange corresponds to a level of individuation that indicates the existence of thresholds. Unlike physical individuation, biological individuation involves the existence of the whole species, colony, or society; it is not indefinitely extendable like physical individuation. If physical individuation is unlimited, we must seek where there is a transition between physical individuation and biological individuation. Yet the biologically unlimited is found in the species or in the group. What we call individual in biology is really something like a sub-individual much more so than an individual; in biology it seems that the notion of individuality is applicable to several stages or according to different levels of successive inclusion. But analogically, it would be necessary to consider the physical individual as a biological society, and the latter alone would be the image of a (albeit very simple) totality.

The first consequence of this manner of thinking establishes that the level of organization contained in a physical system is inferior to that of a biological system, but that a physical individual can possibly have a level of organization superior to that of an individual biological system integrated into a vaster ensemble. Nothing is theoretically opposed to the fact that there is a possibility of exchanges and alternations between a physical system and a biological system; but if this hypothesis is valid, it will be necessary to suppose that a physical individual unit transforms into a biological group, and that what makes the living being appear is in a sense the suspension of the development of the physical being and its analysis, not a synthetic relation which unites completed physical individuals. If this is the case, then we will have to say that only very complex physical edifices can transmute into living beings, which truly limits the possible cases of spontaneous generation. According to this view, the unit of life would be the complete organized group and not the isolated individual.

This doctrine is not a materialism since it supposes a sequence leading from physical reality to the higher biological forms without establishing a distinction between classes and genera; but, if it is complete and satisfactory, this doctrine must be able to explain why and in what sense there is the possibility of inductively observing the genus-species (or even the species-individual) relation. This distinction must be situated in a broader reality that can account for both the continuity and the discontinuities between species. This discontinuity seems comparable to the quantum characteristic that appears in physics. The criterion of syncrystallization that allows us to recognize chemical species (by indicating in which system they crystallize) indicates a type of rapports of real analogy founded on an identity of ontogenetic dynamism; the process of the crystal's formation is the same in both cases; there can be a sequence during the growth of a crystal composed of different chemical species, so that its growth is continuous despite the specific heterogeneity of the different levels. The unity created by the continuity of an operation of individuation that encompasses species which seem heterogeneous to one another according to an inductive classification indicates a profound reality pertaining to the nature of these species as rigorously as what is called specific characteristics; the possibility of syncrystallization does not however indicate the existence of a genus, because, starting from the criterion of syncrystallization, we cannot go back down to the particular characteristics of each syncyristallizable body by adding on specific differences. Such a property, which indicates the existence of a process of information during an operation of individuation, does not belong to the systematics of genera and species; this property indicates other properties of the real, properties which the latter presents when we consider it relative to the possibility of the spontaneous ontogeneses that can occur in it depending on its own structures and potentials.

Such are the properties that can be studied in order to characterize the living being rather than the specific form, which does not allow for us to go back down to the individual, since this form has been obtained by abstraction and therefore by reduction. This kind of research supposes that we consider legitimate the usage in biology of a paradigm taken from the domain of the physical sciences and particularly from the processes of morphogenesis that occur within this domain. In this sense, it is necessary to suppose that the elementary levels of the biological order contain an organization of the same order as the one that the most perfectly individuated physical systems contain, for example those that generate crystals or the large metastable molecules of organic chemistry. Indeed, such a research hypothesis can seem quite overwhelming; custom in fact prompts us to think that living beings cannot result from physical beings since they are superior to the latter due to their organization. Nevertheless, this very attitude is a consequence of an initial postulate according to which inert nature cannot contain a high level of organization.[3] If, on the contrary, we posited right from the beginning that the physical world is already highly organized, we wouldn't be capable of committing this basic error that results from a devaluation of an inert matter; in materialism, there is a doctrine of values that supposes an implicit spiritualism: matter is given as less richly organized than the living being, and materialism seeks to show that the superior can emerge from the inferior. It constitutes an attempt at the reduction of the complex to the simple. But if from the start it is estimated that matter constitutes systems provided with a very high level of organization, then we cannot so easily hierarchize life and matter. Perhaps it would be necessary to suppose that the organization is conserved but is transformed in the passage from matter to life. If this were the case, then we would have to suppose that science will never be complete, since this science is a relation of beings that by definition have the same degree of organization: a material system and an organized living being attempting to think this system by means of science. If it were true that organization is neither lost nor created, we would conclude that organization cannot but be transformed. A type of direct relation between the object and the subject manifests in this affirmation, for the relation between thought and the real becomes a relation between two organized reals that can be analogically linked by their internal structure.

However, even if organization is conserved, it is untrue to say that death is nothing; there will be death, evolution and involution, and the theory of the rapport between matter and life must be able to account for these transformations.

According to this theory, there would be a determined level of organization in each system, and these same levels could be found in a physical being and in a living being. This is why it would be necessary to suppose that when beings like an animal are composed of several superposed ranks of relays and systems of integration, there is no single organization within them that would have any exterior cause, origin, or equivalent: since the level of organization belonging to each system is limited, it can be thought that if a being seems to possess a high level of organization, this is because it actually integrates already informed and integrated elements and because its own integrative task is quite limited. Its individuality would then be reduced to a fairly restrained organization, and the word nature, which is applied to what in the individual is not the product of its activity, would have a very important meaning insofar as each individual would be indebted to its nature for the rich organization it seems to possess on its own. It could then be supposed that the external richness of the relation to the milieu is equal to the internal richness of organization contained in an individual.

Internal integration is made possible by the quantum nature of the relation between (interior and exterior) milieus and the individual as a definite structure. The individual's characteristic relays and integrators could not function without this quantum regime of exchanges. The group exists as an integrator and differentiator relative to these sub-individuals. The relation between the singular being and the group is the same as between the individual and sub-individuals. In this sense, we could say that there is a homogeneity of relation between the different hierarchical scales of the same individual and similarly between the group and the individual. The total level of information is then measured by the number of stages of integration and differentiation as well as by the relation between integration and differentiation (which can be called transduction) in the living being. In the biological being, transduction is not direct but indirect according to a twofold ascending and descending chain; along each of these chains, transduction is what allows for signals of information to pass, but this passage, instead of being a simple conveyance of information, is integration or differentiation, and it is produced by a preliminary labor due to which the final transduction is made possible, whereas in the physical domain this transduction exists in a system as a weak or elevated internal resonance;[4] if integration and differentiation alone were real, life would not exist, for there would also have to be resonance, but then it would be a question of a particular type of resonance that allows for a preliminary activity which requires an elaboration.

If we utilize psychological terms to describe these activities, we will see that integration corresponds to the usage of representation and differentiation corresponds to the usage of activity, which distributes in time energies acquired progressively and kept in reserve, whereas representation preserves the information acquired through abrupt leaps according to the circumstances in such a way as to create a continuum. Ultimately, transduction is carried out by affectivity and by all the systems that play the role in the organism of transductors on various levels. The individual would therefore always be a system of transduction, but, while this transduction is direct and on a single level in the physical system, it is indirect and hierarchized in the living being. It would be false to think that there is transduction only in a physical system, for there is also an integration and a differentiation, but they are situated on the very limits of the individual and only detectable when it grows. This integration and differentiation at the limits are found in the living individual, but then they characterize its relation to the group or to the world, and they can be relatively independent from the differentiation and integration that take place within the living individual. Such an assertion makes it impossible to understand how these two groups of integration and differentiation are connected. Those that act on the exterior cause structural changes of the ensemble in which they occur, changes which are comparable to those of a corpuscle that absorbs or emits energy in a quantum way by passing from a more excited state to a less excited state, or vice versa. Perhaps the relation between the two types of processes is the basis of this variation in the individual's levels accompanied by a structural change that is the internal correlative of an exchange of information or energy with the outside. Indeed, let's note that effort doesn't just have motor aspects but also has affective and representative aspects; the quantum characteristic of effort, spanning both a continuity and a discontinuity, very clearly represents this integration and this differentiation in the mutual relations of an interior grouping to an exterior grouping.

The problem of individuation would be resolved if we knew what information is in its rapport with other fundamental physical quantities, like the quantity of matter or the quantity of energy.

The homeostasis of the living being does not exist in the purely physical being because homeostasis is related to external conditions of transduction due to which the being utilizes the equivalence in external conditions as safeguards for its own stability and its internal transduction. In physics, heterogeneous transductive characteristics only appear in the margins of this physical reality; on the contrary, interiority and exteriority are everywhere in the living being; the nervous system and the interior milieu guarantee that this interiority is in contact on all sides with a relative exteriority. The equilibrium between integration and differentiation is what characterizes life; but homeostasis is not full vital stability. The quantum nature of discontinuous action will be opposed to the continuous nature of the constructive knowledge of synthesis in order to constitute this mixture of the continuous and discontinuous that is manifested in the regulative qualities which serve as a rapport between integration and differentiation. Qualities appear in the reactivity through which the living being evaluates its own action; however, these qualities do not allow us to reduce this rapport to a simple consciousness of the discrepancy between the end and the result, and thus to a simple signal. This is what the automaton lacks in order to be a living being; the automaton can only adapt in a manner convergent with a set of conditions by increasingly reducing the gap that exists between its action and its predetermined end; but it does not prevent and does not discover ends during its action, for it does not carry out any veritable transduction since transduction is the expansion of an initially very restricted domain that increasingly takes on size and structure; biological species are endowed with this capacity of transduction due to which they can indefinitely expand; crystals are also endowed with this capacity to indefinitely expand; but, whereas the crystal has its whole power of growing localized on its limit, this power in the species has fallen to an ensemble of individuals that grow for themselves, from the interior as well as the exterior, and that are limited in time and space but reproduce and are unlimited due to their capacity to reproduce. The most conspicuous biological transduction is thus essentially the fact that each individual reproduces analogues. The species advances in time like a physico-chemical modification that would proceed by degrees with a marginally weak recovery of generations, i.e. like active molecular levels on the edge of a crystal undergoing formation.[5] In some cases, an edifice comparable to that of the crystal is left behind by the generations that come after it.[6] Furthermore, the growth of the living individual is an ongoing and localized type of transduction that has no analogue in physics; a particular individuality combines with speciated individuality.

Life would therefore be conditioned by the recurrence of causality due to which a process of integration and a process of differentiation can receive a coupling while remaining distinct in their structures. Thus, life is not a distinct substance of matter; it supposes processes of integration and differentiation that cannot in any way be given by something other than physical structures. In this sense, there would be a profound triality of the living being through which we would find in it two complementary activities and a third activity that carries out the integration of the preceding as well as their differentiation via the activity of causal recurrence; indeed, recurrence does not add a third relation to the preceding, but the qualification it authorizes and constitutes provides a relation between activities that could not have any other commonality. The basis of unity and affective identity is therefore in the affective polarity due to which there can be a relation of the one and the multiple, of differentiation and integration. What qualification constitutes is the relation of two dynamisms; it is already this relation on the lowest level, and it remains on the higher level of the affectivity of human feelings. Beginning with pain and pleasure understood in their concretely organic nature, relation manifests as a closure of the reflex arc, which is always qualified and oriented; higher up in sensible quality, a similar polarity, which is integrated as a global and particularly dense constellation, characterizes the acquired personality and allows for it to be recognized. When a subject wants to express its internal states, what it resorts to is this relation through the intermediary of affectivity, which is the principle of art and of all communication. In order to characterize an exterior thing that cannot be shown, it is through affectivity that we can pass from the continuous totality of knowledge to the singular unity of the object to be evoked, and this is possible because affectivity is present and available to establish relation. Each association of ideas passes through this affective relation. Thus there are two possible types of utilization of relation already constituted by going from the unity of knowledge to the plurality of action or from the multiplicity of action to the unity of knowledge; these two complementary paths are joined together in certain symbolisms, like poetic symbolism, and due to this double relation poetic symbolism can become self-enclosed in aesthetic recurrence, which does not benefit the integration of the entire subject since it is in fact already virtually contained in the premises of the symbol-object to be contemplated and utilized as a mixture of activity and knowledge.

The anatomo-physiological study of vital processes reveals the distinction between the motor and receptor organs, at least in the arrangement of the cortical areas and in the functioning of the brain; but we also know that the brain is not just composed of areas of projection; a large part of the frontal lobes takes part in the association between the receptor and motor areas; the neurosurgical practice of lobotomy, which consists in dampening the recurrence of causality linking integration and differentiation, deeply modifies the subject's affectivity, whereas, in principle, this lobotomical intervention perfectly leaves intact the center or centers of affectivity situated in the region of the pituitary stalk, i.e. in regions quite different from those that constitute the neocortex; according to this hypothesis, it would be necessary to distinguish between instantaneous affectivity, which is perhaps indeed localizable in the region of the pituitary stalk, and relational affectivity, which concerns what is produced by the integrative activity and differentiated activity, which could be called affective activity, since it characterizes the individual in its singular life and not in its relation to the species. The region of the archicortex would then concern more so the regulation of drives than the regulation of elaborated affectivity; it would manifest in the relation between the subject's tendencies and the qualities it discovers in the milieu, more so than in the conscious elaboration of this transduction characterized by the activity of the neocortex, which is the affectivity of the individual qua individual.

We would also understand in this sense that affectivity is the sole function (due to its relational aspect) capable of giving a meaning to negativity: the nothingness of action and the nothingness of knowledge are indiscernible without a positive context in which to intervene as a limitation or a pure lack; whereas for affectivity, nothingness can be defined as the contrary of another quality; as Plato noted, every realized quantity appears to be inserted according to a measurement into an indefinite dyad of contrary and absolute qualities; qualities become pairings of opposites, and this bipolarity of each qualitative relation is constituted as an ongoing possibility of orientation for the qualified and qualifying being; nothingness has a meaning in affectivity, because two dynamisms confront one another at each instant; the relation of integration to differentiation is constituted as the bipolar conflict in which forces are exchanged and reach equilibrium. The being conserves its identity due to its orientation with respect to itself and to this affective polarization of every content and every psychical constituent. Identity seems to be founded on the permanence of this orientation in the course of existence, an orientation which is deployed due to the qualification of action and knowledge. Certain very profound intuitions of the pre-Socratic philosophers reveal how a qualitative dynamism exchanges actions and structures in existence, either within a being or from one being to another. Heraclitus and Empedocles in particular defined a relation of the structure and of the operation which supposes a bipolarity of the real according to a multitude of complementary paths. Affectivity realizes a type of relation which would be conflict (in terms of action) and incompatibility (in terms of knowledge); this relation can only exist on a level of affectivity, since its bipolarity allows it to unify the heterogeneous; quality is transductive by nature, for each qualitative spectrum links with and distinguishes terms that are neither identical with nor foreign to one another; the subject's identity is precisely a transductive type of identity, particularly across the first of all transductivities, that of time, which can furthermore be fragmented as much as desired into instants or grasped as a continuity; each instant is separated from those that can follow or precede it through time by precisely what unites these instants and constitutes its continuity relative to them; distinction and continuity, separation and relation are the two complementary aspects of the same type of reality. The fundamental type of vital transduction is the temporal series, which is both integrative and differentiating; the identity of a living being is composed of its temporality. An error could be made by conceiving temporality as a pure differentiation, as the necessity of an ongoing and renewed choice; individual life is differentiation to the extent that it is integration; here there is a complementary relation that cannot lose one of its two terms without itself ceasing to exist by transforming into a false differentiation, which is in reality an aesthetic activity through which, within a dissociated personality, each choice is known as a choice by way of the subject's consciousness and becomes an information to be integrated, whereas it was an energy to be differentiated: choice is what is chosen, more so than the object of choice; the affective orientation loses its relational capacity within a being whose choice constitutes the whole relational activity, which in some sense comes to support itself through its own reactivity. The choice must be conspicuously discontinuous to represent a veritable differentiation; a continuous choice in a subject that is conscious of the fact that it chooses is in reality a mixture of choice and information; from this simultaneity and from the information results the elimination of the element of discontinuity characteristic of action; an action mixed with information by this type of recurrence actually becomes a mixed existence, simultaneously continuous and discontinuous, quantum, proceeding through abrupt leaps that introduce a reversal in consciousness; this type of action cannot end up in a veritable constructive affectivity but merely in a precarious stability within which an illusion of choice is produced by a recurrence that ends in oscillations of relaxation. Relaxation differs from the constructive choice insofar as choice never links the subject back to previous states, whereas relaxation periodically relates the subject back to a neutral state that is the same as the previous neutral states; feeling like that of the empty absurd (which we seek to distinguish from the mysterious absurd) precisely corresponds to this state of a return to nothingness in which each reactivity or recurrence is abolished by an absolute inactivity and absence of information; that is because in this neutral state activity leads to an increase in the value of information, and the absence of activity causes a complete lack of information: if elements of information are then presented as coming from the outside, then they are abandoned as absurd because they are without value; they are not qualified because the subject's direct affectivity no longer performs and has been replaced by a recurrence of information and action. This existence is the feature of every aestheticism; the subject in the state of aestheticism is a subject that has replaced its affectivity with a reactivity of action and information according to a closed cycle that is incapable of accepting a new action or a new information. In a certain sense, aestheticism could be treated as a vicarious function of affectivity; but aestheticism destroys the recourse to affectivity by constituting a type of existence that eliminates the circumstances in which a veritable action or a veritable information could arise; the temporal series is replaced by a series of cyclochronic units that succeed one another without being continuous and that carry out a closure of time according to an iterative rhythm. Every artificiality that renounces the creative aspect of vital time becomes a condition of aestheticism, even if this aestheticism does not utilize the construction of the object to carry out the return of causality from action to information and is more simply content with a recourse to an action that iteratively modifies the conditions of grasping the world.

2. Successive Levels of Individuation:
Vital, Psychical, Transindividual

How is the psychical distinguished from the vital? According to this theory of individuation, the psychical and the vital are not distinguished as two substances or even as two parallel or superposed functions; the psychical intervenes as a slowing down of the individuation of the living, a neotenic amplification of the first state of this genesis; the psyche exists when the living being does not completely become concretized and conserves an internal duality. If the living being could be entirely pacified and satisfied in itself with what it is as an individuated individual within its somatic limits and through its relation to the milieu, there would be no appeal to the psyche; but instead of having the capacity to overlay and unify the duality of perception and action, it is when life becomes parallel to an ensemble composed by perception and action that the living being problematizes itself. All the problems of the living being cannot be resolved by the simple transductivity of regulative affectivity; when affectivity can no longer intervene as a power of resolution, when it can no longer carry out this transduction which is an individuation perpetuated within the already individuated living being, affectivity gives up its central role in the living being and becomes situated alongside the perceptive-active functions; a perceptive-active problematic and an affective-emotional problematic then suffuse the living being; the appeal to psychical life is like a slowing down of the living being, which conserves this slowing down in an extended and metastable state rich in potentials.[7] The essential difference between simple life and the psyche consists in the fact that affectivity does not perform the same role in these two modes of existence; in life, affectivity has a regulative value; it dominates the other functions and guarantees this ongoing individuation that is life itself; in the psyche, affectivity is pressed on all sides; it poses problems instead of resolving them and leaves the problems of the perceptive-active functions unresolved. The entrance into psychical existence essentially manifests as the appearance of a new problematic which is higher and more difficult and which cannot receive any veritable solution from within the living being, properly speaking, conceived within its limits as an individuated being; psychical life is therefore neither a prompting nor a higher rearrangement of the vital functions that continue to exist under it and with it, but a new plunge into pre-individual reality followed by a more primitive individuation. Between the life of the living being and the psyche, there is the interval of a new individuation; the vital is not a matter for the psychical; it is not necessarily taken up again and resumed by the psyche, for the vital already has its own organization, and the psyche can do nothing but disrupt it by attempting to intervene in it. A psyche that attempts to be constituted by dealing with the vital and by taking it as a matter in order to give it a form merely ends up with malformations and an illusion of functionality.

In fact, the veritable psyche appears when the vital functions can no longer resolve the problems posed to the living being, i.e. when this triadic structure of perceptive, active, and affective functions is no longer able to be utilized. The psyche appears or at the very least is postulated when the living being no longer has enough being in itself to resolve the problems posed to it. It should not be surprising to find purely vital motivations at the basis of psychical life: but it should be noted that they exist as problems and not as guiding or determining forces; thus, they do not exert a constructive determinism onto the psychical life that they call upon to exist; they provoke it but do not positively condition it. The psyche appears as a new stage of the being's individuation, whose correlative in the being is an incompatibility and a decreasing supersaturation of vital dynamisms and, outside the being as a limited individual, a recourse to a new charge of pre-individual reality is capable of bringing a new reality to the being; the living individuates more precociously, and it cannot individuate by being its own matter to itself, like the larva that metamorphoses by feeding off itself; the psyche expresses the vital and, correlatively, a certain charge of pre-individual reality.

Such a conception of the rapport between vital individuation and psychical individuation leads to representing the existence of the living being as playing the role of a source for psychical individuation, but not the role of a matter relative to which the psyche would be a form. Moreover, such a conception requires the following hypothesis to be posited: individuation does not follow a law of all or nothing; it can occur in a quantum way, by sudden leaps, and an initial stage of individuation leaves around the constituted individual, associated with it, a certain charge of pre-individual reality, which can be called associated nature and which is still rich in potentials and organizable forces.

Thus, when the psychical appears, there is a relation between the vital and the psychical that is not a relation of matter to form but of individuation to individuation; psychical individuation is a dilation, a precocious expansion of vital individuation.

What results from such a hypothesis is that the entrance into the path of psychical individuation forces the individuated being to surpass itself; the psychical problematic, which calls upon pre-individual reality, results in functions and structures that are not achieved within the limits of the living individuated being; if the living organism is called individual, the psychical leads to an order of transindividual reality; indeed, the pre-individual reality associated with individuated living organisms is not segmented like them and does not have limits comparable to those of separate living individuals; when this reality is grasped within a new individuation initiated by the living being, it conserves a relation of participation that connects each psychical being to other psychical beings; the psychical is the nascent transindividual; for a certain amount of time, it can appear as the pure psychical, an ultimate reality that could consist in itself; but the living cannot borrow the potentials that produce a new individuation from the associated nature without entering into an order of reality that makes it participate in an ensemble of psychical reality which surpasses the limits of the living; psychical reality is not self-enclosed. The psychical problematic cannot be resolved in an intra-individual way. Emergence into psychical reality is an emergence into a transitory path since the resolution of the intra-individual psychical problematic (that of perception and that of affectivity) leads to the level of the transindividual; the complete structures and functions resulting from the individuation of the pre-individual reality associated with the living individual are only accomplished and stabilized in the collective. Psychical life goes from the pre-individual to the collective. A psychical life that would like to be intra-individual would not be able to overcome a fundamental disparation between the perceptive problematic and the affective problematic.[8] The psychical being, i.e. the being that achieves as completely as possible the functions of individuation by not limiting individuation to this first stage of the vital, resolves the disparation of its internal problematic to the extent that it participates in the individuation of the collective. This collective, which is a transindividual reality obtained by the individuation of the pre-individual realities associated with a plurality of living beings, is distinguished from the pure social and from the pure inter-individual; the pure social indeed exists in animal societies; in order to exist, it does not require a new individuation that expands upon vital individuation; it expresses the manner in which living beings exist in society; the vital unit is literally what is directly social; information that is attached to social structures and functions (for example, the functional differentiation of individuals in the organic interdependence of animal societies) is lacking in individuated organisms qua organisms. This society supposes as a condition of existence the structural and functional heterogeneity of different individuals in society. On the contrary, the transindividual collective groups together homogeneous individuals; even if these individuals present some heterogeneity, it's only to the extent that they have a basic homogeneity that they are grouped together as a collectivity and not insofar as they are complementary with respect to one another in a superior functional unity. Society and transindividuality can also exist by being superposed in the group, just as the vital and the psychical are superposed in individual life. The collective is distinguished from the inter-individual insofar as the inter-individual does not necessitate a new individuation in the individuals in which it is established, but merely a certain regime of reciprocity and exchanges that suppose analogies between intra-individual structures without challenging individual problematics. The birth of the inter-individual is progressive and does not suppose the interaction of emotion, the capacity of the individuated being to provisionally disindividuate in order to participate in a broader individuation. Inter-individuality is an exchange between individuated realities that remain in their same level of individuation and that seek in other individuals an image of their own existence parallel to this existence. The addition of a certain coefficient of inter-individuality to a society can give the illusion of transindividuality, but the collective only truly exists if an individuation establishes it. It is historical.

II. Specific Form and Living Substance

1. Insufficiency of the Notion of Specific Form; Notion of the Pure Individual; Non-univocal Nature of the Notion of the Individual

Life can exist without individuals being anatomically and physiologically or merely physiologically separate from one another. Let's consider the coelenterate as a type of this kind of existence in the animal kingdom; these beings are characterized by the fact that they have no general cavity; the cavity that hollows out their body and expands into more or less complicated canals is a digestive cavity. Their symmetry is radial, since their organs are mirrored around the axis that passes through their mouth. The majority of coelenterates are apt to bud and form colonies; individuals formed by this budding are called blastozooids, and they can remain in communication with the initial being, which is called an oozoid because it hatches from an egg; corals, hydroids, and gorgonians form extremely numerous colonies. However, continuous formations can appear between individuals, thus constituting a solid material unity of the colony; this is what is seen in polyps joined together in a colony when the coenenchyme fills the spaces that separate individuals; this deposit of limestone, whether compact or spongy, deprives the polyp of its branchy form and gives it a massive aspect; individuals will no longer appear except through their calyces, which are open on the level of the colony's shared surface. A coenosarc then joins the individuals of the same colony, giving birth to new individuals through budding and by secreting the coenenchyme. In certain colony formations, the individuals manifest a differentiation that winds up in some sense transforming them into organs: some have a nutritive role, others have a defensive role, while others have a sexual role, and it could be claimed in some sense that veritable individuality is transferred to the colony if an impregnable residue of individuality didn't remain in the differentiated beings that compose the colony, namely the absence of synchronization in particular births and deaths; temporally, there remains a distinction between individuals that is not canceled out by the high degree of interdependence of their complementary relations. Certainly, it could be said that in a superior organism there are particular births and deaths of cells; but what is born and dies without synchronization in this superior animal is not the organ but the constituent of the organ, the elementary cell.[9] We would like to show that the criterion that allows for the recognition of real individuality here is not the material and spatial bond or separation of beings in a society or a colony, but the possibility of life apart and of migration outside the first biological unit. The difference between an organism and a colony is the fact that the individuals of a colony can die one after another and be replaced without jeopardizing the colony; what constitutes individuality is non-immortality; each individual can be treated as a quantum of living existence; conversely, the colony does not possess this quantum characteristic; in some sense, it is continuous in its development and its existence. What makes individuality remarkable is its thanatological nature. Because of this, it should be said that amoebae, as well as a large number of infusoria, are not strictly speaking veritable individuals; these beings are capable of regeneration by exchanging one nucleus with another being, and after a period of time they can reproduce by dividing into two parts; certain holothuria can also divide into a plurality of segments when conditions of life become poor, each segment afterwards reconstituting a complete unit, i.e. a holothuria similar to the previous entity. In this case and properly speaking, there is no distinction between the individuals and the species; individuals do not die but divide. Individuality can only appear with the death of beings; death is the correlate of individuality. A study of pre-individual life has a theoretical interest, since the passage from these pre-individual systems of existence to individual systems allows us to grasp the correlate or correlates of individuation and their biological signification; in particular, the vast domain of coelenterates reveals a transitional zone between non-individuated life systems and totally individuated systems; the study of these mixed types makes it possible to establish valuable functional equivalences between individuated systems and non-individuated systems on the same level of biological organization and in somewhat equivalent circumstances, either in the same species or from one species to another closely related species.

An interesting point that deserves to be noted before a general study is the following: sexual reproduction seems most directly associated with the individual thanatological characteristic starting from this very level: colonies of coelenterates in certain cases lay eggs that produce jellyfish, and reproduction is guaranteed by these jellyfish; but in certain cases an entire individual detaches from the colony, and it will lay eggs much later after having led a detached life and then die, whereas a new colony is founded by the budding of a source-individual that emerges from this egg; thus a free individual exists, having the capacity to die, between two colonies capable of an indefinite development in time; here, with respect to the colonies, the individual plays a role of transductive propagation; in its birth it emanates from a colony, and before its death it generates the starting point for a new colony after a certain displacement in time and space. The individual is not a part of a colony; it is inserted between two colonies without being integrated in either, and both its birth and its end reach an equilibrium to the extent that it emanates from one community but engenders another; *it is relation.*[10] However, such a function is very difficult to perceive on the superior and highly differentiated level, because the individual, in the individuated forms of life systems, is in fact a mixture: two things are taken up in it: the nature of pure individuality, comparable to what is seen at work in the relation between two colonies, and the nature of continuous life, which corresponds to the function of organized simultaneity such as we see it at work in a colony; the drives[11] of the individual and its tendencies define the distinction between these two functions that may not be represented together in the individual; the drives are indeed relative to the pure individual, insofar as the latter is what transmits vital activity through space and time; conversely, the continuous and everyday tendencies do not possess this irreversible aspect of creative nature that the drives define through successive "stinging blows," which displace the constituted individual and can be in contradiction with its tendencies; tendencies involve the common and the continuous, since there can easily be a synergy between tendencies shared by a very large number of individuals, whereas drives can be much more atypical insofar as they correspond to a transfer function of the individual and not to an integration into the vital community; drives can even be seemingly devitalizing, precisely because they do not belong to the everyday continuity of existence; drives generally reveal themselves by way of their characteristic as consequences without premises; they introduce a transductive dynamism that borrows nothing from the continuity of the tendencies and that can even inhibit it; human communities build up a whole defense system against the instinct-ual drives by seeking to define tendencies and drives in univocal terms, as if they shared the same nature; this is where the error comes from; if ten-dencies and drives shared the same nature, it becomes impossible to distin-guish the transductive characteristic[12] from that of belonging to a society; the manifestations of the sexual drive are, for example, treated as testifying to the existence of a tendency, and then we start talking about a sexual need; the development of certain societies perhaps incites the confusion of needs and tendencies in the individual, since the hyper-adaptation to communal life can be expressed by the inhibition of drives on behalf of tendencies; indeed, since tendencies are continuous and therefore stable, they are able to be integrated into communal life and even constitute a means for the inte-gration of the individual, which is incorporated into the community by its nutritive and defensive needs, both of which transform it into a user and a consumer. Freud's doctrine does not distinguish between drives and tenden-cies clearly enough. His doctrine seems to consider the individual univo-cally, and although it distinguishes between a certain number of zones in the individual from the structural and dynamic point of view, it leaves behind the idea that the individual can manage a complete integration through the construction of the superego, as if the being could discover a condition of absolute unity in the passage to the act of its virtualities; since it is too hylo-morphic, this doctrine cannot account for an essential duality in the individ-ual except by resorting to an inhibiting alienation, insofar as the rapport to the species cannot be conceived except as an inclusion of the individual; but Aristotelian entelechy cannot account for the full sense of the individual and leaves out the properly instinctual aspect through which the individual is a transduction that takes place and not a virtuality that is actualized. Even if it must be said that the metaphysical is still physiological, we must recognize the aspect of the individual's duality and characterize through its trans-communal functioning this existence of instinctual drives. The thanatological nature of the individual is incompatible with everyday tendencies, which can conceal this nature or defer its manifest existence but cannot annihilate it. This is why a psychical analysis must take into account the complementary nature of the tendencies and drives in the being that we call individual, a being which, in

all individuated species, is in fact a mixture of vital continuity and instinctual trans-communal singularity. The "two natures" that classical moralists
find in man are neither an artifact nor the translation of a mythological creationist dogma into the framework of current observation; in fact, the easiness here would be on the side of the biological monism of the tendencies
according to an operative thought that believes to have done enough by
defining the individual as the non-analyzable being that cannot be the object
of consciousness except through its inclusion in the species. Aristotle's doctrine, which is the prototype for all vitalisms, in fact arises from an interpretation of life oriented around "superior" (i.e. totally individuated) species;
this doctrine could not be otherwise in a time when so-called inferior species were very difficult to observe. Aristotle takes into account certain species
of coelenterates and worms, but mainly to discuss the characteristics of the
soul's inherence to the body according to totality or part by part, for example
in ringed worms, which can regenerate after an accidental segmentation, both
segments of which continue to live on. In fact, the model of living beings is
in the superior forms, and, insofar as "beings do not want to be poorly governed," the aspiration of all beings towards a single form leads Aristotle to
consider the superior forms before all else. It is not vitalism properly speaking that has led to the confusion of drives and tendencies, but a vitalism
founded on a partial inspection of life that puts more value on the forms closest to the human species by constituting a *de facto* anthropocentrism more
so than a veritable vitalism.

Furthermore, a vitalism that ignores the distinction between functions
relative to the tendencies and those relative to the drives cannot establish
a difference between functions in themselves and the structural dynamisms
that allow for the operation of these functions by maintaining the stability
of vital characteristics; thus "the death drive"[13] cannot be considered symmetrical with the life drive; instead, the death drive is the dynamic limit of
the operation of the life drive and is not another drive; it appears as the mark
of a temporal threshold beyond which this positive drive no longer operates,
either because the transductive role of the isolated individual is achieved, or
because it is complete, or because it has failed and because the pure individual's quantum of duration has been exhausted; it marks the end of the pure
individual's dynamism. The tendency for beings to persevere in their being,
in the sense of the Spinozist *conatus,* pertains to an instinctual ensemble that
leads to the "death drive." It is in this sense that a relation of the reproductive drive and the death drive can be discovered, since they are functionally
homogeneous. Conversely, the reproductive drive and the death drive are

heterogeneous with respect to the different tendencies, which are tendencies of continuity and socially integrable reality.[14] In superior species, the alternation of the individual stage and the colony stage is replaced by the simultaneity of individual life and society, something which complicates the individual by placing in it a twofold bundle of individual (drive) and social (tendencies) functions.

2. The Individual as Polarity; Functions of Internal Genesis and of External Genesis

The method that emerges from these preliminary considerations requires us not to be primarily preoccupied with hierarchically organizing the levels of vital systems, but to distinguish them in order to see what the functional equivalences are that allow for vital reality to be grasped throughout these different systems by developing the whole range of vital systems instead of classifying them in order to hierarchize them. According to our initial hypothesis, life is deployed through transfer and neotenization; more than a continuous or dialectical progress, evolution is a transduction. Vital functions should be studied according to a method of equivalence that posits the principle by which there can be an equivalence of structures and functional activities. From pre-individual forms to individualized forms, relations of equivalence can be revealed by passing through the mixed forms that include alternating individuality and transindividuality according to the interior or exterior conditions of life. On the other hand, it should be supposed that there is a relative interdependence of species which makes a hierarchization quite abstract, at least when it only considers the anatomo-physiological characteristics of the individual; a rational study of species would have to integrate a sociology for each species.

Certainly, it is difficult to somewhat abstractly define a method for the study of vital individuation; however, it seems that this hypothesis of functional duality makes it possible to account for two types of relations and two kinds of limits discovered in the individual; in a first sense, the individual can be treated as a particular fragmentary being, an actual member of a species, a detachable or not currently detachable fragment of a colony; in a second sense, the individual is what is capable of transmitting the life of the species and constitutes the depository of specific characteristics, even if it should never be called upon to actualize them in itself; as a carrier of virtualities which do not necessarily take on a sense of actuality for it, it is limited both in space and in time; it thereby constitutes a quantum of time for vital activity, and its temporal limit is essential to its function of relation. Often this individual is free in space, since it guarantees the transportation of the specific seeds of the species, and the counterpart to its temporal brevity is its extreme spatial mobility. According to the first form of existence, on the contrary, the individual is a fragment of a currently existing whole in which it is inserted and which limits it spatially; as a fragmentary being, the individual possesses a structure that allows it to grow; it is *polarized* inside itself, and its organization allows it to incorporate alimentary matter, either through autotrophy or by starting from already elaborated substances; the individual as a fragmentary being possesses a certain corporeal schema according to which it grows through differentiation and specialization, which determine the parts during their progressive growth starting from the egg or initial bud; certain studies on regeneration, particularly those dedicated to the freshwater planarian, show that the capacity of regeneration comes from the elements that conserve a germinative capacity even when the individual is an adult and that these elements have a kinship with the sexual cells; nevertheless, the capacity of development does not suffice to explain regeneration, even if we introduce the action of a hypothetical substance like the organism, which is meant to explain induction exerted by a terminal element, for example a head that can be grafted anywhere onto the body of a flatworm; in order for this induction to be able to be carried out, a certain number of secondary elements, probably including physical mechanisms and hormonal dynamisms, must be present; yet above all, after the segmentation of the egg, there needs to be the intervention of a principle of organization and determination that leads to the production of different organs of the being. This principle of spatial determination is what cannot be confused with the principle of production outside of other beings, either by budding or sexual reproduction; even if certain cells can indistinctly aid the regeneration of the particular being or generate other beings, even if there is a link between regeneration and reproduction, a difference of orientation intervenes in the manner in which this fundamental activity is carried out, either toward the interior or toward the exterior; this is the very criterion that allows to distinguish pre-individuality from individuality properly speaking, for in the state of pre-individuality, these two functions are joined together, and the same being can be considered as an organism, society or colony; reproduction through scissiparity is both a phenomenon of modification of the fragmentary individual's corporeal schema and of reproduction; budding is still quite partially a mixture of two types of generation, growth and reproduction properly speaking; but when we progress along the animal series, this distinction between two generations becomes increasingly clear: on the level of mammals for example, the distinction becomes so clear that it is compensated by a relation of exteriority between parents and the young, somewhat similar to a parasitic relationship, at first internal and then external, through gestation and then breastfeeding; the female is a being that is capable of being parasited on, and any type of parasiting can create in a male the appearance of female sexual characteristics, as the study of the barnacled crab shows. Everything happens as if the complex forms necessitated a rigorous distinction between the functions of external genesis and those of internal genesis. External genesis, or reproduction, indeed introduces an amplificative function prominently linked to the operation of individuation: since it can exist in a continuous regime, simple growth on the contrary belongs to the colony and does not necessitate individuation.

This distinction is made clear by the extremely precocious detachment of the young which, instead of developing as a bud, is an independent being, a parasite of the parent but entirely distinct from it in its internal organization; gestation corresponds to this anatomical separation compensated by a nutritive relation; the quantity of organized matter that detaches from the body of a mammal in order to form an egg is less considerable than what detaches from a bird. Gestation, which makes possible the anatomical separation of the young while maintaining the alimentary relationship, authorizes the slowing of the growth of the young and accentuates foetalization, according to the hypothesis of Bolk, who sees in this principle one of the reasons behind evolution; the less rapid maturation of the individual allows it to be dedicated to a longer formation through learning during the time when the nervous centers are still receptive, i.e. before adulthood. However, if we consider these various characteristics of vital organizations, we see that the two functions of the individual conserve their distinction and that this distinction increases when the individual becomes more developed; in a simple vital organization, these functions are antagonistic; they can only be fulfilled successively or entrusted to different forms;[15] when the individual is sufficiently developed, it can guarantee the simultaneous fulfillment of two functions due to a more complete separation of operations relative to each of these functions; reproduction then becomes the act of all individuals, all of which also possess the exercise of other functions. The individual is therefore the system of compatibility of these two antagonistic functions that correspond, for the former, to the integration into the vital community and, for the latter, to the amplificative activity of the individual through which it transmits life by generating its young. Internal organization corresponds to another type of being than reproduction; in totally individualized species, reproduction and the actual organization are joined together in the same being; somatic and germinal functions are made compatible in individual existence, since the stage of life in colonies has disappeared.

For these different reasons, we shall distinguish three vital systems: pure pre-individual life, in which somatic and germinal functions are not distinct, as in certain protozoa and poriferans; meta-individual forms, in which somatic and germinal functions are distinct but need to be carried out by a specialization of individual action that involves a specialization of the individual according to somatic or germinal functions; and lastly, totally individualized forms, in which the germinal functions are delegated to the same individuals as those that carry out the somatic functions; then there is no longer colonies but a community or a society. Transitional forms can be found among these three groups, particularly in insect societies, which are often constituted due to the organic differentiation of the members, some of whom are reproducers, soldiers, workers, etc.; in certain societies, the age in individual development intervenes as a principle of selection between the different functions that are thereby successively fulfilled, which is a principle of unity requiring a lesser complexity of individual structures than when the individual simultaneously fulfills somatic functions and germinal functions. In this sense, we can consider lifeforms singularly represented by individual beings as equivalent to alternating forms (colony and separate individual) in which the passage to the colony stage would never occur, since the individual generates other individuals instead of founding a colony that will emit separate individuals. In the alternating form, the colony is like the completion of the individual; the individual is *younger* than the colony, and the colony is the adult state *after* the individual, which, *mutatis mutandis,* is comparable *to a larva of the colony.* From then on, instead of founding the colony, when the individual is reproduced as an individual, the vital functions of continuity (nutrition, growth, functional differentiation) should be fulfilled by a new layer of the individual's behaviors, i.e. social behaviors.

3. Individuation and Reproduction

The essential function of the living individual qua individual, distinct from a colony, is amplification, discontinuous propagation, for example with the change of location. It can then be asked: what is at stake in reproduction? Death is the fatal termination of every multicellular organism, but the former results from the latter's functioning and not from an intrinsic property of living matter. For Rabaud, the intrinsic property of living matter resides in "this incessant process of destruction and reconstruction in accordance with exchanges with the exterior, which constitutes its metabolism."[16] In a uni-cellular organism, if reconstruction compensated destruction, and assuming that in this process non-assimilated materials do not accumulate to the point of hindering its functioning, the organism would remain indefinitely comparable to itself.

However, according to Rabaud, this illusion of the immortal individual merely corresponds to a mental construction; two facts modify the individual: the first is that metabolism is effectuated in constantly changing conditions; new masses of protoplasm identical to the preceding masses do not necessarily result from the reconstruction of living matter, since not only the quantity and quality of the materials in question but also the natures of the external influences vary incessantly. The second fact is that the rapports between the elements of which the individual mass consists change depending on their influences, and their change sometimes leads to a sort of disequilibrium; this particularly includes the nucleoplasmic rapport, i.e. the one established between the bulk of the nucleus and the cytoplasm.[17]

This is the rapport that regulates reproduction. Rabaud wants to show that the reproduction of the individual does not introduce any finality and is explained in a purely causal manner. It is necessary to study this explanation in order to appreciate the extent to which the disequilibrium that causes death differs from the disequilibrium that causes reproduction. For it is necessary to note that the profound modification that affects the individual in reproduction is not the same as in death; even if the individual loses its identity through a splitting into two individuals of equal size, it becomes other, since two individuals now replace the single individual, but it does not die; no organic matter decomposes; there is no cadaver, and the continuity between the single individual and the two individuals to which it has given birth is complete. Here there is not an end but a transformation of the topology of the living being that makes two individuals appear instead of one.

Rabaud establishes the fact that it is only the value of the nucleoplasmic rapport that makes the cell divide into two independent parts without an intervention of a mysterious influence (despite the cell's volume). An analysis of reproduction in metazoans allows us to clearly confirm this fact due to the relative anatomical simplicity of the individuals that constitute them.

Schizogony takes place as a cellular division: the individual divides into two equal or unequal parts, and each part, having become independent, constitutes a new individual; with multiple variations, the nucleus traverses the series of ordinary phases that consist of the following: first, its division into fragments, i.e., chromosomes (barely distinct in protozoa), then the division of these chromosomes and their separation into two equal groups, and finally the splitting of the cytoplasm, transversally for infusoria and longitudinally for flagellates. Each of the new individuals becomes complete; each regenerates a mouth, a flagellum, and so on.

In other cases, the individual first secretes a layer of cellulose within which it divides into a series of individuals considerably reduced in size, and these individuals either resemble the initial individual or are different from it, but each of them afterwards rapidly resumes its specific aspect. Schizogony consists in the fact that the individual multiplies in isolation without the intervention of the fertilizing action of another individual of the same species.

On the contrary, in still other cases multiplication only begins after the union of two individuals. Depending on the milieu, this conjugation or pairing can be temporary, as in infusoria. After interlocking on a portion of their surface, the two individuals exchange a pronucleus with each of their partners, and then they separate and multiply through simple division. In these infusoria, the two modes of reproduction, gamogony and schizogony, alternate according to the conditions of the milieu. Furthermore, in gamogony, the two individuals are perfectly similar; neither can be qualified as male or female. The conjugation can also lead to the fusion not only of two pronuclei, but also of two whole individuals that are in a state of total fusion, at least for a while; it is furthermore quite difficult to say if the individuality of two beings that fuse is conserved; in fact, their nucleus undergoes two successive divisions; all the products of division degenerate, except one; the remaining two non-degenerated products of the two nuclei fuse, but this mutual nucleus immediately divides, and the fused mass in turn divides and produces two new complete individuals. Would there be a conservation of the individual identity of two infusoria in the non-degenerated masses of nuclei at the moment of the fusion of two nuclei? It is hard to answer this question. This example is taken from the case of the actinophyrid. Fusion can be even more complete in the amoeba, particularly in *Sappinia diploidea,* which normally possesses two nuclei. The nuclei of each individual, and then the two individuals, fuse together, but each nucleus divides separately while losing a part of its substance; then the rest of each of the nuclei gather together away from the rest of the nucleus of the other individual without fusing; a single binuclear individual forms in this way and then multiplies. In this case, the nucleus of each initial individual remains (or rather the rest of this nucleus) in the individuals that arise from multiplication through the division of the intermediary binuclear individual. Male and female cannot be distinguished in this procedure.

The appearance of the distinction between male and female takes place in vorticella, which are basically infusoria anchored to the substrate. The male gamete is an individual of reduced size that arises from a vorticella that has progressively undergone two successive divisions. This individual interlocks with a fixed vorticella and fuses with it entirely. After the disappearance of the macronuclei and the division and degeneration of micronuclei, except for a fragment that remains behind and produces a pronucleus, the pronuclei, which constitute the only remainder of the initial macronuclei, exchange, and then the male pronuclei regenerate, and the male gamete itself is absorbed; the nucleus fragments into eight equal parts, seven of which constitute the macronucleus, while the eighth constitutes the micronucleus. It just so happens that this gamogony alternates with a schizogony according to a veritable evolutionary cycle. This includes sporozoans, particularly haematozoons and coccidias. The cycle of haematozoons at first involves an amoeba anchored in a human blood cell; this individual divides along the planes of radial division; new individuals (merozoites) propagate in the blood and will anchor onto new red blood cells; after a certain time period, the merozoites stop multiplying, which, according to Rabaud, must be attributed to a modification of the host acted upon by a parasite. If, on the other hand, a modification of the milieu occurs (absorption by a mosquito), these merozoites become macrogametocytes or microgametocytes; after shedding a part of their nucleus, macrogametocytes become macrogametes; the microgametocytes emit extensions that envelop, taken together, the whole substance of the nucleus, and these extensions are microgametes. The conjugation of macrogametes and microgametes yields an element surrounded by a thin membrane that grows and divides into sporoblasts, which give rise to elongated elements called sporozoites that are inoculated by the mosquito into human beings, thereby allowing the cycle to recommence. Thus, there is an alternation of a certain number of forms and of two types of reproduction. The reproduction of coccidias occurs in the same way but without an intermediary host. In gregarines, agamous reproduction barely exists, and sexuality is marked particularly clearly. And yet, in the fusion of two individuals that become encysted together, only a part of the nucleus is involved in reproduction. The encysted individuals (macrogametocyte and microgametocyte) divide and form macrogametes and microgametes; after being fertilized, the egg multiplies by dividing into spores, and these spores divide into eight sporozoites that in the end develop into adult gregarines. In this case, the two procedures of reproduction are interlinked to the point of only constituting a single complex process; it seems that gamogony has absorbed schizogony, because in the groups formed by two gregarines encysted together, there is a veritable schizogony that passes from the microgametocytes and from the macrogametocyte that constitute these two gregarines to the microgametes and macrogametes; the spores divide into sporozoites in the same way.

According to Rabaud, reproduction essentially consists in schizogony. This schizogony generally produces equal parts, except in certain cases. Schizogony continues indefinitely in a constantly renewed milieu, as the researches of Baitselle, Woodruff, Chatton, and Metalnikov have shown. Sexuality appears under the action of the milieu: a differentiation is established between individuals, and each division no longer occurs without the preliminary conjugation of two individuals and the fusion of their nuclei. Rabaud does not accept the conclusions of Maupas's study, which supposes that an overly prolonged schizogony involves the individuals' death, whereas sexuality would allow for a rejuvenation; sexuality would therefore be an obligatory process. Maupas also supposes that conjugation only occurs between individuals of different lineages. Rabaud opposes against this thesis the works of Jennings, who shows that conjugation also takes place between individuals with fully related parents. Furthermore, asexual reproduction does not in any way involve the aging of the individuals or their death. The experimental research of Mr. and Mrs. Chatton shows that sexuality is or is not established according to the quality of the nutritive exchanges to which infusoria are submitted. Rabaud states that we can provoke the conjugation of *Colpidium colpoda* or of *Glaucoma scintillans* by adding to the infusion in which these protozoans live a certain quantity of Cl_2Ca and by feeding them with *Pseudomonas florescens*. For Rabaud, sexuality appears "not as an indispensable process, but as a complication that does not bring with it any obvious advantage." The fusion of two completely comparable protoplasms, equally and supposedly old and worn out, can only lead to a rejuvenation.

Ultimately, Rabaud does not want to accept the idea according to which sexual multiplication would be superior to asexual multiplication just because it would give rise to the combination of substances that come from two independent generators and would thus generate a new living organism endowed with the characteristics belonging to its kin, whereas asexual reproduction would be nothing but the continuation of the same individual fragmented into a large number of distinct parts. Asexual multiplication does not give rise to individuals that resemble each other in an exactly identical way. According to Woodruff, there is a veritable recasting of the nucleoid which, produced periodically at the end of a certain number of generations, indicates that the organism, even in the case of asexual reproduction, far from remaining similar to itself, undergoes more or less important modifications.

According to Rabaud, sexuality does not bring anything particularly useful to the protozoans' existence; fissiparous multiplication remains the most direct process and highlights the fundamental nature of reproduction. In fact, the division of the nucleus is always equal, but sometimes the division occurs in such a way that the fragmentation of the cellular body yields very unequal parts; the little cell, or daughter cell, that separates from the large or mother cell is an unspecified part of the latter and is capable of reproducing an individual similar to it. Sexuality is nothing but a particular case of a general phenomenon, a case in which the element that stems from an individual only multiplies after the union with an element that stems from another individual. We will note, however, that what multiplies is the element that stems from two individuals.

In metazoans, the processes are the same, but they pose the problem of individuation in a more complex way, for here the phenomenon of reproduction is hard to detach from association and dissociation, since it can intervene in various degrees and thus create a web of rapports between descendant individuals, or between ascendant and descendant individuals, or the ensemble formed by ascendant and descendant individuals. Here, unlike with protozoans, reproduction is no longer merely the genesis of an individual by way of a process that Rabaud likens to schizogony; here, reproduction is a perpetuation of intermediate conditions and of mediated states between the complete separation of independent individuals and a mode of life within which there would be nothing but growth without reproduction or the appearance of new individuals; it is therefore necessary to study these lifeforms that indicate a transition between mere individuation via schizogony and life without individuation in order to understand if there can be conditions of ontogenetic individuation at this level. Sometimes a methodical prejudice remains in our study: we are seeking to grasp the criteria of individuality in biology by defining the conditions of individuation for species in which the individuated state and the non-individuated state are in a variable rapport. This genetic method can allow some characteristic to remain that will not have been grasped; we should only judge it based on its results, and for the moment we are supposing that genesis can account for the being, the individuation of the individual.

The fission of an individual (whether adult or not) into two equal parts that complete each other on their own account—i.e. schizogony—exists in numerous metazoans within which, despite appearances, it is comparable to what occurs in protozoans. According to Rabaud, the only veritable difference is that the process brings about a fragment that includes many cells; but these cells form a whole that is just as coherent as the components of a protozoan: "In both cases, division results from a process that involves perfectly comparable physiological units."[18] In certain cases, the individual does not split into two appreciably equal parts; this is the case that comes closest to resembling schizogony in protozoans. This case presents itself in various coelenterates, including hydra and several sea anemones; the plane of fission usually passes through the longitudinal axis of the body but sometimes rarely through the transversal axis; this is also found in certain jellyfish *(Stomobrachium mirabile)*. This rupturing lasts one to three hours; the breaking apart of sea anemones begins at the level of the foot, then moves up all along the body and penetrates into its depths; the two halves separate, the edges of the wound come closer together, the stripped cells multiply and produce new parts that replace the absent parts: schizogony implies regeneration. This process exists in various echinoderms, for example starfish *(Asterias tenuispina)* and ophiuroids *(Ophiactis, Ophiocoma, Ophiothela)*. The plane of fission passes through two interradii and divides the animal into two appreciably equal parts with, however, an extra arm on one part than another when the number of arms is unequal (for example, the pentamerous starfish); after separation, each fragment of the disc becomes round, the liquid of the general cavity flows into the wound, coagulates, and closes it; the integument scars over, and the subjacent tissues, which are actively proliferating, sprout forth two or three arms and form two complete individuals from two fragments. This division can yield four complete individuals, for example in holothuria such as *Cucumaria lactea* and *Cucumaria planci*; an initial transversal sectioning yields two halves, and these two halves section yet again, thus yielding four individuals similar to the first.

Rabaud likens scissiparity (the case in which fission yields equal or sub equal parts) to cases in which the fragments that separate are unequal, even extremely unequal. "Indeed, these cases only differ from scissiparity through the relative importance and number of the parts that separate; the processes of regeneration and the ultimate result remain the same: the multiplication of individuals at the expense of a single one."[19] Perhaps it can be remarked, however, that in the case of scissiparity there is no remainder to the division; the individual does not die properly speaking; it multiplies; on the contrary, an individual like a fish lays eggs a certain number of times, then dies. What is important here is obviously not the rapport of dimensions between the different parts that appear during reproduction; instead, what is important is the fact that the two parts are or are not contemporaneous with one another; if, in a division into two equal parts, one of the parts were viable and the other non-viable, either immediately or after a period of time, it would be necessary to say that this process is different from scissiparity, wherein the two halves are contemporaneous with one another or have the same age. The veritable limit is thus situated between all the processes of division that generate individuals of the same age and the processes of division that generate a young individual and leave behind an older individual, which is not rejuvenated when it generates more young beings. Animals that possess reproduction via scissiparity can generally fragment in such a way that only a strip detaches and yields a new individual as a result. Some sea anemones (like *Aiptasia larerata* or *Sagartioides*) are torn to pieces; in others, the tentacles spontaneously detach, for example in *Boloceroides* (studied by Okada and Komori), and these fragments regenerate. A stony coral *(Schizocyatus fissilis)* divides longitudinally into six equal segments that regenerate and yield six complete individuals. The arms of several starfish, after separating from the body, bud into a complete animal after having passed through the so-called "comet" stage, which is characterized by the fact that the young arms are smaller than the old arms. For certain species *(Linckia multifora, Ophidaster, Brinsinga, Labidaster, Asterina tenuispina, Asterina glacialis),* a fragment of the disc must remain attached to the arm for regeneration to take place. Some planarians, such as *Policelis cornuta,* some oligochaete worms, such as *Lumbriculus,* some polychaetes, such as *Syllis gracilis,* and many others dislocate under certain conditions into a variable number of fragments. Tunicates multiply constantly via the transversal fragmentation of their postabdomen; the heart, which is in this terminal segment, disappears and reforms in each segmentation. In hydras, a tentacle section regenerates if it represents at least 1/200th of the total weight; below this weight, a section regenerates less easily. The same principle applies for a fragment of planarian or oligochaete. When the amputation is quite minimal, reproduction, from the point of view of the animal that remains almost intact, takes on the appearance of a simple reconstitution.[20] Rabaud asserts that autotomy, a case in which the animal spontaneously mutilates itself following an external excitation and then becomes whole again while the detached fragment disintegrates without proliferating, is a case of schizogony. From the point of view of the old individual, it is possible that autotomy and schizogony have identical consequences, namely the necessity of regeneration to replace the detached fragment. But the same cannot be said from the point of view of the detached fragment; there are many cases of autotomy in which the detached fragment cannot regenerate at all in such a way as to yield a new individual. Autotomy is in general a process of defense. In the stick insect *Carausius morosus,* for example, autotomy occurs when a member is pinched; this autotomy occurs in certain places in which there are special muscles that contract abruptly when the member is excited by pressure in a particular point, thereby breaking off the member. These member fragments do not produce a new *Carausius morosus*; the lizard's tail, broken by reflexive autotomy, also does not produce a new lizard. It indeed seems that the autotomy reflex undertakes a defensive behavior and is not directly linked to schizogonic reproduction as a particular case. Let us further note that autotomy, which is provoked systematically by a reflexive trigger on the stick insect and other insects, produces a degree of mutilation such that any regeneration becomes impossible, since the animal can be, for example, deprived of all its legs; in this case, autotomy involves the death of the individual without any reproduction; it is thus a reflex of the individual that detaches an article or a member but does not divide the individual qua individual and does not include the involvement of the essential function of amplification.

The existence of schizogony as a fundamental fact and fundamental schema of reproduction takes on great importance relative to the nature of the individual with respect to its specific lineage: according to Weismann, there would be two parts in the ensemble of the body of the individual: one of the parts, which is perishable and strictly linked to the individual, is the soma; the other, which is continuously uninterrupted from one generation to another insofar as the lineage is prolonged, is the germen. According to Weismann, in each generation the germen produces a new soma and gives it its own characteristics; it is essentially hereditary; the soma never produces the slightest bit of germen, and a modification undergone by the soma does not redound on the germen but remains individual. Thus, the individual is strictly distinguished from the species; the soma is nothing but the bearer of the germen, which continues to propagate the species without anything to retain from its passage throughout different successive individuals.

On the contrary, according to Rabaud, the examination of schizogony allows us to refute this unjustified distinction between soma and germen. All the parts of a being that are capable of schizogony are soma and germen; they are soma and germen with respect to one another; they are made of the same substance: "All the tentacles, all the tentacle fragments of a hydra produce the same number of hydras similar between them, for all these tentacles are made of the same substance. If one of them, in isolation and under a local action, experiences the slightest modification, the other tentacles would not experience the same modification. Separated from the body, the modified tentacle would perhaps produce an individual bearing a new disposition; but the other tentacles would certainly produce young fully comparable to the original hydra. All these tentacles are equally *hereditary substance.*"[21]

For Rabaud, every reproduction is a regeneration; it thus stems from the individual itself, which is hereditary substance in all its parts. The schizogonic mode of reproduction is the fundamental mode; it yields regeneration in the pure state, i.e. the intense proliferation of elements that constitute the schizogonic germs. In fact, it is with this name "germs" that we can, according to Rabaud, qualify the fragments that proliferate and separate from the parent, even if it is a question of two halves of a sea anemone or of an echinoderm; no essential particularity is attached to the dimensions of the fragments, since the processes of regeneration do not change with size. From the same animal, fragments separate that are very unequal in size and that nevertheless regenerate in the same way, as can be seen in the planarian, for example. Thus, there is a continuity between the case in which the animal is cut into two halves and the case in which it loses just a small fragment that afterwards becomes a complete individual. These fragments, which can be called schizogonic germs and which sometimes, due to a particular formation, deserve to be called buds, originate from any part of the body whatsoever. The property of regeneration due to which they transform into a complete individual is therefore not the privilege of the determined elements of the body within which the germen would reside to the exclusion of the other elements that would be the pure soma. All the elements of the body, indifferently and under certain conditions, are endowed with the same property. Regeneration would therefore be the fundamental vital mode of amplification.

This conclusion, which is relative to the schizogonic nature of every reproduction, insofar as every reproduction is a regeneration, is of the utmost importance for the notion of the individual. This notion loses hereditary substantiality in Weismann's thesis; the individual would become nothing but a simple unimportant accident without any veritable density throughout the genealogical series. According to the theory that leads every reproduction back to a schizogonic regeneration, the individual becomes substantial and not accidental; the capacity of reproducing is really, indivisibly, and completely in the individual, and not in a germen that would be sheltered from every mixture and every attack that would be borne by the individual without being of the individual. In the fullest sense of the term, the individual is living substance; its power of regeneration, the principle of reproduction, expresses the basis of the process of amplification that vital phenomena manifest.

In other cases, it is interesting to consider a mode of agamous reproduction that is quite significant because it utilizes a single individual which detaches as a link between two colonies; in this case, everything happens as if individuation simply appeared between two states in which it is diffuse, because it simultaneously resides in the whole and in each of the more or less autonomous parts; it could then be said that individuation appears in the pure individual, which is the form that operates the transition from one colony to another.

Sponges emit certain gemmules, and bryozoa emit statoblasts; in both cases, it is a question of buds that do not differ from other unspecified buds; however, the statoblast is charged with inert substances, separates from its founder, and hibernates without significantly modifying; the statoblast is indeed a "dormant bud," for example in *Stolonica socialis,* according to the studies of Sélys-Longchamps. In this case, Rabaud does not accept the nutritive role of the enclaves; but he cites other cases, for example that of the plumatella and entoprocta, which form statoblasts that fall into the general cavity and are only relinquished by the death of the parent.[22] The gemmules that originate from freshwater sponges and calcareous sponges are groupings of embryonic cells that contain a large quantity of enclaves, all of which is surrounded by a sheath. These gemmules form within the sponge by way of a gathering of free cells that stem from different regions of the sponge and accumulate from each place. Around them, other cells are positioned in epithelial membranes that secrete a spongy sheath and disappear; the gemmule remains included in the sponge's tissues until the parent's death. In certain cases, the gemmules have a central mass composed of differentiated tissues; they take on the name of sorites.[23] This is the case of hexactinellids, tethyids, and desmacids. This procedure of reproduction may not exist. But it is worth noting that in colonies wherein this reproduction does exist, due to its mode as well as its role, it represents and replaces the colony in its totality; it only comes into play in the case of the colony's death, an event that can never take place; the statoblast is therefore a concentrated, individualized form that is the depository of the capacity to reproduce the colony.

It can ultimately be said that even during agamous reproduction, a reduction of the complex organism occurs that primes the formation of the gametes; no doubt, the whole organism reproduces itself, but it does so via elementary individuated beings: gametes (spermatozoids in particular) are comparable to tiny living units that can exist autonomously; there is a passage of the complex organism's reproduction through a phase of elementary individuation that has an autonomous fate, is obviously very limited in time, and is made dependent on the conditions of the bio-chemical milieu, yet nevertheless constitutes an elementary phase of individuation. For these different reasons, the dualism of the soma-germen opposition, as well as Rabaud's monistic theory according to which the individual is hereditary substance, could perhaps be softened; the individual is indeed hereditary substance, but only like a gamete in an absolute way; however, the gamete in the sexual reproduction of complex organisms is hardly a single gamete: it is a gamete with respect to a partner; the pair of gametes is what is both hereditary substance and the reality capable of ontogenesis.

4. Undifferentiation and Dedifferentiation as Conditions of Reproductive Individuality

Due to a sort of law of opposition that appears in every problem concerning the individuated being, what the individual gains in density and in substantiality when reproduction is defined as a regeneration and not as a transmission of the germen from soma to soma, it loses in independence relative to other individuals. Those species in which the individual's substantiality is most solid and obvious—going all the way to the capacity of never dying, insofar as each individual can divide without remainders—are also those in which the individual's boundaries are the most difficult to trace, because all the modes of association exist in it and because reproduction often gives rise to intermediary forms between an organism and a society, forms which are hard to name insofar as they are basically mixtures.

This disappearance of the independence of the individual can either occur provisionally, in budding, or definitively, thereby leading to a colony; even in the colony, various degrees of independence are possible.

Budding produces independent individuals, but it only produces them slowly, and the various fragments first proliferate before separating from one another, as if regeneration were consequently prior to schizogony instead of following it. This preliminary regeneration via proliferation gives birth to a mass of indefinite contours, which protrude weakly at first, then increasingly, and which is then called a bud: amplification is contemporaneous with the beginning of the process.

The region in which the bud occurs is more or less narrowly localized in general, which, according to Rabaud, does not imply a special type of properties, opposing it to all the other regions (and which would designate it as the support of a possible germen). Localization "certainly arises from some secondary arrangement that reverberates throughout the local metabolism";[24] localization is a "secondary incident." It is necessary to merely remark that the parts of the body most capable of detaching and proliferating—like the hydra's tentacles, which play the role of the germ—are not the buds' birthplace. On the contrary, the outer lining of the body is what easily produces buds, which eventually separate from their point of origin. According to Rabaud, only local, purely contingent conditions would be able to restrict an absolutely general possibility "in its essence" to certain elements of the body. This possibility of proliferation would not be the privilege of certain elements of the body to the exclusion of certain other elements.

What the two modes of reproduction have in common (budding and schizogony) is the existence of undifferentiated and dedifferentiated elements that play the role of reproductive elements while remaining unspecified elements of the body: before the proliferation of the schizogonic germ, like at the moment of a bud's formation, the elements that prepare the formation of this germ or of this bud conserve or recuperate embryonic properties, i.e. remain undifferentiated or dedifferentiated.[25]

The localization of budding and its essential characteristics manifest in the coelenterates of the hydrozoan group; in the hydra, the bud is a diverticulum of the outer lining that spreads out, expands, and then pierces its vacant extremity, from which tentacles appear; the bud seems to originate from undifferentiated cells that actively multiply and insinuate themselves between elements of the endoderm and between those of the ectoderm for which they are substituted; these cells would therefore not be dedifferentiated but non-differentiated; they play the role of veritable generative cells. What would give birth to this localized budding would be these cells' distribution under the integumentary epithelium due to unknown influences. The substantiality of the whole individual would be absolutely certain if it could be confirmed that dedifferentiation is the sole procedure of budding; it is less clear in the case in which, like in the hydra, there is an undifferentiation in question. But Rabaud points out that these undifferentiated elements are not unified into special organs; these are dispersed elements that originally belong to the integuments with which they are in contact.

Let's note that to completely clarify this question of undifferentiated elements and to understand their role in reproduction, it would be helpful to see if there is a difference between schizogonic properties and properties relative to the budding of the schizogonic germ; when it is notable in size, like the arm of a starfish or serpent star, this germ is integrated into the new individual without rejuvenating it; this new individual therefore has a part of its body that is old, while the other parts are new. During a new schizogony, does this old part have the same properties as those that have been newly formed? Can it still give birth by way of regeneration to a new individual? Systematic experiments in this sense do not seem to have been undertaken from the perspective of a study of *neotenization*.

The localization of budding is also quite distinct in saltwater hydrozoans. In some hydrozoans, stolons form, which are non-differentiated buds; the coenosarc thins and ultimately separates from the original branch when the stolon spreads out; the perisarc thins, and the bud, whether propagule or frustule, becomes free with a substrate to which it adheres and on which it slowly creeps; it is only at this moment that it proliferates out somewhat from its length; the proliferation rapidly grows perpendicularly to the longitudinal axis of the frustule, and two days later it transforms into a hydranth. The same frustule in this way produces several hydranths that remain linked together. We should note that in this procedure of reproduction, there is a veritable synthesis of schizogony and budding; indeed, the formation of the stolon begins as a budding; but instead of proliferating, this bud detaches, which corresponds to a schizogony; then the detached bud starts to proliferate, which corresponds to a budding; we should further note that this synthesis of schizogony and budding leads to a lifeform that is intermediate between pure individualization and a life that is so collective and with such strong bonds between individuals that the latter would no longer be anything but the different organs of a single whole constituting the veritable individual. Other coelenterates, such as campanularia, produce a frustule that, by detaching from the hydrocaulus, drags along the hydranth under which it has formed; but this hydranth is reabsorbed and disappears as the frustule emits buds; everything happens as if the activity of budding that generates a new ensemble were incompatible with the conservation of an already formed individual. Perhaps it is necessary to see in this disappearance of the hydranth a consequence of the dedifferentiation we have seen at work in every reproductive activity, either via schizogony or via the formation of a bud.

There is also budding in tunicates, where it is complicated by the fact that the bud develops at the end of a stolon and grows in the lower part of the body on an undifferentiated tissue that belongs to the mesenchyme and is quite narrowly localized in the region of the postabdomen.

This stolon is a tube limited by the ectoderm and divided lengthwise into two parts by a mesenchymal partition; the stump of the stolon emits several buds, each of which grows and produces an independent ascidian. The active part of the bud is a block of mesenchymal cells originating from the partition; the entire individual is differentiated starting from these cells; the other elements are reabsorbed. In this case, the procedure thus conserves an aspect of budding; it is a budding at a distance that takes place through the intermediary of the stolon; yet this is nevertheless a budding, since the separation only occurs after the differentiation.

Budding presents itself in another form that poses the problem between the founding individual and the young individual, for example in aquatic oligochaete worms in the naididae group. Indeed, budding occurs in quite a narrowly localized zone in the posterior part of the worm behind a septum. At this level, the elements of the external integument multiply starting with the ventral side, and what results is a thickening of this wall that propagates around the somite at the same time as a superficial constriction appears following the transversal median plane, revealing a relative morphological discontinuity between two individuals; the non-differentiated cells of the intestines multiply along with the elements of the mesoderm that line the segment's cavity. The various organs of a new individual, a zooid, differentiate within the embryonic tissue formed by these cells, with the head appearing in the anterior part of the bud in immediate contact with the tissues of the parent. Often this new zooid, before separating from its parent, in turn buds in the same way; it then constitutes a chain of several single-file individuals linked together one after another. Each individual buds in an approximately continuous way; it even happens that a second zone of proliferation occurs in one of the segments situated in front of the posterior segment. Moreover, it may happen that the undifferentiated zone is established in the last somite, higher up; then the following somites, already differentiated before the establishment of the undifferentiated zone, do not dedifferentiate in order to form the new individual; they immediately form an integral part of the zooid and unite with the homologous tissues originating from the bud; the founder regenerates the removed parts.

Thus, a definitively undifferentiated zone separates the individuals that remain aggregated in a chain; these individuals can remain linked together long enough to become almost adults; we find this in certain turbellarians from the rhabdocoela subclass, which are non-segmented worms related to planarians. We can see in this sense how the mode of reproduction is significant in the individual's relation to other individuals; the relation of dependence or independence expresses to a large extent the way the individual has been generated, which is why an important aspect of the interindividual relation is a form of reproduction, even when it spans the whole life of each individual.

This is what is particularly important to study in the case where various modes and degrees of individuation appear in colonies.

Colonial budding is not always established following the same mode. In fact, there are all kinds of transitions between a proliferation that is nothing but a growth of substance and a proliferation that, after producing anatomically and physiologically distinct individuals, on the other hand leaves them grouped in a mechanical unity. The two borderline cases can be represented in terms of ascidians and sponges. The ascidian represents the borderline case in which individuals, while separating from one another, nevertheless remain quite strictly grouped together; on the contrary, sponges represent the borderline case in which an active proliferation yields a simple growth of substance, whereas the new parts seem to be a certain number of individuals. However, even in this case, the individuated state is not completely nullified; it can appear if the mode of reproduction changes; the individuated state temporarily reappears if the sponge produces a bud that detaches, something that occurs every now and then; this would confirm the hypothesis according to which there is a link between the appearance of the well-characterized living individual and the functions of amplifying reproduction: the individual is essentially the bearer of the capacity to reproduce (not necessarily to reproduce *itself*, for it can, on the contrary, reproduce a colony that is not at all comparable to it).

As we have seen, the reproduction of ascidians is performed by a stolon; this stolon expands while anchoring onto a substrate, and then its extremity develops into an individual that detaches from its founder but remains anchored in place. All the stolons originating from the same founder behave in the same way and produce a certain number of buds: what ensues is a grouping of individuals anchored side by side but independent from one another.

Conversely, the sponge, which is at first simple, begins to ramify, and each ramification takes on the aspect of the initial sponge, with a new osculum and inhalant pores; morphologically, these new parts seem to represent a series of individuals; but the external morphological criterion here is lacking and is shown to be insufficient; these ramifications remain in complete and definitive continuity with the sponge's mass; none of them have the value of a bud; the various regions of the sponge form a new mass, each comprising part of the whole in which no element possesses a veritable autonomy. Let's note however that the ensemble of the sponge can hardly be called individual more so than each of its parts; the various parts are not organs of the individual that would be the sponge, since these various parts are not merely continuous but also homogeneous; the appearance of new parts is a growth of the quantity of the sponge's living matter but does not bring about a significant differentiation. Since there is not more in the whole than in the parts, it is difficult to call the whole an *individual* simply because it is the whole. This whole is not indivisible at all; if we remove a part of this sponge that multiplies, the sponge is not mutilated but diminished. Here, we are faced with an absence of structure that does not allow us to give the name individual to the whole more so than to the parts, nor does it allow us to remove this name from the parts in order to give it to the whole, since the whole is nothing but the sum of its parts, the heap they form. In fact, this extreme case is the one in which individuality belongs equally to the parts and to the whole; the parts do not have a veritable individuality, since they are not independent; but they nevertheless have a defined form, with an osculum, inhalant pores, and a certain orientation with respect to the whole, an orientation that is more prominent in certain species. Thus, there is no absolutely complete continuity between the various parts, and a relative unity belongs to each part, despite their lack of independence; each part is complete by itself and could be self-sufficient; each part therefore possesses a certain virtual individuality that the mode of reproduction does not highlight. Furthermore, the whole also possesses a relative individuality that is complementary to that of the parts; this individuality consists of the rudiments of orientation that seem to direct the genesis of new parts: they do not come absolutely at random from the old parts but according to certain directions of privileged growths. The studies that have been carried out until now are not sufficient for us to say with certainty by what force the whole acts on the parts so as to orient them, which thereby produces, despite the randomness of proliferation, ensembles that are not organized but ordered, the first degree of individuation prior to which there is nothing but pure continuity. Indeed, what is quite remarkable is the fact that the individuality of the whole only appears here as a form and not as an organization; but this existence of a form is not negligible, since the individuality of the whole consists of precisely what is removed from the parts in terms of their freedom and their capacity to grow in all senses; however slight this influence may be, it is nevertheless a subordination of the generation of the parts and of their growth to the existence and arrangement of the whole; it is the origination of a structure. The slightest appearance of individuation is therefore contemporaneous with the manifestation of a dynamic structure in the process of a being's reproduction, a reproduction which, moreover, is still not distinguished from growth.

Furthermore, let's note that if two sponges are very close to one another, the budding that they emit indeed lacks a distinction between the two groups-individuals; this dynamic structure of growth does not pass from one individual to the other; the extensions of each sponge remain distinct and do not influence one another, as if this morphological dominance exerted by the whole onto the parts were reserved for them alone and would not be transmitted, even by the narrowest proximity. The morphological criterion is therefore important, since it appears at the very first degree of individuality, in a state in which individuality is still fragmentary and does not exist in the whole except in the slightest perceivable way. Everything happens as if individuality were a measurable physical parameter or quantity with the ability to distribute between the parts and the whole; the more the whole is individualized, the less individualized the parts are; on the contrary, if the parts are almost complete individuals, virtually detachable without requiring regeneration afterwards, the whole is poorly individualized; the whole nevertheless exists as an inhibitor or accelerator of the growth of the parts; it plays a morphological role through its dominance, which is exerted on reproduction. We must regret that studies on the genesis of forms have not been pushed far enough for us to say by which agent these accelerating or inhibiting influences exert themselves and constitute a veritable field of growth in which the individual develops and which it itself involves. The same type of phenomena is prominent in the vegetal world: lichens, an association of algae and fungi, do not develop anarchically; in certain species, the extremities are calloused and endowed with a hardness; when light is not very abundant, the forms become comparable to those of plant leaves, such that this vegetal association could be mistaken for a single living plant in the same type of milieu (for example, sedges and ferns).

Between the two extreme forms of the ascidian and the sponge, there are a multitude of degrees of individualization of the ensemble, i.e. according to our hypothesis, a multitude of values of rapport between the degree of individualization of the parts and the degree of individualization of the whole. Other ascidians produce stolons arrayed more or less regularly but without their own membrane; these stolons ramify and tangle together in the particularly thick membrane of the parent and then bud within this membrane; the buds partially emerge while developing; the region of the thorax, which includes the pharynx and the peribranchial chamber, has its own membrane and emerges from the parent's membrane. Once they have fully developed, the adults remain in continuity with the original stolon but lose all functional relation with it; only the shared membrane joins and maintains them. There is, however, a certain regularity to the grouping: the mere fact of having a membrane and more so a common origin suffices to define for all these developed buds an incorporation in the individuality of the whole. Since each individual buds in turn, the colony, which envelops the products of several generations, branches out and can acquire fairly large dimensions. We should nevertheless note that this dynamic structure of the ensemble seems to have a certain limit; the whole colony is not organized all of a piece; when it is large, it is formed by several groups distributed at random; but each group presents a certain order; these groups, which truly indicate the dimension of the group's individuality for the species considered, are called coenobia.

A similar process of reproduction takes place in *Heterocarpa glomerata,* which generates stolons reabsorbed when the new individual has been born; a single membrane remains that strictly maintains the products of several successive generations tied together. Here again, the mode of reproduction is indeed what determines the specific degree of individuality linking the regime of individuation back to that of reproduction. Reproduction in golden star tunicates *(Botryllus schlosseri)* takes place in a different way and leads to a different regime of individuation: reproduction takes place through a very short stolon (whereas in polystyelines it grows to 1.5 cm) that integrally transforms into an individual; the buds then form clearly delimited coenobia: the whole colony derives from a first individual that begins to bud before having reached adulthood. Afterwards, this budding occurs symmetrically until four buds of the same generation alone remain (those that would support them having been reabsorbed); these buds are arranged into crosses in such a way that their cloacae converge and coalesce into a shared cloaca around which the successive generations are grouped as and when older generations disappear: what results is an important agglomeration of individuals that completely possesses all the organs (most notably the heart) that make an autonomous life possible.

However, the autonomy of the individuals is not full-fledged: they conserve vascular relations between each other; a circular vesicle surrounds the coenobium. Yet each individual has a heart whose beating is not synchronous with the beating of the others. In this sense, this regime of reproduction—in which a clear morphological dominance of the whole over the parts manifests by way of a fairly rigorous symmetry in budding and then by way of the circular form of the coenobium during its development—corresponds to a colony in which the individuality of the whole is quite clearly prominent, to the point of creating vascular relations between the individuals.

In coelenterates, the formation of colonies is a frequent phenomenon. The majority of hydroids produce a large number of stolons that arise beneath the hydranth and then stretch out and ramify without detaching from the founder; by ramifying, they emit lateral buds that transform into hydranths and, in turn, sprout a stolon. This ramification is *indefinite,* and an equally indefinite colony corresponds to the *indefinite* process of reproduction. We should however note a very important but poorly studied fact in order to be able to found a theory on it alone: certain ruptures are produced in this indefinite ramification that lead to collective individuals and limited colonies, as in the previous cases in which we saw the colony produce via proliferation not a single colony of indefinite dimensions, but coenobia of limited dimensions: everything happens as if a certain quantitative limit produced an elementary morphological induction that divided the colony into restricted groups; a certain phenomenon of individuation therefore seems to arise even within the processes of growth, which here are not separate from those of reproduction. Rabaud considers these ruptures as accidental and not physiological.[26] He separates them from the ruptures of short stolons, which he qualifies as "physiological ruptures"; but the conditions of these "physiological ruptures" are as poorly understood as the ones that interrupt the continuity of development. Thus, there is no irrefutable reason that forces us to oppose so-called accidental ruptures to physiological ruptures; perhaps they depend on one another in the same way as the processes of reproduction considered in its dynamic structure, which presides over the establishment of the anatomical or physiological structure of the colony or groupings of individuals. Within one of the groups of hydranths, a coenosarc remains continuous along the hydrocaulus, thereby relating all the hydranths through the system of channels that crosses it; in this sense, certain physiological bonds and a nutritive community in particular are established by this morphological continuity that is itself accompanied by a continuity in the process of reproduction. And yet the indirect nature of this continuity leaves the hydranths with a certain degree of functional autonomy.

The form of the colony is in general correlative to the mode of reproduction: thus, in other coelenterates, like hydractiniids, the stolon creeps along and ramifies while remaining strictly in contact with the substrate; this is how it forms a network without any erect branches; the buds are born and grow perpendicular to this network, thereby transforming into elongated hydranths.

In hexacorallia, buds arise directly at the expense of the wall of the body above the skeleton that serves as a point of support. Colonies take on quite varied forms, but these forms are in relation with the mode of generation, thereby allowing for the recognition of species. In the immense colonies of madrepores, which form coral reefs, the existence of a polarity is quite prominent. Development often takes on the form of extremely ramified branches that follow an orientation of the whole, which indicates a relative morphological individuality of the colony. The aesthetic aspect of these coral ramifications seems to indicate that this morphology is not arbitrary. This morphology could be likened to the way in which certain complex efflorescences form, like those of ice, which is not independent from the characteristics of the substrate on which it forms yet which deploys forms in harmony with the laws of crystallization. Perhaps it would be necessary to seek in the kinship of form the functional analogies that link together a large number of processes of individuation belonging to extremely different domains; one aspect would be shared by all: the identity of the process of growth, which would be the creation of organized ensembles based on a self-constitutive schema that responds to a dynamism of growth and to the initial givens depending on chance; the same law could then be found again in the growth of an efflorescence, in the development of a tree, in the formation of a colony, and even in the genesis of mental images, as if a dynamic dominance would give a structure to ensembles based on a singularity. A morphological analogy could reveal an identity of the process of formation of collective individualities; in each case the structure of the individual would be linked to the schema of its genesis, and the criterion, perhaps the very foundation, of the individuated being would reside in the autonomy of this genetic schema.

III. Information and Vital Individuation

1. Individuation and Regimes of Information

A question can then be posed that is perhaps more formal than profound, since it can only be answered by a recasting of commonplace concepts: does colonial budding consist in an excessively proportioned, simple growth of a single individual? Does it on the contrary give birth to distinct yet interlinked individuals? In a word, what is an individual? We respond to this question that we cannot rigorously speak of the individual but of individuation; we must come back to the activity, to the genesis, instead of attempting to grasp the fully formed being in order to discover the criteria by means of which we will know whether or not it is an individual. The individual is not a being but an act, and the being is an individual as an agent of this act of individuation through which it appears and exists. Individuality is an aspect of generation, is explained by the genesis of a being, and consists in the perpetuation of this genesis; the individual is that which has been individuated and continues to be individuated; it is the transductive relation of an activity, both result and agent, the consistency and coherence of this activity through which it has been constituted and through which it constitutes; the individual is hereditary substance, according to Rabaud's expression, since it transmits the activity it has received; it is what makes this activity pass through time in a condensed form as information. It stores, transforms, reactualizes, and carries out the schema that has constituted it; it propagates the schema by individuating. The individual is the result of a formation; it is an exhaustive recapitulation and can reproduce a vast ensemble; the existence of the individual is this operation of amplifying transfer. This is why the individual is always in a double and amphibological relation with what precedes it and what follows it. Growth is the simplest and most fundamental of these operations of transfer that establish individuality. The individual condenses information, transports it, and then modulates a new milieu.

The individual assimilates a genesis and in turn carries it out. When the nervous system is sufficiently developed, this genesis can be assimilated by the nervous system and can expand into creative acts, like the imagery that the being invents according to a law of development that has roots in experience but would not exist without a self-constituting activity. Learning does not differ from genesis profoundly, but learning is a genesis that requires a very complex somatic formation. The individual is what it is in accordance with this activity of amplifying transfer, which is an active genesis and not a genesis passively undergone; degrees of individuality are relative to the density of this activity. This criterion alone is fundamental, i.e. the exercise of an amplifying and transductive activity. If this activity is distributed between the whole of a colony and the parts of this colony, it should be said that the parts are incomplete individuals, yet the whole should not be considered an organism whose individuals would be nothing but organs; indeed, these incomplete individuals are increasingly incomplete the more dependent on one another and virtually less detachable they are; however, it can be noted that in morphology the interdependence of incomplete individuals is marked by the importance of the functions of the shared relations that belong to the whole. If this relation between the parts of the whole is only nutritive, the individuality of the parts can still be considered noteworthy; for these individuals, a bond is formed by the very fact that they all partake in the same interior milieu establishes a bond between them, but this bond nevertheless leaves behind a certain independence. On the contrary, if nerve fibers link the different parts to one another, the functionality of these different parts is bound by a much stricter interdependence; a strict functional bond exists with the community of information; the individuality of the parts becomes very weak. What needs to be introduced to determine the degree of individuality is therefore not the morphological criterion alone, but the morphological criterion and the functional criterion. For example, as Rabaud indicates,[27] the cells of an organism like a metazoan are defined by well-determined contours, but they are nevertheless not individuals, since each of them only functions under the direct, constant, and unavoidable influence of its neighbors; each cell involves very strict rapports of dependence with the others, such that its functional activity is nothing but an element of the functional activity of the whole. This loss of functional individuality produces a very low level of individuality. Thus, independent of any genesis, individuality can be presented as characterized by functional autonomy; but this is only true if the word autonomy is given its full meaning: self-regulation, the state of obeying nothing but its own law and developing according to its own structure; this criterion coincides with hereditary substantiality; beings are autonomous when they themselves regulate their own developments and store information and regulate their action themselves by means of this information. The individual is the being that can conserve or increase a content of information. It is the autonomous being in terms of information, since information is what grants it veritable autonomy.[28] If individuals that were bound together by a coenosarc had nothing in common but nourishment, they could still be called individuals. But if chemical messages pass with this nourishment from one individual to another, and consequently if there is a state of the whole that regulates the different parts, then the autonomy of information becomes very weak in each part and individuality lowers correlatively. What needs to be studied is the regime of information in a being in order to know what the degree of individuality of the parts with respect to the whole is; the individual is characterized as the unit of a system of information; when one point of the ensemble receives an excitation, this information will be reflected in the organism and will come back in the form of a more or less generalized motor or secretory reflex; this reflection of information sometimes takes place in the same part in which the excitation occurs or in a part that constitutes with it the same organic unity; but this reflex is nevertheless made dependent upon a center if the whole is individualized;

this center creates facilitation or inhibition. In this case, there is a center in which the individual stores past information and by means of which it commands, monitors, inhibits, or facilitates (in the English way of speaking, "controls") the passage from a centripetal information to a centrifugal reaction. What defines individuality is the existence of this center by means of which the being regulates itself and modulates its milieu. The stronger the center's control, the more individualized the whole, and the less the parts can be considered autonomous individuals. A regime of fragmentary information reveals a weak individualization of the whole. In animals whose parts are quite differentiated, such as mammals, the regime of information is very centralized; the information received by any one part of the body immediately reverberates throughout the central nervous system, and all the parts of the body respond in a short enough time with an appropriate action, at least those that depend directly on the central nervous system. In animals that have a poorly centralized nervous system, the relation is established between the different parts more slowly; there is a unity of the system of information, but its speed sharply decreases. We can obtain a notion of this less coherent, less rigorously unified individuality by analyzing what our individuality would be if we only had sympathetic and parasympathetic systems: a unity of information would remain, but the reactions would be slower, more diffuse, and less perfectly unified; this difference is so great between the two regimes of information that we are sometimes hard-pressed to make coincide within us the reverberation of an information in the central nervous system with its reverberation in the sympathetic system, and this difficulty can sometimes veer toward splitting, as if individuality were indeed defined by a regime of information; a being that would have two totally independent regimes of information would have two individualities. What complicates the problem in the case of colonies of metazoans is the fact that every alimentary relation is also a chemical relation and that the importance of chemical messages is greater in proportion to how elementary the being is; this chemical sensitivity is what forms the unity and guarantees the individuality of a plant, allowing for the self-regulation of exchanges in accordance with its needs, the opening and closing of pores, perspiration, and the movements of the sap, as the studies of Sir Bose have shown. We can therefore suppose that in the animal the existence of a community of chemical information lowers the level of the individuality of the parts but nevertheless leaves a certain individuality intact. In sum, the regime of information is what defines the degree of individuality; in order to appreciate it, we must establish a rapport between the propagation speed of information and the duration of the act or event to which information is relative. Therefore, if the duration of information propagation is small relative to the duration of the act or event, an important region of the being, indeed the whole being, will have to take on attitudes and carry out the modifications suitable for this act; in the contrary case, the event or act will remain a local reality, even if there is a reverberation for the whole colony afterwards; individuality is marked with respect to a type of act or event determined by the possibility of reaction and thus of control of the usage of information in accordance with the state of the organism, and consequently the possibility of autonomy; the autonomous zone, i.e. the zone in which information has the time to propagate in a centripetal direction and then in a centrifugal direction quickly enough for the self-regulation of the act to be able to take place effectively, is the zone that belongs to the same individuality. What marks the limits of individuality is the recurrence of centripetal and then centrifugal information. This limit is functional by nature; but it can be anatomical, for anatomical limits can impose a critical delay to information. This criterion applies to colonies. A colony whose parts are linked only by circulatory pathways has no means other than chemical means to convey information. Chemical messages propagate either through convection (and the speed then depends on the speed of the currents, generally several centimeters per second) or through the diffusion of molecules in liquid; this diffusion depends on the temperature and the bodies present, but it is fairly slow (almost at the same order of magnitude as the speed of convection); in small organisms, this mode of information transmission can be quite fast; in organisms of several centimeters, it becomes quite slow. Therefore, the majority of the acts of defense and capture can only receive a self-regulation, the basis of autonomy, if information is conveyed by the nerves, within which the conduction speed of nervous impulses is generally several meters per second, and thus around five times faster than conduction by chemical means. Practically, for the life acts of relation in animals, the limits of the individual are also the limits of the nervous system. Yet it must always be specified that it is only for the life acts of relation that this individuality is limited by the nervous system. Certain other activities can require reactions slow enough such that the colony then behaves as an individual; this is the case, for example, when a toxic substance gets captured by an individualized part of a colony. This capture merely involves a local process, for example a reflex of contraction or relaxation when the toxic body has excited the individualized part; but, after several seconds, the chemical messages produce a global reaction of the whole colony that interrupts or reverses the movement of water pumping or retracts all the hydranths, without any contact with the toxin having taken place except in the part in which the capture reflex occurred. In this case, it will have to be said that the colony is an individual in terms of alimentation but a society for the other functions. Individuality is essentially linked to the regime of information for each subset of vital activities.

Due to this criterion, we can see individuality establish itself progressively: in naidomorph oligochaetes, the new parts, which remain attached to their founder for quite a while, take on the appearance of a complete worm, while budding continues and other parts differentiate, such that it forms a chain of zooids; the new cerebral ganglion is grafted onto the sections of the pre-existing ventral chain. The nervous system forms a continuous whole along the chain that includes several heads with their respective ganglia; in the same way, the new intestinal tube is inserted into the old parts.

The physiological activity is perfectly coordinated; only the intestinal tube of the founder functions; all the movements of the animal are perfectly linked together: the peristaltic waves of the intestines regularly propagate back and forth without discontinuity. The circulation mutually belongs to the whole file; the bristles over the whole ensemble are animated by synchronous oscillations: consequently, we see that this ensemble of zooids includes nothing but a single zone of autonomy coextensive with the nervous system. This ensemble is therefore a single individual.

On the contrary, when the anatomical links that bind the parts begin to dissolve, the tissues enter into histolysis following the same line in which the nervous system of the founder is welded to the new cerebral ganglions. Muscular coordination then breaks down little by little; the contractions become incongruous, and the incongruities accelerate the separation. It can therefore be said that each zooid would already possess its own individuality before the separation, with its functional autonomy and particularly its nervous autonomy. Here individuality is not created by the anatomical separation; it is from the start individuality that appears as the independence of the regime of information and accelerates the separation when the movements are put into disarray. It is interesting to note that the nervous and circulatory connections would still partially exist at the moment in which the contractions would already become antagonistic. Thus independence, even the independence of the neural pathways, is not what creates individuality; instead, individuality is created by the regime of information conditioned by these pathways; it's because the zooid's nervous system is developed enough to have its own rhythmic activity and to inhibit the nervous impulses coming from the nervous system of the founder that individualization can be continued; the mark and foundation of individualization in the nervous system of the zooid is the recurrent regime of information signals;[29] a certain individualization is required in order for this recurrence to be possible, but as soon as it is possible, this recurrence is established and accelerates individualization; the zooid's individualization can be dated the moment that it can inhibit the nervous messages coming from its parent. Let's note that a cyclical activity like that of an oscillation is the very type of nervous functionality that can be produced by the recurrence of signals in an element of the nervous system or in a completely different network in which signals propagate. Anatomical independence is therefore indeed far from constituting the criterion of individuality; what constitutes the criterion of individuality is independence, or better yet functional autonomy; in fact, autonomy is not synonymous with independence; autonomy exists before independence, since autonomy is the possibility of functioning according to a process of internal resonance that can be inhibitory with regard to the messages received from the rest of the colony and that can create independence.

The independence of individuals with respect to one another is moreover rare and almost impossible: even when individuals have no anatomical bond between one another, they undergo the influence of the milieu that surrounds them, and, among these influences, there are those originating from the other individuals, which are components of the milieu; each individual determines the reactions of the neighboring individual to a certain extent; this interaction, which is ongoing and unavoidable, establishes a certain rapport; but the individuals remain autonomous; there is no functional coordination among them; information does not pass from one individual to the other; the zone of the conservation and recurrence of information is limited to individuals; whatever the intensity of reciprocal action may be, each individual reacts in its own way, sooner or later, more slowly or more quickly, for longer or more briefly; in order for information to pass from one individual to another, the centripetal information signals that have detached from the centrifugal information signals within an individual would have to be received as centrifugal by the other individuals;[30] however, any information that emanates from an individual is received as centripetal by another individual, which responds to this information via its own centrifugal reaction; in order for the interaction to become communication, one of the individuals would have to govern the others, i.e. the others would have to lose their autonomy, and the centrifugal information signals emanating from one individual would have to remain centrifugal within the individuals that receive them; this organization, which implies that one individual becomes a leader, does not seem to exist in colonies.

When material obstacles persist and limit the displacements of individuals, functionally autonomous and anatomically distinct but materially interdependent organisms remain attached to the same support: they are nevertheless individuals; even if they are attached to one another, they play the role of a substrate with respect to one another.

In conclusion, regarding the attempt to determine this functional criterion of individuality, it can be said that the hydranths of a colony of coelenterates possess the individuality of local and rapid reactions, such as the contractions and movements of cilia; there is no nervous system that establishes a functional synchronization between the hydranths. In contrast, the individuality of the slow reactions belongs to the colony; hydranths communicate with one another via the system of hollow canals in the coenosarc, canals that directly culminate in the various gastric cavities and thereby establish among the hydranths an obvious functional dependence:[31] the products of the digestion and assimilation of hydranths flow into a sort of mutual circulation; each hydranth is nourished by and also nourishes the ensemble of the others.

In certain cases, the individuality of the parts of a colony can become temporarily complete; this is the case of millepores and hydrocorals: all the hydranths are unified by a system of interlinked canals in a rich hollow network within the calcareous mass; but, since the hydranths do not stop expelling limestone, which accumulates around them, from time to time they dislodge from the bottom of the chamber, go back up toward its orifice, and lose all relation with the system of canals; but soon they again begin to proliferate and produce around them a series of buds linked together by a new system of canals. From then on, each hydranth becomes the center of a coenobium associated with other coenobia, each one originating from the complete yet fleeting individualization of hydranths detached from older coenobia.

In colonies of bryozoans, there can either be a simple juxtaposition of individuals or a circulatory unity of the ensemble, since each bryozoan lacks a heart.

In colonies of tunicates and golden start tunicates, the individuality of the parts is complete, despite the existence of a shared cloaca in the golden star tunicates; in fact, the shared cloaca cannot regularly convey information.

2. Regimes of Information and Rapports between Individuals

Is individualization linked to specialization? This question can be posed by considering polymorphic colonies.

Polymorphism is often a consequence of budding, and if it is considered that individuality depends on conditions of reproduction, it indeed seems that polymorphism must be considered as linked to individuality. In fact, it turns out that the various buds in a colony of coelenterates do not all develop in the same way. The colony is then composed of individuals that are different from one another due to their form and their mode of functioning. In some hydranths, like *Hydractinia* and *Clava,* the hydrorhiza spreads out on a support (a shell inhabited by a hermit crab) in a very tight network and in superposed strata; the hydranths are born directly from this inclined stolon and stand vertically; in the *Clava,* a short hydrocaulus serves as a peduncle for the hydranths. One part of the hydranths has a mouth and tentacles; these are the gastrozooids or nourishing individuals. The other parts, without a mouth, are sterile and very contractile and contort in a spiral (spiral zooids or dactylozooids) and then relax and strike the surrounding bodies with their extremity, which contains nematocysts; these would be the defenders of the colony; the others, which are short, sterile, and spine-shaped, are called acanthozooids and are considered to provide shelter; still others, the gonozooids, yield sexual products. These various parts form a continuous whole; the coenosarc, furrowed by canals, fills the hydrorhiza and binds together the various hydranths without any discontinuity. Gastrozooids, dactylozooids, and gonozooids are also distinguished in millepores. In siphonophores, polymorphism is taken even further: these are floating colonies whose various elements originate at the expense of an initial jellyfish, from which the manubrium extends and buds; nectozooids are found here, which are gastrozooids endowed with a large oscular orifice and very long tentacles; there are also dactylozooids, to which a defensive role is attributed, and gonozooids; sometimes a flat or leaf-like lamina, or phyllozooid, is supposed to protect the ensemble. According to Rabaud, the finality indicated in the names is too accentuated; the role of the zooids is not too clear.[32] It cannot be said that polymorphism results from a "physiological division of labor"; indeed, the majority of the functions have been attributed without a veritable examination of the mode of life of these colonies; the acanthozooids are completely useless and lacking in the majority of species; the "aviculars" of the bryozoans of the cheilostome group are merely simple abnormal variations and not defensive organs. Rabaud concludes by saying that the polymorphism of coelenterates amounts to localized variations dependent on the general metabolism of the siphonophore or hydractinia; thus, the difference between the life of a polymorphic colony and the life of a non-polymorphic colony is weak; the difference in look is considerable, but the mode of life and the functional properties are almost the same. Polymorphism arises neither from the influence of individuals on one another, nor from the necessity of existence, nor from another influence that determines polymorphism; only the gastrozooids and gonozooids are individuals that fulfill a function; all the others result in nothing but a deficit.

Furthermore, it can be wondered if the relation among individuals allows us to define different degrees of individuality. Relative to reproduction, gestation, viviparity, and ovoviviparity represent different modes and different types of relation. It is important to note that these relations are also found in cases that do not concern reproduction but a certain form of association, like parasitism. There is even a profound functional analogy between the gestation of viviparous animals and cases of parasitism, like that of monstrilloida or sacculina. There are even cases of association constituted by a reciprocal parasitism of two animals contemporaneous with one another. These cases are valuable for the theory of information systems; in some sense they allow us to establish identities (concerning the regime of information in the inter-individual relation) where a morphological examination would find nothing but superficial resemblances that we wouldn't dare to qualify as analogies, since the identity of rapports, which are constitutive for analogy, wouldn't appear to be very clear here. According to this path, it becomes possible to characterize quite a few relations relative to a single type of inter-individual rapports taken as a basis: that of reproduction. We are hypothetically treating the elementary forms of association (parasitism) as complements of reproduction. Indeed, when an individual has become completely autonomous, like an alevin that both swims and nourishes itself all on its own, this new individual is born absolutely; in contrast, when a relation continues to exist between the parent and the young in the form of humoral, nutritive interdependence, like when the fertilized ovule becomes implanted in the uterus according to a definite mode of placentation until birth properly speaking, a phase of association that diminishes the embryo's degree of individualization will be inserted between reproduction properly speaking (division of the egg) and the moment of full individuality. Even after birth, the young individual must be considered as still imperfectly individualized: the relation to the parent extends for a longer or shorter time in the suckling phase, sometimes in an ongoing means of transportation (the marsupial pouch; bats), which is still akin to parasitism with an external fixation. We should further note that certain cases of parasitism are made possible by the fact that several animals have organs, folds, or appendices meant to allow for the easy fixation of their young; there can then be a replacement of the young by an individual of another species, and in this case it produces, in place of the homophyseal[33] complex constituted by the union of the parent and the young, a heterophyseal complex constituted by the assemblage of an individual and its parasitic host. The modifications of metabolism, as well as all the morphological modifications that accompany them, are approximately the same in the case of the heterophyseal complex and in that of the homophyseal complex: a sacculinated male crab takes on a form comparable to that of a female. A pregnant female has the same reactions as a parasited animal. Moreover, the asymmetrical relation of parasitism leads the parasite to a regression; in the majority of parasitic species, it is impossible to speak of an "adaptation" to parasitism, since this adaptation is a destruction of the organs that guarantee the being's individual autonomy: for example, the loss of the intestines frequently occurs in animals that, after having sought a host, settle themselves and nourish themselves at the expense of their host; it is not a question of an adaptation in the absolute sense of the term, but of a regression of the parasite's level of organization that ends up transforming the entire heterophyseal complex into a being that does not have a level of organization superior to that of a veritable individual. It even seems that the level of organization of the heterophyseal complex is inferior to that of a single individual, since, in the parasited being, there is no progress, but instead phenomena of anamorphosis;[34] perhaps it should be said that in this case the general level of information of the heterophyseal complex is equal to the difference between that of the parasited individual and that of the parasite.[35] This parasite can also be a society of individuals; when the difference tends toward zero, the heterophyseal complex is no longer viable, and it dissociates either with the death of the parasited being and the liberation of the parasite or with the parasite's death. Thus, it would be necessary to consider a heterophyseal complex as being *less* than a complete individual. Should we consider the homophyseal complex in the same way? Rabaud tends to do so by assimilating gestation to a veritable illness; however, this point deserves to be examined; in fact, while the conclusion of the level of organization is approximately stable in the case of a heterophyseal complex, this conclusion is not always the same throughout the duration of the homophyseal complex; pregnancy can correspond in certain cases to a greater resistance to infectious diseases and to cold temperatures, as if a veritable heightening of vital functions were involved; sensitivity to chemical agents is greater, and reactions are more lively, which seems to indicate an increase in and an adaptive polarization of sensory activity. Motor activity can also be heightened, which seems paradoxical due to the thickening of the body and the greater expenditure of energy. It therefore seems that in this case the relation can be somewhat additional and somewhat subtractive depending on the circumstances and the metabolism of the embryo and of the mother.

Ultimately, we must distinguish asymmetrical parasitism from the symmetrical forms of association that are symbioses, as can be seen in lichens, which are compounds of an alga that "parasites" a fungus and of a fungus that "parasites" an alga. Indeed, in this case the total quality of organization of the beings constituted in this manner exceeds that of a single individual; the morphological regression of each of the two beings is much less than in the case of pure parasitism, for a reciprocal causality binds the two beings according to a positive reaction; the activity of each being is translated by a greater capacity of activity for the partner;[36] on the contrary, parasitism is founded on a negative reaction that constitutes a mutual inhibition, or at the very least an inhibition exerted by the parasite on the host (thus, in the case where a parasited male presents the characteristics of a female, this analogy is due to the inhibitory influence exerted by the parasite on its host; the secondary sexual characteristics seem to be due to a dimorphism resulting from an inhibition in the female of corresponding characteristics that develop in the male alone; this inhibition, for example that which impedes the development of skin appendages, appears in parasitism).[37] In the reciprocal association of symbiosis, like that of an alga and a fungus, this double inhibition does not appear; here, the recurrent causality is positive, which leads to an increase in the capacities of the formed ensemble; lichens manage to thrive and prosper with a great luxuriance where no algae or fungus can, like on a smooth concrete block, exposed to frost and the intense sun in a dry atmosphere, subsisting between winter and summer in temperature differences of around 60°C and considerable differences in humidity.[38] We even encounter luxuriant lichens in the tundra, where the snow covers the ground for several months at a time. These kinds of associations also describe the relationship between the hermit crab ensconced in a shell and sea anemones that settle onto the shell; the anemones would have an influence on the crab's prey, either because they attract them with their lively colors or because they paralyze them with their stinging elements, thus facilitating capture for the hermit crab, which is not very mobile when it is in a shell. Moreover, and inversely, the scraps of the hermit crab's food are consumed by the sea anemones; this latter detail is more certain than that which concerns the usefulness of the anemones for the hermit crab. Nevertheless, we should note that the hermit crab has a tendency to put anemones on the shell it is sheltered in and, more generally, all objects, whether living or not, that it encounters with a lively color; in captivity, this crab grabs all the colored scraps of paper offered to it and positions them on its back; should this reflex be considered finalized? It is quite difficult to say, and yet it seems that the crab itself is what constitutes the association, perhaps through a mimetic behavior (this is how certain zoologists interpret the reflex that ensures that this crab positions lively colored objects onto its back), but it should be recognized in this case that mimicry is quite clumsy, because on a background of gray or black sand the crab allows itself to be covered with red or yellow, which makes it quite visible; in fact, it can be supposed without irrationality that the hermit crab constitutes this association, and that, once inserted into this cycle of causality (whatever the type of reflex or tropism may be that makes the crab act), the sea anemone develops due to conditions of life richer than the ones offered to it by the crab's food; lastly, we should note that here it is not a question of veritable parasitism; the sea anemone does not degenerate but on the contrary exhibits an outstanding development; indeed, it is nourished not due to the probosces or suckers that inhale the substance of its host but in a normal and habitual way; the proximity of the crab's claws and feelers merely puts it in a milieu richer in small assimilable debris; but it remains a separate individual without any physiological continuity with the crab. Furthermore, the crab does not utilize the substances elaborated by the sea anemone, which is on the shell that the crab dwells in, and yet it could be on any other shell or on a rock. Between the crab and the anemone, there is water and the shell, and this is why in this case we have a veritable society; each individual remains individual but modifies the milieu in which the two individuals live; the relation between the individuals that form a society is established by way of the exterior milieu, and this is why there is a great difference between the cases of parasitism and those of association in the regime of causality and the exchange of information. The regime of inter-individual causality is completely different. We should also note that an alga and a fungus associated as a lichen are, in fact, for one another elements of the exterior milieu and not of the interior milieu; following Schwendener's theory, the alga assimilates carbon through its chlorophyll, which is beneficial to the fungus, and the fungus protects the alga against desiccation by means of its filaments, which shelter it and allow it to live where it would have certainly died alone.[39] This relation of two beings that are an equivalent of the exterior milieu through one another can include different topological modalities but always with the same functional role; the thallus is differentiated from the apothecia; in certain species, the fungal filaments can be more concentrated in the periphery, constituting what is called the lichen's "cortex," while the center is the "medulla," and the intermediate region is what contains the gonidia, cells of green algae analogous to those of rocks and soil; this lichen is called heteromeric. On the contrary, in homomeric lichen, such as gelatinous lichen, the distribution of the fungal filaments and algae cells is homogeneous. Lastly, it should be noted that this association goes up to the reproductive elements, including both the algae and the fungus: the soredia contain both the cells of the algae and the filaments of the fungus; these fragments detach from the lichen and are used for its multiplication; in contrast, the fructifications seem to belong to the fungus alone: they are composed of a hymenium, as in ascomycetic fungi, whose cells are asci intermixed with other sterile cells (the paraphyses) and are where spores form. Here, the association constitutes like a second individuality that is superposed on the individuality of the beings that are associated without destroying this individuality; here, there is a reproductive system of society qua society and a reproductive system of the fungus qua fungus; the association does not destroy the individualities of the individuals that constitute it; on the contrary, the parasitic type of relation reduces the individuality of the beings; that of placentation is intermediate; it can evolve in one of two directions, both toward that of society as well as that of parasitism; furthermore, it is highly evolutive and, in this sense, is transformed; like parasitism, the association is static; it is important to note this aspect both in the case of stable states as well as in the case of placentation, i.e. the homophyseal parasitism that tends to become a temporary society. It seems in this sense possible to consider all forms of association as mixtures of parasitism and of the perfect society that ends in the formation of a veritable secondary social individuality, a compound like the one that appears in the algae-fungus grouping; there is no association exempt from a certain parasitism and thus from a certain regression that reduces the individuality of the beings grouped together; but, moreover, pure parasitism is rare, since it tends to destroy itself through a sort of internal necrosis it develops in the group within which parasitism takes place, making this group's level of organization fall to a very low level. The concrete group can be considered as intermediate between complete society and pure parasitism, where the level of organization that characterizes the group is the difference between that of the parasited and that of the parasite.

3. Individuation, Information, and the Structure of the Individual

A very important question that is yet to be posed is one that consists in knowing what the structure of individuality is: where does the organizing dynamism of the individual reside? Is it consubstantial with the individual? Or instead, is it localized in some of the fundamental elements that would regulate the ensemble of the individual organism? This is the question posed for all individuals and also particularly for those that undergo metamorphoses, which is a sort of reproduction of the being on the basis of itself, a reproduction without multiplication, a reproduction of unity and identity but without similarity during which the being becomes completely other while remaining an individual, which seems to show that individuality does not reside in self-resemblance and in the fact of not being modified, thus leading us to exclude the idea of an individuality fully consubstantial with the whole being.

The research conducted by biologists have borne either on the development of the egg (Dalcq's studies on the egg and its organizing dynamism) or on the metamorphoses of certain animals, particularly those of insects in which the passage through the nymph stage implies an important reorganization of the organism after a quite extensive dedifferentiation. In the first case, it seems that differentiation by far precedes the appearance of anatomically and cytologically distinct regions; in the stage of the division into macromeres and micromeres, an ablation of one part of the egg already produces the disappearance or atrophy of a particular part of the body, although we might think it would operate on a continuous mass: the continuum is already heterogeneous, as if a veritable polarity appeared in the egg barely beginning to be segmented. In the nymph, several "imaginal discs" direct the reorganization of a mass that has undergone a profound dedifferentiation. The individual structure can therefore be reduced to several elements starting from which it extends to the whole mass. This theory of "organizers" seems to indicate that living matter can be the basis of certain fields that are poorly known and that can neither be measured nor revealed by any currently known procedure; they can only be compared to the formation of crystals or rather crystalline figures in a supersaturated milieu or a milieu that is in other conditions favorable to crystallization;[40] but this case is not absolutely analogous, since the crystal is indefinite in its growth in principle, whereas the individual seems to have limits; truly speaking, the formation of crystals would instead be comparable to the growth of a colony, which doesn't develop in any specific direction and any specific way but according to directions that it favors during its development; there is an orientation at the basis of these two processes, a polarity that makes it such that the individual being is capable of growing and even reproducing with a certain polarity, i.e. analogically with respect to itself, based on its organizing germs, in a transductive way, insofar as this property of analogy is not exhausted; analogy relative to itself is characteristic of the individual being, and it is the property that allows us to recognize the latter.[41] There is a preparation of individuality every time that a polarity is created, every time that an asymmetrical qualification, an orientation, and an order appear; the condition of individuation resides in this existence of potentials that allow matter to be polarized, whether living or not; furthermore, there is a reversibility between the condition of polarity and the existence of potentials; every field makes polarities appear in initially non-oriented milieus, like a field of mechanical forces in a portion of glass, which modifies its optical properties, for example. However, until now, studies on the polarization of matter, as interesting and suggestive as they may be, have remained fragmentary and partially uncoordinated; an entire theory of polarization is to be made that would no doubt further clarify the rapports of what we call living matter (or organized matter) and inert or inorganic matter;[42] it indeed seems that non-living matter is already organizable and that this organization precedes any passage to functional life, as if organization were a sort of intermediate static life between inorganic reality and functional life properly speaking. The latter would be that in which a being reproduces itself, whereas in non-living matter the individual indeed produces effects on other individuals but does not generally produce individuals similar to it: the physical individual does not convey any other message than its own capacity to grow; it is not "hereditary substance," to use the expression by which Rabaud designates the living individual; thus, a photoelectron falling onto a target can emit secondary electrons, which are many from a single photoelectron; but these secondary electrons are not the descendants of the first electron or photoelectron; they are the descendants of other electrons emitted at the moment of the photoelectron striking against a metal plate (photomultiplier tubes) or against a molecule of gas (ionization chamber).

In these conditions, the individuality and origin of the first electron hardly matters; it can involve a photoelectron, but also a thermoelectron (thyratron) or an electron emitted by some other procedure, for example with the ionization of a gas (a Geiger counter): the result does not change for the emission of secondary electrons, and, for example, there is no way to discriminate the secondary electrons originating from the multiplication of the electrons of the dark current of an ionization chamber or of a photomultiplier from those that originate from veritable photoelectrons; there is no individual marking of electrons and not even a specific marking in terms of their origin, at least with the procedures of measurement at our disposal. On the other hand, this marking is possible in physiology, and it seems to constitute one of the profound characteristics of individuality linking the individual back to its particular genesis. Regeneration, which supposes an immanence of the organizing schema for each individual and a conservation within it of the dynamism by which it has been produced, does not seem to exist in physics; a sawed-off crystal does not regenerate when it is put back into a mother liquor; it continues to grow but without favoring the side that was amputated; on the contrary, a living being is activated or disturbed by a severance, and its growth occurs much more actively on the side of the amputation than on the surfaces that remain intact, as if the immanence of an organizing dynamism distinguished the surface that has undergone a severance.

Perhaps it is not possible to predict the point on which research would have to bear in order to clarify this relation between individuality and polarization; nevertheless, another aspect of the question is beginning to emerge that is different from the previous one but no doubt connected to it; a possible path of study is situated in the interval that separates these two directions and in the sector that they mark out without structuring it; this second research is the one that is preoccupied with determining the relation between quanta and life. The quantum aspect of physics is found in biology and is perhaps one of the characteristics of individuation; it could be that one of the principles of organization is a functional quantum law that defines the thresholds of the functioning of the organs and thus effectuates organization: the nervous system, whatever its degree of complexity may be, is not merely composed of an array of chemical conductors; between these electrochemical conductors there is a relational system on several levels, a systemics t hat presents characteristics of operation akin to what is called relaxation in physics and what is sometimes called in physiology the "all or nothing"; Anglo-American biologists and neurologists willingly use the expression *to fire* (to discharge like a gun) in order to characterize this operation, which supposes that a certain quantity of potential energy is accumulated and then exerts its effect completely and all of a sudden, not continuously. Not only do the different effectors appear to function according to this law, but the centers themselves, which are organized as an interconnection of relays that facilitate or inhibit one another, are regulated by this law. Thus, although in an organism everything is linked back to everything else physiologically speaking, various and structured regimes of causality can be established due to the laws of quantum functionalities. A quantity that does not reach a certain threshold is virtually null for all the relays that are temporarily at a certain level of triggering, and the message transmitted by this information is guided only down the paths where passage is possible with an operation of relays that have a threshold below the energetic level of the message considered; these characteristics of operation can furthermore be something besides the pure quantity of energy; a temporal modulation can intervene, for example a frequency, but certainly less universally than Lapicque would think at the time when he established the theory of synaptic relays with the notion of chronaxie. It would seem that this operation, which creates a structured regime of information in an individual, should require a preliminary morphological differentiation with a nervous system in particular. Yet, it could be precisely that quantum actions exerted on the level of the large molecules of organic chemistry find a facilitation or an inhibition in certain directions according to a law of thresholds based on the quantum properties of energy exchanges, and then there would be a root of organization as a heterogeneity of paths of exchange in a mass that is nevertheless continuous. Before any anatomical differentiation, the heterogeneously continuous supplies (through a slight quantity of energy) the first elements of a regime of the conditioning of the exercise of a greater quantity of potential energy, which is the starting point of a regime of information in a milieu and makes processes of amplification possible.

Perhaps the separation between the physical individual and the living individual could be established by means of the following criterion: information in the operation of physical individuation is not distinct from the supports of the potential energy actualized in the manifestations of organization; in this sense, there would be no remote relays without life; on the contrary, individuation in the living being would be founded on the distinction between the modulating structures and the supports of potential energy implied in the operations characterizing the individual; the structure and dynamism of relays would therefore be essential to the living individual; this is why according to this hypothesis it would be possible to define different levels in the regime of information for the physical individual and for the living individual: the living being is itself a modulator; it has a power supply in energy, an input or a memory, and an effector system; the physical individual requires the milieu as a source of energy and as an effector charge; the milieu supplies information, the received singularity.

IV. INFORMATION AND ONTOGENESIS

1. Notion of an Ontogenetic Problematic

The ontogenesis of the living being cannot be thought based on the notion of homeostasis alone, i.e. the perpetuation of metastable equilibrium through self-regulations. This representation of metastability could be suitable for describing a fully adult being that would merely maintain itself in existence, but it would not be sufficient for explaining ontogenesis.[43] This notion must be joined with that of an internal problematic of being. The state of the living being is like a problem to be resolved, to which the individual becomes the solution through successive assemblages of structures and functions. The young individuated being could be considered a system that carries information as pairs of antithetical elements linked together by the precarious unity of the individuated being whose internal resonance creates a cohesion. The homeostasis of the metastable equilibrium is the principle of cohesion that links these domains through an activity of communication and between which there is a disparation. Development could then appear as successive inventions of functions and structures that resolve, step by step, the internal problematic carried by the individual as a message. These successive inventions, or partial individuations which could be called stages of amplification, contain significations that ensure that each of the being's stages is presented as the solution of the previous states. But these successive and fractioned resolutions of the internal problematic cannot be presented as a nullification of the being's tensions. Gestalt theory, which uses the notion of equilibrium, supposes that the being seeks to discover its most stable state of equilibrium in the good form; Freud also thinks that beings tend toward a pacification of their internal tensions. In fact, a form is not a good form for the being unless it is constructive, i.e. unless it veritably incorporates the foundations of the previous disparation[44] in a systematic unity of structures and functions; an achievement that would merely be an unconstructive relaxation would not be the discovery of a good form but simply an impoverishment or a regression of the individual. What becomes a good form is that of the individual which is not yet individuated. Only death would be the resolution of all tensions; and death is not the solution to any problem. The resolving individuation is one that conserves the tensions in the equilibrium of metastability instead of nullifying them in the equilibrium of stability. Individuation makes tensions compatible but does not relax them; it discovers a system of structures and functions within which tensions are compatible. The equilibrium of the living being is an equilibrium of metastability, not an equilibrium of stability. Internal tensions remain constant as the cohesion of the being relative to itself. The being's internal resonance is the tension of metastability; it is what confronts the pairs of determinations between which there is a disparation that can only be significative through the discovery of a higher structural and functional ensemble.

It could be said that ontogenesis is a perpetuated problematic that rebounds from resolution to resolution up to complete stability, which is that of the adult form; however, complete maturation is not reached by all the functions and structures of the being at the same time; many paths of ontogenesis are pursued sometimes in parallel with an alternation of activity that makes it such that the process of growth affects one set of functions, then another, and then a third, after which it ultimately returns to the first; it seems that this capacity of resolving problems is limited to a certain extent and appears as an operation of the being on itself, an operation that has a systematic unity and cannot affect all the aspects of the being simultaneously. According to Arnold Gesell, the ontogenesis of living individuals manifests a process of growth founded on the coexistence of a principle of unity and a principle of duality. The principle of unity is that of the *direction of development,* which is revealed as a gradient of growth. Somatic and functional development is effectuated by a series of successive waves oriented according to the cephalocaudal axis, which is fundamental, and radiates from the different levels of this axis following the secondary proximodistal schema. This first principle of unity through the polarity of development is completed by that of lateral dominance: the bilateral symmetry of the body, and particularly that of the sense organs and neuromuscular effectors, does not prevent the existence of a functional asymmetry both in the development and in the anatomo-physiological symmetry. On the other hand, there is a principle of duality, that of the bilateral symmetry of the majority of the organs and that of the sense organs and of the effectors in particular. Somatic and functional development ("development of behavior," according to Gesell's expression) is effectuated according to a process of reciprocal intertwining that blends unity and duality through a sort of weaving that separates, keeps together, organizes, differentiates, relates, and structures the different somatopsychic functions and assemblages. Development is a behavior upon behaviors, a progressive weaving of behaviors; the adult being is a dynamic web, an organization of separations and reunifications of structures and functions. A double movement of integration and differentiation constitutes this structural and functional web. A progressive individuating maturation divides up increasingly detached and precise schemata within the global unity of reactions and attitudes. But this detachment of schemata of action is only possible to the extent that these schemata are individuated, i.e. are formed as a synergistic unity that structures many elements which could be separate. A precise and adapted movement is, with respect to the whole organism, in fact the result of an individuating maturation, but this individuating maturation cannot constitute a functional unity through pure analysis: the individuation of what Gesell calls a *pattern*[45] (structural and functional schema) does not originate from the mere analysis of a preexisting global whole, but also and simultaneously from a structuration that systematically integrates several functions. Each motion and each behavior implicate the whole body, but they are not obtained by the analysis and specialization of a global process that would implicitly contain them; the initial organismic unit does not act as the reservoir of all possible behaviors but as the power of cohesion, reciprocity, unity, and symmetry; maturation makes individuation possible, but individuation does not result from maturation. It is not a pure synthesis, a pure learning by way of the conditioning of responses entering into a natural and preformed relational schema. Development takes place through successive learning procedures, which are occasions for the integration of processes during the organism's maturation. The organism's relation to the world takes place through the self-regulating fluctuation of behavior, a schema of differentiation and integration more complex than learning through respondent conditioning alone. The resolution of the problems the individual bears takes place according to a process of constructive amplification.[46]

Gesell's description of human ontogenesis and the principles by means of which he interprets it extend, according to Gesell, the results of general embryology; these principles are not merely metaphorical and descriptive; according to the author, they translate a fundamental aspect of life. In truth, this duality, which is maintained by a unity manifested by the principles of bilateral symmetry and functional asymmetry, or better yet the direction of development and individuating maturation, is at the heart of the principle of ontogenesis in the chromosomal structure. Gesell cites Winch's theory according to which the chromosome is a *structure* constituted by two elements: long filaments of identical protein molecules, distributed parallel to one another, surrounded by groups of molecules of cyclized nucleic acid, all of which is interlinked like a weft. The symbol of the chain and of the weft could thus be invoked as the structural and functional foundation of development; ontogenesis would take place starting from the duality of the pairs of protein molecules. A hereditary characteristic would not be a predetermined element but a problem to be resolved, a pair of two distinguished and rejoined elements in a relation of disparation. The individuated being would therefore contain a certain number of disparation pairs that are generative of problematics. Structural and functional development would be a result of the resolution of problems: a stage of development is the solution to a problem of disparation; by way of the temporal dimension of the successive, which brings with it differentiation and integration, a stage of development supplies the unique signification within which the pair of disparate elements

constitutes a continuous system. Development is therefore neither pure analysis nor pure synthesis, nor a mixture of the two aspects; development is the
discovery of significations, the structural and functional *realization* of significations. In the form of pairs of disparate elements, the being contains an
implicit signification that is realized, discovered in development; but development is not merely an unfolding, an explication of characteristics contained
in a complete individual notion that would be a monadic essence. There is
no single essence of the individuated being, because the individuated being
is not substance, not a *monad*: its entire possibility of development comes to
it from what is not completely unified or systematized; a systematized being,
which has an essence just like a series has its reason, could not develop. The
being is not fully contained in its principle, or rather in its principles; the
being develops on the basis of its principles, but its principles are not given
in a system; there is no first essence of an individuated being: the genesis
of the individual is a discovery of successive *patterns* that resolve the incompatibilities inherent to the basic pairs of disparation; development is the discovery of the dimension of resolution, or better yet of signification, which is
the dimension not contained in the disparation pairs and due to which these
pairs become systems.[47] Thus, each retina is covered with a two-dimensional
image; the left image and the right image are disparate; they cannot overlap, because they represent the world seen from two different points of view,
which creates a difference of parallaxes and of field overlaps; certain details
hidden by a first field in the left image are, on the contrary, exposed in the
right image and vice versa, such that certain details only figure on a single
monocular image. However, a third image that would unify these two images
is not optically possible; they are disparate by essence and not superposable
in the axiomatic of bi-dimensionality. In order for them to make a coherence appear that incorporates them, they must become the foundations of a
world perceived from within an axiomatic in which the disparation (condition of impossibility of the direct two-dimensional system) precisely becomes
the index of a new dimension: there are no longer two images in the three-
dimensional world, but the system integrates two images, a system that exists
according to an axiomatic on a superior level to that of each of the images
but which is not contradictory relative to them. Tri-dimensionality integrates
bi-dimensionality; all the details of each image are present in the system of
significative integration; details that are concealed by the overlap of fields and
consequently only exist on a single image are retained in the system of integration and perceived completely, as if they belonged to both images; here,
we wouldn't be able to think of a process of abstraction and generalization

that would merely conserve in the perceptive signification what is mutual to the two separate retinal images: far from retaining what is mutual, perception retains everything that is particular and incorporates it into the whole; furthermore, it utilizes the conflict between two particulars in order to expose the superior system within which these two particulars are incorporated; the perceptive discovery is not a reductive abstraction but an integration, an amplifying operation.

Yet, it is possible to suppose that perception is not fundamentally different from growth and that the living being operates similarly in every activity. As an activity, growth is amplification via differentiation and integration, not a simple continuity or unfolding. In every complete vital operation, the two aspects of integration and differentiation are joined together. Thus, perception would not exist without the differential utilization of sensation, which is sometimes considered as a proof of subjectivity and a justification of the critique of the validity of a knowledge obtained from perception; sensation is not what contributes a confused continuum to the *a priori* of the perceiving subject and matter for the *a priori* forms; sensation is the differential play of the sense organs indicating a relation to the milieu; sensation is the capacity of differentiation, i.e. the apprehension of relational structures between objects or between the body and objects; but this operation of sensory differentiation can only be coherent with itself if it is made compatible by another activity, the activity of integration, which is perception. Sensation and perception are not two activities that follow one another, with the former providing matter to the latter; they are two twin and complementary activities, two versions of this amplifying individuation that the subject operates according to its relation to the world.[48] Furthermore, growth is not a separate process: it is the model of all vital processes; the fact that it is ontogenetic truly indicates its central, essential role, but this does not mean that there is not a certain ontogenetic coefficient in each of the being's activities. An operation of sensation-perception is also a relative and restrained ontogenesis; but it is an ontogenesis that effectuates itself by utilizing preformed structural and functional models: it is supported by the already existing living being and oriented by the content of memory and activated by instinctual dynamisms. All the functions of the living being are ontogenetic to some extent, not just because they ensure an adaptation to an external world, but because they participate in this ongoing individuation that life is. The individual lives to the extent that it continues to individuate, and it individuates by way of the activity of memory as well as the imagination or abstract inventive thought. In this sense, the psychical is vital, and it is also true that the vital is psychical, but on condition of understanding the *psychical* as the activity of the construction of systems of integration within which the disparation of pairs of elements takes on a sense. Adaptation, the particular case in which the disparation pair includes an element of the subject and a representative element of the external world, is an insufficient criterion for providing an account of life. Life includes adaptation, but for there to be adaptation, there must be an already individuated living being; individuation is anterior to adaptation, and the latter does not exhaust the former.[49]

2. Individuation and Adaptation

Adaptation is a correlate of individuation; it is only possible in accordance with individuation. The whole biologism of adaptation, upon which an important aspect of nineteenth-century philosophy depends and which persists in our day in the form of pragmatism, implicitly supposes the already individuated living being as a given; the processes of growth are partially set aside: this is a biologism without ontogenesis. In biology, the notion of adaptation represents the projection of the relational schema of thought with a dark zone between two clear terms, just like in the hylomorphic schema; furthermore, the hylomorphic schema itself appears in the notion of adaptation: the living being finds in the world certain forms that structure the living being; in addition, the living being gives form to the world in order to appropriate it for itself: adaptation, which is passive and active, is conceived as a complex and reciprocal influence based on the hylomorphic schema. However, since adaptation is taken for granted by biology as the fundamental aspect of the living being, it is quite natural that psychology and the poorly structured disciplines (which lack principles) have believed to borrow from biology a faithful and profound expression of life by utilizing the principle of adaptation in other domains. But if it were true that the principle of adaptation does not express vital functions in depth and does not account for ontogenesis, it would be necessary to reform all the intellectual systems founded on the notion of adaptation. It would be particularly advisable not to accept the consequences of Kurt Lewin's social dynamics, which represents a synthesis of German Gestalt theory and American pragmatism. Indeed, the personality is represented as the center of the tendencies; the milieu is essentially constituted by a goal toward which the being strives and by a set of forces opposed to the movement of the individual toward the goal: these forces constitute a barrier that exerts a reaction proportionate in strength to the intensity of the individual's action; consequently, the different possible attitudes are behaviors relative to this barrier that seek to attain the goal in spite of this barrier (for example, detour is one of these behaviors). Such a conception appeals to the notion of force fields; behaviors and attitudes are understood as possible pathways within these force fields, these *hodological* spaces; animals and children project a simpler hodological space than that of adult humans; each situation can be represented by the structure of the force field that constitutes it. However, this doctrine supposes that the essential activity of the living being is adaptation, since the problem is defined in terms of the opposition of forces, i.e. a conflict between the forces emanating from the subject oriented toward the goal and the forces emanating from the object (from the object for the living subject) as a barrier between subject and object. The discovery of a solution is a new structuration of the field that modifies the topology of this field. However, what seems to be lacking in the topological and hodological theory is a representation of the being as capable of operating successive individuations *within it*;[50] for the topology of force fields to be modified, a principle must be discovered, and the old configurations must be incorporated into this system; the discovery of significations is necessary for the given to be modified. Space isn't just a force field, and it isn't merely hodological. For the integration of elements into a new system to be possible, there must be a condition of disparation in the mutual relation of these elements; if elements are as heterogeneous as Kurt Lewin supposes, if they were opposites like a barrier that repulses and a goal that attracts, the disparation would be too great for a mutual signification to be discovered. Action, the individuation enveloping certain elements of the milieu and certain elements of the being, can only occur starting from nearly similar elements. Action isn't just a topological modification of the milieu; it modifies the very weft of objects and subject much more finely and delicately; what is modified is not the abstract topological distribution of the object and the forces: in both a global but more intimate and less radical way, the incompatibilities of disparation are overcome and integrated due to the discovery of a new dimension; the world before actions isn't just a world where there is a barrier between the subject and the goal; it is above all a world that does not coincide with itself, because it cannot be seen from a single point of view. The obstacle is indeed rarely just one object among objects; it is only such symbolically and for the needs of a clear and objectifying representation; in real lived experience, the obstacle is the plurality of ways of being present in the world. Hodological space is already the space of the solution, the significative space that integrates the various possible points of view into systematic unity, the result of an amplification. Before hodological space, there is this overlap of perspectives that does not allow for the apprehension of the determined obstacle, since there are no dimensions with respect to which the single ensemble would be organized. The *fluctuatio animi*[51] that precedes the resolute action is not a hesitation between several objects or even several paths, but an unstable collection of incompatible, almost similar, and therefore disparate, ensembles. The subject before action is caught between several worlds, between several orders; action is the discovery of the signification of this disparation, of that through which the particularities of each ensemble are integrated into a broader and richer ensemble, which has a new dimension. It is not by way of the dominance of one of the ensembles constraining the others that action manifests as organizing; action is contemporaneous with the individuation by which this conflict of planes is organized in space; the plurality of ensembles becomes a system. The schema of action is nothing but the subjective symbol of this new significative dimension that has just been discovered in the active individuation. Therefore, such an incompatibility can be resolved as a systematic signification by a schema of succession and conditioning. Action indeed follows paths, but these paths can only be paths because the universe becomes ordered by individuating: the path is the dimension according to which the life of the subject in the *here and now* is integrated into the system by individuating it and by individuating the subject: the path is simultaneously world and subject, it is the signification of the system that has just been discovered as a unity that integrates the different anterior points of view, the singularities borne. The perceiving being is the same as the acting being: action begins with a resolution of the problems of perception; action is the solution to the problems of the mutual coherence of perceptive universes; it takes a certain disparation between these universes for action to be possible; action is impossible if this disparation is too great. Action is an individuation above perceptions, not a function without links to perception and independent from it in existence: after perceptive individuations, an active individuation will give a signification to the disparations that appear between the universes resulting from perceptive individuations. The relation that exists between action and perceptions cannot be thought according to the notions of genus and species. Pure perception and pure action are the extreme terms of a transductive series oriented from perception toward action: perceptions are partial discoveries of significations that individuate a limited domain with respect to the subject; action unifies and individuates perceptive dimensions and their content by finding a new dimension, that of action: in fact, action is this course that is a dimension, a manner of organizing; the paths do not preexist action: they are the very individuation that makes a structural and functional unity appear in this conflictual plurality.[52]

The notion of adaptation is poorly formed to the extent that it supposes the existence of terms as preceding that of relation; what deserves to be critiqued is not the modality of relation such as the theory of adaptation envisions it; what deserve to be critiqued are the very conditions of this relation coming after the terms. The theory of active adaptation according to Lamarck nevertheless presents an important advantage over that of Darwin: it considers the activity of the individuated being as playing an extremely important role in adaptation; adaptation is an ongoing ontogenesis. However, Lamarck's doctrine does not make enough room for this conditioning via the problematic aspect of vital existence. The striving of the living being is not simply conditioned by needs and tendencies; in addition to needs and tendencies, which have an individual and specific origin, there appear ensembles in which the individuated being is engaged by perception and which are not compatible with these needs and tendencies according to their internal dimensions. In both Darwin and Lamarck, there is the idea that the object is object for the living being, a constituted and detached object that represents a danger or a food or a refuge. In the theory of evolution, the world relative to which perception takes place is a world already structured according to a unitary and objective system of reference. Yet it is precisely this objective conception of the milieu that creates the notion of adaptation. There is not merely a food object or a prey object but a world pursuant to the search for nourishment and a world pursuant to the avoidance of predators or a world pursuant to sexuality. These perceptive worlds do not coincide but are nevertheless not that different from one another; they have some elements that belong to each (objects designated as predator, prey, mate, food), just as monocular images each possess several fringes that belong to each image.[53] Adaptation is a resolution to a superior degree that must engage the subject as the bearer of a new dimension. The objective dimensions are adequate for each perceptive universe: three-dimensional space pairs together two disparate two-dimensional images. But different perceptive universes cannot be reduced to a system of a superior dimensional axiomatic according to a principle of objectivity; the living being consequently enters into the axiomatic by supplying it with a new condition that becomes a dimension, i.e. action, the course, the succession of phases of the rapport to the objects that modifies the latter; the hodological universe integrates disparate perceptive worlds in a perspective that makes the milieu and the living being mutually correlative according to the being's becoming in the milieu and the milieu's becoming around the being. The very notion of milieu is misleading: there is only a milieu for a living being that manages to integrate perceptive worlds in a unity of action. The sensory universe is not given all at once: there are nothing but sensory worlds waiting for action so that they can become significative. Adaptation creates the milieu and the being relative to the milieu, the being's paths; before action, there are no paths, there is no unified universe within which the directions and intensities of forces can be indicated in order to find a result: the physical paradigm of the parallelogram of forces is not applicable, for it supposes a single space, i.e. dimensions valid for this single space, axes of reference valid for every object that is in this field and for every movement that will take place there. In this sense, Gestalt theory and its extension via the work of Kurt Lewin's dynamic Field Theory are retroactive representations: it is easy to explain action when the being is given in a single structured milieu; but action is precisely the condition of the coherence of the axiomatic by means of which this milieu is singular: Adaptation theory, Gestalt theory, and the dynamics of fields reject, before action and in order to explain it, what action creates and conditions; these three doctrines suppose a structure of action before action to explain action: they suppose the problem resolved; however, the problem of the living being's action is precisely the problem of the discovery of compatibility. This problem is a problem of individuation to a superior degree. It cannot be resolved by means of notions which, like that of the stable state, suppose preliminary axiomatic coherence. What is common to the three notions of adaptation, good form, and hodological space is the notion of stable equilibrium. However, stable equilibrium, that which is realized when all potentials are actualized in a system, is precisely what supposes that there is no incompatibility, that the system is perfectly unified because all possible transformations are realized. The system of stable equilibrium is one that has attained the highest degree of homogeneity possible. It cannot explain action to any extent, for it is the system within which no transformation is possible, since all potentials have been exhausted: it is a dead system.

To account for the activity of the living, we must replace the notion of stable equilibrium with that of metastable equilibrium, and we must replace the notion of good form with that of information; the system in which the being acts is a universe of metastability; the preliminary disparation between perceptive worlds becomes a condition of structure and operation in a state of metastable equilibrium: the living being is what maintains, transposes, prolongs, and sustains this metastable equilibrium through its activity. The complete universe only exists so long as the living being enters into the axiomatic of this universe; if the living being is removed or disengaged, the universe breaks down into perceptive worlds of new disparates. The living being, which enters among these perceptive worlds to transform them into a universe, amplifies the singularity it bears. Perceptive worlds and the living being individuate together into a universe of vital becoming.[54]

Only this universe of vital becoming can be grasped as a veritable total system; but it is not given all at once; it is the meaning of life, not its condition or origin. Goldstein has indeed indicated the meaning of this systematics of the whole; but, by treating it as an organismic unity, he has been forced to a certain extent to take it as a principle and not as a meaning: whence the Parmenidean aspect of his conception of being: the whole is given at the origin, such that vital becoming is difficult to grasp as an effective dimension of this systematics. The structure of the organism would be understood better at the level of perceptive worlds in Goldstein's theory than at the level of activity properly speaking. Holistic dominance is at the beginning, such that totality is the totality of the living being, rather than the totality of the universe including the living being inserted through activity into the perceptive worlds that have taken on a meaning for the becoming of this activity. Sensory systems are difficult to think in their relative distinction; however, the structural and functional distinction of the senses is the basis for action, insofar as they are a basis for the significations residing in the pairs of forms that are the only ones starting from which information can exist. Sensibility, the plurality of sensations, therefore cannot be unified under a global function, since this plurality is the foundation for future significations as a plurality of points of contact based on which significations will be possible during the course of further individuations.

3. Limits of the Individuation of the Living. Central Characteristic of the Being. Nature of the Collective

This theory does not suppose that all vital functions merge together and are identical; but it tends to designate all these functions by the operation of individuation that they carry out; thus, individuation would be a much more general and widespread operation than what is usually considered as an individuation. The fact that the living being is a separate individual in the majority of species is nothing but the consequence of the operation of individuation; ontogenesis is an individuation, but it is not the only individuation that is carried out in the living being or that takes the living being as a basis and incorporates it.[55] To live consists in being agent, milieu, and element of individuation. Perceptive, active, and adaptive behaviors are aspects of the fundamental and perpetuated operation of individuation that constitutes life. According to such a conception, in order to think the living being, life must be thought as a transductive result of operations of individuation or, better yet, as an interlinking of successive resolutions, insofar as each previous resolution can be taken back up and reincorporated in subsequent resolutions. In this sense, we could consider that life in its entirety seems like a progressive construction of increasingly elaborate forms, i.e. forms capable of containing increasingly elevated problems. The vital axiomatic is complicated and enriched through evolution; evolution is not a perfecting properly speaking but an integration, the maintenance of a metastability that increasingly settles on itself and thereby accumulates potentials and assembles structures and functions. Individuation as generative of perishable individuals submitted to aging and to death is only one of the aspects of this generalized neotenizing vital individuation that incorporates an increasingly rich axiomatic. In fact, the individual as a limited being submitted to the *here and now* and the precariousness of its isolated condition expresses the fact that it remains something unsolvable in the vital problematic; it is because life is the resolution of problems that it remains something residual, a detritus that cannot take on signification, a remainder after all the operations of individuation. What remains in the old being is what has been unable to be integrated, the unassimilated. From the ἄπειρον [ápeiron] before individuation to the ἄπειρον[56] after life, from the undetermined of the before to the undetermined of the after, from the first dust to the last dust, an operation is carried out that does not break down into dust; life is in its present, in its resolution, not in its remainder. And death exists for the living being in two senses that do not coincide: it is hostile death, that of the rupture of metastable equilibrium, which is only maintained through its own functioning and its capacity of ongoing resolution: this death construes the very precariousness of individuation, its confrontation with the conditions of the world, the fact that it is engaged and takes risks and cannot always succeed; life is like a posed problem that may not be resolved or may be resolved badly: the axiomatic collapses in the very course of the resolution of the problem: a certain risk or happenstance from outside therefore exists in every life; the individual is not self-enclosed, and there is no destiny contained in it, for what it resolves is simultaneously the world and itself, the system of the world and itself.

But death also exists for the individual in another sense: the individual is not pure interiority: it is burdened with the weight of the residues of its operations; it is passive by itself; it is to itself its own exteriority; its activity

weighs it down, charges[57] it with an unusable indetermination, an indetermination in stable equilibrium whose nature is exhausted, deprived of potentials, and can no longer be the basis for new individuations; the individual
little by little takes on elements of stable equilibrium that charge it and prevent it from going toward new individuations. The entropy of the individuated system increases throughout the successive operations of individuation,
particularly in those that are not constructive. The results of the past that lack
potential accumulate without becoming the seeds for new individuations;
this heatless dust and this unenergized accumulation are the rise of passive
death within the being, a death which does not originate from confronting
the world but from the convergence of internal transformations. It can nevertheless be wondered if aging is not the counterpart of ontogenesis. Tissues
cultivated *in vitro* and transplanted frequently enough to never yield large
masses live indefinitely; it is generally said that these tissues owe their unlimited longevity to the fact that transplantation prevents the accumulation of
toxic waste products within the ensemble of the living matter. But it can also
be noted that transplantation always maintains the portion of living tissue in
a state of undifferentiated growth; as soon as the portion is large enough, it
differentiates, and the differentiated tissues die after a certain period of time;
however, differentiation is a structuration and a functional specialization; it
is the resolution of a problem, whereas the undifferentiated growth of frequently transplanted tissues takes place before any individuation on the
level of the portion: perpetual transplantation always brings the tissue back
to the same point in its evolution as an ensemble that can be the support
of an individuation. The tissue's longevity is no doubt due to this absence
of individuation: there is an iteration of the growth process, an externally
provoked iteration. The fact that a large enough ensemble differentiates and
dies seems to show that every differentiation leaves behind a certain residue
that cannot be eliminated and places a burden on the individual, thereby
diminishing the chances for future individuations. Aging is indeed this lesser
capacity of renewal, as studies on the healing of wounds show; the individual that is structured and specializes its organs or its automatic habitual frameworks becomes increasingly less capable of recreating new structures if the
old ones are destroyed. It's as though the majority of initial potentials proceeded by diminishing and the inertia of the being proceeded by increasing:
the being's viscosity increases through the effects of individuating maturation.[58] This increase in inertia, rigidity, and viscosity is apparently compensated by the increasingly pronounced richness of the acquired arrangements,
i.e. of adaptation; but adaptation is precarious in the sense that if the milieu

is modified, new problems may not be resolved, and then the previously elaborated structures and functions will encourage an unfruitful iteration. In this sense, the fact that the individual is not eternal seems like something that should not be considered accidental; life in its entirety can be considered a transductive series; death as the final event is nothing but the consummation of a process of amortization that is contemporary with each vital operation insofar as they are operations of individuation; every operation of individuation deposits death in the individuated being, which is therefore progressively charged with something it cannot eliminate; this amortization is different from the degradation of the organs; it is essential to the activity of individuation. The being's inborn indetermination is little by little replaced by the indetermination of the past, deprived of tension, a pure inert charge; the being goes from the plurality of initial potentials to the indistinct and homogeneous unity of ultimate dissolution across successive structurations of metastable equilibria: individuated structures and functions make the two indeterminations between which life is inserted communicate.

If the individual has a meaning, it is certainly not just in terms of the being's tendency to persevere in its being; the individual being is transductive, not substantial, and the being's tendency to persevere in its being seeks the equivalence of a substantialization, even if the individual is only composed of modes. In fact, the meaning of the living being cannot be found in its unconditional integration into the species; the species is a reality that is as abstract as the individual would be if it were taken as substance. Between the substantialization of the individual being and its absorption in the superior continuum of the species—wherein it is like the leaves of a tree, according to the expression that Schopenhauer has taken up from Homer (Οίηπερ φυλλων γενέη, τοινδε καί ανδρῶν [the race of men is related to that of leaves])[59]— there is a possibility of grasping the individual, insofar as it is limited, as one of the sides of essential vital individuation; the individual is a transductive reality; through the span of its active existence in the temporal dimension, it increases life's capacity to solve problems; the individual bears an axiomatic or rather a dimension of the vital axiomatic; the evolution of individuation— this binding of a functional structuration and of an amortization paired together and constituting each active and perceptive operation—transforms the individual into a being that translates potentials which are incompatible with one another into metastable equilibria that can be maintained by means of successive inventions. Like any transductive series, the individual's existence must be grasped within its milieu in order to be comprehended in its full reality; the complete individual is not merely the being that goes from its birth to its death: it is essentially the *being of maturity*, with the status of existence that is between two extremes and that gives meaning to the two extremes; birth and death and then ontogenesis and destruction (which are anabolic processes and catabolic processes) are extremes relative to the center of maturity; the real individual is the mature individual, the median individual. The individual continues in maturity, not by again becoming eternally young or by transmutating beyond an ultimate death; the individual corresponds to its function most fully in its center of existence via these individuations that resolve the world and resolve the individuated being. Young and old, the individuated being is isolated; mature, it is structured in the world and structures the world within it. The structures and functions of the mature individual link it back to the world and insert it into becoming; significations are not like individuated beings: they are not contained or enclosed in an individual circumference that will degrade; only realized significations, the paired structures and functions of the mature individual, surpass the *here and now* of the individuated being; the mature individual, the one that resolves perceptive worlds into action, is also the one that participates in the collective and creates it; the collective exists as the individuation of the charges of nature transported by individuals. What accumulates this translation of the structures and functions elaborated by the individuated being is not just the species as a phylum but also the collective unity of the being.[60] It could be said that a second birth in which the individual participates is that of the collective, which incorporates the individual itself and constitutes the amplification of the schema it bears. The individual is translated into the collective as an effectuated signification, as a resolved problem, as information: it is therefore prolonged across and above but not within its individual enclosure. With respect to this discovered signification, the individual is itself in the *here and now*, a progressive amortization, a detritus, and it incrementally detaches from the movement of life. The individual is neither complete nor substantial; the individual has no meaning except in individuation and through individuation, which deposits it and stores it as much as assumes it by way of participation. Individuation does not merely occur in the individual and for it; it also occurs around it and above it. The individual is translated through its center of existence, converted into signification, perpetuated in information, whether implicit or explicit, vital or cultural, thereby waiting on successive individuals to reach maturity and resume the signs of information left behind by their predecessors: the individual encounters life in its maturity: entelechy is not merely internal or personal; it is an individuation in accordance with the collective. Lucretius represents living beings as relay runners that pass on torches; this is no doubt how he understands the flame of life given at birth; but this can also be understood as what is passed on to the interior of the collective, recreated and renewed through time by successive individuals. For species in which complete and distinct individuals do not exist, this inactuality[61] of young and old never forms to the same extent; the colony or vital ensemble circulates a perpetual actuality in the different parts of the being. In superior species, accentuated ontogenesis and its correlate in old age phase-shift the individual from one end to the other with respect to this actuality of the collective: the individuated being is not in phase with life properly speaking except in its maturity. And this is precisely the resolution of the problem that only the individuation of separate beings can achieve: the colony is fixed in its perpetual actuality; it cannot detach from itself or phase-shift from end to end relative to its present; it can only react and develop according to continuity. Life, which discovers ontogenesis and aging through the invention of the separated individual, creates this end-to-end phase-shift of each individuated being relative to the collective and to the actual.[62] The mode of being of the collective of individuals differs from the perpetual present of the colonies of primitive living beings due to the fact that it is the encounter of individual becomings in a present that dominates the advance of youth and the delay of old age and incorporates them into a real entelechy. The collective finds and realizes the signification of these two temporal decenterings that constitute the forward phase-shift of growth and the backward phase-shift of aging. The collective, the functional equivalent of the colony, is the signification of the two inverse and contradictory aspects of ontogenesis and destruction, which are incompatible in the individual. The individual finds the signification of perceptive disparations through action. By way of this superior analogue of action that is presence, the collective finds in the individual's signification of disparation the pair of anabolic processes and catabolic processes, of ontogenesis and degradation, a pairing of the ascent toward existence and of the descent toward the definitive stability of the equilibrium of death. The definitive and only metastability is that of the collective, since it is perpetuated without aging throughout successive individuations. Inferior species may not involve separate individuality: metastability can be immanent to the individual, or instead it can traverse the whole imperfectly portioned into individuals. In superior species, the permanence of life is also found on the level of the collective; but it is found there at a superior level; it is rediscovered there as signification, as the dimension within which the ascent and degradation of the individuated being is integrated; the collective is borne by the maturity of individuals, a maturity that is the

superior dimension relative to which youth and old age are organized and
that is not a transitional state between youth and old age; the individual is
mature to the extent that it is integrated into the collective, i.e. to the extent
that it is simultaneously old and young, *prior to* and *coming after* relative to
the present, thereby containing within itself both future potentials and traces
of the past. Maturity is not a state but a signification that integrates the twin
anabolic and catabolic sides of life. The individual finds its meaning in this
phase-shift via which it offers the bi-dimensionality of time (coming to be
then passing away, swelling with potentials toward the future, then being
insularly structured in the past) to the integration of the collective; with the
present, the collective is the resolution of the incompatible bi-dimensionality
within the individual in accordance with the tri-dimensionality that coheres
in the present. This is because there is a great difference between the future
and the past as they are for the separate individual, and the future and the
past as they are in the three-dimensional system of collective presence. The
future and the past become dimensions *through the presence of the present*;
before the individuation of the collective, the future is the isolated signification of anabolic processes, and the past is the isolated signification of catabolic processes. These two processes do not coincide: relative to one another,
they are disparate and yet paired together, for each action implies both the
one and the other. In the collective, individual action takes on a meaning
because it is present. The present of the collective is comparable to the third
dimension of space for perception; the future and the past of the individual
find a coincidence in this dimension and are organized there into a system due
to an axiomatic of a superior degree. The individual bears within it the conditions of temporal depth, but not this dimension of depth; alone, it would
be held between its future and its past, which means that it would not be
fully living. For any vital signification to be found, the temporal duality of
the individual must be organized according to the tri-dimensionality of the
collective. In the collective, the pairing of the future and the past becomes
signification, for the individuated being is recognized as integrated: it is
integrated not only according to its future or its past, but according to the
direction of the condensation of its future and its past: the individual is present in the collective, it *is unified in the present* through its action. The collective is not a substance or a form anterior to the individuated beings that
would compel them, penetrate them, or condition them: the collective is the
communication that envelops and resolves individual disparations as a presence that is the synergy of actions, the coincidence of futures and pasts as
an internal resonance of the collective. Indeed, collective synergy supposes

a unity that creates a domain of transductivity from what is not yet individuated within each individual being, something which could be called the charge of nature associated with the individuated being; the collective is that in which an individual action has a meaning for other individuals as a symbol: each action presented to the others is a symbol of the others; it belongs to a reality that individuates into totality as capable of involving the simultaneous and successive plurality of actions.

The collective is not merely the reciprocity of actions: within it, each action is signification, insofar as each action resolves the problem of separate individuals and is constituted as a symbol of other actions; the synergy of actions is not merely a *de facto* synergy, an interdependence that ends in a result; it is due to the fact that it is structured as symbolic of the others that each action has this capacity of making the individual past coincide with the individual present. In order for the dimension of presence to exist, it requires not only several individuals gathered together: it also requires this union to be inscribed in their own dimensionality and requires that, within them, present and future be corelative of the dimensions of other beings through this unity of the present; the present is that in which there is signification, that through which a certain resonance of the past toward the future and of the future toward the past is created: the exchange of information from one being to another passes through the present; each being becomes reciprocal with respect to itself to the extent that it becomes reciprocal with respect to the others. Intra-individual integration is reciprocal with transindividual integration. The category of presence is also the category of the transindividual. A structure and a function exist both in individuals and from one individual to another, without them being able to be defined as merely external or internal. This relation between individuals and through individuals expresses the fact that individuals are amplified in a vaster reality via the intermediary of something that is a problematic tension within them, i.e. information: this reality can be called the pre-individual charge within the individual. Action, the resolution of perceptive pluralities into a dynamic unity, implies the intervention of this pre-individual reality: the being qua pure individuated being has nothing within it to go beyond perceptive worlds in their plurality. The individual being would remain incompatible with itself if it had nothing but perception, and it would have nothing but perception if there were nothing available to resolve these problems than what the being is, qua individuated individual, as the result of an anterior operation of individuation. The being must be able to appeal within it and outside it to a not yet individuated reality: this reality is the information that it contains relative to a pre-individual real: this charge is the very principle of the transindividual; it communicates directly with other pre-individual realities contained in other individuals, just as the links of a network communicate with one another by each link being surpassed in the following link.[63] Participating in an active reality within which it is nothing but a link, the individuated being acts in the collective: action is this networked exchange between the individuals of a collective, an exchange that creates the internal resonance of the system formed in this way. The group can be considered as substance with respect to the individual, but only in an inexact fashion. Indeed, the group is reached starting from the charge of pre-individual reality of each of the grouped individuals; the group does not directly incorporate individuals but their charges of pre-individual reality: it is through the latter, and not as individuated individuals, that beings are included in the transindividual relation. The transindividual is that which (in non-provisional individuals) is equivalent to the transformation of provisional beings used for genetic transfer into colonies or to the seed's development into a plant.

4. From Information to Signification

It could then be questioned how we should represent the function of individuation when it develops in the living being. It would be necessary to be able to define a notion that would be valid for thinking individuation in physical nature as well as in living nature and, afterwards, for defining the internal differentiation of the living being that extends its individuation by separating vital functions into physiological and psychical functions. However, if we take up again the paradigm of technological form-taking, we find a notion that seems to be able to pass from one order of reality to another due to its purely operative nature, which is not linked to any particular matter and is only defined relative to an energetic and structural regime: the notion of information. Form, for example the rectangular parallelepiped, does not act on matter directly; it does not even act after being materialized as the parallelepipedic mold; the mold only intervenes as a modulator of the energy that bears the clay in a particular way at a particular point; the mold is the bearer of information signals; the form must be translated into information signals to be able to effectively encounter the matter when it is originally external to the latter. Individuation is a modulation. Yet the notion of information is delivered separately by certain technologies, known as information technologies, on whose basis information theory has been built. But it is difficult to extract a univocal notion of information from these multiple technologies in which the notion of information is utilized and which have led to the usage of quantities. Indeed, the notion of information appears in two almost contra-dictory ways. In the first case, information, as Norbert Wiener says, is what is opposed to the degradation of energy or the increase of entropy in the system; it is essentially negentropic. In a system in which all possible transformations would have been effectuated, in which all potentials would be actualized, no other transformation would be possible; nothing would be distinguished from anything else. Thus, in the transmission of a message, information is what is opposed to the general flattening of energy modulated by the signal; it is what guarantees that it is possible to distinguish in a Morse code transmis-sion between the moment when the current passes and the moment when the current does not pass. If during the course of the system's electrical iner-tia of transmission *(self-inductance)*[64] the current is established very slowly and diminishes very slowly, it becomes impossible to discern whether the cur-rent passes or not, or whether we are dealing with a dash, a dot, or an inter-val between a dot and a dash; the information signal is the decision between two possible states (for example, current or non-current in the aforemen-tioned case); to transmit a message in Morse code clearly, one must manipu-late slowly enough at the start so that, despite the inertia of the apparatus, the signals are still distinct to the receiver, i.e. so that one can clearly distinguish the moments of the current passing and the moments without a current, the indecisive periods of establishment and rupture remaining brief relative to the total duration of a sign or an interval between signs. The information signal provides the decision among possibilities in this first sense; it supposes a possible variety of states, non-confusion, and distinction. It is opposed in particular to background noise, i.e. to what occurs randomly, like the thermal agitation of molecules; when the energetic medium of the signal is essen-tially discontinuous, like an electrical current consisting of elementary charges in transit, each element of the signal must modulate a large number of ele-mentary units of carried energy in order for the message to be transmitted correctly; an electronic tube of small dimensions has a higher background noise than one with large dimensions, since it allows less electrons to pass per unit of time; in order not to be inconvenient, this quantum discontinuity due to the type of carried energy in use must remain extremely inferior to the significative variations that have a meaning for the transmission of infor-mation. The information signal is therefore the capacity to decide, and the "quantity of information" that can be transmitted or registered by a system is proportionate to the number of significative decisions that this system can transmit or register. In this sense, a fine-grained photographic emulsion has a power of resolution greater than that of a coarse-grained emulsion; for the same unreeling speed of the recording head and playback head, a fine-grained magnetic strip can register the sound more faithfully by reproducing the high-pitched sounds and the harmonics of the low-pitched sounds (which is analogous to fine details for photography).

In this sense the information signal is what is not predictable and what sections off the predictable to the point that the energy that conveys this signal or the supports that record it must have states that, compared to the order of magnitude of the information signal (long or wide according to the case), can be considered as predictable, such that the unpredictability of the states of the support or of the modulated energy does not interfere with that of the information signal. If we wanted to transmit a background noise considered as a signal by means of an apparatus that already has a background noise, it would be necessary that the background noise belonging to the system of transmission be extremely slight relative to the background noise to be transmitted as a signal. An area of fine, very flat, and uniformly lit sand is very difficult to photograph: the grain of the photographic film must be much smaller than the average magnitude of the image of a grain of sand on the film, or else the granulation of the developed film could equally be due to the image or to the grain of the film: decision, which is characteristic of the information signal, will no longer exist. One cannot duplicate the image of the grain of a photographic film by means of the same type of film; a more fine-grained film must be used.

However, in another sense, information is what implies regularity and periodic occurrence, i.e. predictability. The more easily predictable the signal is, the more easy it is to transmit; thus, when an oscillator has to be synchronized by means of another oscillator, the more the oscillators are stable on their own, the easier it is to synchronize one of the oscillators by means of the other: even if the synchronization signal is very weak and almost on the same level as the background noise, it is possible to receive this signal without error by means of the phase comparison apparatus, which supposes that the time during which the receptive oscillator is sensitive to the signal is extremely reduced within the total duration of a period. That is because in this case the signal is not just emitted or transmitted by the modulation of an energy: it is also received by an apparatus that has its own operation and that must integrate the information signal within its own operation by making it perform the role of effective information: the information signal is not merely what is to be transmitted without a deterioration caused by the background noise and the other aspects of chance and the degradation of energy; it is also *what must be received*, i.e. take on a signification and have an effectiveness for an ensemble that has its own operation. Since the problems related to information are problems of transmission in general, the only aspects of information retained and submitted to technological evaluation are those related to the non-degradation of signals during transmission; the problem of the signification of signals is not posed, since the non-degraded signals have upon arrival the signification that they would have had at the point of departure if they had not been transmitted but delivered directly; the human subject is the receiver at the end of the transmission relay, just as it would be if there were no distance separating it from the origin of the signals. In contrast, the problem is quite different when the signals are not simply technologically transmitted but also technologically received, i.e. received by a system endowed with its own operation and which must integrate them into this operation. It is then seen that the physical dimensions relative to the *transmission* of signals and those relative to their *signification* are antagonistic. Signals are transmitted better when they merge less with the uniformization of the predictable; but in order for signals to be received and integrated into the operation of a system, they must present an analogy as perfect as possible with those that could be emitted by the receptive apparatus if it were used as an emitter; they must be almost predictable; two oscillators synchronize more easily when the signals emitted by one and by the other are closer in frequency and in form (sinusoidal signals, relaxed signals, sawtooth waves, pulse trains). This possible aspect of reciprocity is illustrated by the coupling of oscillators: when two oscillators allowed to radiate a part of their energy are brought closer to one another, they mutually synchronize in such a way that it can only be said that one guides the other; they no longer form anything but a single oscillating system. In addition to the quantity of information signals transmissible by a given system, one must therefore consider their aptitude for being received by a receptive apparatus; this aptitude cannot be expressed directly in terms of quantity. It is also difficult to call it quality, since quality seems to be an absolute property of a being, whereas here it is a question of a relation; a certain modulated energy can become information signals for a defined system and not for some other system. This aptitude of information, or rather what founds this aptitude, could be called the haecceity of information: the latter is what makes it such that *this* is information and received as information, while *that* is not received as information;[65] the term quality is overly indicative of generic characteristics; that of haecceity overly particularizes and shuts into a concrete characteristic what a relational aptitude is. It is only important to indicate that this relational aptitude is attached to the schema of the predictability of information signals; in order for signals to take on a meaning in a system, they must not contribute anything entirely new to it; a set of signals is only significative on a background that almost coincides with it; if signals expose the local reality exactly, they are no longer information but merely an external iteration of an internal reality; if they differ from it too much, they are no longer grasped as having a meaning, are no longer significative, and cannot be integrated. In order to be received, signals must encounter the *preliminary forms* with respect to which they are *significative*; signification is relational. This condition for the reception of information signals could be compared to what creates the binocular disparation in depth perception. In order for the relief and layering of fields in depth to be effectively perceived, it merely requires the image formed on the retina of the left eye to be different from the image formed on the retina of the right eye; if the two images are completely independent (like when we look at one side of a sheet of paper with one eye and the other side with the other eye), no image appears, because then there is no point in common; the two images must not be superposable, but their difference must be slight and they must be able to become superposable by means of a certain number of actions fractioned on a number of finite planes corresponding to simple laws of transformations. Relief intervenes as a signification of this duality of images; the duality of images is neither felt nor perceived; only the relief is perceived: it is the meaning of the difference of the two givens. In the same way, for a signal to receive a signification not only in a psychological context but also in an exchange of signals between technical objects, there must be a disparation between a form already contained in the receiver and an information signal provided from the outside. If the disparation is null, the signal corresponds to the form exactly, and the information, as a modification of the state of the system, is null. On the contrary, the more the disparation increases, the more the information increases, but only up to a certain point, for beyond certain limits and depending on the characteristics of the receiving system, information becomes null abruptly when the operation through which disparation is assumed qua disparation can no longer be carried out. By increasing the gap between the lenses in a stereoscopic shoot, the impression of relief and the successive staggering of fields are increased, since the disparation is increased (this apparatus is also used for direct observation at a distance: the sights are produced by means of two periscopes whose lenses can be separated as far apart as desired, which ends up increasing the gap between both eyes): but if the gap between the lenses exceeds a certain limit (which is variable with the real gap between the first field and the second field), the subject perceives two different images that blur together, with a fleeting dominance sometimes for the left eye, sometimes for the right eye, in an indefinite instability of perception that no longer conveys information as a staggering of the fields and relief of objects. Similarly, a synchronizable oscillator that receives signals strictly of the same frequency as the local oscillation and without any phase difference does not receive any signal properly speaking, since there is an absolute coincidence of the local operation and the external operation translated by the signals. If the difference of frequency increases, information grows due to the effectively integrated signals; but if the received signals have a frequency that is too different from the local frequency, there is no longer any synchronization; signals are no longer utilized as mediums of information and can be nothing more for the oscillator than what amount to irregular external disturbances (feedback or background noise, the electronic noise of thermal agitation). The condition of frequency is fundamental, but there are other conditions that can be reduced to the following: the integration of signals into a functioning system is easier when the distribution of energy in a single period of the signal is more closely related to the distribution of energy in local exchanges; thus, a relaxation oscillator is more easily synchronized by the steep-front impulse voltages originating from another relaxation oscillator than by a sinusoidal signal of the same frequencies as the impulses. We can call *signal* that which is transmitted, *form* that with respect to which the signal is received in the receiver, and *information* properly speaking that which is effectively integrated into the functioning of the receiver after the experience of disparation involving the extrinsic signal and the intrinsic form. A recording of information is in fact a determination of signals, not a veritable recording of information; the magnetic strip or photographic film records signals as a set of local states but without an experience of disparation; the magnetic strip or the film then must be used as a secondary source of signals in front of a veritable receiver that will or will not integrate them according to the existence or nonexistence within it of adequate forms for the experience of disparation; the magnetic strip must be reactualized as signals, and the photographic film must be exposed to light; the film then modulates the light point by point in the same way the photographed objects modulated the film. If the disparation between two external signals is necessary for perception, the recording must deliver two sets or series of signals separately: it takes two separate photographs to produce the perception of depth, and it takes two tracks on the magnetic strip to produce depth of sound. This necessity of two truly separate recordings shows that the recording conveys *signals* but not directly integrable *information*: disparation is not made and cannot be made, since it is not on the level of signals and does not give rise to a *signal* but to a *signification,* which only has meaning in an operation; an operating receiver is required for disparation to take place; what's needed is a system with structures and potentials. The conditions for the good transmission of signals should no longer be confused with a system's conditions of existence. The signal does not constitute relation.

5. Topology and Ontogenesis

To this day, the problem of the rapports between life and inert matter has primarily focused on the difficulty concerning the fabrication of living matter from inert matter: the properties of life have been situated in the chemical composition of living substances; many synthetic bodies have been elaborated since the synthesis of urea; not only can chemical synthesis produce rather small molecular bodies from catabolic transformations, it can also produce bodies that participate directly in anabolic functions. Nevertheless, there is still quite a gap between the production of substances utilized by life and the production of the living being: to say that we are getting closer to life, we would need to produce the topology of the living being, its particular type of space, the relation between a milieu of interiority and a milieu of exteriority. The bodies of organic chemistry do not bring with them a different topology than that of the usual physical and energetic relations. However, perhaps the topological condition is primordial in the living being qua living being. There is no evidence that we can think the living being adequately by way of Euclidean rapports. Perhaps the space of the living being isn't a Euclidean space; the living being can be considered in Euclidean space, where it is then defined as one body among other bodies; the very structure of the living being can be described in Euclidean terms. But nothing proves that this description is adequate. If there were a set of topological configurations necessary for life and if they were untranslatable into Euclidean terms, then every attempt to make a living being with the matter elaborated by organic chemistry would have to be considered insufficient: perhaps the essence of the living being is a certain topological arrangement that cannot be known based on the physics and chemistry that typically use Euclidean space.

Currently, we can do nothing but remain content with conjectures in this domain. It is nevertheless interesting to observe that the properties of living matter manifest more as the maintaining and self-sustaining of certain topological conditions than as pure energetic or structural conditions. In this sense, one of the properties at the basis of all the functions—be it the conduction of nerve impulses, muscular contraction, or assimilation—is the polarized asymmetrical nature of cellular permeability. The living membrane, which is anatomically differentiated or merely functional when no particular formation materializes its limit, is characterized as what separates a region of interiority from a region of exteriority: the membrane is polarized and therefore allows the passage of some particular body centripetally or centrifugally while blocking the passage of some other particular body. No doubt the mechanism of this permeability can function in a single direction for a definite type of chemical substance; this is how we have explained the activation of the muscles through the intermediary of the neuromuscular junction by an unleashing of acetylcholine, which momentarily breaks down the potential of the polarized membrane; but this just pushes the problem back, since the membrane is living precisely in the sense that it always repolarizes, as if it were, according to Gellhorn's expression, a "sodium-potassium pump" that recreates the polarization of the membrane after functioning; an inert membrane would very quickly be reduced to the neutral state in its functioning as a selective membrane; on the contrary, the living membrane conserves this property; it regenerates this characteristic asymmetry of its existence and functioning. It could be said that the living substance within the membrane regenerates the membrane but that the membrane is what guarantees that the living being is alive each moment insofar this membrane is selective: it is what maintains the milieu of interiority as a milieu of interiority relative to the milieu of exteriority. It could be said that *the living being lives at the limits of itself, on its limit*; in a simple and unicellular organism, there is a direction toward the inside and a direction toward the outside relative to this limit. In a multicellular organism, the existence of the interior milieu complicates topology in the sense that there are several stages of interiority and exteriority; thus, an endocrine gland empties the products of its activity into the bloodstream or some other organic liquid: the typical organism's interior milieu is in fact a milieu of exteriority relative to this gland. Likewise, the intestinal cavity is an exterior milieu for the assimilating cells that perform selective absorption within the intestinal tract. According to the topology of the living organism, the interior of the intestines is in fact exterior to the organism, even though within this space a certain number of transformations conditioned and controlled by the organic functions are performed; this space is an annexed exteriority; thus, if the contents of the stomach or the intestines are harmful to the organism, the coordinated movements that aid in expulsion will empty these cavities and evacuate into the completely exterior (independent) space the harmful substances that were in the exterior space annexed to the interiority. Similarly, the progression of chyme is regulated by the different successive degrees of the biochemical activities of this chyme, which is controlled by interoceptors that are in fact sense organs that would more appropriately be called medioceptors, since they apprehend an information relative to the exterior annexed space and not relative to veritable interiority. We therefore find various levels of interiority in an organism; the space of the digestive cavities is a space of exteriority with respect to the blood that floods the intestinal walls; but the blood in turn is a milieu of exteriority with respect to the endocrine glands that empty the products of their activity into the blood. It can therefore be said that the structure of a complex organism is not just integration and differentiation; it is also this establishment of a transductive mediation of interiorities and exteriorities going from an absolute interiority to an absolute exteriority through different mediators of relative interiority and exteriority; organisms could be classified according to the number of mediations of interiority and exteriority that they utilize to carry out their functions. The simplest organism, which can be called elementary, is the one that does not possess a mediate interior milieu but merely an absolute interior and an absolute exterior. For this organism, the characteristic polarity of life is on the level of the membrane; it's here that life essentially exists as an aspect of a dynamic topology that itself maintains the metastability through which it exists. Life is the self-sustaining of a metastability, but this metastability requires a topological condition: structure and function are linked together, since the deepest and most initial vital structure is topological. The structure of integration and differentiation only appears in complex organisms with the appearance of the nervous system and the distinction between sense organs, effectors, and neural centers; this non-topological structure of integration and differentiation appears as a means of mediation and organization in order to support and extend the first structure, which remains not only subjacent but also fundamental. Thus, we do not grasp the structure of the organism when we start from the organismic unity of the complex ensembles of evolved organisms, since we run the risk of attributing a privilege to the organization of integration and differentiation. We can no longer account for the veritable structure of the living being by considering the cells that compose a complex organism, according to the atomistic method, as architectonic units of this organism. The totalizing vision and the elementary vision are equally inadequate; we have to start with the basic function that depends on the first topological structure of interiority and exteriority, and then we have to see how this function is mediated by a chain of intermediary interiorities and exteriorities. At the two ends of the chain, there is still the absolute interior and the absolute exterior; the functions of integration and differentiation are in the function of metastable asymmetry between absolute interiority and absolute exteriority. This is why living individuation must be thought according to topological schemata. Furthermore, topological structures are those by means of which the evolving organism's spatial problems can be resolved: thus, the development of the neocortex in superior species essentially occurs through a folding of the cortex: this is a topological solution, not a Euclidean solution. It is then understood why the cortical homunculus is nothing but a very approximate representation of the cortical areas of projection: projection in fact converts a Euclidean space into a topological space, such that the cortex is not adequately represented in a Euclidean fashion. All things considered, we should not speak of projection for the cortex, even though there is, in the geometrical sense of the term, projection for the small regions; we should say: a conversion of Euclidean space into topological space. The basic functional structures are topological; the corporeal schema converts these topological structures into Euclidean structures through a mediate system of relations that is the very dimensionality of the corporeal schema.

If living individuation is a process that essentially unfolds according to topological structurations, then it is understood why the borderline cases between inert matter and the living being are precisely cases of processes that unfold according to the dimensions of exteriority and interiority. These cases include the individuation of crystals. The difference between the living being and the inert crystal consists in the fact that the interior space of the inert crystal does not serve to keep extending the individuation carried out at the limits of the crystal undergoing growth: there is only interiority and exteriority from one molecular layer to another, from an already deposited molecular layer to a layer about to be deposited; a crystal could be deprived of an important part of its substance without stopping its growth; the interior is not homeostatic in its entirety relative to the exterior or, more exactly, relative to the limit of polarity; in order for the crystal to individuate, it must continue to grow; this individuation is superficial; the past doesn't serve a purpose in the crystal's mass; it merely plays a role of bare support and does not provide the availability of an information signal: the succession of time is not condensed. Conversely, in the living being the space of interiority with its content plays a role for the perpetuation of individuation throughout the whole being; there is and can be resonance because what has been produced by individuation in the past belongs to the content of the interior space: the whole content of the interior space is topologically in contact with the content of the exterior space at the limits of the living being; indeed, there is no distance in topology; the whole mass of living matter in the interior space is actively present to the exterior world at the limit of the living being: all the products of the past individuation are present immediately and without distance. The fact of belonging to the milieu of interiority does not merely signify "being inside" in the Euclidean sense but being on the interior side of the limit without a delay in functional efficacy, without isolation, without inertia. The living being doesn't just interiorize by assimilating; it condenses and presents everything that has been elaborated in the successive: this function of individuation is spatiotemporal; in addition to a topology of the living being, it would be necessary to define a chronology of the living being associated with this topology, which would be as elementary as it and as different from the physical form of time as topology is different from the structure of Euclidean space. In the same way that there are no distances in topology, in chronology there is no quantity of time. This in no way means that the time of vital individuation is continuous, as Bergson claims; continuity is one of the possible chronological schemata, but it is not the only one; schemata of discontinuity, contiguity, and envelopment can be defined in chronology as well as in topology. Whereas Euclidean space and physical time cannot coincide, the schemata of chronology and of topology are applicable to one another; they are not distinct, and they form the first dimensionality of the living being: every topological characteristic has a chronological correlate, and vice versa; thus, for living substance, the fact of being within the interior of the selective polarized membrane means that this substance has been held in the condensed past. The fact that a substance is in the milieu of exteriority means that this substance can come forth,[66] put itself forward for assimilation, and possibly breach or harm the living individual: the substance is to come [à venir]. The interior past and the exterior future confront each other at the level of the polarized milieu: this confrontation in the operation of selective assimilation is the present of the living being, which is formed by this polarity of passage and obstruction between past substances and substances to come that are present to one another via the operation of individuation; the present is this metastability of the rapport between interior and exterior, past and future; the exterior is exterior and the interior is interior relative to this mutual allagmatic activity of presence. Topology and chronology coincide in the individuation of the living being. It is only later on and according to psychical and collective individuations that the coincidence can be broken. Topology and chronology are not a priori forms of sensibility, but the very dimensionality of the living being undergoing individuation.

We would therefore need a word to designate this initially singular dimensionality that later splits into a separate temporal dimensionality and a separate spatial dimensionality. If not only this word but also the set of unified representations allowing for it to have a precise meaning existed, it would perhaps be possible to think morphogenesis, to interpret the signification of forms, and to understand this first relation of the living being to the universe and to other living beings that can be understood neither according to the laws of the physical world nor according to the structures of the complicated psyche; even before sensorimotor structures, there must be chronological and topological structures, namely the universe of tropisms, tendencies, and drives; the psychology of expression, which is still too detached and arbitrary albeit grounded in its research, would perhaps find a path for axiomatization in a similar topological and chronological research.

Furthermore, this type of research could perhaps allow us to understand why there are intermediary processes between those of the inert world and those of the animate world, like the formation of crystallizable viruses, such as, for example, the mosaic virus of tobacco. This virus develops like a living being within the sap of the plant: it assimilates, because if the tobacco plant is inoculated with a certain quantity of this virus, the quantity of virus increases; after extracting sap from the plant and then crystallizing the virus, we obtain a greater quantity of crystallizable virus. In contrast, when this virus is crystallized, nothing allows us to say that it is alive: it is no more alive than hemoglobin or chlorophyll. If chemical bodies are found that are capable of assimilating into the state of the solution without requiring a crystalline germ in a supersatured or supercooled solution, a part of the gap that separates living processes from physicochemical processes would be bridged. The case of viruses indeed seems to be intermediary between the two orders of processes; however, it should be noted that the mosaic virus of tobacco only assimilates into a living milieu; the potentials of the living plant can therefore be utilized by the virus, a virus which in this sense would not be veritably alive if its activity of assimilation is in reality a borrowed activity sustained and nourished by the plant's activity. The problem has not been resolved to this day: it can just be said that it would certainly be necessary to consider this problem as implying a formation of an axiomatic according to chronology and topology and not merely according to physicochemical knowledge. The study of elementary operations does not imply an atomism. It is regrettable that the holistic systematics of biologism, such as it is presented by Goldstein, is conceived necessarily as macrophysical and is fixated on the totality of a complex organism. Goldstein's Parmenidean ontology prevents any relation between the study of the living being and the study of inert beings, whose processes are microphysical. There can be an intermediary order of phenomena between fragmentary microphysics and the macrophysical organismic unit; this order would be that of genetic, chronological, and topological processes, i.e. processes of individuation belonging to all the orders of reality in which ontogenesis takes place: an axiomatic of ontogenesis remains to be discovered, at least if this axiomatic is definable. It could be that ontogenesis is not able to be axiomatized, which would explain the existence of philosophical thought as perpetually marginal with respect to all other studies, since philosophical thought is what is driven by the implicit or explicit research of ontogenesis in all orders of reality.

CHAPTER TWO

Psychical Individuation

I. Signification and the Individuation of Perceptive Units

1. Segregation of Perceptive Units; the Genetic Theory and the Theory of Holistic Grasping; Determinism of Good Form

From the outset, a problem of individuation can be defined relative to perception and knowledge taken in their totality. Without prejudging the nature of perception, which can be considered as an association of elements of sensation or as the grasping of a figure on a ground, it is possible to contemplate how the subject perceives separate objects and not a confused continuum of sensations and how it perceives objects as having an already given and consistent individuality. The problem of the segregation of units is solved neither by associationism nor by Gestalt psychology, since the former does not explain why the individualized object possesses an internal coherence, a substantial bond that gives it a veritable interiority that cannot be considered the result of association. Habit, which is then invoked to guarantee the coherence and unity of perception, is in fact a dynamism that can communicate to perception only what it possesses by itself, namely this temporal unity and continuity inscribed in the object as a static unity and static continuity of the *perceptum*. Associationism, which is the genetic theory of pure appearance, involves the recourse to habit (or, more indirectly, a link of resemblance or analogy, i.e. a dynamism grasped statically) and in fact borrows from a hidden innatism. Association alone via contiguity was not able to explain the internal coherence of the object individualized in perception. The latter would remain a mere accumulation of elements without cohesion, without mutual attractive force, and these elements would remain *partes extra partes* relative to one another. But the perceived object doesn't merely have the unity of a sum or a result passively constituted by a "*vis a tergo*," i.e. habit and the series of repetitions. Far from being passive, the perceived object has a dynamism

The Individuation of Living Beings

that allows it to transform without losing its unity; it has not only a unity but also an autonomy and a relative energetic independence that renders it a system of forces.

Gestalt theory has replaced the genetic explanation of the segregation of perceptive units with an innatist explanation: unity is grasped immediately by virtue of a certain number of laws (like the laws of pregnancy or of good form), and this psychological phenomenon shouldn't be surprising, insofar as the living world with its organisms and the physical world in general manifest phenomena of totality.[1] Seemingly inert matter contains the virtuality of forms. A supersaturated solution or a liquid in a state of supercooling will allow crystals to appear whose form is predestined in the amorphous state. However, Gestalt theory leaves an important problem up for debate, which is precisely that of the genesis of forms. If form were truly given and predetermined, there would be no genesis, plasticity, or uncertainty relative to the future of a physical system, an organism, or a perceptive field; but this is precisely not the case. There is a genesis of forms just as there is a genesis of life. The state of entelechy is not fully predetermined in the bundle of virtualities that precede it and preform it. What Gestalt theory and associationism both lack is a rigorous study of individuation, i.e. this critical moment when unity and coherence appear. A veritable sense of totality forces us to assert that Gestalt theory does not consider the *absolute ensemble*. In the physical world, the absolute ensemble is not just the solvent and the dissolved body; it is the solvent, the dissolved body, and the ensemble of forces and potential energies characterized by the word metastability, which is indicative of the state of the supersaturated solution at the moment when crystallization takes place. In this moment of metastability, there is no determinism of "good form" that can sufficiently predict what occurs: phenomena such as epitaxy show that at the critical instant (the moment when the potential energy is maximum) there is a sort of relative indetermination of the result; the presence of the smallest external crystalline germ, even the presence of another chemical species, can then initiate crystallization and orient it. Before the appearance of the first crystal, there is a state of tension that leaves a considerable amount of energy available for the slightest local accident. This state of metastability is comparable to a state of conflict in which the instant of highest uncertainty is precisely the most decisive instant, the source for determinisms and genetic sequences that find their absolute origin in this instant. In the living world, a genesis of forms also takes place that supposes a calling into question both of prior forms and their adaptation to the vital milieu. Not

every transformation can be considered a genesis of form, because a transformation can also be a degradation. When crystals form, erosion, abrasion,
crumbling, and calcination modify the crystal's form, but they are not in
general geneses of form; some consequences of the form generated during
crystallization can remain, such as, for example, the privileged directions of
the cleavage due to the crystal's reticular structure, which consists of a large
number of elementary crystals; but then we are observing a degradation of
form and not a genesis of forms. In the same way, not all the transformations
of a living species can be interpreted as geneses of forms. There is a genesis
of forms when the relation of a living ensemble to its milieu and to itself
passes through a critical phase rich in tensions and virtuality, a phase that
ends with the disappearance of the species or the appearance of a new lifeform. The situation in its entirety is constituted not only by the species and
its milieu, but also by the tension of the ensemble formed by the relation of
the species to its milieu wherein the relations of incompatibility become
increasingly strong. Moreover, the species isn't the only thing that is modified, for the entire ensemble of the vital complex formed by the species and
its milieu also discovers a new structure. Finally, in the psychological domain,
the ensemble in which perception takes place—and which, following Kurt
Lewin, can be called the psychological field—is constituted not just by the
subject and the world, but also by the relation between the subject and the
world. Lewin indeed says that this relation, with its tensions, conflicts, and
incompatibilities, is integrated into the psychological field. But, according to
our theory, this is precisely where Gestalt theory reduces to two terms what
is an ensemble of three independent, or at the very least distinct, terms: it is
only after perception that tensions are effectively incorporated into the psychological field and become part of its structure. Before perception, before
the genesis of the form that perception precisely is, the relation of incompatibility between the subject and the milieu only exists as a potential, similar
to the forces that exist in the phase of metastability of the supersaturated
solution or the supercooled solid, or even in the phase of metastability of the
relation between a species and its milieu. Perception is not the grasping of
a form but the resolution of a conflict, the discovery of a compatibility, the
invention of a form. This form that perception is modifies not only the relation between the object and the subject, but also the structure of the object
and the structure of the subject. Like all physical and vital forms, it is susceptible to degrading, and this degradation is also a degradation of the whole
subject, because each form is part of the subject's structure.

2. Psychical Tension and Degrees of Metastability. Good Form and Geometrical Form; the Different Types of Equilibrium

Perception would therefore be an act of individuation comparable to those in physics and biology. But for us to be able to consider perception in this way, we must introduce a term that could be called "psychical tension" or, better yet, degree of metastability, because the first expression has already been used to designate a reality that is quite different, insofar as it does not begin with the notion of crisis. Consequently, the laws of good form are not enough to explain the segregation of units in the perceptive field; indeed, they don't consider how a solution to a problem arises from perception. These laws apply for the transformation and degradation of forms more so than their genesis. In particular, many laboratory experiments that use a fairly relaxed, perfectly secure subject do not produce the conditions under which the genesis of forms takes place. We should note the ambivalent characteristic of the notion of "good form." A form like the circle or the square easily emerges from a web of incoherent lines upon which it is superimposed as an image. But, in spite of their simplicity, is the circle or square superior to a form invented by an artist? If this were true, the most perfect column would be a cylinder. On the contrary, according to da Vignola's *Orders,* the most perfect column is a rotating figure that is both narrowed down and reduced at both ends as well as non-symmetrical relative to its center, with the largest diameter situated below the middle of its height. The author of this work considers the proportions he gives to be the result of a veritable invention that was unachievable for the Ancients. The ancient architects also thought of themselves as inventors, and Vitruvius shows how the three classical orders were successively invented under conditions in which the prior forms were inadequate. It is necessary to establish a distinction between *form* and *information*; a form like the square can be quite stable (pregnant) and contain a small quantity of information, in the sense that it can only very rarely incorporate different elements of a metastable situation; it is difficult to discover the square as a solution to a perceptive problem. The square or the circle, or more generally all simple and pregnant forms, are structural schemas rather than forms. It may be that these structural schemas are innate, but they are not enough to explain the segregation of units in perception; the human figure with its friendly or hostile expression and the form of an animal with its typical external characteristics are just as pregnant as the circle or the square. In his work *Animal Forms and Patterns,* Portmann notes that the perception of a lion or a tiger does not fade away, even if it takes place only once and in a

young child. This supposes that the simple geometrical elements do not matter much: it would be very difficult to define the form of the lion or tiger and
the patterns of their skin using geometrical figures. In reality, there is a relation between a very young child and an animal that does not seem to borrow
from the "good forms" of perceptive schemata: the child shows an astonish-
ing aptitude for recognizing and perceiving the different parts of the body
in animals he sees for the first time, even though the very slight similarity
between the human form and the form of these animals forces us to rule out
the hypothesis of an external analogy between the human form and animal
forms. What is in fact engaged in this perception is the corporeal schema of
the child in a situation deeply suffused with fear or sympathy. What is structured into a perception of the animal's corporeal schema is the tension (the
degree of metastability) of the system formed by the child and the animal in
a determined situation. Here, perception grasps not just the form of the object,
but its orientation within the ensemble, its polarity, which determines whether
it is lying down or standing on its legs, whether it stands tall or takes flight,
and whether it adopts a hostile or trusting attitude. If there were no preliminary tension (potential), perception wouldn't be able to produce a segregation of units that is simultaneously the discovery of the polarity of these
units. The unit is perceived when the reorientation of the perceptive field
can be effectuated in line with the object's own polarity. To perceive an animal is to discover the cephalocaudal axis and its orientation. To perceive a
tree is to see in it the axis that goes from its roots to the end of its branches.
Every time the tension of the system cannot be resolved into a structure, into
an organization of the subject's polarity and of the object's polarity, an uneas-
iness remains that habit is hard pressed to destroy, even if every threat has
been removed.[2]

3. Relation between the Segregation of Perceptive Units and the Other Types of Individuation. Metastability and Information Theory in Technology and Psychology

The psychological problem of the segregation of perceptive units indicates a
fact that had been perfectly revealed by the founders of Gestalt theory: individuation is not a process restricted to a single domain of reality, for example that of psychological reality or physical reality. This is why any doctrine
is insufficient if it limits itself to privileging a field of reality in order to turn
it into the principle of individuation, whether it be the domain of psychological reality or that of material reality. It may even be possible to say that
there is individualized reality only in a mixture. In this sense, we will attempt

to define the individual as transductive reality. By transductive reality, we mean that the individual is neither a substantial being like an element, nor a pure rapport, but the reality of a metastable relation. There is no veritable individual except in a system in which a metastable state occurs. If the appearance of the individual makes this metastable state disappear by reducing the tensions of the system in which it appears, the individual becomes in its entirety a motionless and non-evolving spatial structure: the physical individual. On the other hand, if this appearance of the individual does not destroy the system's potential of metastability, then the individual is a living being, and its equilibrium is that which maintains metastability: in that case, it is a dynamic equilibrium, which generally supposes a series of new successive structurations, without which the equilibrium of metastability could not be maintained. A crystal is like the fixed structure left by an individual that lived for a single instant, the instant of its formation, or rather the instant of the formation of the crystalline germ around which successive layers of macroscopic crystalline network have clustered. The form that we encounter is merely the vestige of individuation that was already achieved in a metastable state. The living being is like a crystal that would maintain an ongoing metastability around it and in its relation to the milieu. This living being can be endowed with an indefinite life, as in certain extremely elementary forms of life, or on the contrary it can be limited in its existence because its own structuration is opposed to the upkeep of an ongoing metastability of the ensemble formed by the individual and the milieu. Little by little the individual loses its plasticity, its capacity to render situations metastable, to turn them into problems with multiple solutions. It could be said that the living individual increasingly structures within itself and therefore tends to repeat its previous conditions as it moves further from its birth. In this sense, the limitation of a lifespan is not absolutely linked to individuation; it is merely the consequence of very complex forms of individuation, wherein the consequences of the past are not eliminated from the individual and provide it with an instrument for resolving future difficulties and also with an obstacle for accessing new types of problems and situations. The successive characteristic of learning, the utilization of successiveness in the fulfillment of different functions, provides the individual with superior possibilities of adaptation but requires an internal structuration of the individual that is irreversible and forces it to conserve within itself, along with the schemata discovered in past situations, the determinism of these very situations. Only an individual whose transformations would be reversible could be considered immortal. From the moment the functions of the succession of behaviors and the temporal sequences of acts appear, an irreversibility that specializes the individual becomes the consequence of this appearance of temporal laws: for each *type* of organization, there is a threshold of irreversibility beyond which all progress made by the individual (every acquired structuration) is a chance of death. Only beings with a superficial innervation and a barely differentiated structure have no limit to their lifespan. These beings are generally also the ones for which it is the most difficult to determine the limits of the individual, particularly when several individuals live in clusters or symbiotically. The degree of structural individuality, which corresponds to the notion of a limit, to that of a boundary of one being with respect to other beings or to that of an interior organization, is consequently to be put on the same level as the characteristic of temporal structuration that involves irreversibility, even though the former is not the direct cause of the latter; the common origin of these two aspects of the individual's reality seems to be in fact the process according to which metastability is conserved or increased in the individual's relation to the milieu. The essential problem of the biological individual would thus be relative to this characteristic of the metastability of the ensemble formed by the individual and the milieu.

The physical problem of individuality is not just a problem of topology, for what topology lacks is the consideration of potentials; precisely because they are potentials and not structures, potentials can be represented as graphical elements of the situation. The situation in which physical individuation arises is spatiotemporal insofar as it is a metastable state. Under these conditions, physical individuation (and more generally the study of physical forms) involves a theory of metastability that contemplates the processes of exchange between spatial configurations and temporal sequences. This theory can be called allagmatics. Allagmatics must be related to information theory, which contemplates the translation of temporal sequences into spatial organization or vice versa; yet, since it proceeds on this point like Gestalt theory, information theory instead contemplates already given sequences or configurations and can hardly define the conditions of their genesis. On the contrary, what must be contemplated is absolute genesis, like the mutual exchanges of forms, structures, and temporal sequences. Such a theory could then become the shared foundation of information theory and Gestalt theory in physics. These two theories in fact cannot be used in the study of the individual because they employ two mutually incompatible criteria. On the one hand, Gestalt theory privileges the simplicity and pregnancy of forms; on the contrary, the quantity of information defined by information theory rises with the number of decisions involved; corresponding to an elementary mathematical law, the more predictable the form, the easier it can be transmitted with a small quantity of signals. On the contrary, what is hard to transmit and requires an elevated quantity of information is anything that avoids all monotony and stereotypy. The simplification of forms, the elimination of details, and the increase of contrasts correspond to a loss in the quantity of information. However, the individuation of physical beings is neither assimilable to simple geometrical good form nor to the high quantity of information understood as a large number of transmitted signals: it consists of two aspects (form and information) joined together in a unity; no physical object is merely a good form, but, moreover, the cohesion and stability of the physical object are not proportional to its quantity of information, or more exactly to the quantity of information signals that must be utilized to correctly transmit a knowledge to its subject. Whence the necessity of a mediation; the individuation of the physical object is neither that of the pure discontinuous (like the rectangle or the square) nor that of the continuous, i.e. structures that require almost an infinite number of information signals to be transmitted.

4. Introduction of the Notion of Quantum Variation into the Representation of Psychical Individuation

It seems that a research path can be discovered in the notion of quantum. Subjectively, it is possible to quite paradoxically increase the quantity of useful signals by introducing a quantum condition, which in fact diminishes the system's veritable quantity of information within which there is information. Thus, by increasing the contrast of a photograph or a television image one enhances the perception of objects, although one loses information in the sense of information theory.[3] What humans perceive in objects when they grasp them as individual is therefore not an indefinite source of signals, an inexhaustible reality, like matter, which allows itself to be analyzed indefinitely; what they perceive is the reality of certain thresholds of intensity and of quality maintained by objects. If it were pure form or pure matter, the physical object would be nothing; if it were an alliance of form and matter, it would merely be a contradiction; the physical object is an organization of thresholds and of levels maintained and transposed throughout various situations; the physical object is a bundle of differential relations, and its perception as individual is the grasping of the coherence of this bundle of relations. A crystal is an individual not because it possesses a geometrical form or an ensemble of elementary particles, but because all of its (optical, thermal, elastic, electrical, piezo-electrical) properties undergo an abrupt variation when we pass from one facet to another; without this coherence of a multitude of properties with highly variable values, the crystal would be nothing but a geometrical form associated with a chemical species and not a veritable individual. Hylomorphism here is radically insufficient, since it cannot define this characteristic of unified plurality and pluralized unity consisting of a bundle of quantum relations. This is why at the very level of the individual the notion of polarity is prominent; without it, the unity of these quantum relations could not be understood. Moreover, it could be that this quantum condition allows us to understand why the physical object can be perceived directly in its individuality: an analysis of physical reality cannot be separated from a reflection on the very conditions of knowledge.

5. The Perceptive Problematic; Quantity of Information, Quality of Information, Intensity of Information

It is necessary to define more precisely what can be understood by quantity of information and by form. Two fairly different senses are presented by information theory and Gestalt theory. Gestalt theory defines good forms by pregnancy and simplicity: the good form, the one that has the capacity to impose itself, prevails over forms that have less coherence, clarity, and pregnancy. Thus, the circle and the square are good forms. By contrast, information theory responds to an ensemble of technical problems which are contemporary with the usage of low currents in the transmission of signals and in the usage of the different modes of the recording of light and sound signals. When a scene is recorded via photography, film, tape recorder, or video tape, the overall situation must be decomposed into a set of elements that are recorded by a modification imposed upon a very large number of physical individuals ordered according to a spatial, temporal, or mixed (i.e. spatiotemporal) organization. Photography can be taken as an example of spatial organization: in its active part, a photographic surface, which is the support of signals, is constituted by an emulsion that contains a multitude of silver grains in the basic form of a chemical combination. If the optical system were supposed as perfect and given that the optical image is projected onto this emulsion, we obtain a more or less accentuated chemical transformation of the chemical combination that constitutes the emulsion; but the capacity of this emulsion to record small details depends on the fineness of the particles: the translation of a continuous optical line into chemical reality within an emulsion is constituted by a discontinuous trail of sensible grains; the rarer and coarser these grains are, the more difficult it is to pin down a small detail with sufficient fidelity. Examined under a microscope, an emulsion that should reveal new details (if it had a continuous structure) shows nothing but an unformed mist of discontinuous grains. What is known as an emulsion's degree of definition or resolving power can thus be measured by the number of distinct details capable of being recorded on a determined surface; for example, on a current type of emulsion, one square millimeter can contain five thousand distinct details.

On the other hand, if we consider a sound recording on a covered strip of magnetic iron oxide coating, on steel wire, or on disc, here we see that the order becomes an order of succession: the distinct physical individuals whose modifications translate and transmit the signals are oxide grains, steel molecules, or clusters of plastic ordered in a line that unreels in front of the air gap of a polarized electromagnet or under the sapphire or diamond of a turntable. The quantity of details that can be recorded per unit of time depends on the number of distinct physical individuals that unreel during this unit of time in front of the place where the recording is carried out: the details engraved on a disc must be smaller than the order of magnitude of the molecular chains that constitute the plastic; furthermore, frequencies cannot be recorded on a magnetic tape when the number of details (particles magnetized to variable degrees) is larger than the number of particles; lastly, the variations of a magnetic field cannot be recorded on a steel wire whose sections are too small to receive a magnetization particular to each one. If we attempt to go beyond these limits, the sound would coincide with the background noise constituted by the discontinuity of the elementary particles. On the contrary, if an adequately high unreeling speed is adopted, this background noise is pushed back into the higher frequencies; this noise corresponds quite exactly to the indistinct fog of silver grains that appears when a photograph is examined under a microscope;[4] the sound is recorded as a series of particle masses that are more or less magnetized or arranged in a groove, similar to the way photography consists of a juxtaposition and distribution of more or less concentrated silver grain masses. The limit to the quantity of signals is in fact the discontinuous characteristic of the information support, i.e. the finite number of distinct representative elements organized according to space or time and in which information finds its support.

Ultimately, when a movement is to be recorded, the two types of signals (the spatial and the temporal) enter into a sort of conflict, such that one type of signal can be obtained only by partially sacrificing the others and such that the result is a compromise: cinematography or television can be used to break movement down into fixed images or to transmit it; in both cases, temporal sequences are cut into a series of snapshots that are then successively fixed or transmitted; in television, each separate view is transmitted point by point using the exploring movement of an analyzing "spotlight" that scans the entire image, generally according to successive straight-line segments, just like we read with our eyes. The faster the movement to be transmitted, the higher the number of images required to render it correctly; for a slow movement (e.g. a man walking), five to eight images per second suffice; for a more rapid movement, such as that of an automobile, the rate of twenty-five complete images per second is insufficient. Under these conditions, the quantity of signals to be transmitted is represented by the number of details to be transmitted per unit of time, similar to the measurement of a frequency. Thus, in order to make full use of all the advantages of its definition, the 819-line television needed to be able to transmit around fifteen million details per second.

This technical notion of quantities of information conceived as a number of signals is therefore quite different from what Gestalt theories have elaborated: good form is distinguished by its structural quality, not by a number; by contrast, what requires a high quantity of signals in order to be transmitted correctly is a datum's degree of complication. In this respect, the quantity of signals required for the transmission of a determined object does account for the characteristic of "good form" it may have: the transmission of the image of a heap of sand or the irregular surface of granite requires the same quantity of signals as the transmission of the image of a well-aligned regiment or the columns of the Parthenon. The measurement of the quantity of signals that must be utilized neither allows us to define nor compare the different contents of objective data: there is a considerable gap between information signals and the form. It could be said that the quantity of signals appears to increase as the qualities of the form are lost; it is technically easier to transmit the image of a square or a circle than that of a heap of sand; in terms of the quantity of signals, there is no difference between the transmission of an image of text with a meaning and that of an image of text composed of randomly distributed letters.[5]

It would therefore seem that neither the concept of "good form" nor that of the quantity of pure information are perfectly adequate for defining the reality of information. Above information as quantity and information as quality, there is what could be called information as intensity. The simplest and most geometrical image is not necessarily the most expressive; the image that has the most meaning for the perceiving subject is not necessarily the image that is most elaborated and meticulously analyzed in its details. The entire subject (with its tendencies, drives, and passions) must be considered in a concrete situation and not as a subject in the laboratory, i.e. a situation that generally has little emotive value. It then appears that the intensity of information can be increased using a voluntary reduction of the quantity of signals or of the quality of the forms: a high-contrast photograph with extreme light and dark areas or one that is slightly out of focus can have more value and intensity than the same photograph with perfect gradation for every detail or a geometrically centered and undistorted photograph. The geometrical rigor of a contour often has less intensity and meaning for the subject than a certain irregularity. A perfectly round or oval face that would embody a good geometrical form would be lifeless and remain cold for the subject who would perceive it.

The intensity of information supposes a subject oriented by a vital dynamism: information is then what allows the subject to be situated in the world. Every received signal in this sense possesses a possible coefficient of intensity due to which we constantly correct our situation relative to the world we inhabit. Pregnant geometrical forms do not allow us to orient ourselves; they are innate schemata of our perception, but these schemata do not introduce a preferential meaning. Information takes on an intensive, predominant meaning at the level of the various gradients (whether they be luminous, colored, dark, olfactory, thermal, etc.). The quantity of signals only produces an unpolarized ground; the structures of good forms only provide frameworks. It's not enough to perceive details or ensembles organized in the unity of a good form: these details and ensembles must have meaning with respect to us and be grasped as intermediaries between the subject and the world, as signals that allow for the coupling of the subject and the world. The object is an exceptional reality; what is usually perceived is not the object but the world, which is polarized in such a way that the situation has a meaning. The object properly speaking only appears in an artificial situation that is somewhat exceptional. However, the very rigorous and absolute consequences of Gestalt theory relative to the spontaneous nature of perceptive processes deserve to be examined with more precision. It is undoubtedly true that the grasping of forms takes place immediately without a learning process or without resorting to a formation that would be carried out due to habit. But perhaps it is not true that grasping the meaning of a situation is this primitive and that no learning process intervenes. Affectivity can be qualified, transposed, and modified. In certain cases, it can also be inverted: one aspect of defeatist behavior is the general negativism of subsequent behavior; everything that attracted the subject before its failure is rejected; all spontaneous movements are refused and transformed into their opposite. Situations are grasped backwards and read in reverse. Failure neuroses manifest this inversion of polarity, but the training of an animal that presents definite tropisms or taxes already shows this possibility of the inversion of polarity.

This existence of a perceptive polarity plays a dominant role in the segregation of perceptive units; neither good form nor the quantity of signals can account for this segregation. The subject perceives in such as a way as to be oriented relative to the world. The subject perceives to increase not the quantity of information signals nor the quality of information, but the intensity of information, i.e. the information potential of a situation.[6] As Norbert Wiener puts it, to perceive is to struggle against the entropy of a system, to organize, maintain, or invert an organization. It is not enough to simply say that perception consists in grasping organized wholes; in fact, perception is the act that organizes wholes; it introduces organization by analogically linking the forms contained in the subject to the signals received: to perceive is to retain the greatest possible quantity of signals inside the forms most deeply rooted in the subject; perception is not merely grasping forms or recording multiple juxtaposed or successive data; neither quality, quantity, the continuous, nor the discontinuous can explain this perceptive activity; perceptive activity is the mediation between quality and quantity; it is intensity, the grasping and organization of intensities in the relation of the world to the subject.

Several experiments on the perception of forms through vision have shown that quality is not enough for perception; it is very difficult to perceive forms represented by colors with the same luminous intensity; on the contrary, these same forms are quite easily perceived if they are marked by a slight difference in intensity, even when the colors are identical or absent (shades of gray). The differential thresholds of intensity are remarkably low for vision (6/1000), but the thresholds of frequency are even lower in differential perception; the phenomenon mentioned above thus cannot be attributed to peripheral organic conditions. What is at stake is the central perceptive process of the grasping of forms. In the same way, a weak frequency modulation of a sound cannot be easily distinguished from a modulation of intensity or from very short interruptions in the sound's emission, which could be called phase modulation: the different types of modulation converge toward the modulation of intensity, as if the dynamisms involved in perception essentially retained this type of modulation.

If to perceive consists in increasing the information of the system formed by the subject and the field in which it is oriented, the conditions of perception are analogous to those of every stable structuration: a metastable state must precede perception. Kant wanted to explain perception through the synthesis of the manifold of sensibility, but in fact there are two types of manifold: the qualitative manifold and the quantitative manifold, the hetero-geneous manifold and the homogeneous manifold; Gestalt theory showed that perception cannot be explained by the synthesis of the homogeneous manifold: a cloud of elements cannot produce a unity through simple addi-tion. But there is also an intensive diversity that renders the subject-world system comparable to a supersaturated solution; perception is the resolution that transforms the tension that affected this supersaturated system into an organized structure; it could be said that every veritable perception is the resolution of a problem of compatibility.[7] Perception reduces the number of qualitative tensions and makes them compatible by transforming them into a potential of information, a mixture of quantity and quality. A figure against a ground is not yet an object; the object is the provisional stabilization of a series of dynamisms that proceed from tensions to the aspects of the deter-mination that characterizes a situation. By orienting in this situation, the sub-ject can unify the aspects of qualitative and intensive heterogeneity and carry out the synthesis of the homogeneous manifold; this act of orientation indeed reacts on the milieu, which becomes simplified; the multiple world, a problem posed to the subject of perception, and the heterogeneous world are merely aspects of the time that precedes this act of orientation. Through its percep-tive activity, the subject constitutes the unity of perception in the system formed by the world and the subject. To believe that the subject immediately grasps already fully constituted forms is to believe that perception is a pure knowledge and that forms are fully contained in the real; in fact, a recurring relation is instituted between the subject and the world in which it must per-ceive. To perceive is literally to take through; without this active gesture, which supposes that the subject is part of the system in which the perceptive prob-lem is posed, perception could not take place. Borrowing from the language of axiomatics, it could be said that the world-subject system is an overdeter-mined or supersaturated field. Subjectivity is not deforming, because it is what effectuates the segregation of objects according to the forms it contributes; subjectivity could only be hallucinatory if it is detached from the signals re-ceived from the object. The perceptive act institutes a provisional saturation of the axiomatic of the system that is the subject plus the world. Without this coupling[8] of the subject to the world, the problem would remain absurd or undetermined: by establishing the relation between supersaturation and in-determination, the subject of perception introduces a finite number of nec-essary solutions; in some cases, the problem can involve several solutions (as in reversible figures), but it generally only has one, and this uniqueness con-stitutes the stability of perception.

It is however necessary to distinguish the stability of perception from its pregnancy. The perception of a circle or a square is not pregnant, and yet it can be very stable; this is because the pregnancy of perception is due to its degree of intensity, not its quality or the number of signals; a certain perception can be pregnant for a certain subject, and some other perception for some other subject: the perception will be more pregnant in proportion to how dynamic the prior state of incompatibility is; fear or intense desire yield a great intensity for perception, even if this perception is not very clear; the perception of a smell is often confused and does not include solidly structured elements; nevertheless, a perception that incorporates olfactory data can be very intense. Certain tonalities, certain colors, and certain timbres can be part of an intense perception without even constituting a good form. It thus seems necessary to distinguish between the clarity and the pregnancy of a perception; pregnancy is veritably linked to the dynamic nature of the perceptive field; it is not just a consequence of the form alone, but also and more importantly a consequence of the range of the solution it constitutes for the vital problematic.

What has been said about the segregation of perceptive units can also be applied to the genesis of concepts. The concept does not result from the synthesis of a certain number of perceptions under a relational schema that gives them a unity. The formation of the concept to be possible, there must be an interperceptive tension that involves the meaning of the relation of the subject to the world and to itself. An assemblage of perceptive data cannot be constituted with perceptions alone; nor can it be constituted by the conjunction of perceptions on the one hand and an *a priori* form on the other, even if it is mediated by a schematism. The mediation between the *a priori* and the *a posteriori* cannot be discovered starting from either the *a priori* or the *a posteriori*; the mediation is not of the same nature as the terms: it is the tension, potential, and metastability of the system formed by the terms. Furthermore, *a priori* forms do not rigorously preexist perceptions: just as each perception has its own form, there is already something of this capacity of syncrystallization that manifests at a higher level in the birth of concepts: it could be said in this sense that conceptualization is to perception what syncrystallization is to the crystallization of a single chemical type. Furthermore, like perception, the concept requires an ongoing reactivation in order to be maintained in its integrity; it is maintained by the existence of quantum thresholds that sustain the distinction of concepts; this distinction is not an intrinsic property of each concept but a function of all the concepts present in the logical field. The entrance of new concepts into this logical field can lead to the restructuration of the set of concepts, which is what every new metaphysical doctrine does; before this restructuration, it modifies the threshold of the distinction of all concepts.

II. Individuation and Affectivity

1. Consciousness and Individuation; the Quantum Nature of Consciousness

Such a study requires us to pose the problem of the rapport between consciousness and the individual. This problem seems to have been obscured above all by the fact that Gestalt theory has privileged the perceptive relation over the active relation and the affective relation. If equilibrium is restored by reintroducing the consideration of all the aspects of relation, it becomes clear that the subject effectuates the separation of units in the object-world of perception, which is a support for action or responds to sensible qualities insofar as this subject realizes within itself a progressive individualization through successive leaps. This role of consciousness in individuation has been poorly defined because the psyche has been considered as an undefined plurality (in the atomistic doctrine) or as a pure, indissoluble, and continuous unity (in the doctrines opposed to atomistic psychologism, whether this be Bergsonism or Gestalt theory in its beginnings). In fact, if it is supposed that the individuality of states of consciousness, of acts of consciousness, and of qualities of consciousness is that of a quantum type, it is possible to discover a mediation between absolute unity and infinite plurality; a regime of intermediary causality thereby appears between the obscure determinism that results in the psyche as stripped of interiority and consistency and the tensed and limpid finality that allows for neither exteriority nor accident. The psyche is neither pure interiority nor pure exteriority, but an ongoing differentiation and integration according to a regime of associated causality and finality that we shall call transduction, a regime that seems to us to be a process that is more fundamental than causality and finality, which express the borderline cases of a fundamental process. The individual individuates insofar as it perceives beings, constitutes an individuation through action or through a productive construction, and belongs to the system that includes its individual reality and the objects it perceives or constitutes. Consciousness would thus become a mixed regime of causality and efficiency insofar as it links the individual to itself and to the world. Affectivity and emotivity would thus be the transductive form of the psyche *par excellence*, the intermediary between clear consciousness and subconsciousness, a continual link of the individual to itself and to the world, or rather the link between the relation of the individual to itself and the link of the individual to the world. At the level of affectivity and emotivity, the relation of causality and the relation of finality are not opposed: every affectivo-emotive movement is simultaneously judgment and preformed action; it is really bipolar in its unity; its reality is that of a relation that has a value of auto-position with respect to its terms. Affectivo-emotive polarization feeds on itself insofar as it includes or is a result of an intentionality; it is at once auto-position and hetero-position.

Thus, the individual would be neither a pure relation of exteriority nor an absolute substantiality; it could not be identified with the residue of the analysis that fails when confronted with the indivisible or with the first principle that contains everything in its unity from whence everything follows.

2. Signification of Affective Subconsciousness

The intimacy of the individual should not be sought at the level of pure consciousness or that of organic unconsciousness; it should be sought at the level of affectivo-emotive subconsciousness. In this sense, the thesis we are presenting here would diverge from the doctrine broadly called psychoanalysis. Psychoanalysis has noted that there is indeed an unconscious in the individual. But it considered this unconscious as a complete psyche somewhat copied from a consciousness that can be grasped. On the contrary, we shall suppose that there is a fundamental layer of the unconscious that is the subject's capacity for action: the sequences of action can hardly be grasped by clear consciousness; the subject errs to the greatest extent with respect to what it wants or wills and does not want or will; the succession of acts of will ensues in such a way that the markers of the process appearing to consciousness is quite rare and in no way suffices to constitute a valid foundation. By contrast, representation is much clearer; the unconscious representative elements are not rare but summary, barely sketched out, and generally incapable of veritable invention and progress: they remain fairly crude stereotypes that lack representative reality. At the limit between consciousness and the unconscious, on the contrary, there is the layer of subconsciousness, which is essentially affectivity and emotivity. This relational layer constitutes the center of individuality. The modifications of this layer are the modifications of the individual. Affectivity and emotivity are capable of quantum reorganizations; they proceed through abrupt leaps according to degrees and obey a law of thresholds. They are the relation between the continuous and the pure discontinuous, between consciousness and action. Without affectivity and emotivity, consciousness seems like an epiphenomenon, and action seems like a discontinuous series of consequences without premises.

An analysis of what can be called psychical individuality should therefore be centered on affectivity and emotivity. Here as well, psychoanalysis acted appropriately, although without always using a theory that is adequate to its operative appropriateness, because when the psychoanalyst addresses the individual, he is acting within the affectivo-emotive regime. What Jung discovers in his analysis of the unconscious (or the subconscious) are the affectivo-emotive themes at the basis of myths. If one can speak in a certain sense of the individuality of a group or of a people, it is not by virtue of a community of action, which is too discontinuous and cannot be a solid basis, nor by virtue of an identity of conscious representations, which are too broad and too continuous to allow for the segregation of groups; collective groupings are constituted at the level of affectivo-emotive themes, which are a mixture of representation and action. Interindividual participation is possible when affectivo-emotive expressions are the same. Thus, the vehicles of this affective community are not merely symbolic elements but also effective elements of the life of groups: the regime of sanctions and rewards, symbols, the arts, and collectively esteemed and unappreciated objects.

Finally, it can be noted that this doctrine, which places the quantum regime of affectivity and emotivity at the center of the individual, is in agreement with the teaching of research on the structure and genesis of species and organisms: no living being seems to be deprived of affectivo-emotivity, which has a quantum nature for highly complex beings such as humans and also for beings that are only partially organized. The oldest layers of the nervous system (particularly the midbrain) are the centers of this regulation. Pathology also shows that the dissolution of individuality can occur quite profoundly when the organic foundations of this regulation are affected, particularly in the case of tumors of the midbrain, where it seems that the very foundations of the personality are destabilized. Whereas a weakening of the functions of representative consciousness or of the capacities of action alters the personality without destroying it, and often in a reversible manner, alterations to affectivity and emotivity are rarely reversible.

3. Affectivity in Communication and Expression

Ultimately, this theory of the individuating role played by the affectivo-emotive functions could serve as a basis for a doctrine of communication and expression. Affectivo-emotive instances form the basis of intersubjective

communication; the reality that is called the communication of consciousnesses could more correctly be called the communication of subconsciouses.
Such a communication is established through the intermediary of participation; neither the community of action nor the identity of the contents of consciousness suffice to establish intersubjective communication. This explains
why intersubjective communication can be established between individuals
that are very dissimilar, such as that between a human and an animal, and
why very strong sympathies or antipathies can arise between very different
beings; however, here beings truly exist as individuals and not as specific
realities: a certain animal can be in a relation of sympathy with some other
animal and not with all the animals of that same species. The profound bond
between two draft animals has often been noted, a bond so strong that the
accidental death of one animal leads to the death of its companion. To express this relation of lived sympathy, which is at once so strong and nevertheless silent, the Greeks used, even for the human couple, the term συζυγία
[syzygy], the community of the yoke.

No doubt, such an observation does not allow us to fully define what
content can be transmitted in interindividual communication. Nor does it
completely determine eschatological reality in advance. However, certain
metaphysical consequences are inevitable: the conservation of personal identity after death does not seem possible in the simple form of a continuation
of existence. Spinoza's "sentimus experimurque nos aeternos esse" (we feel and
know by experience that we are eternal) certainly corresponds to a real feeling, but the tenor of this experience is affectivo-emotive and should not be
transposed into a representative definition or into a voluntary decision; we
can neither demonstrate eternity (or even conceive it, properly speaking) nor
wager on eternity's existence; both would be unsatisfactory ways of reasoning
that would be inadequate to their veritable object. The experience of eternity
must be left at the level of what it veritably is: the basis of an affectivo-emotive
regime. If there is a certain sort of reality that is eternal, it is the individual
as a transductive being and not as a subject-substance, body-substance, consciousness, or active matter. Already during its objective existence, the individual, insofar as it experiences, is a being-in-relation. It is possible that something of the individual is eternal and is somehow reincorporated into the
world with respect to which it was individual. When the individual disappears, it is annihilated only relative to its interiority; but for it to be annihilated
objectively, it would have to be supposed that the milieu is also annihilated.
The individual continues to exist and even to be active as an absence with
respect to the milieu.[9] By dying, the individual becomes an anti-individual,

it changes sign but is perpetuated in being as an absence that is still individual; the world is made up not just of actively living individuals, which are real, but also of "holes of individualities," veritable negative individualities composed of a kernel of affectivity and emotivity existing as symbols. At the moment an individual dies its activity is incomplete. One could say that it will remain incomplete for as long as individual beings survive that are capable of re-actualizing this active absence, this seed of consciousness and of action. The responsibility of maintaining dead individuals in being through a perpetual νέκυια [nékuia] (the evocation rites of the dead) depends on living individuals. The subconsciousness of living beings is fully traversed by this responsibility of maintaining in being the dead individuals that exist as absence, as the symbols with which living beings are reciprocal. Many religious dogmas have been constructed around this fundamental feeling. Religion is the domain of the transindividual; the sacred does not have its full origin in society; the sacred is fueled by the feeling of the being's perpetuity, a vacillating and precarious perpetuity with which living beings are burdened and charged. It is fruitless to seek the origin of sacred rites as arising from a fear of the dead; such a fear is founded on the internal feeling of a lack that emerges when the living being feels that it abandons this reality of absence within it, this real symbol. The dead seem to become hostile when they are abandoned not as dead but as living beings of the past whose perpetuation is entrusted to posterity. This feeling was deeply ingrained in the Romans, which is why they wanted an heir.[10] The strong belief in substantial identity that is attached to Christian theology did not destroy this fundamental feeling. In the individual's will to serve some purpose, to do something real, there is in a certain sense the idea that the individual cannot merely consist in itself. An absolute aseity, an absolute closure that could yield a perfect eternity would not be a livable condition for the individual: to subsist would not mean to exist eternally, because this would not be to exist. The study carried out by Franz Cumont in *Lux Perpetua* concerning the beliefs of the beyond is not just an analysis of eschatological mythology but a veritable study of the collective or individual subconscious; myth takes on a profound meaning here, because it is not merely a representation that is useful for action or a facile mode of action; myth can be accounted for neither through representation nor through action, because myth isn't just an uncertain representation or a procedure for acting; the source of myth is affectivo-emotivity, and the myth is a bundle of feelings relative to the becoming of being; these feelings convey representative elements and active movements, but these realities are secondary and not essential to myth. Plato understood this value of myth, and every time the being's becoming was called into question, he made use of myth as an adequate mode for the discovery of becoming.

4. The Transindividual

One can wonder to what extent such a conception of individuation can account for knowledge, affectivity, and, more generally, spiritual life. Spiritual life is spoken of in a sort of abstraction. Yet this adjective does have a meaning; it indicates a value and shows that a certain mode of existence is given priority over other modes; it perhaps should not be said that there is a biological or purely bodily life and then another life, which would be spiritual life in opposition to the first. Substantialist dualism must be kept outside of a theory of individuation. But it is nevertheless true that spirituality exists and that it is independent of metaphysical and theological structures. When Thucydides speaks of a work of the mind [esprit] saying "κτῆμα ες αεί" (a possession for all time) and when Horace says "exegi monumentum aere perennius" (I have raised a monument more permanent than bronze), these men are experiencing as authors an impression of eternity: the idea of the work's immortality is merely the sensible symbol of this internal conviction, of this faith that traverses the individual being and through which the individual feels that it surpasses its own limits. When Spinoza writes "sentimus experimurque nos aeternos esse," he reveals a very profound impression that the individual being experiences. And yet we also feel that we are not eternal, that we are fragile and transitory, that we will no longer exist when the sun will still be shining on the rocks next spring. Facing natural life, we feel that we are as perishable as the leaves of a tree; within us, the aging of the being that passes makes tangible the precariousness that responds to this upsurge, this emergence of life radiating in other beings; the ways are diverse in the paths of life, and we intersect with other beings of all ages that are themselves in all periods of life. And even the works of the mind [esprit] age. The κτῆμα ες αεί crumbles like the walls of dead cities; the monument more durable than bronze follows the crown of laurels into universal desiccation. More slowly or more quickly—prematurely, like Marcellus and cut lilies, or in the fullness of old age and a completed career—beings ascend and descend the slope without remaining long on the plateau of the present. It is only due to illusion, or rather semi-blindness, that spiritual life provides the unique experience of the being's eternity. The *massa candida*, the only tangible remainder of martyrs burned with quicklime, is also a testimony of spirituality through its symbolism of pitiful fragility; it is just like the monument more durable than bronze, the law engraved in tablets, or the mausoleums of the past. Spirituality is not merely what remains, but also what shines forth in the instant between two indefinite depths of obscurity, and then is covered over forevermore; the desperate, unknown gesture of the slave in revolt is just as much spirituality as Horace's writing. Culture gives too much weight to written, spoken, expressed, or recorded spirituality. This spirituality, which tends toward eternity through its own objective forces, is nevertheless not the only one; it is only one of the two dimensions of lived spirituality; the other, that of the spirituality of the instant, which does not seek eternity and shines like the light of a glance only to fade away afterwards, also really exists. Spirituality would have no signification if there were not this luminous adherence to the present, this manifestation that gives an absolute value to the instant and consummates within itself sensation, perception, and action. Spirituality is not another life, nor is it the same life; it is other and same, it is the signification of the coherence of the other and the same in a superior life. Spirituality is the signification of the being as separate and attached, as alone and as a member of the collective; the individuated being is both alone and not alone; it must possess both dimensions; in order for the collective to be able to exist, separated individuation must precede it and still contain the pre-individual, that through which the collective will be individuated by joining the separated being. Spirituality is the signification of the relation of the individuated being to the collective and therefore also the signification of the foundation of this relation, i.e. the fact that the individuated being is not entirely individuated but still contains a certain charge of non-individuated, pre-individual reality that it preserves and respects, living with the awareness of its existence instead of retreating into a substantial individuality, a false aseity. Spirituality is the respect of this relation of the individuated and the pre-individual. It is essentially affectivity and emotivity; pleasure and pain, sadness and joy are the extreme disparities involved in this relation between that which is individual and pre-individual in the subject being; one should not speak of affective states but rather of affective exchanges, exchanges between the pre-individual and the individuated within the subject being. Affectivo-emotivity is a movement between the natural undetermined and the *here and now* of actual existence; it is that through which this rise of the undetermined toward the present occurs within the subject, a rise that will incorporate the subject into the collective. Pleasure and pain are generally interpreted as signifying that a favorable or unfavorable life event emerges and affects the being: in fact, this signification does not exist at the level of the pure individuated being; there may be purely somatic pains and pleasures; but affective-emotive modes also have a signification in the accomplishment of the relation between what is individual and pre-individual: positive affective states indicate the synergy between the constituted individuality and the movement of the actual individuation of the pre-individual; negative affective states are states of conflict between these two domains of the subject. Affectivo-emotivity is not merely the reverberation of the results of action within the individual being; it is a transformation, it plays an active role: affectivo-emotivity expresses the rapport between the two domains of the subject being and modifies action in accordance with this rapport, harmonizing it with this rapport and attempting to harmonize the collective. The expression of affectivity in the collective has a regulative value; pure action would not be able to regulate the manner in which the pre-individual is individuated in different subjects in order to found the collective; emotion is this individuation on the way to being effectuated in transindividual presence, but affectivity itself precedes and follows emotion; within the subject being, it is what translates and perpetuates the possibility of individuation in the collective: affectivity is what leads the charge of pre-individual nature to become the support of collective individuation; it is mediation between that which is pre-individual and that which is individual; it is the manifestation and reverberation in the subject of the encounter and emotion of presence, of action. Without presence and action, affectivo-emotivity cannot be expressed and accomplished. Action doesn't just resolve the perceptive problem through the encounter of perceptive worlds; action qua emotion resolves the affective problem, which is that of the incompatible bi-dimensionality of pleasure and joy; emotion, the individualized side of action, resolves the affective problem that parallels the perceptive problem action resolves. Action is for perception what emotion is for affectivity: the discovery of a superior order of compatibility, of a synergy, of a resolution through the passage to a higher level of metastable equilibrium. Emotion implies the presence of the subject to other subjects or to a world that calls the subject into question as subject; it is thus parallel to action, linked to action; but it assumes affectivity, it is the point where affective plurality is inserted into a unity of signification. Emotion is the signification of affectivity in the same way that action is the signification of perception. Affectivity can therefore be considered as the foundation of emotivity, just as perception can be considered as the foundation of action. Emotion is that which, within action, is turned toward the individual participating in the collective, whereas action is that which, within the same collective, expresses the individual being in the actuality of the realized mediation: action and emotion are correlative, but action is collective individuation grasped from the side of the collective in its relational aspect, while emotion is the same individuation of the collective grasped in the individual being insofar as it participates in this individuation. In the individual being, or rather in the subject, perception and affectivity are more separate than action and emotion are in the collective; but the collective only establishes this reciprocity of action and emotion in presence; in the subject, affectivity has a content of spirituality greater than that of perception (at least seemingly), because perception reassures the subject and essentially makes use of the structures and functions already constituted within the individuated being; on the contrary, affectivity indicates and comprises this relation between the individualized being and pre-individual reality: thus, to a certain extent affectivity is heterogeneous relative to individualized reality and seems to bring to it something from the outside, indicating to it that it is not a complete and self-enclosed ensemble of reality. The problem of the individual is that of perceptive worlds, but the problem of the subject is that of the heterogeneity between perceptive worlds and the affective world, between the individual and the pre-individual; this problem is that of the subject qua subject: the subject is individual and other than individual; it is incompatible with itself. Action cannot resolve the problems of perception nor can emotion solve the problems of affectivity unless action and emotion are complementary, symbolic with respect to one another within the unity of the collective; for there to be a resonance of action and emotion, there must be a superior individuation that envelops them: this individuation is that of the collective. The subject can only coincide with itself in the individuation of the collective because the individuated being and the pre-individual being within it cannot coincide directly: there is disparation between perceptions and affectivity; even if perceptions could find their unity in an action that would systematize them, this systematization would remain foreign to affectivity and would not satisfy the search of spirituality; spirituality is neither in pure affectivity nor in the pure resolution of perceptive problems; even if emotion could resolve affective problems, even if action could resolve perceptive problems, there would still be an impossible gap for the being to bridge between affectivity and perception, which would have become a unity of emotion and a unity of action. But the very possibility of these syntheses is problematic; in their respective isolation, these syntheses would be much more so common perceptions and affective results—common feelings—rather than veritable actions or veritable emotions with their own internal unity. What creates the condition of the unity of veritable action and veritable emotion is the reciprocity between perceptions and affections within the nascent collective. Action and emotion arise when the collective individuates; for the subject, the collective is the reciprocity of affectivity and perception, a reciprocity that unifies these two domains by giving them an additional dimension. In the active course of the universalized world of action, there is an immanence of possible emotion; emotion is the polarity of this world both vis-à-vis the subject and objects; this world has a meaning and direction because it is oriented, and it is oriented because the subject orients itself in the world according to its emotion; emotion is not just an internal change, a turmoil of the individuated being and modification of structures; it is also a certain momentum across a universe that has a meaning and direction; it is the meaning and direction of action. Inversely, in emotion, even internal to the subject, there is an implicit action; emotion structures the being topologically; emotion is prolonged in the world as action, just as action is prolonged in the subject as emotion: a transductive series goes from pure action to pure emotion; this has nothing to do with psychical types, isolated operations, or isolated states; this is the very reality that we grasp abstractly in its two extreme terms by believing that they suffice unto themselves and can be studied. In fact, it would be necessary to be able to grasp action-emotion at its center, at the limit between the subject and the world, at the limit between the individual being and the collective. We would then understand that spirituality is the union of these two opposite sides (of action and emotion) ascending toward the same summit. The side of action expresses spirituality insofar as it emerges from the subject and is established in objective eternity, in a monument more durable than bronze, through language, an institution, art, or an oeuvre. The side of emotion expresses spirituality insofar as it penetrates the subject, flowing back into it and filling the subject in the instant, rendering it symbolic relative to itself, reciprocal relative to itself, comprehended relative to what engulfs it. To oppose the humanism of constructive action with the interiority of a withdrawal into emotion is to divide the subject, to fail to grasp the conditional reality of the collective within which this reciprocity of emotion and action exists. After this division, all that remains is the impoverished image of action, its structure transformed into nothing more than the residual sediment of a monument of indifferent eternity, i.e. science; facing science, internalized emotion, separated from its support and its condition of appearing, which is the collective undergoing individuation, becomes faith, emotion deprived of action, something maintained by means of the voluntary renewal of the collective subjugated to this function of sustaining emotion via rituals or spiritual practice. The rupture between action and emotion creates science and faith, which are two separate existences, two irreconcilable existences, because no individuation can reunite them, and no transductive series can reconnect them; only external rapports can exist between these two ways of being that deny transindividuality in its real form. Science and faith are the debris of a spirituality that has failed and that divides the subject and pits the subject against itself instead of leading the subject to discover a signification relative to the collective. Spiritual unity resides in this transductive rapport between action and emotion; this rapport could be called wisdom, on condition of not thereby understanding it as humanist wisdom. Neither an appeal to immanence nor an appeal to transcendence, neither naturalism nor theology can account for this transductive relation; the being must be distinguished in its own milieu; the individual man does not produce his works starting from his human essence, from man as species according to a classification through common genus and specific differences. Nor is spiritual unity a power that is fully external to man and that would be expressed through man by depriving him of his consistency and interiority. This opposition is futile; it translates the problematic characteristic of the complete human being, but it does not go far enough; it substantializes into terms of an initial bipolarity instead of seeking the meaning of this bipolarity; in the examination of the human being, there are possible foundations for a humanism or for a theory of transcendence, but both of these positions are halting points in the examination that provide these two divergent paths. One exploits man as the subject of science, while the other exploits man as a theater of faith.

5. Anxiety

We can also reflect on the signification of certain feelings that seem to be at the same time emotions, such as anxiety. Anxiety can neither be identified with a feeling nor with an emotion alone; as a feeling, anxiety indicates the possibility of a separation between the nature associated with the individuated being and this individuated being; in anxiety, the subject feels itself to be a subject to the extent that it is negated; it bears its own existence in itself, it is weighed down by its existence as if it had to carry itself—a burden of the earth (ἄκθος αρούρης) [ákthos aroúres], as Homer says, but also a burden to itself, since the individuated being, instead of having the ability to find the solution to the problem of perceptions and the problem of affectivity, feels all problems flowing back into it; in anxiety, the subject feels as if it exists as a problem posed to itself, and it feels its division into pre-individual nature and individuated being; the individuated being is *here and now,* and this *here and now* prevent an infinity of other *here and nows* from coming into existence: the subject becomes conscious of itself as nature, as undetermined (ἄπειρον) [ápeiron], and as something it will never be able to actualize into a *here and now*, that it will never be able to live; anxiety is diametrically opposed to the movement by which one takes refuge in one's individuality; in anxiety, the subject would like to resolve itself without going through the collective; it would like to come to the level of its unity by way of a resolution of its pre-individual being into an individual being, a direct resolution without mediation or delay; anxiety is an emotion without action, a feeling without perception; it is the pure reverberation of the being within itself. Of course, waiting and the passing of time can appear in anxiety, but it cannot be said that they produce anxiety, because, even when anxiety is not present, it is in preparation; the charge of anxiety is in the process of being aggravated before spreading throughout the whole being; the anxious being requests itself, requests this silent and concealed action that can only be emotion because it does not have the individuation of the collective to be resolved as a problem; the subject becomes conscious of itself as subject suffering anxiety, calling itself into question, without being able to really unify itself. Anxiety is always taking itself back up and does not advance or construct, but it profoundly calls upon the being and makes it become reciprocal with respect to itself. In anxiety, the being is like its own object, but an object as important as itself; it could be said that the subject becomes object and witnesses its own expansion according to dimensions it cannot assume. The subject becomes world and fills all this space and time in which problems emerge: there is no longer a world nor problem that is not a problem of the subject; this universal counter-subject that develops is like a night that constitutes the very being of the subject in every point; the subject adheres to everything as it adheres to itself; it is no longer localized, it is universalized according to a passive adhesion that makes it suffer. The subject dilates painfully by losing its interiority; it is here and elsewhere, detached from here by a universal elsewhere; it assumes all space and all time, becomes coextensive with being, spatializes, temporalizes, becomes uncoordinated world.

This immense expansion of the being, this limitless dilation that removes all refuge and all interiority, expresses the fusion, within the being, between the charge of nature associated with the individual being and its individuality; the structures and functions of the individuated being are mixed with one another and dilated, because they receive from the charge of nature this power of being without limits; the individuated is suffused by the pre-individual; all the structures are attacked, and the functions are animated by a new force that renders them incoherent. If the experience of anxiety could be adequately supported and endured long enough, it would lead to a new individuation within the being itself, to a veritable metamorphosis; anxiety already contains the premonition of this new birth of the individuated being based on the chaos that spreads all throughout; the anxious being feels that it might be able to be reconcentrated within itself in an ontological beyond that supposes a change in all dimensions; but in order for this new birth to be possible, the dissolution of the previous structures and the reduction of the previous functions in potential must be complete, which is an acceptance of the annihilation of the individuated being. This annihilation as an individuated being implies a contradictory movement through the dimensions according to which the individuated being poses its perceptive and affective problems; anxiety begins with a sort of inversion of significations; close things appear distant without a link to the contemporary and the actual, whereas distant beings are abruptly present and all-powerful. The present becomes hollowed out while losing its actuality; the plunge into the past and into the future dissipates the weft of the present and deprives it of its density as something lived. The individual being flees itself, deserts itself. And yet in this desertion there is a sort of underlying drive to go recompose oneself elsewhere and otherwise by reincorporating the world such that everything can be lived. The anxious being becomes universe to find another subjectivity; it exchanges itself with the universe, plunges into the dimensions of the universe. But this contact with the universe does not pass through the intermediary of action and the emotion correlative with action, and this contact lacks recourse to the transindividual relation as it appears in the individuation of the collective. Anxiety expresses the condition of the solitary subject being; it goes as far as this single being can go; it is a sort of attempt to replace transindividual individuation (which is impossible due to the absence of other subjects) with an exchange with the non-subject being. Anxiety realizes the highest achievement of the solitary being qua subject; but this realization seems to remain merely a state and does not seem to lead to a new individuation, since it is deprived of the collective. However, there can be no absolute certainty on this point: the transformation of the subject being towards which anxiety tends is perhaps possible in several extremely rare cases. In anxiety, the subject feels that it does not act as it should, that it is moving further and further from the center and direction of action; emotion becomes amplified and internalized; the subject continues to be and operate an ongoing modification within itself, but without acting, without being inserted into or participating in an individuation. The subject becomes distanced from the individuation that is still felt to be possible; it takes the inverse paths of the being; anxiety is like the inverse course of ontogenesis; it unravels what has been woven, it goes backwards in every sense. For the individuated being submerged by pre-individual being, anxiety is a relinquishment and the acceptance to cross the destruction of individuality to venture toward another unknown individuation. It is the being's departure.

6. The Affective Problematic: Affection and Emotion

Affectivity has a problematic status because it does not merely consist in pleasure and pain; pleasure and pain are perhaps the dimensions according to which the initial polarity of affectivity operates on the world and on the subject, but affectivity can no more be reduced to pleasure and pain than sensation can be reduced to lines and angles; there are sensations in a world that is oriented and polarized according to lines and angles, just as affectivity consists in affective qualities that are oriented according to pleasure and pain; however, we can no more extract affective qualities from pleasure and pain than we can produce sensations from the dimensions according to which they are organized; the dimensions of sensations are the field of movement that are in harmony with them, just as pleasure and pain are the field of insertion of affective qualities into the living being; pleasure and pain are the taking-root of actual experience in the existence of the living being, in the structures and potentials that constitute it or that it possesses. Pleasure and pain are not just the reverberation of what the being has experienced; they are not just effect, they are also active mediations that have a functional sense; even by considering affectivity as a reaction, it can be asserted that the sense of this reverberation is the dimension according to which the affective state polarizes the living being; for each affective experience, pleasure and pain are the sense of affectivity; affections have a sense, just as sensations have a sense; sensation is organized according to the bipolarity of light and darkness, up and down, interior and exterior, right and left, warm and cold; affection is organized according to the bipolarity of joyful and sad, happy and unhappy, exhilarating and depressing, bitterness or bliss, the degrading and the ennobling. Pleasure and pain are already secondary aspects elaborated based on affection; they are dimensions relative to the whole being, whereas the primary affective qualities may not be strictly compatible among one another without mutual integration according to pleasure and pain; to put this relation into the vocabulary of critique, pleasure and pain are the "*a priori* forms" of affectivity, rather than the affective given. Each affection is polarized simply according to a directivity internal to a qualitative dyad. Multiple qualitative dyads are initially uncoordinated; they each constitute a relation between the subject and the initial experienced; a coordination between the different experiences makes possible an integration into the subject that proceeds according to frameworks (or rather, dimensions) constituting a veritable affective universe. However, affective universes (or rather. nascent affective universes) lead only to distinct subsets that do not coordinate together, as long as action, or the analogue of action in its aspect of interiority, does not intervene. The coordination of the initial affective dimensions cannot be fully accomplished in the subject without the intervention of the collective, since the collective is necessary for emotion to be actualized; in affectivity, there is a continual pre-emotivity, but emotion cannot emerge from affections by means of simplification or abstraction; abstracting from affectivity could only lead to an inferior synthesis that would be impoverishing and reductive; affections, no more than sensations, do not contain their own key within themselves; an extra-being *[plus-être]* or a new individuation is necessary for sensations to be coordinated into perceptions; an extra-being of the subject is also required for affections to become an affective world; sensations not only give rise to perception, but also something of the subject, something of the being of the subject; similarly, the condition of the initial integration relative to pleasure and pain or the different affective categories are not affections alone, but something of the subject; sensation and affection correspond to two types of the being's calling into question by the world; sensations correspond to the being's calling into question as an individuated being with sense organs, and a being which therefore can be oriented according to various polarities in a world, that which corresponds to unidimensional and bidirectional tropism; sensation is this presence to the world of gradients, and its correlate is the response to tropism, not reflex. For tropism is total and corresponds to a calling into question of the entire individuated individual; but tropism does not correspond to a calling into question by the singular world; there are several worlds of tropisms, contradictory or divergent worlds that incite tropisms without a common vanishing point. Perception seeks the sense or direction of tropisms, i.e. the sense or direction of responses coordinated with sensations; sensation is the basis of tropism; it is a calling into question of the living being by the world according to a presupposed unidimensional schema; the unidimensional structure of the response is already prefigured in the nature of the calling into question, in the structure of sensation; the problematic that exists on the level of sensation is a problematic of orientation according to an axis that is already given. The structure of the sensorial world, and consequently also of the tropism that corresponds to it, is the indefinite dyad of cold and hot, heavy and light, dark and bright; sensation is the expectation of tropism, an information signal for tropism; it is what orients the living being vis-à-vis the world; sensation does not contain the object, since it does not localize, it does not attribute to a definite being the power of being the source of the effects experienced in sensation; there is a manner in which the being is called into question by the world that is anterior to any consistency of the object; objectivity is not first, nor is subjectivity or syncretism; what is first is orientation, and what contains the sensation-tropism couple is the totality of orientation; sensation is the grasping of a direction, not of an object; it is differential, which implies the recognition of the sense or direction according to which a dyad manifests; thermal, tonal, or chromatic qualities are differential qualities anchored around a center that corresponds to an average state, to a maximum of differential sensibility. For each type of reality there is a center relative to which the relation is deployed. There is not just the highest pitched and the lowest pitched, the hottest and the coldest; there is higher pitched and lower pitched than the human voice, hotter and colder than the epidermis, lighter and darker than the optimal lighting needed by the human eye, more yellow and green than the yellow-green of the maximum sensitivity of human chromatic sensation. The real *medium*[11] of each species is in each dyad, and the polarity of the world of tropism is grasped with respect to this *medium*. The constant error that has distorted the relational theory of sensation consisted in thinking that relation was the grasping of two terms: in fact, the polarity of tropism implies the simultaneous grasping of three terms: the *medium* of the living being between the hottest and the coldest, the brightest and the darkest. The living being seeks in the gradient the *optimal* zone; the living being evaluates the two directions of the dyad relative to the center in which it resides and which it occupies. The first usage of sensation is more *transductive* than relational: sensation allows us to grasp how the *medium* extends into the colder of one side and into the hotter on the other; the *medium* of temperature is what extends and splits directionally into hotter and colder; the dyad is grasped starting from its center; it is not synthesis but transduction; hotter and colder are deployed symmetrically relative to the center; in the same way, green and yellow occur symmetrically with respect to the *medium* of color; and the qualities of the dyad proceed in both directions toward the extreme terms beyond which there is merely pain or the absence of sensation. Sensation relates to the state of the living being grounded in an *optimal* region of each qualitative dyad, coinciding with a gradient of the world; it is the grasping of the middle [*milieu*] of a bipolarity. *Medium* and bipolarity are part of the same unity of being, which is that of sensation and tropism, that of sensation for the orientation of tropism; sensation is already tropism, for it grasps the structure according to which tropism is actualized; a disadaptation doesn't need to produce the necessity of a movement for there to be tropism; there is tropism in immobility as well as in readjustment. Sensation is tropistic in itself, it makes the living being coincide with the *medium* of a gradient and indicates the sense or direction of this gradient to the living being. In sensation, there is no intention to grasp an object in itself for it to be known, nor the rapport between *an object* and the living being; sensation is that through which the living being adjusts its insertion into a transductive domain, into a domain that includes a transductive reality, the polarity of a gradient; sensation is part of an ensemble that in a certain sense splits into pure sensation and pure reaction but that normally includes tropistic unity, i.e. sensation, which is tropism actualized. A psychology of behaviors leads to ignoring the role of sensation because this type of psychology only considers separate reactions as reflexes; reflex is an abstract element of reaction grasped in the tropistic unity, just as sensation is an abstract relational element grasped in the same tropistic unity from which the active side has been removed.

Comparable to the structures of veritable sensation, affectivity contains structures involved in tropistic unity. Affection relates to a subjective transductive reality (belonging to the subject) in the same way that sensation relates to an objective transductive reality. There are modes of the living being that are not modes of the world and that develop according to their own dimensions without implying a causal reference to this world and without directly organizing according to the dimensions of a gradient, i.e. without being part of sensation. An interoceptive sensation is often treated as a type of reality that does not consist in sensations and that in reality consists in affectivity. Affections constitute an orientation of a part of the living being with respect to itself; they bring about a polarization of a particular moment of life relative to other moments; they make the being coincide with itself through time, but not with the totality of itself and the totality of its states; an affective state is one that has a unit of integration into life; it is a temporal unit that is part of a whole according to what could be called a gradient of becoming. The pain of hunger is not just what is felt and what reverberates within the being; it is also and above all the way hunger as a psychological state endowed with the power of being modified is inserted into the subject's becoming; affectivity is the self-constitutive integration into temporal structures. Desire, the onset of fatigue, and the intensification of cold are aspects of affectivity; affectivity is much more than just pleasure and pain; it is a way for the being to be instantaneously situated according to a vaster becoming; affection is the index of becoming, just as sensation is the index of gradients; each mode, each instant, each action, and each state of the living being are between the world and the living being; this being is polarized in accordance with the world on the one hand and in accordance with becoming on the other. And just as the different dimensions according to which orientation in the world is effectuated do not necessarily coincide together, the different affective aspects constitute insertions into the subsets of the living being's becoming, not into a single becoming. Both an affective problem and a perceptive problem remain; the plurality of tropistic orientations calls for perceptive unification and knowledge of the object, just as the plurality of affective subsets calls for the birth of emotion. Emotion arises when the integration of the current state into a single affective dimension is impossible, just as perception arises when sensations call for incompatible tropisms. Just as perception is sensorial contradiction, emotion is affective contradiction overcome. Moreover, we shouldn't speak of *affective* contradiction and *sensorial* contradiction, for sensations and affections in themselves are not what are contradictory with respect to other sensations or affections: what are contradictory are the tropistic subsets and the subsets of becoming that compose these sensations and these affections with respect to other sensorial and tropistic subsets. There is no contradiction on the level of sensations properly speaking or affections properly speaking; they cannot be apperceived if this encounter of subsets does not take place; sensations and affections are incomplete realities taken outside the subsets to which they belong and within which they operate. The non-coincidence of affections promotes emotion, just as the non-coincidence of sensations fosters perception. Emotion is a discovery of the unity of the living being, just as perception is a discovery of the unity of the world; these are two psychical individuations that extend the individuation of the living being, completing it, perpetuating it. The interior universe is emotive, just as the exterior universe is perceptive. It shouldn't be said that affection flows from emotion felt facing the object, for emotion is integrative and richer than affection; affection is like emotion in slow motion, i.e. emotion not yet constituted in its unity and in the capacity to become the master of its own development; emotion is like an insular temporal unity with its own structure: it drives the living being, gives it a direction, polarizes it, takes up its affectivity, and unifies it; emotion unfolds, whereas affectivity is merely felt as the belonging of the actual and current state to one of the modalities of the living being's becoming; emotion responds to a being's calling into question that is more complete and more radical than affection; it tends to take time for this calling into question, it presents itself as a totality and possesses a certain internal resonance that allows it to perpetuate itself, to sustain itself, and to prolong itself; it imposes itself as a self-maintained state, whereas affection does not have any active consistency and allows itself to be penetrated and to be driven off by another affection;[12] there is a certain closure of emotion, whereas there is no closure of affection; affection returns, presents itself again, but does not resist; emotion is totalitarian, just as much as perception, which, after having discovered forms, perpetuates them and imposes them as a system that acts as its own support; there is a tendency of the being to persevere in its being on the level of perception and on the level of emotion, but not on the level of sensation or affection; sensation and affection are realities that befall the individuated living being without assuming a new individuation; these states are not self-sustained; they are not determined in themselves by a self-conditioning; on the contrary, perception and emotion are metastable: a perception clings to the present, resists other possible perceptions, and is exclusive; an emotion also clings to the present and resists other possible emotions; the disruption of this metastable equilibrium is what allows for one perception to replace another; one emotion only comes after another emotion due to a sort of internal break. There is a relaxation from one emotion to another. In emotion, what disorganizes the living being is not emotion itself, since emotion is the organization of affections; what disorganizes it is the passage from one emotion to another. However, it could be said that perception also brings about a disorganization: but this disorganization is less appreciable, since it is merely a rupture between two successive perceptive organizations relative to the world; since the disorganization that exists between two emotions involves the living being, it is more appreciable than the one that separates two perceptions. Nevertheless, perception and emotion are still activities that correspond to a transitory mode of activity; due to their plurality, perception and emotion require a higher integration, an integration that the being cannot effectuate with its pure constituted individuality; in the perceptive contradiction and in the emotional ruptures, the being experiences its limited nature facing the world through perception and becoming through emotion; perception imprisons the being in a point of view, just as emotion imprisons it in an attitude. Points of view and attitudes are mutually exclusive. To unlock the possibility for the formation of a network of key points that integrates all possible points of view and for the formation of a general structure of the manner of being that integrates all possible emotions, a new individuation must occur that includes the rapport to the world and the rapport of the living being to other living beings: emotions must go toward the perceptive points of view, and the perceptive points of view must go toward emotions; a mediation between perceptions and emotions is conditioned by the domain of the collective, i.e. the trans-individual; for an individuated being, the collective is the mixed and stable kernel within which emotions are perceptive points of view and within which points of view are possible emotions. The unity of the modification of the living being and the modification of the world depends on the collective, which brings about a convertibility of the orientation relative to the world into an integration into vital time. The collective is the stable spatiotemporal; it is a milieu of exchange, the principle of conversion between these two sides of the being's activity (perception and emotion); by itself, the living being could not go beyond perception and emotion, i.e. perceptive plurality and emotive plurality.

III. Psychical Individuation and the Problematic of Ontogenesis

1. Signification as Criterion of Individuation

The difference between signal and signification is important because it constitutes an accurate and essential criterion for the distinction between a veritable individuation or individualization and the functioning of a non-individuated subset. Static criteria (like those of material limits and those of the body of each individual) are not sufficient. Certain cases (e.g. association, parasitism, and gestation) cannot be studied using spatial or purely somatic criteria in the usual (i.e. anatomo-physiological) sense of the term. According to the distinction between signals and signification, we will say that there is an individual when there is a process of real individuation, i.e. when significations appear; *the individual is that through which and in which significations appear,* whereas there are only signals between individuals. The individual is the being that appears when there is signification; reciprocally, there is signification only when an individuated being appears or persists in the being undergoing individualization; the genesis of the individual corresponds to the resolution of a problem that could not be resolved in accordance with the previous data, since they had no axiomatic in common; *the individual is the self-constitution of a topology of the being that resolves a previous incompatibility via the appearance of a new systematics*; what was tension and incompatibility becomes functioning structure; fixed and fruitless tension becomes an organization of functioning; instability is transformed into an organized metastability that is perpetuated and stabilized in its capacity to change; the individual is therefore a spatiotemporal axiomatic of the being that makes compatible previously antagonistic data in a system with

temporal and spatial dimensions; the individual is a being that becomes—
according to its structure, in time—and is structured according to its becoming; tension becomes tendency; what merely depended on the instant, before
individuation, becomes order in the successiveness of the continuous; the
individual is what introduces a system according to space and time, with a
mutual convertibility of order according to space (structure) and of order
according to time (becoming, tendency, development, and aging; in a word,
function). Signals are spatial or temporal; a signification is spatiotemporal;
it has two senses, one with respect to a structure and the other with respect
to a functional becoming; significations constitute something of the individual being, although they require a preliminary existence of the partially individuated being; a being is never completely individualized; to exist, it must
have the power to continue individualizing by resolving the problems of the
milieu that surrounds it and that is its milieu; the living being is a being that
perpetuates itself by exerting a resolving action on the milieu; it brings with
it the initiations of resolution, since it is alive; but when it effectuates these
resolutions, it effectuates them at the limit of its being and thereby continues
the individuation: this individuation after the initial individuation is individualizing for the individual to the extent that it is resolving for the milieu.
According to this manner of viewing individuation, a specific psychical operation would be a discovery of significations in an ensemble of signals, since
signification would extend the being's initial individuation and, in this sense,
have a rapport both to the ensemble of exterior objects as well as to the being
itself. Insofar as it contributes a solution to a plurality of signals, a signification has a bearing toward the exterior; but this exterior is not foreign to the
being as the result of an individuation; this is because before the individuation this being was not distinct from the ensemble of the being that separated
into milieu and individual. In the same way, the discovery of a significative
solution has a bearing toward the interior of the being and increases for it
the intelligibility of its relation to the world; the world is merely the individual's complementary with respect to an initial indivision; individualization
continues individuation. Each thought, each conceptual discovery, each affective emergence is a recurrence of the initial individuation; each develops as
a recurrence of this schema of the initial individuation of which it is a distant,
partial, but faithful rebirth. If knowledge rediscovers the lines that allow the
world to be interpreted according to stable laws, this is not because in the
subject there are *a priori* forms of sensibility whose coherence with the raw
data emerging from the world through sensation would be inexplicable; this
is because the being as subject and the being as object arise from the same

initial reality, and because the thought that now seems to establish an inexplicable relation between the object and the subject in fact merely extends this initial individuation; the *conditions of possibility* of knowledge are in fact the individuated being's *causes of existence.* Individualization differentiates beings with respect to one another, but it also weaves relations among them; it links them to one another, because the schemata according to which individuation follows its course are shared by a certain number of circumstances that can be reproduced for several subjects. The *de jure* universality of knowledge is indeed a *de jure* universality, but this universality passes through the mediation of conditions of individualization, which are identical for all beings placed in the same circumstances and with the same foundations of individuation from the start; because individuation is universal, just like the foundation of the relation between subject and object, knowledge is validly given as universal. The opposition of the empirical subject and the transcendental subject overlaps that of the subject reached *here and now* at a certain result of its personal individualization and that of the same subject as expressing a single act—carried out once and for all—of individuation. The subject as the result of an individuation that it incorporates is a milieu of *a prioris*; the subject as the milieu and agent of the progressive discoveries of signification in the signals that come from the world is the principle of the *a posteriori.* The individuated being is the transcendental subject, and the individualized being is the empirical subject. However, it is not absolutely legitimate to attribute to the transcendental subject a responsibility in the choice of the empirical subject's character; the transcendental subject does not operate a choice; it is itself choice, the concretization of a founding choice of the being; this being exists to the extent that it is a solution, but it is not the being qua individual that existed prior to the choice and that is the principle of choice; this is the ensemble, the system from which this being has emerged and in which it did not preexist as individuated. The notion of transcendental choice introduces individuality too far upstream. There is no transcendental character, and this is precisely why knowledge is universalizable; problems are problems for the transcendental ego, and the sole character, the empirical character, is the set of these problems' solutions. The schemata according to which problems can be resolved are true for every individuated being relative to the same mode of individuation, whereas the particular aspects of each solution contribute to constructing the empirical character. The only character that is constituted is the empirical character; the transcendental subject is that through which there is a problem; but for there to be problems, there must be experience, and the transcendental subject cannot operate a choice before all experience. There can be no choice of the principles of choice before the act of choice. We could call personality everything that connects the individual qua individuated being to the individual qua individualized being. The individualized being tends toward singularity and incorporates the accidental as singularity; the individual qua individuated being itself exists relative to the system of being from which it arises, on which it is formed, but it is not opposed to other individuals formed according to the same operations of individuation. The being insofar as it is individualized diverges from other beings that are individualized; by contrast, this mixture of individuation and individualization that constitutes personality is the differentiated and asymmetrical relation with others. A relation on the level of individuation is a relation of the sexuality type; a relation on the level of individualization is of the type concerning the contingent events of everyday life; lastly, a relation on the level of personality is one that integrates sexuality and the events of the individual's history into a single situation. What constitutes the human concretely is neither pure individuation nor pure individualization, but a mixture of the two. The character that pure individualization would be is never a detached result; it only becomes so if this relational activity that the permanence of personality constitutes stopped being able to unite individuation and individualization. In this sense, the unstable person *[le caractériel]* is not one who has troubles concerning their character, but one in whom the character tends to become detached, since the personality can no longer assume its dynamic role; what is ill in the unstable person is the personality, not the character. Personality is thus a relational activity between principle and result; personality is what produces the being's unity between its foundations of universality and the particularities of individualization. The interindividual relation is not always interpersonal. It is quite insufficient to appeal to a communication of consciousnesses to define the interpersonal relation. An interpersonal relation is a common mediation between the individuation and individualization of a being and the individuation and individualization of another being. In order for this single mediation that is valid for two individuations and two individualizations to be possible, there must be a separate community of individuations and individualizations; the interpersonal relation does not exist on the level of constituted personalities but on the level of the two poles of each of these personalities: the community cannot intervene after the personalities are constituted; a preliminary community of the conditions of the personality allows for the formation of a single mediation, of a single personality for two individuations and two individualizations. This is why it is rare that the domain of the interpersonal is in fact veritably coextensive with the entire reality of each of the personalities; the interpersonal relation only involves a certain zone of each of the personalities; but the particular coherence of each of the personalities makes it seem like the community exists for the whole ensemble of the two personalities; the two personalities have a part that is veritably in common but also a part that is not: the two parts that are not in common are joined by the part in common; this is a question of partial identity and of the connection through this identity, rather than a question of communication. Consciousnesses would not be enough to guarantee a communication; there must be a communication of the conditions of consciousnesses for there to be a communication of consciousnesses.

2. The Relation to the Milieu

The interpersonal relation shares some resemblance with the relation to the milieu; however, the relation to the milieu forms either on the level of individuation or on the level of individualization. It is established on the level of individuation through emotion, which indicates that the individual being's principles of existence are called into question. Fear and cosmic admiration affect the being in its individuation and situate it within itself once again relative to the world; these states consist of forces that challenge and call on the being to affirm its existence as an individuated being. This relation is situated on the level of individualization when it touches the being in its particularity through the property of familiar things or habitual and regular events, i.e. things and events that are integrated into the rhythm of life, are unsurprising, and can be integrated into prior frameworks. The impression of deep participation or normal perception are the aspects of these two rapports. These two types of relation rarely combine but instead succeed one another in life. On the contrary, the personality involves the presence of the two aspects, and the experience that corresponds to the personality is relative to two conditions: it partially involves challenging and questioning individuation as well as a modification of individualization, thereby resulting in an integration into acquired frameworks. The relation to others calls us into question as an individuated being; it situates us in an encounter with other people as being young or old, sick or healthy, weak or strong, male or female: however, one is not absolutely young or old in this relation but younger or older than another; and one is also stronger or weaker; to be man or woman is to be man in a rapport to a woman or woman in a rapport to a man. To speak of simple perception is insufficient here. To perceive a woman as a woman is not to introduce a perception into preestablished conceptual frameworks but to situate oneself both in terms of individuation and individualization with respect to her. This interpersonal relation involves a possible relation of our existence as an individuated being with respect to her own. The perceived and the felt are only split off from one another in the illness of the personality. Minkowski brings up the case of a young schizophrenic who wonders why seeing a woman in the street causes him a specific emotion: he sees no relation between the perception of the woman and the emotion he feels. However, the specific characters cannot suffice to explain the unity of the felt and the perceived, no more than habit or any other principle of exterior unity. The being's individuality can be effectively perceived: a woman can be perceived as having a specific particularity that distinguishes her from every other person; but it isn't as a woman that she is distinguished in this way: she is distinguished qua human being or living being. The concrete knowledge corresponding to a complete haecceity (this woman here, this very woman) is that in which individuation and individualization coincide; it is a certain expression, a certain signification that makes it such that this woman is this very woman; all the aspects of individuality and of individuation are incorporated into this fundamental expression that the being cannot have unless it is really unified. Gestalt psychology, which developed into a psychology of expression, considered signification as a basic reality; signification is in fact given by the coherence of two orders of reality, that of individuation and that of individualization. The expression of a being is indeed a veritable reality, but it is not a reality that is graspable otherwise than as expression, i.e. as personality; there are no elements of expression, but there are bases of expression, since expression is a relational unity maintained in the being by an incessant activity; this is the very life of the individual manifested in its unity. On the level of expression, the being is to the extent that it manifests itself, which is something that is not true for individuation and individualization.

3. Individuation, Individualization, and Personalization. Bi-substantialism

It could be asked if there are individuals other than physical or living individuals and if it is possible to speak of psychical individuation. In fact, it actually seems that psychical individuation is an individualization rather than an individuation, if we agree to designate by individualization a type of process that is more restricted than individuation, insofar as it requires the support of the already individuated living being in order to develop; psychical functioning is not a functioning separate from the vital, but, after the initial individuation that provides a living being with its origin, there can be in the unity of this individual being two different functions, functions which are not superposed but which are (functionally) relative to another, just like the individual with respect to the associated milieu; thought and life are two complementary, rarely parallel functions; everything happens as if the living individual could once again be the theater of successive individuations that divide it into distinct domains. It is correct to assert that thought is a vital function with respect to a living being that would not be individualized by separating into a physiological being and a psychical being; the physiological and the psychical are like the individual and the complement of the individual at the moment in which a system individuates. Individualization, which is the individuation of an individuated being and results from an individuation, creates a new structuration within the individual; thought and organic functions are the vital split along an asymmetrical rift that is comparable to the first individuation of a system; thought is like the individual of the individual, whereas the body is the complementary associated milieu of thought with respect to the already individuated σύνολον [súnolon] that the living being is. When the individuated living system is in the state of internal resonance, it individualizes by splitting into thought and body. Before individualization, psychosomatic unity is a homogeneous unity; after individualization, it becomes a functional and relational unity. Individualization is merely a partial splitting (in normal cases), for the psycho-physiological relation sustains the unity of the individuated being; furthermore, certain functions never become solely psychical or solely somatic, and, in this way, they maintain in the living being the status of the individuated but not individualized being: this is the case for sexuality; this is also generally the case for the concrete interindividual functions (like social relations) that concern the individuated being. According to this path of study, the ensemble of psychical contents could be considered as the result of the resolution of a series of problems posed to the living being, problems the latter must resolve by individualizing; psychical structures are the expression of this fractured individualization that has separated the individuated being into a somatic domain and a psychical domain. There is no identity of structures between the somatic and the psychical; but there are pairs of complementary realities that constitute living subsets on the level of the individuated being; the individuated being is expressed in partially coordinated, successive somatopsychic pairs. Initially, the individuated being does not have *a* soul and *a* body; it is constructed as such by individualizing, by gradually splitting. There is no psychical individuation properly speaking, but there is an individualization of the living being that gives rise to the somatic and the psychical; this individualization of the living being is expressed in the somatic domain by specialization and in the psychical domain by the schematization that corresponds to this somatic specialization; each psychical schema corresponds to a somatic specialization; the body can be called the ensemble of the specializations of the living being to which psychical schematizations correspond. The psychical is the result of an ensemble of sub-individualizations of the living being, and this holds for the somatic as well; each individuation reverberates within the living being by partially splitting it in a way that produces a pair formed by a psychical schema and a somatic specialization; the psychical schema is not the form of the somatic specialization but the individual that corresponds to this complementary reality relative to the anterior living totality. If the living being were to individualize completely, its soul would be a society of schemas, and its body would be a society of specialized organs, each carrying out a specific function. The unity of these two societies is maintained by that which does not individualize in the living being and consequently resists splitting in two. Individualization is all the more accentuated as the living being is subjected to increasingly critical situations in which it manages to triumph by splitting within itself. The individualization of the living being is its real historicity.

Personality appears to be more than relation: it is what maintains the coherence of individuation and of the ongoing process of individualization; individuation takes place only once; individualization is as continual as perception and everyday behaviors; by contrast, personality concerns the domain of the quantum, of the critical: structures of personality are established that last a certain amount of time, resist the difficulties they must take on, and then, when they can no longer maintain individuation and individualization, collapse and are replaced by others; personality is constructed by successive structurations that are replaced, with the new structurations integrating the subsets of the old ones and also leaving a certain number of the latter aside as unusable debris. Personality is constructed via successive crises; its unity is increasingly strong the more this construction resembles a maturation in which nothing of what has been built is definitively rejected but is, sometimes after a latency period, reintroduced into the new edifice. Individuation is unique, individualization continual, and personalization discontinuous. But the discontinuity of genesis includes the unity of the process of organizational construction; in the actual expression of the harmonious personality, one can identify the anterior stages that it takes back up by integrating them into its functional unity. Saint Augustine's expression *etiam peccata* ("even sins") is true solely on the level of the personality's construction. Indeed, it can be said that the personality integrates *even sins* without supposing that there is the occasional aspect of the *felix culpa* ("blessed fault"), which is inexplicable without resorting to a transcendence.

The foundation of the problem of transcendence lies in the successive rapport of these phases of personality; all the schemata that seek to explain the inherence of a transcendent principle in man or, on the contrary, that want to show that everything emerges genetically from experience, ignore the initial reality of the operation of individuation. It's true that the being, to the extent that it is individuated, does not have and will never have the complete course of its explication within it; the individuated being cannot account for itself or for everything that is within itself, no more than it can account for its emotion facing the starry sky and the moral law within it or the principle of true judgment. This is because in its ontogenetic limits the individuated being has not retained within it the whole real from which it has emerged; it is an incomplete real. But it also cannot search outside itself for another being that would be complete without it. Whether according to creation or procession, the being that has allowed the individual to form has split, i.e. has become the individual and the complement of the individual. The first reality anterior to individuation cannot be recovered whole outside the existing individual. The genesis of the individual is not a creation, i.e. an absolute advent of the being, but an individuation within the being. The concept of transcendence mistakes anteriority for exteriority. The complete being, which is the origin of the individual, is both within the individual and outside it after individuation; this being has never been outside the individual, for the individual did not exist before the being has individuated; it cannot even be said that the being has individuated: there has been individuation within the being and individuation of the being; the being has lost its unity and its totality by individuating. This is why the study of transcendence finds outside the individual and before it another individual that both has the appearances of the individual and those of actual and contemporaneous nature, i.e. this complement of the individual. But the image of the Supreme Being cannot become coherent because it is impossible to make coincide or even to render compatible aspects like the personal character of the Supreme Being and its character of positive eternity and omnipresence, which give it a cosmicity. The study of immanence is doomed to the same ultimate failure, for it would like to recreate a world starting from what is found in the individuated being; the aspect of personality is then predominant, but the cosmicity is obscured; the individuated being is thus found to be relative to the ensemble of the world in a double relation, as a being that includes nature qua naturing nature and

as a being that is a mode of natured nature. The relation of naturing nature
and of natured nature is graspable with just as much difficulty in the study
of the immanence within the individuated being as that of God as personal
being, active agent, and God as omnipresent and eternal, i.e. as endowed with
cosmicity. Both the search for transcendence and the search for immanence
aim to recreate the whole being with one of these two symbols of the incomplete being that individuation separates. Before posing the critical question
prior to any ontology, philosophical thought must pose the problem of complete reality, which is anterior to the individuation from whence the subject
of critical thought and of ontology emerges. Veritable first philosophy is not
that of the subject, nor that of the object, nor that of a God or Nature searched
for according to a principle of transcendence or immanence, but that of a
real anterior to individuation, a real that cannot be sought in the objectivated object or in the subjectivated subject but at the limit between the individual and what remains outside it, i.e. according to a mediation suspended
between transcendence and immanence. The same reason that makes the
study according to transcendence or immanence futile also makes the search
for the essence of the individuated being in the soul or in the body futile.
This search has led to materializing the body and spiritualizing consciousness, i.e. to substantializing both terms after having separated them. The term
body after this separation conserves elements and functions of individuation
(like sexuality); it also conserves aspects of individualization, like wounds,
illnesses, and infirmities. Nevertheless, it seems that individuation dominates in the body insofar it is a separated body, one that has its life and its
death apart from other bodies and that can be wounded or diminished without another body being wounded or diminished. Conversely, consciousness
grasped as spirit contains the basis of personal identity, first as an independence of consciousness with respect to the known material elements or
objects of action; body and consciousness then in some sense become two
separate individuals between which a dialogue is established, and the total
being is conceived as a reunification of two individuals. The materialization
of the body consists in seeing in it nothing but a pure given, a result of the
capacity of the species and of the milieu's influences; the body is then like
an element of the milieu; it is the closest milieu for the soul, which becomes
the being itself, as if the body enveloped the soul (this is what Saint Augustine calls *carneam vestem,* "fleshly clothing"). Consciousness is spiritualized
in the sense that expression becomes clear, deliberate, and reflective thought,
willed according to a spiritual principle; expression is fully uprooted from
the body; in particular, the gaze—which is perhaps what conveys the most

profound and refined expression of the human being—becomes "the eyes of the flesh"; however, the eyes as the seat of the gaze's expression cannot be said to be of flesh; they are the support and milieu of expression, but they are not of flesh in the way that a stone is of quartz or of mica; they are not merely organs of a body but the intentional transparency of one living being to other living beings. The body can only be said to be of flesh as a possible corpse and not as a real living being. Every somatopsychic dualism considers the body to be dead, which is what allows it to be reduced to a matter: *soma sema* ("the body-prison"), as Plato calls it (*Cratylus*, 400b). The spiritualization of consciousness operates inversely to that of the materialization of the body. The body is materialized to the extent that it is identified with its instantaneous and consequently unexpressive physical reality; consciousness is spiritualized to the extent that it is identified with a timeless reality; while the body is drawn toward the instant and reduced to it, consciousness expands into eternity; it becomes spiritual substance tending toward the state of non-becoming; death, which severs the soul from the body, leaves the body to essential instantaneity, whereas the soul is freed into absolute eternity. To consider that death is the separation of the soul and the body, to know the being through the prescience of its death, and to preface the knowledge of the being with the description of its bi-substantiality after death is in some sense to consider the being as already dead during its very existence. For bi-substantialism would only be true in the hypothesis of a death that would conserve consciousness intact. This reductive reversal of time that permits seeing the living being in terms of what it will be after death implies begging the question, insofar as one sets out, despite everything, from the living being, from this edifice of life that the expression of a personality in somatopsychic unity is. The experience of what is rarest and most elevated in vital becoming is what's used to enact this dissociation of the soul and the body. The bi-substantialist reduction broadly makes use of vital experience at first, then turns its back on this initial experience and turns back against it by way of the abstract schema of the dead being. The notion of body and the notion of soul are two reductive notions, since they replace the individual being (which is not a substance) with a pair of substances; but adding as many substances together as one likes with schemata of interaction as subtle as one could imagine will not succeed in recreating the initial broken unity. The somatopsychic distinction cannot go further than that of the pair of symbols.[13] In the living individual, there are almost purely somatic structures and functions, at least in the sense in which materialism could understand it; there are also almost purely psychical functions;

but above all, there are psychosomatic functions; the model of the living being is the psychosomatic; the psychical and the somatic are merely borderline cases that are never available in the pure state. What is eliminated from the living being via bi-substantialist reduction is precisely the set of median structures and functions, like the unitary functions of expression and integration. Thus, Bergson's bi-substantialism has led to the bisection of a function, like that of memory in the distinction between pure memory and habit-memory. But the same study of memory shows that pure memory and habit-memory are merely borderline cases. Pure memory and habit-memory are subtended by a network of significations that holds for the living being and other living beings. The opposition of sensation and perception still expresses the bi-substantialist preoccupation: sensation would be sensorial, i.e. somatic, while perception would involve a psychical activity that collects and interprets sense data. This opposition even extends to that between feeling and affection. However, this opposition is not caused by their belonging to two separate substances but by two types of functioning. On the contrary, if one compares science to perception, perception is what becomes somatic, while science is psychical. Both science and perception are in fact psychosomatic; they both suppose an initial encounter of the subject being and the world in a situation that calls the being into question; the only difference involves the fact that perception corresponds to the resolution of an encounter without a preliminary technical elaboration, while science stems from an encounter by way of the technical operation: science is technical perception, and it extends vital perception in a circumstance that supposes a preliminary elaboration but actually responds to a new engagement; when water rises into the barrel pump, technics suffices; but when water stops rising, science is necessary. Technical excess is profitable for the development of the sciences, just as the *élan* of the tendencies is necessary for the development of perception, since this excess and this *élan* make man once again face the need to stabilize the rapport between subject and world by way of perceptive signification or scientific discovery. Finally, the opposition between man and animal, which is erected into a dualistic principle, originates within the somatopsychic opposition itself. With respect to man who perceives, the animal perpetually seems to feel without being able to elevate itself to the level of the representation of the object separated from contact with the object. However, in the animal there is also a relative opposition between instinctual behaviors (which draw their direction and their orientation from pre-given schematisms) and behaviors of organized reaction, thus revealing the establishment of a definite presence to the world, along with the possibility of conflict. Instinctual behaviors are those that unfold, not without adaptation—since behavior does not negate adaptation—but without preliminary conflict; it could be said that instinctual behavior is one in which the elements of the solution are contained in the structure of the ensemble constituted by the milieu and the individual; on the contrary, a behavior of organized reaction is one that implies the invention of a structure on behalf of the living being. Nevertheless, organized reactions suppose drives, but they add something to the situation on the level of the resolution; drives, with the tendencies that derive from them if objects are present, always play the role of motors. The difference from so-called human behaviors resides in the fact that motivation by instincts generally remains visible in behaviors when an animal is concerned and the observer is a human, whereas motivations that drive human behavior cannot be easily detected for another human as an observer. The difference is more so of level than of nature. By conflating simple instinctual behaviors in the animal with the conflictual reactions that overcome them, we improperly join the aspects of individuation and the aspects of individualization. However, it is correct that the behaviors arising from individuation are more numerous and more easily observable than the behaviors of individualization, but it is incorrect that the former are the only behaviors; every individualization supposes an individuation, but the former adds something to the latter. The error stems from the fact that we search for behaviors that would not be instinctual; nevertheless, when an absolute absence of drives leaves the being in an anorexic state, no further behavior is possible; the finality of behaviors is replaced by absolute indistinction, prostration, and the absence of orientation. This opposition between man and animal, which is unfounded, adds a new implicit substantialism to the basic substantialism by means of which we give individuality to the body and the soul in man.

Furthermore, there is a form of monism that is merely a bi-substantialism in which one of the terms has been obliterated. To say that only the body is determinative or that only the mind [esprit] is real is to suppose implicitly that there is another term in the individual, a reduced term deprived of its whole consistency but nevertheless real as a useless or negated understudy. The loss of the role is not the loss of the being, and this being exists sufficiently to subtract from the dominant term a certain number of functions and to expel them back outside the representation of the veritable individual; materialist monism or spiritual monism are in fact asymmetrical dualisms: they impose a mutilation of the complete individual being. The only veritable monism is the one in which unity is grasped at the time when the possibility of a diversity of functioning and structures is perceived. The only veritable monism is that which, instead of following an implicit dualism that it seems to refuse, contains the dimension of a possible dualism but against a background of the being that cannot be overshadowed. This monism is genetic, for genesis alone presupposes unity that encompasses plurality; becoming is grasped as a dimension of the individual starting from the time in which the individual did not exist as an individual. Dualism can only be avoided if one starts from a phase of the being anterior to individuation in order to relativize individuation by situating it among the phases of the being. The only compatibility of duality and unity is in the genesis of the being, in ontogenesis. In a certain sense, it can thus be said that the different notions of monism and of pluralism arise from a shared postulate, one according to which the being is substance in the beginning, i.e. exists as individuated before every operation and every genesis. Both monism and dualism therefore put themselves in the impossible situation of rediscovering an effective genesis, since they wish to make a genesis emerge from the already individuated being as a result of individuation; nevertheless, the individual emerges from individuation, but the former neither contains the latter nor fully expresses it. This does not mean that the individual must be devalued relative to an initial reality that is richer than it; but the individual is not the only aspect of the being; it is only the whole being when it is associated with its complement, the milieu, which is engendered at the same time as the individual. Furthermore, the irreversibility of the ontogenetic process prohibits one from going back from the system posterior to individuation toward the system anterior to individuation. There are two errors in substantialism: that of mistaking the part for the origin of the whole by seeking in the individual the origin of individuation, and that of wanting to reverse the course of ontogenesis by making individuating existence emerge from individuated substance.

4. Insufficiency of the Notion of Adaptation to Explain Psychical Individuation

One of the most characteristic traits of modern psychology and psychopathology is that they contain an *implicit sociology* that is inherent particularly to the normativity of their judgments. Certainly, these disciplines claim not to be normative and want to be merely objective; they are objective no doubt, but from the moment that the necessity of the distinction between the normal and the pathological appears, from the moment that it is merely necessary to determine a hierarchy by classifying behaviors or states according to a scale of levels, normativity once again arises. If we define this implicit normativity, it is not to argue against it in this part of our study, but because it obscures a whole aspect of the representation of the individual. If dynamics is included in the implicit normativity, one will be able to construct a psychological theory of the individual within which it will seem that no dynamics is presupposed; in fact, this dynamics is present in implicit normativity, but it does not appear as a dynamics inherent to the object studied. If we analyzed the complete content of the dynamic notions employed by modern psychology (such as the normal and the pathological, high-level states and low-level states, states of elevated psychical tension and states of low psychical tension), we would find that this implicit normativity conceals a sociology and even a sociotechnics that do not belong to the explicit foundations of psychology. Perhaps this remark would even be valid for the psychological doctrines of previous centuries, since they seem to be exempt from any theory of society and because sociology had not been constituted as an autonomous discipline; in Malebranche for example, we can discover a certain conception of human freedom and of individual responsibility founded on the fact that each being has "movement to always go further"; in Maine de Biran, the hierarchy of three lives supposes a certain representation of interindividual relation. Lastly, even in the work of Rousseau, whom we are taking as a general example of the authors that sought to construct a doctrine of the individual grasped in his solitude, virtue and consciousness involve an implicit presence of relation.

But this incapacity of psychological thought facing the analysis of its presuppositions is particularly notable in the most recent developments of this discipline. As an example, if we take the address of Dr. Kubie to the 1949 Macy Conference of Cybernetics, we find that the author legitimizes his distinction of the normal and the pathological in individual behavior through the criterion of adaptation. This is indicated by the title of his study, "Neurotic Potential and Human Adaptation"; he attempts to show that a behavior governed by neuropathic forces and presenting certain analogies with a normal behavior is ultimately exposed due to the fact that the subject cannot be satisfied with any of his successes. Neuropathic potentials are distinguished from normal forces by the continual disadaptation of the subject that they animate; this subject is neither happy nor satisfied, even if, seen from outside, his behavior seems to involve success. As the author states, this is because there is an immense gap between the goal pursued by the neuropathic potentials and the conscious goal that the subject seeks and can effectively attain. When the overarching and consciously sought goal is finally reached, the subject understands that he has been the victim of an illusion and that this is not yet his true goal; he is not satisfied, and he sees that he never will be. This may then be the moment of despair, which is incomprehensible for someone who sees from outside this drama of the neuropathic quest. At the height of their career, an engineer or a writer commit suicide without any apparent cause; their success was not a veritable adaptation.[14] At least for a time, neurotics often seem to excel normal subjects; this is because they work and act under the influence of neuropathic potentials. But sooner or later, neurosis manifests. Dr. Kubie cites several cases to illustrate his thesis, particularly the case of a man who, during World War II, was awarded several military medals for his heroic conduct and his remarkable aggressiveness; he had managed to leave the desk job to which he was assigned in order to partake in battle in an extremely courageous way. However, after the end of the war, this man's severe neurosis manifested and forced him to seek psychiatric help. Similarly, according to the author, one often finds in universities certain "campus heroes" (an expression whose literal meaning is "heroes of the university grounds," but this expression has a value similar to phrases like "heroes of the honor roll" or "heroes of the court of honor"). These heroes are neurotics who mask their inability to adapt by excelling in the intellectual or athletic domain and who find in the laurels they receive a provisional means of ensuring their integration into the society in which they live. Later on, neurosis manifests.

Nevertheless, this criterion of adaptation or adaptability, which is taken by Dr. Kubie as a principle of distinction between the normal and the pathological, presents a very serious possibility of confusion. Should adaptation be grasped in the relation of the individual to the group or in the relation of the individual to himself? At the beginning of his address, Dr. Kubie establishes the nature of the logical and physical necessity of this criterion by assimilating it with the law of gravitation; it would be absurd to ask if any norm whatsoever requires matter to attract matter, for without this natural law, the world would not exist. Similarly, it is absurd to ask whether there is a norm that requires man to adapt to society: the very fact that the human world exists proves the existence of this norm of adaptation; it is a norm because it is a law that expresses the existence of a human world whose condition of possibility it is. However, this analogy is much too condensed to be considered a principle. Indeed, the physical world is not merely constituted by neutral matter, i.e. each particle attracting all the others and being attracted by them according to Newton's law; there are also electrical charges that polarize matter and make particles capable of a mutual repulsion stronger than Newtonian attraction, as can be seen currently in certain stable or unstable plasmas; there is a considerable difference between a field like the gravitational field and a field like an electrical field or magnetic field: the latter actually involve a polarity, whereas the field of gravity does not. Finally—over and above electrical charges (be they associated with matter or not) and appearing as electron or ion, potential or potential well—there is electromagnetic radiation, which can be grasped in all the degrees of the vast domain of transductivity it constitutes. If the physical universe were only constituted by neutral particles without polarity and without radiation, its properties would be totally different from what they are. The problem of physical individuality certainly would not be posed with such acuteness: there would then be no explanation for why a corpuscle like an electron, which repels other electrons with a force inversely proportionate to the distance between the corpuscles, is not dislocated by forces that should, by virtue of the preceding law, tend to dissociate its parts from one another. If the individual unity of the electron remains despite this law, this is because a reality distinct from attraction at a distance and from repulsion at a distance enters into play on the level of the particle.[15] The physical individual cannot be treated according to laws derived from the study of interindividual relations, since, if the individual exists, this is because the laws (whose action is not observable on the interindividual level) become predominant on the individual level. If there were only one type of relation, the individual would not be isolated from the whole into which it is integrated. In the same way, in psychology the normality of the individual cannot be defined by a law that expresses the coherence of the world, because if this law alone were valid, there would be no individual reality, and thus no problem of normality could intervene.

Furthermore, in the description of the neuroses he recounted, Dr. Kubie indeed shows that the adaptation in question, which defines normality, is an adaptation of the individual not only to the human world but also to himself, because in formal terms, success, achievement, an enviable and envied situation, an honorable position, and wealth do not constitute satisfaction, without which there is no adaptation. However, a law comparable to that of gravitation in the physical world cannot determine in the human world whether a specific role suits a specific personality. The neurotic is one for whom no role is suitable and who therefore suffers from a constant disadaptation, not between his role and society, but between himself and his role in society. One can be disadapted without being neurotic and neurotic without being disadapted, because the compatibility or incompatibility in the relation of the individual to himself is not determined by the law of interindividual relation. An implicit sociology is not a guarantee of objectivity in psychology; it only keeps us from posing the problem of the relation of the individual to himself. Nevertheless, this question is posed on the level of physical thought itself; it is posed all the more in psychology due to the higher level of organization and the greater complexity of the individual within this domain.

5. The Problematic of Reflexivity in Individuation

For psychosociology, the difficulty of situating individual reality and defining adaptation seems to stem from the same origin as the difficulty that plagues scientific thought when it seeks to define physical individuality: wanting to grasp the being's structure without operation and operation without structure, it either leads to an absolute substantialism or to an absolute dynamism that does not leave room for relation within the individual being; relation becomes inessential. Even Bergson, who has made a remarkable effort to think the individual without allowing himself to be ensnared by a mental habit imported into psychology by a spirit accustomed to treating other problems, has remained too close to pragmatism; like pragmatism, he has privileged intraindividual dynamism at the expense of structural realities that are just as intraindividual and important. It would be difficult to account for a properly *mental* illness in Bergson's philosophy.

According to the doctrine we are expounding, the psychological individual, like the physical individual, is a being constituted by the coherence of a domain of transductivity. In particular and as a direct consequence of this nature, it is impossible to constitute in the study of the individual two types of forces or behaviors, i.e. normal behaviors and pathological behaviors; certainly not because behaviors would be identical to one another, but precisely because they are so different from one another to be able to constitute two types alone; according to the point of view in which we are situated, either an infinity of types can be constituted or one alone, but never two alone. The constitution of two types does nothing but express the bipolarity of normativity essential to a psychological classification that conceals an implicit sociology and sociotechnics. In fact, as in every domain of transductivity, there is in the psychological individual the unfolding of a reality that is simultaneously continuous and multiple. Bergson has seized upon this characteristic in one of its dimensions, i.e. the temporal dimension; but, instead of studying the characteristics of relation according to the order of simultaneity more deeply, he has remained prejudiced against spatiality (no doubt due to the abuses of psychological atomism) and has remained content with opposing the characters of the "superficial self" to those of the "deeper self." However, transductivity on the psychological level is expressed by the relation between the transductive order of the simultaneous and the transductive order of the successive. Without this relation, psychological reality would not be distinct from physical reality. In the psychological domain, the relation that has the value of being is that of the simultaneous and the successive; the different modalities of this relation are what constitute the domain of properly psychological transductivity; but they cannot be divided into kinds; they can only be hierarchized according to a given type of function.

Ultimately, the very center of individuality therefore appears as *reflexive* self-consciousness, this expression being taken in its fullest sense; a nonreflexive consciousness, one incapable of introducing a normativity derived from behavior into behavior itself, would not effectuate this domain of transductivity that constitutes the psychological individual; indeed, the characteristic polarity of teleological behavior already exists on the biological level; but then it lacks this reciprocity (between the order of the simultaneous and the order of the successive) that constitutes psychological reality. Moreover, we do not mean by this to assert that there is a radical distinction between the biological order and the psychological order; by hypothesis alone, we are saying that pure biological reality would be constituted by the nonreciprocity of the relation between the domain of the simultaneous and that of the successive, whereas psychological reality is precisely the establishment of this reciprocity that can be called reflection. The pure living being indeed integrates its past experience into its present behavior, but it cannot carry out the inverse integration, because it cannot introduce reflection due to which the present behavior, already imagined in its results and analyzed in its structure, is placed on the same ontological level as the past behavior. For the pure living being, there is a heterogeneity between experience and behavior; for the psychological individual, there is a relative and progressive homogeneity of these two realities; instead of sinking into the past by becoming pure experience, the past behavior conserves the characteristics of interiority that make it a behavior; it conserves a certain coefficient of presence; inversely, the present behavior, consciously represented as that which will have consequences as effective as those that now constitute the real experience of the past, is already an experience in advance. The possibility of foresight and the possibility of remembering converge because they share the same nature and have a single function: to establish the reciprocity of the order of the simultaneous and the order of the successive.

The domain of psychological individuality thus appears to be affected by a certain precariousness, for it is defined not only by the composition of a certain number of elements that constitutes a partially unstable idiosyncrasy, but also by a self-constitutive dynamism that exists only to the extent that it supports itself and maintains itself in the being; an activity that constructs itself and conditions itself develops on a biological underpinning that provides a more or less abundant, concordant, or discordant idiosyncrasy. This self-constitutive character develops as a problematic without a solution on the level of personal idiosyncrasies; the character is not yet the individual, because it is what poses problems but not what resolves them; if the solution of problems were given in experience, the individual would not exist; the individual exists the moment that a reflexive becoming-conscious of the posed problems has allowed the particular being to introduce its idiosyncrasy and its activity (including that of its thought) into the solution; the proper characteristic of the solution on the level of the individual resides in the fact that the individual plays a double role, on the one hand as an element of the data and on the other hand as an element of the solution; the individual intervenes twice in its problematic, and it is through this double role that it calls itself into question; if, as Vladimir Jankélévitch says, every problem is essentially thanatological, this is because the axiomatic of every human problem can only appear to the extent that the individual exists, i.e. establishes a finitude within itself that confers a recurrent circularity onto the problem of which it becomes conscious; if the individual were posited as eternal, none of the problems that appear to it could receive a solution, because the problem could never be dissociated from the subjectivity that the individual confers on it by figuring among the data and elements of the solution; the problem must be able to be freed from its inherence to individuality, and this requires that the individual only intervene provisionally in the question that it poses; a problem is a problem to the extent that it includes the individual, since it includes the individual doubly in its structure, although the individual seems to appropriate the problem; the individual and the problem surpass one another and sort of intersect according to a schema of mutual inherence; the individual exists to the extent that it poses and resolves a problem, but the problem only exists to the extent that it forces the individual to recognize its temporally and spatially limited nature. The individual is the being that joins within it and outside it an aspect of the simultaneous and an aspect of the successive; but in this act through which it brings a solution to an aspect of a problem, it becomes determined in order to make a compatibility between these two orders occur, and it is localized and temporalized by becoming universalized. Every individual act is essentially ambiguous, since it is at the point where there is a chiasmus of interiority and exteriority; it is at the limit between interiority and exteriority; interiority is biological, exteriority is physical; the domain of psychological individuality is at the limit of physical reality and biological reality, between the natural and nature, as an ambivalent relation with the value of being.

The domain of psychological individuality therefore does not have its own space; it exists as a superimpression relative to the physical and biological domains; it is not inserted between them, properly speaking, but joins them and includes them partially, all while being situated within them. The nature of psychological individuality thus is essentially dialectical, since it only exists to the extent that it establishes a compatibility that passes through itself between nature and the natural, between interiority and exteriority; biological reality is anterior to psychological reality, but psychological reality takes the biological dynamism back up after being decentered with respect to it. The psychological detour is not an abandonment of life but an act through which psychological reality becomes decentered relative to biological reality to be able to grasp in its problematic the rapport of the world and of the ego, the rapport of the physical and of the vital; psychological reality unfolds as a transductive relation of the world and of the ego. The direct communication of the world and of the ego is not yet psychological; for psychological reality to appear, the implicit link between the world and the ego must be broken and then reconstructed solely through this complex act of two mediations that suppose one another and are mutually called into question in reflexive self-consciousness.

Whence results for the psyche the necessity to unfold through mediations endowed with reciprocity; since its domain is that of relation but not of possession, it can only be constituted by what it constitutes. This reciprocity of the subject and the object appears in the individual problematic, because what the object of the problem is for the consciousness that posits it, the subject of this consciousness is for the world that contains this object. This double situation is inherent to the opposition of realism and nominalism. However, the dialectical relation of the individual to the world is transductive, because it unfolds a homogeneous and heterogeneous, consistent and continuous, but diversified world, a world which neither belongs to physical nature nor to life but to this universe in the process of constitution that can be called mind [esprit]. Yet this universe constructs the transductivity of life and of the physical world through knowledge and through action; the reciprocity of knowledge and of action allows this world to be constituted not just as a mixture but as a veritable transductive relation; everything that is constructed by the individual, everything that is apprehensible by the individual is homogeneous, whatever the degree of spatial and temporal diversity that affects the elements of this constructed universe may be; all individual realities can be ordered in continuous series without radical heterogeneity. Every reality can be understood either as physical being, as vital gesture, or as individual activity; this third order of reality establishes a transductivity that partially and incompletely joins the preceding orders that are commensurate with the existence of psychological individuals. The inclusion of the elements of the first two orders in the third is the work of the individual and expresses the individual. Nevertheless, this inclusion is never complete, because it requires the existence of physical and biological underpinnings; just as there cannot be an entirely biological world, there cannot be an entirely psychological world.

The psychological individual could also appear to belong to a psychological world. But here an illusion arising from an overly facile analogy must be prevented: properly speaking, a psychological world within which individuals would be distinguished and defined after the fact does not exist. The psychological world is constituted by the relation of psychological individuals; in this case, the individuals are anterior to the world and are constituted based on non-psychological worlds. The relation of the physical and biological worlds to the psychological world passes through the individual; the psychological world must be called the transindividual universe rather than the psychological world, since the latter does not have an independent existence; for example, culture is not a reality that subsists of itself; it only exists to the extent that cultural monuments and expressions are reactualized by individuals and included by them as bearers of significations. What can be transmitted is nothing but the universality of a problematic, which is in fact the universality of an individual situation recreated through space and time.

Yet the psychological world exists to the extent that each individual finds before it a series of mental schemata and of behaviors already incorporated in culture that compel the individual to pose its particular problems according to a normativity previously elaborated by other individuals. The psychological individual must choose among the values and behaviors from which it receives examples: but not everything is given in culture, and we must distinguish between culture and transindividual reality; culture is neutral in a certain sense; it has to be polarized by the subject that calls itself into question; on the contrary, there is in the transindividual relation a requirement of the subject to be called into question by himself, because this calling into question is already begun by others; the decentering of the subject relative to himself is carried out in part by others in the interindividual relation. However, it should be noted that the interindividual relation can obscure the transindividual relation, to the extent that a purely functional mediation is made available as an easy option that avoids the veritable position of the problem of the individual by the individual himself. The interindividual relation can remain a simple rapport and avoid reflexivity. Pascal has felt and noted quite vividly the antagonism between diversion and the reflexive consciousness of the problem of the individual; to the extent that the interindividual relation offers a prior validation of the ego grasped as a persona through the functional representation that others have formed of it, this relation avoids the acuteness of the calling into question of oneself by oneself. On the contrary, the veritable transindividual relation only begins beyond solitude; it is constituted by the individual who called himself into question and not by the convergent sum of interindividual rapports. Pascal discovers transindividuality in the reciprocal relation with Christ: "I have shed my blood for thee," Christ said; and the man who has managed to remain alone understands that Christ is in agony until the end of time; "there must be no sleeping during that time," Pascal said. The veritable individual is one who has traversed solitude; what the individual discovers beyond solitude is the presence of a transindividual relation. The individual finds the universality of relation at the end of the trial that is imposed on him, and this trial is one of isolation. We believe that this reality is independent of any religious context, or rather, it is anterior to any religious context and is in fact the common basis for all religious forces when it is translated into religion. The source of all religions is not society, as certain sociological thoughts have wanted to show, but the transindividual. This force is socialized, institutionalized only afterwards; but it is not social in its essence. Nietzsche shows Zarathustra taking refuge in his cave at the top of the mountain to find solitude, which allows him to foresee the enigma of the universe and to speak to the Sun; he isolates himself from other men to the point of being able to say: "You great star, what would your happiness be had you not known those for whom you shine?". The transindividual relation is that of Zarathustra to his disciples or that of Zarathustra to the tightrope walker who lies broken on the ground in front of him and who has been abandoned by the crowd; the crowd only considered the funambulist in terms of his function; it abandons him when he ceases to perform his function after his death; on the contrary, Zarathustra feels himself to be this man's brother, and he carries off his corpse to give him a proper burial; it is with solitude, in this presence of Zarathustra to a dead friend abandoned by the crowd, that the trial of transindividuality begins. What Nietzsche describes as the event of wanting "to climb onto his own shoulders" is the act of every man who undergoes the trial of solitude to discover transindividuality. However, Zarathustra does not discover a creator

God in his solitude but the pantheistic presence of a world submitted to eternal return: "Zarathustra dying holds the earth in his arms." The trial is thus anterior to the discovery of the transindividual, or at the very least anterior to the discovery of all the transindividual; the example of Nietzsche's Zarathustra is invaluable, for it shows that the trial itself is often guided and initiated by the flash of an exceptional event that makes man conscious of his destiny and leads him to feel the necessity of the trial; if Zarathustra hadn't felt this absolute and profound fraternity with the tightrope walker, he would not have left the village to seek refuge in the cave at the top of the mountain. A first encounter between the individual and transindividual reality is necessary, and this encounter can only be an exceptional situation that externally presents the aspects of a revelation. But, in fact, the transindividual is self-constitutive, and Pascal's phrase "you would not seek me, if you have not found me," if it accounts for the role of the individual's activity in the discovery of the transindividual, seems to presuppose the transcendent existence of a being in which the origin of all transindividuality resides. Neither the idea of immanence nor the idea of transcendence can account completely for the characteristics of the transindividual with respect to the psychological individual; transcendence or immanence are indeed defined and determined before the moment that the individual becomes one of the terms of the relation into which it is integrated, and whose other term was already given. However, if it is admitted that the transindividual is self-constitutive, it will be seen that the schema of transcendence or the schema of immanence only account for this self-constitution through their simultaneous and reciprocal position; each moment of self-constitution involves the definition of the rapport between the individual and the transindividual as that which *surpasses the individual by extending it*: the transindividual is not exterior to the individual and yet becomes detached from the individual to a certain extent; furthermore, this transcendence that takes root in interiority (or rather, at the limit of interiority and exteriority) does not bring about a dimension of exteriority but a dimension of excess relative to the individual. The fact that the trial of transindividuality was able to be interpreted sometimes as a recourse to a superior and exterior force and sometimes as a deepening of interiority—according to Augustine's formulas, *In te redi; in interiore homine habitat veritas* ("return to yourself, truth resides in everyone"), or even, *Deus interior intimo meo, Deus superior superrimo meo* ("God is higher than my highest and more interior than my innermost self")—shows that at the very start this fundamental ambiguity exists: the transindividual is neither exterior nor superior; it characterizes the true relation between every exteriority and every interiority relative to the individual; perhaps the dialectical formula according to which man must go from the exterior to the interior and from the interior to the superior could also articulate the passage from interiority to exteriority prior to the access to superior things. For it is in the relation between exteriority and interiority that the starting point of transindividuality is constituted.

Thus, psychological individuality appears to be what is elaborated by elaborating transindividuality; this elaboration rests on two interconnected dialectics, one of which interiorizes the exterior, the other of which exteriorizes the interior. Psychological individuality is therefore a domain of transductivity in this sense; it is not a substance, and the notion of the soul must be revised, since it seems to imply in some of its aspects the idea of a substantiality of the psychological individual. However, beyond the notion of the soul's substantiality and also beyond the notion of the inexistence of any spiritual reality, there is the possibility of defining a transindividual reality. The afterlife of the soul is then no longer presented with the characteristics that the quarrel between materialism and spiritualism have given it; the most delicate question is undoubtedly that of the "personal" nature of the afterlife of psychological individuality. None of the alleged reasons for proving this personal character are definitive; all these reasons and this whole search simply show the existence of the desire for eternity, which is indeed a reality qua desire; and a desire is obviously not a simple notion; it is also the emergence of a dynamism of the being, of a dynamism that makes transindividuality exist by suffusing it with value. It nevertheless seems possible to affirm that the path of research here is indeed the examination of this transindividual reality that psychological reality is; in a certain sense, every human act achieved on the level of transindividuality is endowed with the power of indefinite propagation that confers on it a virtual immortality; but is the individual itself immortal? The interiority of the individual cannot be immortal, since it has too many biological roots to be able to be immortal; the pure exteriority attached to the individual, with its deeds or its works insofar as they materialize its action, also cannot be immortal; they survive it but are not eternal; what can be eternal is this exceptional relation between interiority and exteriority, which is designated as supernatural and which must be maintained above any interiorist or communal deviation. Just as the excellence of the sacred is something enviable for cementing the greatness of establishment or for legitimizing the promotion of a certain interiority to the rank of spirituality, there is a strong tendency to the interiorist or communal deviation of transindividual spirituality. No solution in this domain can be absolutely clear: the notion of the soul and that of matter merely provide the false simplicity of what habit presents and manipulates without clarifying the implicit meanings; the notion of the afterlife through transindividuality is more unfashionable and less common than that of the completely personal afterlife of the soul or that of cosmic afterlife in a pantheistic union, but it is not more confused; like them, it can only be grasped by intuitions formed in an active and creative contemplation.

Wisdom, heroism, and sainthood are the three paths for studying this transindividuality according to the predominance of representation, action, or affectivity; none of them can lead to a complete definition of transindividuality, but each designates in some way one of the aspects of transindividuality and contributes a dimension of eternity to individual life. The hero is immortalized through his sacrifice, just like the martyr in his bearing witness and the sage in his radiant thought. The excellence of action, the excellence of thought, and the excellence of affectivity, moreover, are not exclusive with respect to one another; Socrates is a sage, but his death is a heroic testimony of affective purity. Martyrs are saints become heroes. Every path of transindividuality initiates the other paths. Furthermore, each of them has something in common that marks the category of the transindividual specifically and manifests it without, however, sufficing to define it: what they each share is a certain sense of inhibition, which is like a negative revelation that puts the individual into communication with an order of reality superior to that of everyday life. According to the cultural basis of each path, these inhibitions that orient action are presented as emanating from a certain transcendent being or from a "spirit" [génie], such as Socrates's *daimon*; but what is most important is the existence of this inhibition; in sainthood, it manifests through the refusal of everything that is judged impure; in heroism, abject and ignoble actions are refused; and in wisdom, the refusal of the useful and the affirmation of the necessity of disinterest has this same value of inhibition; the lack of this inhibition was seen in the Sophists by Plato, and this is what allowed him to oppose Socrates against them. There is a negative and inhibitive aspect of ascesis that prepares the way to wisdom. The being surpasses itself specifically to the extent that this inhibition is exerted, either according to a search for transcendence or by being "immortalized in the sensible." It should be noted that this inhibition can take on different forms, but it only transforms the better to subsist. Thus, in Nietzsche, the ancient and classical aspects of this inhibition are refused and fiercely critiqued: violence replaces sainthood, and the inspired frenzy of Dionysus compensates the cold lucidity of Apollo with the creation of the gay science; but what remains is contempt, which becomes the attitude of Nietzsche's hero and which, under the auspices of a feeling of the overman's superiority, in fact contains an extremely strong inhibition; the overman is denied happiness and any sort of easiness.

Psychological individuality introduces certain norms that do not exist on the biological level; whereas biological finality is homeostatic and seeks to obtain a satisfaction for the being in a state of greater equilibrium, psychological individuality exists to the extent that this biological equilibrium and this satisfaction are judged insufficient. Apprehensiveness and concern in vital security mark the arrival of psychological individuality, or its possibility of existence at the very least. Psychological individuality cannot be created by a devitalization of the vital rhythm or by a direct inhibition of tendencies, since this would then lead to nothing but an interiority and not a spirituality. Psychological individuality is superimposed on biological individuality without destroying it, since spiritual reality cannot be created by a simple negation of the vital. We should note that the distinction between the vital order and the psychological order is particularly revealed by the fact that their respective normativities constitute a chiasmus: worry appears during a time in which biological calm dominates, and during times of pain spirituality transforms into defensive reflexes; fear transforms spirituality into superstition.

Ultimately, the appeal to transcendence that sees in spiritual reality a being distinct from the living individual is still too close to immanence; there is still too much biological reality in a pantheistic or creationist conception of spirituality.

Indeed, pantheistic or creationist conceptions place the individual in an attitude whose initial participation is undertaken with great difficulty; participation requires a sort of self-abnegation and a sort of self-departure, both through the negation of individual reality (as in the thought of Spinoza) as well as through the detachment of the individual from the biological milieu (as in certain aspects of creationist mysticism). This is because too much individuality remains in the conception of the transindividual; the relation between the biological individual and the transindividual then can only intervene through a disindividuation of the individual; here, the error properly speaking is not one of anthropomorphism but of the individualization of the transindividual; perhaps only negative theology has made an effort not to think the transindividual in the manner of a superior individuality that is vaster but just as individual as that of the human being; the most difficult anthropomorphism to avoid is that of individuality; nevertheless, pantheism does not avoid this anthropomorphism, for it can do nothing but expand the singular individual to the dimensions of the cosmos; but the analogy between microcosm and macrocosm, which remains present throughout this infinite expansion of unique substance, sustains the individuality of the macrocosm. It is no doubt because of this ineradicable individuality that every pantheism leads to this difficult conception of freedom within necessity, whose infinitely subtle Spinozist form, however, is reminiscent of the Stoic image of the dog attached to the cart: the dog is a slave when its will is not in unison with the rhythm of the carriage, while it is free when it has been able to synchronize the movements of its will with the cart's successive stops and starts. What is oppressive in every type of pantheism is the valorization of the cosmic law as both the rule of thought and of the individual will; however, this valorization of universal determinism intervenes because there is an implicit presupposition: the universe is an individual. Theodicy can be opposed to pantheism as well as creationism and the doctrine of a personal God, because in both cases facts become norms, insofar as the mutual foundation of the fact and the norm is a law, that of the internal organization of the supreme individual. The transcendence or immanence of this individual relative to the world does not change the fundamental schema of its constitution, which thereby confers value on each determination.

Furthermore, we should ask to what extent the phenomenon that psychologists call "split personality" comes up in the study of transindividuality. Indeed, the splitting of the personality is quite clearly a pathological aspect of self-consciousness and of behavior. However, there is nevertheless an aspect of the study of spirituality that cannot fail to bring splitting to mind: this aspect is the separation in itself between good and evil, between beast and angel, which is a separation accompanied by the awareness of man's twofold nature and is projected outside in mythology as a Manichaeism that defines a principle of good and a principle of evil in the world; the very idea of demons, with the description of the means they use to tempt someone's soul, is merely the transposition of this duality accompanied by an implicit technique of exorcizing the evil one has within oneself; for the Devil is not just the principle of evil; the Devil is also the scapegoat that pays for all the sins and weaknesses that one does not wish to attribute to oneself and to whom one attributes responsibility; in this way, bad conscience is transformed into hate against the Devil. Temptation is the imminence of the personality's split, the moment when the being feels that it will allow its effort and its tension to be released to fall into a lower level of thought and action; this fall of oneself away from oneself gives the impression of an alienation; it is put back into a perspective of exteriority. No doubt the splitting would not exist if man always lived and thought on the same level; but how can one explain that the fall from a higher level to a lower level gives the impression of an alienation? This is because the presence of the transindividual then is found lacking and because the subject understands that its existence is realigned or defined by new values that are not properly speaking more mediocre than the old ones or absolutely antagonistic, but foreign to them; these new values do not contradict the old values, for to contradict is still to recognize, yet they do not speak the same language. The fall to a lower level could not cause the splitting on its own if there weren't at the same time a decentering of the system of references. If the lower values were in an analogical rapport relative to the higher values, if there were but a vertical leap from one level to the other, the profound *disorientation* that arises in temptation would not manifest. By resorting to a more simplified expression, one can turn the notion of *disorientation* into an invasion of evil and the notion of evil into a correlate of the good with respect to a neutrality of values. If evil were the correlate of the good, the ego would never be foreign to itself; here, there is an essentially *asymmetrical* relation, and the substantialist idea of two natures is still much too close to a schema of symmetry to be able to account for this relation.

6. The Necessity of Psychical Ontogenesis

According to this perspective, ontogenesis would become the starting point for philosophical thought; it would really be first philosophy, anterior to the theory of knowledge and to an ontology that would follow this theory. Ontogenesis would be the theory of the phases of the being, anterior to objective knowledge, which is a relation of the individuated being to the milieu after individuation. The existence of the individuated being as subject is anterior to knowledge; a first study of the individuated being must precede the theory of knowledge. The science [savoir] of ontogenesis is prior to any critique of knowledge [connaissance]. Ontogenesis precedes ontology and critique.

Unfortunately, it is impossible for the human subject to witness its own genesis, for the subject must exist in order for it to think. The geneses of the conditions of the validity of thought in the subject cannot be mistaken for a genesis of the individuated subject; the Cogito, with the methodological doubt that precedes it and with the development that follows it ("but what am I, I who am?"), does not constitute a true genesis of the individuated subject: the subject of doubt must be anterior to doubt. One can only say of the Cogito that it approaches the conditions of individuation by assigning the return of the subject to itself as a condition of halting doubt: the subject grasps itself simultaneously as a doubting being and as an object of his doubt. Doubting and doubt are a single reality grasped via two aspects: it is an operation that returns to itself and grasps itself from two facets. It is a privileged operation that objectivates the subject facing himself, because in the operation of doubting, it objectivates the doubting subject; doubt is both the doubt subject, i.e. the doubt *operation* in the first person, and also the doubt that detaches from the operation of actual doubting as doubted doubt, an already accomplished objectivated operation, i.e. already matter for another operation of doubting that immediately follows it. Between doubting doubt and doubted doubt, a certain relation of distancing is constituted through which, nevertheless, the continuity of the operation is sustained. The subject recognizes himself as a subject of the doubt he just put forth, and nevertheless this doubt as an accomplished reality is already objectivated and detaches by becoming the object of a new doubt. In order for reaction to exist, there must be memory, i.e. at the same time and through a shared reality or operation, a distance-taking and a joining-together; the operation of doubt, which in this instance adheres to the subject, must distance itself relative to the center of activity and of consciousness, and it must form as an independent and autonomous unity of the being, all while remaining through this distance a thing of the subject, a thing expressing the subject. Memory is a distance-taking, an acquisition of objectivity without alienation. It is an extension of the limits of the subjective system that takes on an internal duality without separation or rupture: it is alterity and identity progressing together, forming and becoming distinguished in the same movement. The content of memory becomes the symbol of the present ego; it is the other part; the progress of memory is an asymmetrical splitting of the subject being, an individualization of the subject being. The mental matter that has become memory (or rather, the content of memory) is the milieu associated with the present ego. Memory is the unity of the being as totality, i.e. as a system that incorporates this splitting and resists it, such that this splitting can be repeated and taken up again by the being. To remember is to find oneself again. But what finds is not homogeneous with what is found; what finds is like the individual, and what is found is like the milieu. The unity of the being that remembers is the unity of the joining of symbols. The being that remembers is more than the ego; it is more than the individual; it is the individual plus something else. The same applies for the imagination; the difference between memory and the imagination resides in the fact that the principle of encounter between the ego and the symbol of the ego aligns with a dynamic tendency of the ego in the imagination, whereas in memory the principle of encounter is in the symbol of the ego; there is symbolization in both cases, but in the operation of memory, symbolization takes the complementary symbol of the ego for the individual and the ego for the milieu; in the imagination, the ego is the individual, and the symbol of the ego is the milieu. Finally, in the dialogue with oneself, the two roles alternate, such that a quasi-reciprocity is established between the ego and the symbol of the ego. But this reciprocity is illusory: it cannot be equivalent to a veritable reciprocity except in the cases of splitting, i.e. when a certain coalescence is effectuated between the two symbols of the ego, the symbol relative to which the ego is an individual and the symbol relative to which it is a milieu; a counter-personality is therefore constituted at the expense of the first, which increasingly loses its power of actuality and consequently its freedom; freedom is in fact essentially constituted by this double adequation of the ego to its symbols, that of memory and that of the imagination. What psychoanalysis considers to be an unconscious should in fact be considered a counter-ego, a double that is not a true ego, since it is never endowed with actuality; it can only be expressed in dreams or automatic acts, not in the state of integrated activity. Janet's idea of the personality splitting is perhaps closer to reality than that of the unconscious, which has been accepted since Freud. However, it would be more appropriate to speak of a *doubling [doublement]* of personality, of a phantom-personality, than of a *splitting [dédoublement]* of personality. What splits is not the actual personality, but another personality, a personality equivalent that is constituted outside the field of the ego, like a virtual image is constituted beyond a mirror for the observer without ever really being there. If there were a veritable splitting of the personality, one could not speak of a first state and a second state; even if the second state occupies a time frame longer than the first state, it does not have the same structure and can be recognized as the second state.

Yet Descartes chooses the development of memory as the privileged case in which the existence of the subject is deciphered: the reciprocity of the doubt that *just occurred* relative to the doubt that *is* currently being constituted as doubt establishes the substantial unity of the subject in a conditional and causal circularity. Nevertheless, this circularity is a borderline case; there is already distance, and there must be distance for there to be circularity; but the circularity conceals and obscures the distance; this is why Descartes can substantialize what is not a substance properly speaking, i.e. an operation; the soul is defined as *res* and as *cogitans*, the support of the operation and the operation in the process of being accomplished. However, the unity and homogeneity of this being formed by a support and by an operation can only be affirmed if the being-operation ensemble continues to be perpetuated in the same mode. If the activity stops or seems to stop, the permanence and identity of substance thus defined is put at risk: whence the problem of sleep and loss of consciousness for Descartes relative to the conception of the nature of the soul.

Descartes has legitimately considered the self-return of doubt as indicating the consistency and unity of the individuated being; circularity indeed should be considered as indicating the consistency of the individuated being; but perhaps there is an error in considering that the return of actualized doubt as an object of actual doubt is a veritable circularity; assimilating this return to a circularity in his proof of the Cogito, Descartes does not account for the growing distance between actualized doubt—which has become the object of memory—and actualizing doubt, relative to which this anterior doubt is an object to the extent that it is no longer already actual: individuation is not achieved, it is in the process of taking place, but there is already more than the actual subject ego to the extent that there is enough distance between *doubt* and *ego* for doubt to be able to be the object of the ego: doubt becoming object is doubt passing and not doubt actualizing. Through this first assimilation, through this first encroachment unrecognized as encroachment, the adjacent symbol of the ego is attached to and assimilated with the ego: by gradually proceeding in this way Descartes attaches the whole symbolic content to the actual ego; the attachment of actualized doubt to the subject of actual doubt authorizes the attachment of willing, feeling, loving, hating, and imagining to thinking substance; the fact of suffering is homogeneous relative to the act of thinking. The most distant aspects of reflecting thought are then attached to this reflecting thought that has helped define the essence of the *res cogitans*. This radical affirmation of homogeneity can only be effectuated by pushing back the limit between the *res cogitans* and the *res extensa*: the break is thus so abrupt between the aspects of thought most attached to the body and the body itself that the gulf between substances is insurmountable. Descartes has not just separated the soul from the body; he has also, within the very interior of the soul, created a homogeneity and a unity that prevent the conception of a continuous gradient of distancing relative to the actual ego, thereby joining it, in its most decentered zones at the limit of memory and the imagination, with somatic reality.

Psychically, the individual continues its individuation by means of memory and imagination, the function of the past and the function of the future according to mundane definitions. Indeed, it is only after the fact that one can speak of past and future for memory and imagination: memory is what creates the past for the being, in the same way that the imagination creates the future; the product of this psychical individuation is in fact only psychical at the center; the pure psychical is the actual; the distant future and the past that has become distant past are realities that tend toward the somatic; the past is incorporated as well as the future into the form of anticipation. By distancing from the present, the past becomes a state against the ego and is available for the ego but is not directly related to the ego and is not adherent to the ego. The future projected is all the more distanced from actualization as it is broadly pushed back into the future; but progressive becoming evokes it and renders it imminent, little by little gives it a status that is closer to the status of the present, i.e. more directly symbolic relative to the actual present.

According to this manner of envisioning the reality of the individuated being, it could be said that the body plays a double role with respect to consciousness; with respect to imagining consciousness, the body is milieu and not individuated reality; it is the real virtual, i.e. a source of reality that can become symbolic with respect to the present: this reality splits into present and future as though into individual and milieu. Conversely, the body results from the splitting that creates memory as an individuated being relative to a consciousness milieu of individuation: the consciousness of memory is thus always as though it were below what it remembers, whereas imagining consciousness is above what it imagines; the past—and therefore the body—is what directs and chooses the present in the consciousness of memory, while the present chooses the future in imagining consciousness. The body provides access to memory while consciousness provides access to imagination.

Consciousness is attached to the body through memory and through imagination at least as much through functions generally considered psychosomatic; the complementary opposition of memory and imagination indicates psychophysiological relation. But this relation cannot be assimilated to bisubstantial relation; the aspect of the soul and the aspect of the body are merely extreme cases; the pure soul is the present; the pure body is the soul infinitely past or infinitely distanced into the future. This is why the soul is univalent, while the body is bivalent; the body is pure past and future; the soul makes the near past and near future coincide; it is present; the soul is the being's present; the body is its future and its past; the soul is in the body, just as the present is between the future and the past that radiate out from it. The body is past and future, but not the soul; in this sense, the soul is timeless as pure soul; but this timelessness is nevertheless lodged between two temporal realities; this timelessness temporalizes toward the past by becoming body, and it arises from a corporeal reality that approaches the state of the present. The reality of the being comes from the future toward the present by becoming soul, and it is reincorporated by passing. The soul emerges and is built between two corporeities; it is the extremity of anima-tion and the origin of incorporation.

Consciousness is therefore a mediation between two corporeal becomings, an ascending movement toward the present and a descending movement from the present. One could say that this movement of becoming—proceeding step by step—is transductive. The true schema of real transduction is time, the passage from state to state that is formed by the very nature of the states, by their content, and not by the exterior schema of their succession: time thus conceived is the being's movement, real modification, reality that mod-ifies and is modified, being simultaneously what it leaves behind and what it takes, real insofar as it is relational to the middle [*milieu*] of two states; being of passage, a passing reality, reality insofar as it passes—such is transductive reality. The individuated being is that for which there exists this ascent and this descent of becoming relative to the central present. There is no living and psychical individuated being except to the extent that it assumes time. To live as an individuated being is to exert memory and anticipation. The present is psychosomatic at the limit, but it is essentially psychical. Relative to this present that is psychical, the future is like an immense possible field, a milieu of virtualities associated with the present through a symbolic rela-tion; on the contrary, the past relative to this very present is an ensemble of individualized, localized, defined points. The present is a transduction between the field of the future and the interconnected points of the past. The field of the future is reticulated through and by the present; it loses its ten-sions, its potentials, its implicit energy that expands in its full extension and is coextensive with it; it crystallizes into individuated points in a neutral void; whereas the tendency of the future is expanded through the whole milieu (like the energy of a field not localizable into points) and constitutes a sort of general energy, the past takes refuge in a network of points that absorb its whole substance; it loses the milieu, its own extension, the omnipresent immanence of tension to charged reality; there is nothing in the universe of memory but actions and reactions between points of reality structured in a network; between these points, there is the void, and this is why the past is condensable, since there is nothing in the intervals between these points of reality; the past is isolated relative to itself, and it can become a system only partially through the present that reactualizes it, takes it back up, gives it tendency and living corporeity; the past owes its availability to this structure of molecular isolation; it can be artificialized because it does not hold onto itself; it allows itself to be utilized because it is in pieces. The future does not

allow itself to be condensed, detailed, or even thought; it can only be antici-
pated by a real act, for its reality is not condensed in a certain number of
points; all of its energy exists between possible points; there is a proper am-
bience of the future, a relational capacity and an implicit activity before any
realization; *the being preexists itself through its present.* The present of the
being is thus simultaneously individual and milieu; it is individual relative to
the future and milieu relative to the past; the soul, the active essence of the
present, is both individual and milieu. But it cannot be individual and milieu
without this existence of the total being, the psychosomatic being, which is
both somatic and social, linked to exteriority. The relation of the present to
the past and to the future is analogical vis-à-vis the somatopsychic relation
and to this other, vaster relation of the complete individuated being to the
world and to other individuated beings. This is why one must refrain from
substantializing the soul, for the soul does not possess all its reality within
itself; the present requires the future and the past in order to be present, and
through these two distancings of the future and the past, the soul approaches
the body. The body is the non-present; it is not the matter of a soul-form.
The present arises from the body and returns to the body; the soul crystallizes the body. The present is individuation's operation. The present is not a
permanent form; it is found as form in the operation, it finds form in individuation. This double rapport of the symbolization of the present relative
to the future and to the past allows one to say that the present, or rather
presence, is signification relative to the past and to the future, a mutual signification of the past and of the future through the transductive operation.
The present consists for the being in existing as individual and as milieu in
a unitary way; however, this is only possible through the operation of ongoing individuation, which is analogous in itself to the initial individuation by
which the somatopsychic being constitutes itself within a tensed and polarized systematic whole. The individual concentrates within it the dynamics
that has given birth to it, and it perpetuates the first operation as a continued
individuation; *to live is to perpetuate an ongoing relative birth.* It does not suffice to define the living being as an organism. The living being is an organism depending on the initial individuation; but it can live only by being an
organism that organizes and organizes itself through time; the organization
of the organism is the result of an individual individuation that can be called
absolute; but this organization is a condition of life, rather than life itself; it
is a condition of the perpetuated birth that life is. To live is to have a presence,
to be present relative to oneself and relative to what is outside oneself. It is
indeed true in this sense that the soul is distinct from the body, that it is not

the organism; it is the presence of the organism; to make of consciousness an aspect of the organism, as Goldstein does, is to envelop it in an organismic unity. However, the Parmenidean monism that inspires Goldstein, failing to give temporality a constitutive role in the being, cannot introduce diversification into the being except through the notion of a "folding of being," according to the expression put forth by the author; the soul could then only be a being imperfectly detached from within a totality that would in this way lose its reciprocal unity of circular plenitude. If, by contrast, the soul is conceived as what perpetuates the first operation of individuation that the being expresses and integrates (insofar as it is the result of the latter yet contains and extends it), such that the genesis that has made it be is veritably its own genesis, then the soul intervenes as the extension of this unity; it has a reference to what has not been incorporated into the individual by individuation; it is presence to this symbol of the individual; it is at the very center of the individual, but it is also that through which the latter remains attached to that which is not individual.

CHAPTER THREE

Collective Individuation and the Foundations of the Transindividual

I. THE INDIVIDUAL AND THE SOCIAL, GROUP INDIVIDUATION

1. Social Time and Individual Time

Such a view of individual reality seeking to clarify the problems that psychology is tasked with resolving would nevertheless make it impossible to arrive at a clear representation of the rapport of the individual to society. Society encounters the individual being and is encountered by it in the present. But this present is not the same as what could be called (at the limit) the individual present or the somatopsychic present. The social rapport is indeed to the present from the point of view of each individual. But society encountered in this rapport itself possesses its equivalent of substantiality, its presence, as a correlation between past and future; society becomes; an affirmation of permanence is still a mode of becoming, for permanence is the stability of a becoming that has a temporal dimension. The individual encounters in society a specific demand of the future and a conservation of the past; the future of the individual in society is a reticulated future conditioned according to points of contact with a structure quite analogous to that of the individual past. Engagement in society for the individual directs it toward the fact of being this or that; becoming is no longer effectuated—as in the non-social individual envisioned by hypothesis—from the future toward the present: it is effectuated in the inverse direction *starting from the present*; the individual finds himself proposing goals and roles to choose; he must tend toward these roles, toward types, toward images to be guided by structures that he endeavors to realize by coordinating with them and by accomplishing them; society facing the individual being presents a network of states and of roles through which individual behavior must pass.

What is most important for society is the individual past because the agreement of the individual and the social is formed by the coincidence of two reticulations. The individual is forced to project his future through this social network that is already there; to socialize, the individual must pass; to be integrated is to coincide according to a reticulation and not according to this force that is immanent to the future of the somatopsychic being. The individual draws on tendencies from the social past and an impetus toward a specific action rather than a veritable remembrance; he draws from the social past that which would be associated with the dynamism of his future and not with the reticulation of his individual past; the rapport to the social re-quires that between the individual soul and the social contact a sort of rever-sal, a sort of substitution, is established. Sociality requires presence, but a presence-in-reverse. The social soul and the individual soul operate in inverse directions and individuate opposite from one another. This is why the indi-vidual can appear to himself as fleeing into the social and confirming himself in opposition to the social. The social thus appears as a reality that is quite different from the milieu with respect to the individual; we can speak of the social milieu only imprecisely and by expanding its meaning. The social could be a milieu if the individuated being were a simple result accomplished once and for all, i.e. if he did not continue to live by transforming. The social milieu exists as such only to the extent that it is not grasped as a reciprocal social; such a situation only corresponds to that of children or the sick; it is not that of the integrated adult. The integrated adult, relative to the social, is an equally social being to the extent that he possesses an actual active consciousness, i.e. to the extent that he extends and perpetuates the movement of individu-ation that has given birth to him instead of merely resulting from this indi-viduation. Society does not really emerge from the mutual presence of several individuals, but it is also not a substantial reality that should be superposed on individual beings and conceived as independent of them: it is the opera-tion and the condition of operation through which is created a mode of pres-ence more complex than the presence of the individuated being alone.

2. Interiority Groups and Exteriority Groups

The relation of an individuated being to other individuated beings can form either analogically—the past and the future of each coinciding with the past and the future of the others—or non-analogically—the future of each indi-viduated being finding, within the ensemble of the other beings, not subjects but a reticular structure through which it must pass. The first case is what

American researchers call the *in-group*; the second case is what they call the *out-group*; however, there is no *in-group* that does not supposes an *out-group*. The social is formed by the mediation between the individual being and the *out-group* through the intermediary of the *in-group*. It is useless to proceed like Bergson by opposing an open group and a closed group;[1] up close, the social is open; from afar, it is closed; the social operation is situated at the limit between the *in-group* and the *out-group* rather than at the limit between the individual and the group; the individual's body proper extends up to the limits of the *in-group*; just as there is a corporeal schema, there is a social schema that extends the limits of the ego up to the boundary between the *in-group* and the *out-group*. In a certain sense, the open group *(in-group)* can be considered as the social body of the subject; the social personality extends up to the limits of this group; belief, as a mode of belonging to a group, defines the expansion of the personality up to the limits of the *in-group*; such a group indeed can be characterized by the community of implicit and explicit beliefs in all the members of the group.

In certain cases, it can come about that the open group is significantly reduced around an atypical subject to the point that the social expansion of the personality is null, and that consequently every group is an *out-group*; this is what occurs in cases of delinquency, mental alienation, or in "deviants" within a specific group; it can also come about, through an immense effort of expansion of the personality, that every group, even those that normally seem to be *out-groups,* is accepted by the subject as an *in-group*. Charity is the force of expansion of the personality that does not wish to recognize any limit to the *in-group* and considers it as coextensive with the whole of humanity or even with all of creation; for St. Francis of Assisi, not only men but the animals themselves belong to the *in-group,* the interiority group. Similarly, Christ did not recognize enemies, and he had an attitude of interiority even toward those who struck him.

Between these two extremes that absolutely reduce or infinitely expand the boundaries of the interiority group, there is the status of contemporary life, i.e. everyday social life, which situates the limit between the interiority group and the exteriority group at a certain distance from the individual. This limit is defined by a second zone of presence attached to the presence of the individual. The integration of the individual to the social is formed by the creation of a functional analogy between the operation that defines individual presence and the operation that defines social presence; the individual must find a social individuation that overlaps his personal individuation;

his rapport to the *in-group* and his rapport to the *out-group* are like the future and the past respectively; the *in-group* is the source of virtualities, of tensions, just like the individual future; it is a reservoir of presence because it precedes the individual in the encounter of the exteriority group; it represses the exteriority group. Through belief, belonging to the interiority group is defined as an unstructured tendency that is comparable to the future for the individual: it is conflated with the individual future, but it also assumes the individual's past, for the individual is given an origin in this interiority group, whether it be real or mythical: it is of this group and for this group; future and past are simplified, led to a state of elementary purity.

3. Social Reality as a System of Relations

Thus, it is difficult to consider the social and the individual as clashing directly in a relation of the individual to society. This confrontation corresponds only to an extreme theoretical case to which certain lived pathological situations approach; the social substantializes into society for the delinquent or the alienated, and perhaps for the child; but the veritable social is not substantial, for the social is not a term of relation: it is a system of relations, a system that includes a relation and sustains it. The individual only relates with the social through the social; the interiority group mediates the relation between the individual and the social. The group interiority is a certain dimension of the individual personality, not a relation to a distinct term of the individual; it is a zone of participation around the individual. Social life is a relation between the milieu of participation and the milieu of non-participation.

Psychologism is insufficient for representing social life, insofar as it supposes that the intergroup relations can be considered as an extension of the individual's relations to the interiority group; by partially exteriorizing the relations of the individual to the interiority group, then by partially interiorizing the relations of exteriority groups to the interiority group, one can manage in an illusory manner to identify two types of relation; but this identification misrecognizes the proper nature of the social relation, since it misrecognizes the boundary of relational activity between the interiority group and the exteriority group. Sociologism also misrecognizes the characteristic relation of social life in the same way by substantializing the social based on exteriority, instead of recognizing the relational character of social activity. However, there is not the psychological and the sociological, but there is the human, which, at the extreme limit and in rare situations, can split into the psychological and the sociological. Both psychology and sociology are two viewpoints that fabricate their own object based on interiority or exteriority; the psychological approach to the social is formed by the intermediary of small groups; nevertheless, this manner of approaching the social based on the psychological forces one to load the psychological with something of the social: such is the *affective stability* of the American psychosociologists, i.e. the character of the individual being that is already social or pre-social. In the same way, adaptability and the capacity for acculturation are pre-social aspects of the being. The individual being is seen according to instances that overflow his individual existence.

Similarly, the sociological attitude includes contents of the pre-individual in the social that will allow for individual reality to be recovered by reconstituting it. To this extent, we understand why problems like those concerning the study of labor are invalidated by the opposition between psychologism and sociologism; the human relations that characterize labor or at the very least are introduced by labor can be reduced neither to the play of sociological substantialism nor to an interpsychological schema; they are situated at the boundary of the interiority group and the exteriority group. However, envisioned as interpsychological relations, the human relations of labor are assimilated to the satisfaction of a certain number of needs, the list of which could be drawn up based on an inspection of the individual being by considering it before any social integration, as if there were a pure and complete individual before any possible integration. Labor is consequently considered as the satisfaction of an individual need, as relative to an essence of man, a collective essence but one that defines man as individual, as a being made of soul and body (something also found in the notion of manual labor and of intellectual labor, with a hierarchical distinction between these two levels of labor). Based on sociologism, on the contrary, labor is envisioned as an aspect of *the exploitation of nature by men in society,* and it is understood through the politico-economic relation. Labor then is substantialized as an exchange value in a social system within which the individual disappears. The notion of class is founded on the fact that the group is always considered as an exteriority group; the interiority of one's own class is no longer that of a social body coextensive with the limits of the personality, for class is no longer eccentric relative to the individual; one's class is conceived as one's own class based on conflict with the adverse class; it is through the return of becoming-conscious that one's class is conceived as one's own; becoming-conscious is secondary relative to this first opposition; there is no longer a structure of successive circles but a structure of conflict with a front line.

4. Insufficiency of the Notion of the
Essence of Man and of Anthropology

However, it can be wondered whether an anthropology would be capable of giving a unitary vision of man that can serve as a principle for this study of social relation. But an anthropology does not include this relational duality contained in a unity that characterizes this rapport; it is not based on an essence that one can indicate what man is, for every anthropology will be forced to substantialize either the individual or the social to give an essence of man. By itself, the notion of anthropology already includes the implicit affirmation of the specificity of Man separated from the vital. Nevertheless, it is indeed certain that one cannot make man emerge from the vital if one deducts Man from the vital; but the vital is the vital that includes Man, not the vital without Man; it is the vital up to Man and including Man; there is the whole vital, which includes Man.

The anthropological point of view would thus suppose a preliminary abstraction, similar to the abstraction one encounters in the subdivisions into individual and social and the principle of these further abstractions. Anthropology cannot be the principle of the study of Man; on the contrary, human relational activities, like the one that constitutes labor, can be taken as the principle of an anthropology to be developed. The being as relation is what is first and what must be taken as a principle; the human is social, psychosocial, psychical, and somatic, without any of these aspects being able to be considered as fundamental while the others would be judged as ancillary. In particular, labor cannot be defined solely as a certain rapport of man to nature. There is a labor that is not referred to Nature, for example the labor accomplished on Man itself; a surgeon labors; the exploitation of Nature by associated Men is a particular case of the relational activity that constitutes labor; labor can be grasped in its essence as a particular case only if this essence extracts its particularity from the whole spectrum of possible labor activities; a particular case cannot be taken as a foundation, even if it is encountered very frequently. Labor is a certain rapport between the interiority group and the exteriority group, just like war, propaganda, and commerce. Each group with respect to others can be considered as an individual to a certain extent; but the error of traditional psychosociological conceptions consists in taking the group as a gathering of individuals in the manner in which there are gatherings of individuals in the sciences, i.e. the domain of the biological sciences; in fact, the interiority group—and every group relative to itself exists to the extent that it is an interiority group—is formed by the superposition of individual personalities and not by their agglomeration; the agglomeration, whether organized or inorganic, would presuppose a viewpoint at the level of somatic realities, not at the level of somatopsychic ensembles.

An interiority group does not have a structure that is more complex than a single person; each individual personality is coextensive with what can be called the group personality, i.e. with the shared locus of individual personalities that constitute the group. However, this manner of envisioning the group is not a psychologism, for two reasons: the first is that the word personality is not taken in a purely psychical sense, but in a really and unitarily psychosomatic sense, which includes tendencies, drives, beliefs, somatic attitudes, significations, and expression. The second reason, which is more important and constitutes the foundation of the first, is that this overlapping of individual personalities in the interiority group plays a self-constitutive structural and functional role. This overlapping is an individuation, the resolution of a conflict, the assumption of conflictual tensions in an organic, structural, and functional stability. These are not structures of personalities that are previously defined, i.e. structures that are constituted and fully formed before the moment when the interiority group is constituted, and that come to be encountered and overlapped; the psychosocial personality is contemporaneous with the genesis of the group, which is an individuation.

The group is not what contributes to the individual being a fully formed personality, like a cloak tailored in advance. The individual, with an already constituted personality, is not what is approached by other individuals with the same personality to constitute a group with them. It is necessary to start from the operation of group individuation within which the individual beings are both the milieu and the agents of a syncrystallization; the group is a syncrystallization of several individual beings, and it is the result of this syncrystallization that constitutes the group personality; the group personality is not introduced into individuals by the group, since the individual must be present for this operation to occur; furthermore, it is not just required that the group merely be present; the group must also be tensed and partially undetermined, like pre-individual being before individuation; an absolutely complete and perfect being could not enter into a group; the individual must still be a bearer of tensions, tendencies, potentials, and reality, and this reality it bears must be structurable but not yet structured for the interiority group to be possible; the interiority group emerges when the forces of the future harbored by several living individuals lead to a collective structuration; participation and overlapping arise at this instant of group individuation and of the individuation of grouped individuals. The individuation that gives birth to the group is also an individuation of grouped individuals; without emotion, without potential, and without preliminary tension, there can be no group individuation; a society of monads cannot exist; the contract does not found a group, no more than the statutory reality of an already existing group; even in this borderline case where the already constituted group receives a new individual and incorporates it, the incorporation of the new is a new birth (individuation) for this individual and also a rebirth for the group; a group that cannot be recreated by incorporating new members dissolves as an interiority group.

The member of a group sustains the collective personality in the group by recruiting new beings and by introducing them into the group. The distinction between psychogroups and sociogroups is only valid as a manner of defining a certain polarity within groups: every real group is simultaneously a psychogroup and a sociogroup. The pure sociogroup would have no interiority and would be nothing but a social substance; a group is a psychogroup as soon as it forms; but this momentum of the psychogroup can only be perpetuated by incorporating, by giving birth to sociogroupal structures. Psychogroups and sociogroups can only be distinguished abstractly.

5. Notion of Group Individual

It is therefore not appropriate to speak of the influence of the group on the individual; in fact, the group is not formed by individuals joined together in a group due to certain bonds, but by grouped individuals, *group individuals*. Individuals are group individuals, just as the group is a group of individuals. It cannot be said that the group exerts an influence on individuals, for this action is contemporaneous with the life of individuals and is not independent from the life of individuals; the group is also not interindividual reality but the complement of individuation on a vaster scale joining together a plurality of individuals.

This type of reality cannot be thought if it is not acknowledged that there is a mutual convertibility of structures into operations and of operations into structures, and if the relational operation is not considered as having a value of being. Substantialism forces us to think the group as anterior to the individual or the individual as anterior to the group, which is how psychologism and sociologism arise as two substantialisms on different levels, that of the molecular or the molar. The choice of an intermediate, microsociological, or macropsychical dimension cannot resolve the problem, since it is not founded on the choice of a dimension that is adequate to a particular phenomenon that would be intermediate between the social and the psychical. There is no psychosociological domain that would be the domain of restricted groups; this privileged aspect of certain restricted groups only stems from the fact that the successive crises of individuation, the outbursts of functional structurations through which they pass, are more visible and can be more easily studied. But these phenomena are the same as in larger groups, and they introduce the same dynamic and structural rapports; only the types of mediation between individuals are more complex, since they use modes of transmission and of action that imply a delay and are exempt from real presence; but this development of networks of communication and of authority does not have an essence (apart from macrosocial phenomena insofar as they are social) in their rapport to what can be called the individual being. The rapport of the individual to the group is always the same in its foundation: it depends on the simultaneous individuation of individual beings and of the group; it is presence.

6. Role of Belief in the Group Individual

In the individual, belief is the latent set of references relative to which significations can be discovered. Belief is not the immanence of the group to the individual, who would ignore such an immanence and would falsely believe to be an autonomous individual when he would merely express the group; belief is this collective individuation in the process of existing; it is presence to the other group individuals, the overlapping of personalities; personalities can overlap through belief; more exactly, what is called collective belief is equivalent in the personality to what a belief would be in the individual; but this belief does not exist as belief; there is belief only when some force or obstacle obligates the individual to define and structure his belonging to the group as expressible in intelligible terms for individuals who are not members of the group. Belief supposes a foundation of belief, which is the personality formed in the group individuation; belief develops in the individual as veritable belief when belonging to the group is called into question; belief is veritably interindividual; it supposes a foundation that is not merely interindividual but veritably groupal.

This is why the study of beliefs is a rather bad means of knowing man as a group member. The man who believes defends himself, or he wants to change groups and is in disharmony with other individuals or with himself. Belief is granted a causal privilege in group belonging, since belief is what is the easiest to manifest, project, and consequently grasp in the usual methods of the knowledge of psychosocial reality. But belief is a phenomenon of the dissociation or alteration of groups, not a basis of their existence; it has a provisional value of compensation, consolidation, or reparation rather than a fundamental signification relative to the genesis of the group and to the mode of existence of individuals in the group. Perhaps one could distinguish in this sense between myth (collective belief) and opinion, which would be individual belief. But myths and opinions correspond in symbolic pairs; when the group elaborates myths, group individuals express corresponding opinions; myths are the geometrical sites of opinions. Between myth and opinion, there is merely a difference relative to the mode of inherence: opinion is what can be expressed relative to a precise exterior case; it is the norm of a defined and localized judgment concerning a precise matter; myth is an indefinite reserve of possible judgments; it has the value of a paradigm and is turned toward group interiority, rather than toward beings exterior to judging relative to group norms; myth represents the group and the personality in its internal consistency, whereas opinions are already diversified in definite objectivated situations that are separate from one another.

Myths and opinions are the dynamic and structural extension of the operations of group individuation into situations within which this individuation is no longer actual, possible, or able to be reactivated; opinion is borne by the individual, and it manifests in situations where the individual is no longer in the group, although he is of the group and tends to act as belonging to it; opinion allows the individual to confront other individuals that belong to the exteriority group, all while maintaining his relation to the interiority group and allowing this confrontation to occur as a confrontation with the exteriority group. Myth, on the contrary, would be the shared site of opinions that obey a systematics of group interiority, and this is why myth cannot circulate perfectly in its pure form except in the interiority group; it supposes a logic of participation and a certain number of basic evidences that are part of the group individuation.

7. Group Individuation and Vital Individuation

It is possible to investigate the signification of social reality with respect to the living individual. Can we speak of individuals living in society, i.e. can we suppose that individuals would be individuals even if they didn't live in society? The example of animal species shows us that there are cases in which the life of the solitary individual is possible; in other cases, periods of solitary life alternate with periods of collective life. Finally, in a number of cases, life is almost always social, except in some extremely rare moments (courtship, mating).

Should it then be said that sociality resides in the species and is a part of specific characteristics? If this proposition is admitted, we will have to consider an individual that is not integrated into a social group (in a generally social species) as an unaccomplished, incomplete individual that does not participate in this system of individuation that the group is; if, on the contrary, the group is formed by beings that could be complete individuals by themselves, the isolated individual is not necessarily incomplete.

However, the response to this question seems contained in the morphology and physiology of the species. When a morphological and functional specialization intervenes and models individuals to the point of making it improper for them to live in isolation, sociality should be defined as one of the characteristics of the species; the bee or the ant is necessarily social, because it only exists as a very specialized individual in its inability to live alone. On the contrary, in the species where there is no extremely clear differentiation between individuals that makes them incomplete by themselves, the necessity of social life belongs less directly to specific characteristics; according to ecology or other conditions, temporary isolated life arises or halts; the group can be intermittent; the group is then a mode of behavior of the species relative to the milieu or to other species, rather than the expression of the imperfect and incomplete character of the individual being. This is generally the type of existence for societies of mammals.

For man, the problem is more complex; there is the somatic and functional independence of the individual, as in other mammals; there is both the possibility of a somewhat grouped life and a somewhat solitary life, which is the consequence of this somatic and functional completion of the individual. Under these conditions, there can be groupings that correspond to a mode of behavior relative to the milieu; Marx interprets the characteristic association of labor in this sense. But it seems that in addition to this somato-psychic individuation that permits independence or association on the level of specific behaviors, the human being still remains unachieved, incomplete, evolving individual by individual; there is no specific behavior sufficient for responding to this becoming, which is so strong that, while having a somato-psychic achievement at least as perfect as that of other animals, man resembles a very incomplete being. It is as if, above a first specific individuation, man sought another individuation and required two individuations consecutively. Recognized as living in the world, man can associate together to exploit the world; but something is still lacking for man, there is still a void to fill, something yet to be accomplished. Exploiting Nature alone is not enough for man; the species facing the world is not an interiority group;

another relation is required to make each man exist as a social person, and for that to come about, there must be this second genesis, i.e. the group individuation.

After having been constituted as a complete being, man once again enters into a calling of incompletion in which he seeks a second individuation; Nature or man face to face with Nature are not enough. There still remain forces and tensions that go further than the group face to face with nature; this is why man thinks of himself as a spiritual being, and to a certain degree the notion of spirit is perhaps mythical, insofar as it leads to the substantialization of the spirit and to a somatopsychic dualism. In addition to functional groups, which are like animal groups, or in addition to the functional tenor of groups, there is something hyperfunctional in groups, specifically their interiority; this interiority creates the human individual a second time, recreates him through his existence as an already biologically individuated being; this second individuation is the group individuation; but it is not at all reducible to the specific group, i.e. the exploitation of Nature by associated men; this group, which can be called an action group, is distinct from the interiority group.

Nothing, moreover, proves that human groups are the only ones to possess the characteristics we define here: it could be that animals include a certain coefficient that corresponds to what we are seeking as the basis of spirituality in human groups, albeit in a more transitory, less stable, and less continual way. In this opposition of human groups to animal groups, here we are not taking animals as being veritably what they are, but as responding, perhaps fictitiously, to what the notion of animality is for man, i.e. the notion of a being that has relations regulated by the characteristics of the species with Nature. It is then possible to call the human social group a group whose basis and function would be a specific adaptive response to Nature; this would be the case for a labor group that would be nothing but a labor group, if such a thing could be realized in a pure and stable manner. Social reality thus defined would remain on the vital level; it would not create the relation of group interiority, unless one accepts the Marxist schema of the conditioning of superstructures by the socioeconomic infrastructure.

But it is precisely a question of knowing if one can treat the other types of groups and the other contents of group life as superstructures with respect to this unique infrastructure. There are perhaps other infrastructures than the exploitation of nature by men in society, other modes of relation to the milieu than those that pass through the relation of elaboration, i.e. through labor. The very notion of infrastructure can be critiqued: is labor a structure, or indeed a tension, a potential, a certain manner of being connected to the world through an activity that calls for a structuration without itself being a structure? If it is admitted that socio-natural conditionings are multiple on the specific level, it is difficult to extract one of these conditionings and to assert that it has the value of a structure; perhaps Marx has generalized a real historical fact, i.e. the dominance of this mode of relation to Nature that labor is in the human relations of the nineteenth century; but it is difficult to find the criterion that allows for this relation to be integrated into an anthropology. The man who works is already biologically individuated. On the biological level, labor is like the exploitation of Nature; it is a reaction of humanity as a species, a speciated reaction. This is why labor is so permeable to other interindividual relations: it does not have its own resistance, it does not produce a second, properly human individuation; it is defenseless; in himself, the individual remains a biological individual, a simple individual, a determined and already given individual. But above these biological, biologico-social, and interindividual relations, there is another level that could be called the level of the transindividual: this is what corresponds to interiority groups, to a veritable group individuation.

The interindividual relation goes from individual to individual; it does not penetrate individuals; transindividual action is what makes it such that individuals exist together as the elements of a system that contains potentials and metastability, expectation and tension, then the discovery of a structure and of a functional organization that integrate and resolve this problematic of incorporated immanence. The transindividual passes into the individual as though from individual to individual; individual personalities are constituted together by overlapping and not by agglomeration or by a specializing organization, as in the biological grouping of solidarity and division of labor: the division of labor imprisons the biological unities, i.e. the individuals, into their practical functions. The transindividual does not localize individuals: it makes them coincide; it makes individuals communicate through significations: relations of information are what is primordial, not relations of solidarity and functional differentiation. This coincidence of personalities is not reductive, for it is not founded on the amputation of individual differences or on their utilization toward ends of functional differentiation (which would imprison the individual in its particularities), but on a second structuration based on what the biological structuration that forms living individuals still leaves unresolved.

It could be said that biological individuation does not exhaust tensions, which have aided in its constitution: these tensions pass into the individual;

they pass into the individual from the pre-individual, which is both milieu and individual: it is precisely based on this position of the unresolved in man, within this not-yet-individuated charge of reality, that man seeks out his fellow man to form a group in which he will find presence through a second individuation. In man and perhaps also in animals, biological individuation does not fully resolve tensions: it leaves the problematic latent, subsistent; to say that life is that which carries spirit is not to express oneself correctly; for life is a first individuation; but this first individuation has not been able to exhaust and absorb all forces; it has not resolved everything; we have movement to go ever further, as Malebranche said; in fact, we have tension and potentials for becoming-other, for recommencing an individuation that is not destructive of the first.

This force is not vital; it is pre-vital; life is a specification, a first solution, complete in itself by leaving a residue outside its system. It is not as a living being that man carries with him enough to individuate spiritually, but as a being that contains within itself something pre-individual and pre-vital. This reality can be called transindividual. Its origin is neither social nor individual; this reality is deposited in the individual, carried by the individual, but it does not belong to the individual and is not a part of the individual's system of being. We should not speak of the individual's tendencies that carry it toward the group; for these tendencies are not properly speaking tendencies of the individual qua individual; they are the non-resolution of potentials that have preceded the genesis of the individual. The being that precedes the individual has not been individuated without remainder; it has not been totally resolved into individual and milieu; the individual has conserved the pre-individual with it, and all individuals together thus have a sort of unstructured ground based upon which a new individuation can occur.

The psychosocial is transindividual: it is this reality that the individuated being carries, this charge of being for future individuations. This pre-vital charge should not be called *élan vital*, since it is not exactly in continuity with vital individuation, although it extends life, which is a first individuation. As a bearer of pre-individual reality, man encounters in others another charge of this reality; the emergence of structures and functions that can occur at this moment is not interindividual, since it contributes a new individuation that is superposed on the older one and goes beyond it, linking several individuals into a group that is born. In this sense, it could be said that spirituality is marginal relative to the individual rather than central, and that it does not establish a communication of consciousnesses but a synergy and shared structuration of beings. The individual is not just the individual, for it is also the *being's reserve,* which is not yet polarized but which is available and lies in wait. The transindividual is with the individual, but it is not the individuated individual. It is with the individual according to a more primordial relation than belonging, inherence, or the relation of exteriority; this is why it is a possible contact beyond the limits of the individual; to speak of the soul is to overly individualize and overly particularize the transindividual. The impression of surpassing individual limits and the opposite impression of exteriority that characterize the spiritual have a meaning and find the foundation of their unity of divergence in this pre-individual reality. The divergence of spirituality's transcendence and immanence is not a divergence within the transindividual itself but a divergence with respect to the individuated individual alone.

8. Pre-individual Reality and Spiritual Reality: The Phases of Being

The very notion of psychosomatic unity is not completely satisfying, and we recognize this insufficiency of organismic theory without being able to say what it consists in. However, it in fact seems that the insufficiency consists in this overflowing of pre-individual reality with respect to the reality of the individual. The individual is only itself, but it *exists* as superior to itself, since it carries with it a more complete reality that individuation has not exhausted and that is still new and potential, i.e. animated by potentials. The individual is aware of this fact of being linked to a reality that is over and above itself as an individuated being; with a mythological reduction, one can make of this reality a δαίμων [daímon], a spirit *[génie],* a soul; one then sees in it a second individual that doubles the first, watches over it and can constrain it, lives on after it as an individual. By accentuating the aspect of transcendence, one can also find in this same reality the testimony for the existence of a spiritual individual exterior to the individual.

All these various expressions used for naming this spiritual reality are expressions the individual translates for consciousness and conduct so as not to feel alone inside himself, to not feel limited as an individual to a reality that would be nothing but himself; the individual begins to participate by association within himself before any manifested presence of some other individuated reality. Starting from this first feeling of possible presence, the search begins for this second fulfillment of the being that reveals the transindividual to it by structuring this reality carried with the individual at the same time as other similar realities and by means of them. One can speak neither of the immanence nor transcendence of spirituality with respect to the individual, for the veritable relation is that of the individual to the transindividual:

the transindividual is what is on the outside of the individual as well as inside him; in fact, the transindividual, insofar as it is not structured, traverses the individual; it is not in topological relation with the individual; *immanence or transcendence* can only be said with respect to individuated reality; there is an anteriority of the transindividual relative to the individual that prevents defining a rapport of transcendence or immanence; the transindividual and the individuated do not concern the same phase of the being: there is a co-existence of two phases of being, like the amorphous ice in a crystal. This is why the group can seem like a milieu: the group personality is constituted on a ground of pre-individual reality that includes, after structuration, an individual aspect and a complementary aspect of this individual. The group possesses an analogue of the soul and an analogue of the body of the individual being; but this soul and this body of the group are formed by the reality provided before any splitting by the individuated beings.

Collective consciousness is not formed by the joining of individual consciousnesses, no more than the social body arises from the joining of individual bodies. Individuals carry something that can become collective but is not already individuated in the individual. The union of individuals charged with non-individuated reality, bearers of this reality, is necessary for the individuation of the group; this non-individuated reality cannot be called purely spiritual; it splits into collective consciousness and collective corporeity as structures and limits that determine the individuals. The individuals are both animated and determined by the group. Purely spiritual groups cannot be created without bodies, without limits, or without attachments; like that which is individual, the collective is psychosomatic. If successive individuations become rare and less frequent, the collective body and the collective soul increasingly separate, despite the production of myths and opinions that keep them relatively paired together: whence the aging and decline of groups, which consists in a detachment of the group soul from the group body: the social present is no longer an integrated present, but an erratic one; it becomes insular, detached, just as the awareness of the present in a person of old age is no longer directly linked to the body, is no longer inserted in the body, but sustains itself in an indefinite iteration. One can assert that there is a relation of the collective and the spiritual, but this relation is neither on the level of the interindividual nor on the level of the natural social, if by natural social one means a collective reaction of the human species to the natural conditions of life, for example through labor.

What makes use of already individuated reality, whether somatic or psychical, cannot define a spirituality. Spiritual significations are discovered on the level of the transindividual, not on the level of the interindividual or the social. The individuated being bears with it a possible future of relational significations to be discovered: the pre-individual is that which founds the spiritual in the collective. One could call *nature* this pre-individual reality that the individual bears with it by seeking to rediscover in the word nature the significations that the pre-Socratic philosophers gave it: the Ionian physiologists found in nature the origin of all types of being prior to individuation; nature is the *reality of the possible,* in the form of this ἄπειρον [ápeiron] from which Anaximander makes every individuated form emerge: Nature is not the contrary of Man, but the first phase of the being, while the second phase is the opposition of the individual and the milieu, the complement of the individual relative to the whole. According to the hypothesis presented here, ἄπειρον would remain in the individual, like a crystal that retains its mother liquor, and this charge of ἄπειρον would allow it to go toward a second individuation. However, unlike all the systems that grasp the collective as a joining of individuals and that think the group as a form for which individuals are the matter, this hypothesis would not make individuals into the matter of the group; individuals bearing ἄπειρον discover in the collective a signification, which is expressed, for example, as the notion of destiny: the charge of ἄπειρον is the principle of disparation relative to the other charges of the same nature contained in other beings.

The collective is an individuation that joins the natures that are borne by several individuals but not contained in the already constituted individualities of these individuals; this is why the discovery of the collective's signification is both transcendent and immanent relative to the anterior individual; it is contemporaneous with the new group personality in which the individual participates through the significations that he discovers, i.e. through its nature; but this nature is not veritably the nature of its individuality; it is the nature associated with its individuated being; it is the persistence of the initial and original phase of the being in the second phase, and this persistence implies a tendency toward a third phase, which is that of the collective; the collective is an individuation of the natures linked to individuated beings. Through this ἄπειρον that it carries, the being is not just an individuated being; it is the pair of the individuated being and of nature; through this persistent nature, the being communicates with the world and with other individuated beings, discovering significations concerning which it does not know whether they are *a priori* or *a posteriori.* The discovery of these significations is *a posteriori,* for there must be an operation of individuation in order for these significations to appear, and the individuated being cannot accomplish this whole operation of individuation alone; a presence must be created with some other being than the individuated being alone in order for individuation, the principle and milieu of signification, to be able to appear. But this appearance of signification also supposes a real *a priori*, the link to the subject of this charge of Nature, the persistence of the being in its original, pre-individual phase. The individuated being is the bearer of absolute origin. Signification is the correspondence of the *a prioris* in the individuation that come after the first, i.e. the *a posteriori* individuation.

II. The Collective as Condition of Signification

1. Subjectivity and Signification; the Transindividual Character of Signification

The existence of the collective is necessary for information to be significative. When the original charge of nature borne by individual beings cannot be structured and organized, there can be no form in the being for accommodating the form contributed by signals. To receive an information is in fact for the subject to carry out within itself an individuation that creates the collective rapport with the being from which the signal arises. To discover the signification of the message that comes from one being or several beings is to form a collective with them and individuate through the group individuation with them. There is no difference between discovering a signification and existing collectively with the being relative to which the signification is discovered, since signification is not of the being but between beings, or rather across beings: it is transindividual. The subject is the ensemble formed by the individuated individual and the ἄπειρον [ápeiron] that it carries along with it; the subject is more than individual; it is individual and nature, it is both phases of being at the same time; the subject tries to discover the signification of these two phases of being by resolving them in the transindividual signification of the collective; the transindividual is not the synthesis of the first two phases of being, since this synthesis could only occur in the subject in order to be rigorously synthetic. But the transindividual is nevertheless the signification of these two phases, since the disparation that exists between the two phases of being contained in the subject is enveloped within signification via the constitution of the transindividual.

This is why it is absolutely insufficient to say that language is what allows man to access significations; if there were no significations to sustain language, there would be no language; language is not what creates signification; it is merely what conveys between subjects an information, which, in order to become significative, must encounter this ἄπειρον [ápeiron] associated with the definite individuality in the subject; language is the instrument of expression, the conveyance of information, but it does not create significations. Signification is a rapport of beings, not a pure expression; signification is relational, collective, transindividual, and it cannot be provided by the encounter of expression and the subject. We can say what information is based on signification, but we cannot say what signification is based on information.

There are innate psychosomatic structures and dynamisms that constitute a mediation between the natural (the pre-individual phase) and the individuated. Sexuality is one such mediation; in a sense, it could be said that the fact of being sexuated for the individual is a part of individuation; and sexuality in fact could not exist if the psychosomatic distinction of individuals did not exist; however, sexuality does not belong to the individual, is not its property, and requires the couple to have a signification. Sexuality is the pre-individual still linked to the individual and is specified and dichotomized in order to be conveyed implicitly and psychosomatically by the individual. The dichotomy of the pre-individual allows for a larger integration of this pre-individual charge into the individual; sexuality is more immanent to the individual than the pre-individual, which veritably remains an ἄπειρον; sexuality models the body and the soul of the individuated being, and it creates an asymmetry between individuated beings qua individuals. Sexuality is at an equal distance between the ἄπειρον of pre-individual nature and the limited, determined individuality; it establishes to limited, individuated individuality the inherence of a relation to the unlimited; this is why it can be passed through in two directions, toward individuality and toward nature; it makes individuality and nature communicate. It is not true that sexuality is merely a function of the individual, since it is also a function that makes the individual step outside itself. It is not a specific function placed by the species in the individual as a foreign principle: the individual is sexuated, it is not merely affected by a sexual index; individuation is therefore bimodal qua individuation; and it is precisely not an individuation completely achieved as individuation, because it remains concretely bimodal: there is a halt in the path of individuation that allows for this bimodality to conserve the inherence of a charge of ἄπειρον [ápeiron]; this translation of the unlimited into the limited protects the being from aseity and correlatively deprives it of complete individuation. In this way, it can be understood why this individual bimodality was able to be considered as a principle of dialectical ascension; nevertheless, the myth of the hermaphrodite indeed remains a myth, for the hermaphrodite is bisexual rather than a complete individual: we can wonder if the rigorously unimodal individual can exist apart; in species where sexuality does not exist or is merely episodic for the individual, there are often gregarious forms of existence that mark a halt in individuation. With superior species, the adherence of sexuality to the individual being creates the inherence of a limit of individuation to the interior of the individual. Sexuality can be considered a psychosomatic immanence of pre-individual nature to the individuated being. Sexuality is a mixture of nature and of individuation; it is an individuation in suspense, arrested in the asymmetrical determination of the elementary collective, of the unified duality of the couple.

This is why sexuality can be an introduction to the collective or a withdrawal based on the collective, an inspiration and incitation toward the collective, but it is not the collective, and it is also not spirituality, but the incitation to spirituality; putting the being into movement, it informs the subject that it is not a closed individual, that it does not have aseity; there is sexuality, but it remains a *metaxy* and cannot be detached from the individuated being, since it is deposited in its modality of individuation. Unlike Freud, we cannot identify sexuality with the very principle of the tendencies in the individuated being; the being also cannot be divided into two principles, that of pleasure and that of the death drives, as Freud attempted when he reworked his doctrine and modified it after the First World War. Freud felt that there is both a unity and a duality of the individuated being. But the being can neither be interpreted according to pure unity nor according to pure duality. The difficulty of Freud's whole doctrine stems from the fact that the subject is identified with the individual and that sexuality is placed in the individual as something that the individual contains and includes; however, sexuality is a modality of the initial individuation, rather than a content of the actual individual; it is organized or is not organized in its ontogenetic development with what we have called Nature in the subject, such that it becomes individualized or on the contrary is linked to the world and to the group. Pathogenesis should be linked to a conflict between the modality of individuation in the form of sexuality and the charge of pre-individual reality that is in the subject without being included in the individual. But it is indeed certain that the fulfillment of desires, the satisfaction of tendencies, and the relaxation of all the tensions of the sexuated being do not harmonize the individual with itself and do not halt the pathogenic conflict within the subject between the modality of individuation and nature. Neither the study of the individual alone nor the study of social integration alone can account for pathogenesis. It is the subject who is ill, not the individual alone, for there is within the subject a conflict between nature and the individual.

The only path of resolution is the subject's discovery of significations due to which the collective and that which is individual can be harmonized and develop in a synergistic way. Goldstein appropriately remarks that the normal state of the drives is not resolution, flat calm, but a certain median tension that applies them to the world and attaches them to their object; the subject can find its fulfillment and its equilibrium neither in the pure individual facing itself and its given reality, nor in its insertion into the empirical social. Freud and Karen Horney have generalized two borderline cases. Mental pathology is on the level of the transindividual; it appears when the discovery of the transindividual is lacking, i.e. when the charge of nature that is in the subject with the individual cannot encounter other charges of nature in other subjects with which it could form a transindividual mode of significations; the pathological relation to others is one that lacks significations and dissolves into the neutrality of things, thus leaving life without polarity; the individual then feels itself becoming an insular reality; improperly crushed or falsely triumphant and dominant, the subject seeks to link the individual being to a world that loses its signification; the transindividual relation of signification is replaced by the powerless relation of the subject to neutral objects, some of whom are his peers. With "Fate analysis," Szondi has indeed found this aspect of nature that there is in the subject; but this aspect must also be found in cases where no definite pathogenic forces appear; there is still some pre-individual reality that has guided the subject in its positive choices: indeed, choice is not merely the activity of that which is entirely individuated in the subject; choice supposes the individuation of a part of non-individuated nature, for choice is the discovery of a relation of the being through which the subject is constituted in a collective unity; choice is not the control of a neutral object by a dominant subject, but the individuation that intervenes in a charged pre-individual ensemble formed by two or several subjects; choice is the discovery and institution of the collective; it has a self-constitutive value; it takes several masses of pre-individual nature for choice to be fulfilled; choice is not an act of the subject alone; it is the structuration in the subject with other subjects; the subject is the milieu of choice as well as an agent of this choice. Ontologically, every true choice is reciprocal and supposes an operation of individuation deeper than a communication of consciousnesses or an intersubjective relation. Choice is a collective operation, a group foundation, a transindividual activity.

Thus, the subject more so than the individual is implicated in choice; choice occurs on the level of subjects and involves the constituted individuals within the collective. Choice is therefore the advent of the being. It is not simple relation. It then would be more appropriate to study if there are modes of the pre-individual, i.e. the different aspects of nature that subjects include. The ἄπειρον [ápeiron] is perhaps undetermined only with respect to the individuated being: there are perhaps various modalities of the undetermined, which would explain why specific cases and specific tensions are required for the birth of the collective and in order to have a certain number of chances of stability in all cases. One could perhaps define in this way classes of *a prioris* in possible significations, categories of potentials, stable pre-relational bases. The concepts to conduct such a study are lacking.

2. Subject and Individual

One of the things that seems to emerge from this partial and hypothetical study is that the name individual is improperly given to a more complex reality, that of the complete subject, which, in addition to individuated reality, includes within it an unindividuated, pre-individual, or even natural aspect. This unindividuated charge of reality conceals a power of individuation, which, within the subject alone, cannot conclude, whether due to the being's poverty, isolation, or the lack of a systematic whole. Gathered with other subjects, the subject can correlatively be the theater and agent of a second individuation that gives birth to the transindividual collective and links the subject to other subjects. The collective is not nature, but it supposes the preliminary existence of a nature attached to subjects between which collectivity is established by their overlapping. Beings are linked to one another in the collective not actually as individuals, but as subjects, i.e. as beings that contain the pre-individual.

This doctrine would aim to consider individuation as a phase of being. This phase, moreover, cannot exhaust the possibilities of pre-individual being, such that a first individuation gives birth to beings that still carry virtualities and potentials with them; although they are too weak in each being, these potentials joined together can carry out a second individuation (the collective), thus linking individuated beings via the pre-individual that they conserve and include. The particular being is thus more than an individual; it is first an individual on its own, as the result of a first individuation; a second time it is a member of the collective, which is what makes it participate in a second individuation. The collective is not a milieu for the individual but a set of participations in which it enters through this second individuation that choice is when it is expressed as a transindividual reality. The subject being can be conceived as a more or less perfectly coherent system of three successive phases of being: the pre-individual phase, the individuated phase, and

the transindividual phase, all of which partially but not completely correspond to what is designated by the concepts of nature, individual, and spirituality. The subject is not a phase of being opposed to that of the object, but
the condensed and systematized unity of the three phases of being.

3. The Empirical and the Transcendental. Ontogenesis and Pre-critical Ontology. The Collective as Signification That Overcomes a Disparation

This manner of envisioning the subject allows us to avoid the difficult distinction of the transcendental and the empirical. It also saves anthropology
from the dead end of an absolute point of departure for the knowledge of
man based on an essence. The individual is not everything in man, for the
individual is the result of a preliminary individuation; a pre-individual knowledge of the being is necessary. The being as individuated must not be considered as absolutely given. Ontogenesis must be integrated into the domain
of philosophical examination, instead of considering the individuated being
as absolutely first. This integration would allow for the surpassing of certain
ontological postulates of critique, postulates which are essentially relative
to individuation; it would also allow us to refuse a classification of beings
into genera that do not correspond to their genesis but instead correspond
to a knowledge of beings considered after genesis, concerning which we
have asserted that it was the foundation of every scholasticism. It is therefore
a question of witnessing the genesis of individuated beings based on pre-
individual reality, which contains potentials that are resolved and determined
within systems of individuation.

To try to lead to this institution of a pre-critical ontology that is an ontogenesis, we have wanted to create the notion of phases of being. This notion
to us has seemed to be established on the basis of the notion of information, which is destined to replace the notion of form such as it is implicated
in the insufficient hylomorphic schema; information is not a system of form
and matter, but a system of form and form, which supposes an equality and
homogeneity of both terms, along with a certain discrepancy that founds signification and collective reality (such as visual disparation). The collective is
the signification obtained by the superposition of beings that are disparate
by themselves in a single system: it is an encounter of dynamic forms established into a system, a realized, consummated significative that requires passage to a superior level, i.e. the advent of the collective as a unified system
of reciprocal beings; the collective personality of the individual is what can
become significant relative to other collective personalities evoked at the same
moment by a play of reciprocal causality. Reciprocity, internal resonance, is

the condition for the advent of the collective. The collective is what results from a secondary individuation relative to vital individuation, since it takes back up what the first individuation had left unused of bare nature in the living being. This second individuation does not fully overlap the first; despite the collective, the individual dies as an individual, and participation in the collective cannot save it from this death, which is a consequence of the first individuation. The second individuation, that of the collective and the spiritual, gives birth to transindividual significations that do not die with the individuals by which they are constituted; what there is of pre-individual nature in the subject being can survive the individual that has been a living being as signification; *non omnis moriar* ("not everything dies") is true in a certain sense, but it would be necessary to be able to alter this judgment with an index that deprives it of personality in the first person; for this is no longer the individual, and it is barely the subject that lives beyond itself; the charge of nature associated with the subject, which has become a signification integrated into the collective, is what survives the *here and now* of the individual contained in the subject being. The only chance for the individual (or rather, for the subject) to live beyond itself in some fashion is to become signification, to make it such that something of itself becomes signification. This is still a fairly unsatisfying perspective for the subject, since the task of the discovery of significations and of the collective is submitted to chance. Nevertheless, the subject being can hardly live beyond itself in the generalized collective except as information; participating in collective individuation, the subject infuses something of itself (which is not individuality) into a reality that is more stable than it. There is contact with the being via associated nature. This contact is information.

4. The Central Operational Zone of the Transindividual: Theory of Emotion

The gist of this study is the following: the hylomorphic schema must be abandoned to think individuation; veritable individuation does not amount to a form-taking. The operation of individuation is a much more general and much vaster phenomenon than simple form-taking. Form-taking can be thought based on individuation, but individuation cannot be thought based on the paradigm of form-taking. The hylomorphic schema includes and accepts a dark zone, which is precisely the central operational zone. It is the example and the model of all logical processes through which a fundamental role is attributed to borderline cases, to the extreme terms of a reality organized into series, as if the series could be generated based on its boundaries.

According to the method proposed to replace the hylomorphic schema, the being must be grasped in its entirety, and the milieu of an ordered real is as substantial as its extreme terms. The dark zone conveyed by the hylomorphic schema projects its shadow over every reality known by way of this schema. The hylomorphic schema improperly replaces the knowledge of the genesis of a real; it prevents the knowledge of *ontogenesis*.

In psychology, the median zone of the being is thrust back into the irrational and the unknowable that cannot be experienced or known: the psychosomatic relation poses unsolvable problems. However, perhaps it should be asked whether the notion of psycho-physiological relation is illusory and merely expresses the fact that one has wanted to consider the being as the result of a form-taking and to grasp it by way of the hylomorphic schema after it has been constituted. The impossibility of reaching a clear relation of the soul and the body merely expresses the being's resistance to the imposition of the hylomorphic schema; the substantialized terms of soul and body can be nothing but artifacts that stem from this effort to know the being by way of this schema, which first requires a preliminary reduction of the entire spectrum of reality that constitutes the being in its extreme terms considered as matter and form. The study of groups also reveals the same existence of a dark zone; the body of groups is known by way of social morphology; group representations are the object of inter-psychology and microsociology. But between these two extremes extends the dark relational zone, that of the real collective, the ontogenesis of which seems to be thrust back into the unknowable. According to the attitude of sociological objectivity, to grasp the reality of groups as a fact is to come after the individuation that founds the collective. To start with inter-psychological postulates is to place oneself before the group individuation and to want to extract this group of psychical dynamisms that are internal to individuals or to the individual's tendencies or social needs. However, the veritable collective that is contemporaneous with the operation of individuation cannot be known as a relation between the extreme terms of the pure social and the pure psychical. The collective is the very being that spans the spectrum from social exteriority to psychical interiority. The social and the psychical are nothing but borderline cases; they are not the foundations of reality, the true terms of relation. There is nothing but extreme terms for the gaze of knowledge, insofar as knowledge must be applied to a hylomorphic schema, a pair of clear notions that cling to an obscure relation.

The representation of individuation that grasps the being in its center of activity stands against the hylomorphic schema. But, in order for the notion of individuation to be fully dissociated from the hylomorphic schema, a procedure of thought must be elaborated that does not invoke a classification and that foregoes definitions of essence via the inclusion or exclusion of characteristics. This is because classification, which permits a knowledge of beings via common genus and specific differences, supposes the usage of the hylomorphic schema; form gives to the genus its signification relative to the species, which are its matter. The thought that can be called *transductive* does not consider that the unity of a being is conferred by the form informing a matter, but by a definite regime of the operation of individuation that founds the being absolutely. The being's cohesion forms the being's unity, not the rapport of a form to a matter; the being's unity is a regime of activity that traverses the being, going from part to part, converting structure into function and function into structure. The being is relation, for relation is the internal resonance of the being relative to itself, the manner in which it is conditioned reciprocally within itself, splitting and reconverting into unity. The being's unity can only be understood based on individuation, absolute ontogenesis. The being is one, because it is a symbol of itself, harmonizing with and reverberating within itself. Relation can never be conceived as a relation between preexisting terms, since it is a reciprocal regime of information exchange and of causality in a system that individuates. Relation exists physically, biologically, psychologically, collectively as the internal resonance of the individuated being; relation expresses individuation and is at the being's center.

For being-to-being relation to be possible, there must be an individuation that envelops the beings between which there is relation: this supposes that there is within individuated beings a certain charge of the undetermined, i.e. of pre-individual reality that has passed through the operation of individuation without being effectively individuated. This charge of the undetermined can be called nature; it must not be conceived as pure virtuality (which would be an abstract notion arising to a certain extent from the hylomorphic schema), but as a veritable reality charged with potentials actually existing as potentials, i.e. as an energy of a metastable system. The notion of virtuality must be replaced with that of a system's *metastability*. The collective can emerge based on the charge of pre-individual reality contained within individuated beings and not based on an encounter of previously existing form and matter. The individuation of the collective is the relation between individuated beings; the relation starting from individuated beings and depending on their very individuality taken as a term is not what founds the relation and constitutes the collective; without individuation there can be no being, and without the being there can be no relation. The bonds that can exist between already individuated beings and that would be established between their individualities, grasped on the basis of an individuation of the collective, would merely be an interindividual relation, like the inter-psychological relation. The collective has its own ontogenesis, its own operation of individuation that utilizes the potentials carried by the pre-individual reality contained in already individuated beings. The collective manifests through the internal resonance within the collective; it is real as a stable relational operation; it exists *physikos* and not *logikos*. The birth of an intersubjective relation is conditioned by the existence of this charge of nature within subjects, the persistence of a pre-individuality within individuated beings.

Manifestations like emotion in the individual being seem impossible to explain in accordance with only the content and structure of the individuated being. It is certainly possible to invoke a certain phylogenetic conditioning that influences ontogenesis and to reveal in emotion the characteristics of adaptation to critical situations. In fact, these aspects of adaptation raised by Darwin indeed exist, but they do not exhaust the whole reality of emotion. Through emotion, the being disadapts as much as it adapts, if adaptation is reduced to behaviors that guarantee the security of the individual qua individual. If, in fact, emotion poses problems to psychology that are so difficult to resolve, this is because it cannot be explained in accordance with the being considered as totally individuated. Emotion reveals the persistence of the pre-individual within the individuated being; it is this real potential that, within the natural undetermined, evokes within the subject the relation inside the collective that establishes itself; there is the collective to the extent that an emotion structures itself; in the situation of solitude, emotion is like an incomplete being that will only be able to systematize itself according to a collective that will individuate; emotion is something pre-individual revealed within the subject and can be interpreted as interiority or exteriority; emotion refers to exteriority and to interiority, because emotion is not something individuated; it is the exchange within the subject between the charge of nature and the individuated being's stable structures; exchange between the pre-individual and the individuated, emotion prefigures the discovery of the collective. Emotion is a calling into question of the being in its individual aspect insofar it is the capacity to evoke an individuation of the collective that will overlap and link the individuated being.

Emotion is incomprehensible according to the individual because it cannot find its root in the structures or functions of the individual qua individual: its adaptation to certain acts or to certain behaviors is merely lateral; it seems that emotion creates a disadaptation so as to be able to remedy this disadaptation by way of a certain number of ancillary manifestations. Indeed, the adaptation-disadaptation criterion does not suffice to account for emotions, since it grasps emotion after the fact in its consequences or marginally in the reactions of the individual's adaptation to emotion; the individual communicates with emotion and adapts relative to it, not so as to struggle against emotion, as is generally said, but in order to exist with emotion; there is a correlation of the individual and the charge of pre-individual nature in emotion; but we can only grasp behaviors that do not have their own explanation within themselves if we take on a study of emotion that wants to restrict it to the structures of the individuated being; it will therefore have to rely on a complex set of reductive suppositions (like that of bad faith for Sartre) in order to reduce emotion to a phenomenon of the individual. Emotion also cannot be interpreted correctly by attempting to consider it as social, if the social is conceived as substantial and anterior to the birth of emotion and capable of provoking emotion within the individual by way of an invasive action that comes from outside. Emotion is not the action of the social on what is individual; it is also not the momentum of the constituted individual that would constitute the relation starting from a single term; emotion is the potential that is discovered as signification by structuring itself within the individuation of the collective; it is incomplete and unachieved as long as it is not fulfilled within the individuation of the collective; it does not exist veritably as emotion outside the collective, but is like a conflict between the pre-individual reality and the individuated reality within the subject, which is the latency of emotion and is sometimes confused with emotion itself; this emotion is not a disorganization of the subject, so to speak, but the initiation of a new structuration that will be able to stabilize only within the discovery of the collective. The essential instant of emotion is the individuation of the collective; after this instant or before this instant, the complete and veritable emotion cannot be discovered. Emotive latency, the inadequacy of the subject to itself, the incompatibility of its charge of nature and of its individuated reality, indicates to the subject that it is more than the individuated being and that it contains the energy for a further individuation; but this further individuation cannot take place within the being of the subject; it can only take place through this being of the subject and through other beings as the transindividual collective. Emotion is therefore not implicit sociality or disturbed individuality; it is that which within the individuated being contains the possible participation in further individuations that incorporate the pre-individual reality remaining in the subject.

It is not surprising that emotion is situated within the dark zone of the psychosomatic relation; it cannot be thought whatsoever via the hylomorphic schema. Arising from the pre-individual, emotion seems to be able to be grasped (before individuation) as an invasive disturbance in the individual and (after individuation) as a functionally defined signification on the level of the collective; but neither that which is purely individual nor that which is purely social can explain emotion, which is the individuation of pre-individual realities on the level of the collective established by this individuation. Emotion cannot be grasped by the extreme terms of its development, which it joins together through its own cohesion, i.e. the purely individual and the purely social, insofar as these terms are the extreme terms of emotive individuation only because emotion localizes them and defines them as the extreme terms of a relational activity that it establishes. The purely social and the purely individual exist with respect to transindividual reality as the extreme terms of the entire scope of the transindividual; the individual and the social do not exist as antithetical terms with respect to one another. The transindividual has only been forgotten in philosophical reflection because it corresponds to the dark zone of the hylomorphic schema.

Conclusion

To conceive individuation as *operation* and as an operation of communication—thus as first operation—is to accept a certain number of ontological postulates; it is also to discover the foundation of a normativity, insofar as the individual is not the only reality, being's unique model, but merely a phase. However, it is more than a part of a whole because it is the seed of a totality.

The entrance into the collective must be conceived as a supplementary individuation that calls for a charge of the pre-individual nature borne by living beings. Indeed, nothing makes it possible to assert that the whole reality of living beings is incorporated into their constituted individuality; the being can be considered as an ensemble formed by individuated reality and pre-individual reality:[1] pre-individual reality can be considered as the reality that founds transindividuality. Such a reality is not at all a form within which the individual would be like a matter, but a reality that extends the individual on both sides, like a world into which the individual is initially inserted by being on the same level as all the other beings that make up this world. The entrance into the collective is an amplification of the individual in the form of the collective of the being that would include a pre-individual reality as well as an individual reality. This supposes that the individuation of beings does not completely exhaust the potentials of organization and that there is only a single possible state of the completion of beings. Such a conception therefore depends on a postulate of discontinuity; individuation does not effectuate itself according to the continuous, which would result in making it such that an individuation could only be total or null, since this mode of the appearance of the being qua unity cannot operate via fractions of unity (whereas a plurality joins together with another plurality). The discontinuous is normally conceived as a spatial or energetic discontinuous that only appears in exchanges or in movements for the elementary particles of physics and chemistry. Here, the idea of the discontinuous becomes that of a discontinuity of phases linked to the hypothesis of the compatibility of the being's successive phases: a being, considered as individuated, can in fact exist according to several phases present altogether, and in itself it can change phases of being; there is a plurality in the being that is not the plurality of parts (the plurality of parts would be below the level of the being's unity), but this plurality is a plurality that is even above this unity, since it is that of the being as phase, in the relation of one phase of being to another phase of being. The being qua being is fully given in each of its phases, yet with a certain reserve of becoming; it could be said that the being has several forms and consequently several entelechies, not just one, as the doctrine extracted from a biological abstraction supposes.[2] The relation of the being to its own parts or the consideration of the being's becoming insofar as this becoming alters it cannot provide the key to the rapport between the being's unity and plurality, no more than it can provide the key to the rapport between the individuated being and other beings. Being (whether individuated or not) has a spatiotemporal dimensionality, for, in one instant and in one place, it harbors several phases of being; the being is not merely what it is insofar as it manifests, since this manifestation is just the entelechy of a single phase; while this phase actualizes, other latent and real phases exist (and these can even be actual as energetically present potential), and the being consists in them as well as in its phase through which it attains entelechy. The error of the hylomorphic schema mainly consists in that it merely authorizes a single entelechy for the individuated being, whereas the being must be conceived as having several phases; the being can have several successive phases that are not entelechies of the same phases and are consequently not iterations. The relation of the individuated being to other beings is inconceivable in a doctrine that substantializes the individuated being, because it considers individuation as an absolute appearance of the being, a creation, or as a continued formation based on elements that do not contain something that foresees the individuated being and that prepares it energetically. Ontological monism must be replaced with a pluralism of phases, since the being incorporates, instead of a single form given in advance, successive informations that are a certain number of reciprocal structures and functions. *The notion of form must be dissociated from the hylomorphic schema in order to be able to be applied to the polyphasic being.* Consequently, this being cannot be considered from within the general schema of common genera and specific differences, which supposes the validity of the hylomorphic schema. Dissociated from the hylomorphic

schema, the notion of form can become adequate to the polyphasic nature of
being by structuring itself in a relational way, following the direction of the
Gestalt theorists: this relational signification of form is attained more fully
from within the notion of information, provided that information be understood as the relational signification of a disparation, i.e. as well as a problem
that can only be resolved through amplification. Such a doctrine supposes that
there is communication only within an individuated reality and that information is one of the aspects of the reciprocity of the individuated being relative to itself. The relation of the being with respect to itself is infinitely
richer than identity; identity, an impoverished relation, is the only relation
of the being to itself that can be conceived according to a doctrine that considers the being as having a single phase; in the theory of polyphasic being,
identity is replaced with internal resonance, which, in certain cases, becomes
signification and permits an amplifying activity. Such a doctrine supposes
that the order of realities is grasped as *transductive* and not as *classificatory*.
The grand divisions of the real (marked by genera in hylomorphic theory)
become phases, which are never totally simultaneous in actualization but nevertheless exist either as functional and *structural actuality* or as *potentials*;
the potential becomes a phase of the actually existing real, instead of being
pure virtuality. By contrast, what was considered as the pure indetermination of matter in the hylomorphic theory of the individuated being becomes
an ordered transductive series or the incompatibility of several transductive
series. Transductive order is an order according to which a *qualitative or
intensive staggered spectrum* spreads out on both sides based on a center in
which the qualitative or intensive being culminates: such is the series of colors, which one should not attempt to discern from its extreme, imprecise,
and outstretched limits of infrared and ultraviolet, but which one should
grasp *in its center*, in the yellow-green *in which organic sensibility culminates*;
for the human species, yellow-green is the center starting from which chromatic quality splits toward red and toward violet; there are two tendencies in
the series of colors, tendencies starting from the *center* toward the *extremes*,
tendencies *already contained in the center qua center of the series*. The series
of colors must first be grasped in its *real middle [milieu]*, which is variable
for each species;[3] this also applies for tonal qualities and thermal qualities;
for the individuated being, there is neither matter, which is pure indetermination, nor an infinite diversity of the sensible, but the fundamental bipolarity of transductive series ordered according to an axis. Instead of a relation
between two terms, the transductive series constitutes as a single central
term that splits into two opposite directions starting from itself, distancing

from itself into complementary qualities. Such a representation of the being requires a conceptual reform that can only be obtained based on a revision of the basic schemata; the usage of a certain number of paradigms is necessary for replacing the hylomorphic schema, which is directly imposed by culture. However, the choice of the domain that can provide the first notional paradigms cannot be arbitrary: in order for a schema to be able to be utilized effectively as a paradigm, there must be an operative and functional analogy between the original domain and the domain of application for the paradigm to be possible. The hylomorphic schema is a paradigm extracted from the technical operation of form-taking and then utilized to think the living individual grasped through its ontogenesis. On the contrary, we have attempted to extract a paradigm from the physical sciences by thinking that it can be transposed into the domain of the living individual: the study of this physical domain is meant not only to form notions, but also to serve basically as the study of a first domain within which an operation of individuation can exist; since we suppose that there are various degrees of individuation, we have utilized the physical paradigm without reducing the vital to the physical, because the transposition of the schema is accompanied by a composition of the physical itself. We do not mean to say that physical individuation is what produces vital individuation: we simply mean to say that reality has not clarified and developed all the possible steps of the operation in the physical system of individuation, and that a vital individuation still remains available within the physically individuated real;[4] the individuated physical being can be invested in a further vital individuation without its physical individuation dissolving; perhaps physical individuation is the condition of vital individuation without ever being its cause, since the vital intervenes as an amplifying deceleration of physical individuation; physical individuation is the *resolution of a first problem* underway, and vital individuation is inserted into it after the emergence of a new problematic; there is a pre-physical problematic and a pre-vital problematic; *physical* individuation and *vital* individuation are modes of resolution; they are not absolute points of departure. According to this doctrine, individuation is *the arrival of a moment of the being* that is not first. Not only is it not first, but it brings with it a certain *persistence of the pre-individual phase*; only the pre-individual phase can really be called monophasic; on the level of the individuated being, the being is necessarily already *polyphasic,* for the pre-individual past survives parallel to the existence of the individuated being and remains a seed for new amplifying operations; individuation intervenes in the being as the *correlative birth of the distinct phases* based on that which did not include them, insofar as what did not include them is pure omnipresent potential. The individual, which is the *result* but also the *milieu or milieu* of *individuation,* must not be considered as singular: it is singular only with respect to other individuals, according to a very superficial *here and now.* In fact, the individual is multiple insofar as it is polyphasic, not as if it harbored a plurality of more localized and more momentary secondary individuals, but because it is a provisional solution, a phase of becoming that will lead to new operations. The unity of the individual is the *central and median phase of being,* starting from which other phases arise and diverge into a unidimensional *bipolarity.* The being after individuation is not merely an individuated being; it is the being that entails individuation, the result of individuation, and the movement toward other operations based on a persistence of the initial pre-individual state. After individuation, the being *has a past,* and the pre-individual becomes a phase; the pre-individual is before every phase; it becomes the first phase only based on the individuation that splits the being and phase-shifts it with respect to itself. Individuation is what creates phases, for phases are nothing but this development of the being on both sides of itself, this double decentering based on an initial consistency swarming with *tensions* and *potentials* that made it incompatible with itself. The pre-individual is *being without phases,* while *the being after individuation is phasic being.* Such a conception identifies or at the very least links *individuation and the being's becoming;* the individual is not considered identical to the being; the being is richer, more durable, and larger than the individual: the individual is *individual of the being, individual taken out of the being, not the primordial and elementary constituent of the being;* it is a manner of the being, or rather a moment of the being.

To propose a conception of individuation as the genesis of an individuated being that *is not the first element of the being* is to be forced to indicate the meaning of the consequences that such a conception must have for the entirety of philosophical thought. Indeed, it seems that a certain conception of individuation is already contained within the notion of *term* at least implicitly. When reflection, intervening before any ontology, wants to define the conditions of valid judgment, it resorts to a certain conception of judgment and, correlatively, a certain conception of the content of knowledge, of the object and the subject as terms. However, prior to any exercise of critical thought concerning the conditions of judgment and the conditions of knowledge, it would be necessary to respond to this question: what is relation? What is implied in such a theory of knowledge is a certain conception of relation, and in particular a certain conception of the individuality of terms as anterior to relation. Nevertheless, nothing proves that knowledge is a relation, particularly a relation within which the terms preexist as individuated realities. If knowledge were conditioned by the community of an individuation that envelops the subject and the object within a structural and functional unity, what is said of the conditions of judgment would not be seen to concern the reality of knowledge but a *translation after the fact* of knowledge as a relational schema between separately individuated terms. A theory of individuation must develop into a theory of sensation, perception, affection, and emotion. It must make *psychology* and *logic* coincide, the mutual separation of which indicates a double inadequacy to the studied object rather than a separation of points of view. *The theory of individuation must be first with respect to the other critical and ontological, deductive studies.* It's precisely this theory of individuation that indicates the legitimacy for carving up being in order to make it enter into the propositional relation. Prior to any particular category, there is the category of *being,* which is a response to the problem of individuation: to know *how being can be thought,* one must know how it individuates, for this individuation is the support of the validity of any logical operation that must conform to it. Thought is a certain *mode of secondary individuation* that intervenes after *the fundamental individuation that constitutes the subject*; thought is *not necessarily capable of thinking being in its totality*; it is second relative to the subject's condition of existence; but this condition of the existence of the subject is not isolated and unique, for the subject is not an isolated term with the capacity to constitute itself; the substantialization of the subject as a term is a facility that thought grants itself to be able to witness the genesis and justification of itself; thought seeks to be identified with the subject, i.e. to be identified with its condition of existence so as not to lag behind itself. However, if the individual is itself relative as a phase of being, and if it is richer than unity as the depository of a preindividual situation that it transmits in an amplifying activity, it cannot be grasped as the pure term of relation. The subject is *substantialized by thought* so that thought *can coincide with the subject.* Yet the subject's substantialization, which supposes that the subject can be taken as a term of relation, gives it the status of an absolute term; substance is like the *relational term become absolute,* having absorbed into it everything that was the being of relation. A similar *logical reduction* is tangible in all the cases within which the individual has been thought; for the individual is always to a certain extent *thought* as being a *subject*; man is put in the place of what he thinks as an individual; the individual is what could have an interiority, a behavior, volitions, a responsibility, or at least a certain coherent identity that is on the same order as responsibility. There is an implicit subjectivity to every conception of the individual in contemporary doctrines, whether physical or biological; never-theless, in addition and prior to this projection of the status of subjective individuality into the world, a reduction takes place within the subject that reduces it to being a substance, i.e. a term that has absorbed relation into it; substance is an extreme case of relation, that of the inconsistency of relation. Under these conditions, it seems difficult to consider the notion of the individ-ual as first with respect to every judgment and every critique; the individual being, which is the principle of the notion of substance, must be considered via individuation, the operation that founds it and brings it about; the study of ontogenesis must be anterior to logic and ontology. The theory of indi-viduation must therefore be considered as a theory of the *phases of being,* a theory of the being's becoming insofar as the latter *is essential.* According to the notion of substance, becoming indeed poorly fits together with being's essence; the notion of accident is not very satisfying and requires delicate systematic edifices, like those of Leibniz, who could hardly account for be-coming qua becoming, because, insofar as all the accidents are included in essence conceived as the complete individual notion, there is no longer a veritable becoming for monadic substance, including the power of the future; the Spinozist edifice is not much more satisfying relative to becoming, which is excluded more so than integrated, since the individual is denied as a sep-arate being. In a theory of the phases of being, becoming is something other than an alteration or a succession of states comparable to a serial develop-ment. Indeed, becoming is a perpetuated and renewed resolution, an ampli-fying, incorporating resolution that proceeds via crises, such that *its sense is in each of its phases,* not at its *origin* or its *end* alone. To explain becoming as a series instead of positing it as transduction is to want to make it emerge from its extreme terms, which are the most impoverished and least stable; an individual life is neither the determined unfolding of what it has been at its origin, nor the preparation of a voyage toward a final end; it is also not a tension between a birth and a death, between an *Alpha* and an *Omega* that would be the true terms; the being must also be grasped temporally in its cen-ter, in its present at the moment in which it is, and not reconstituted based on the abstraction of its two parts; the substantialization of the extremities of the temporal series disrupts the being's central consistency; becoming is being as *present* insofar as it actually phase-shifts into past and future, thus finding its sense in this bipolar phase-shifting. It is not the passage from one moment to the other as one would pass from yellow to green; becoming is transduction based on the present: there is only one source of time, the cen-tral source that the present is, just as there is a single source of *chromatic qualities in their bipolarity,* a single source for all intensive and qualitative series. The being's present is *its problematic in the process of resolution,* since as such it is *bipolar according to time, i.e. phasic insofar as it is problematic.* The individuated being is not substance but *the being called into question,* the being across a problematic, divided, reunited, carried within this problematic that posits itself through the being and makes the being become at the same time as it makes becoming. *Becoming is not the becoming of the individuated being but the becoming of the being's individuation:* what happens comes about as a calling into question of the being, i.e. as an *element of an open problematic,* which is what the being's individuation resolves: the individual is *contemporaneous with its becoming,* since this becoming is that of its *individuation;* time itself is essence, not as an unfolding of an origin or a tendency toward an end, but as *the being's resolutive constitution.* Such a conception is possible only if we accept the notion of phases of being. This notion is different from the notions contained and utilized by dialectics: dialectics indeed implies the existence of a significative becoming that has a capacity to constitute *essence;* but dialectical becoming changes the being, opposes it, renews it: on the contrary, phases are phases of the being; the being is not what passes through phases by modifying; it is *the being that becomes the being of the phases,* that proceeds from itself by phase-shifting with respect to its center of reality. The dimensionality of phases is the being's becoming; the being is according to the phases that are its phases, phases relative to the center that it is; the being is not displaced from the center by phase-shifting in two directions with respect to itself; the time of becoming is the direction of the bipolarity according to which the being phase-shifts; the being *individuates* as it *becomes;* to individuate and to become is a single mode of existing. The phases of being are given together, they are part of one manner of being; becoming is a manner of being, it is the being's becoming, not a becoming to which the being is submitted by some violence done to its essence and with which the being could dispense all while remaining what it is. In the conception of dialectics, being requires becoming, but becoming is nevertheless conceived partially as it was when becoming was considered independent of being, foreign to being, *hostile to its essence;* the becoming of dialectics is *not sufficiently integrated into the being that becomes;* the time of the dialectic has remained the time of being, which is timeless *in essence* but thrown into becoming due to *its existence.*[5] The successiveness of dialectical stages can be contracted into the parallelism of the phases of being if becoming is veritably the being's becoming, in such a way that one cannot say that being is in becoming, but that being becomes; becoming is ontogenesis, *physis*. Dialectics overly separates becoming from the existence through which being becomes. It is not becoming that modifies being, it is being that becomes; the modifications of being are not the consequences of becoming but aspects of the phases of being. The existence of phases of being should not be conceived as a simple power of succession: there is succession only on a background of the parallelism of phases, as a dimension of phases; permanence and succession are concepts that cannot account for becoming because they suppose being to be reduced to a single phase, i.e. exempt from phases.

There is a danger in the use of the physical paradigm to characterize life: that of reduction. But this danger can be avoided; indeed, this paradigm can be used by taking the physical domain as a support of structures and functions that depend on non-living characteristics that expand them in their initial phase and amplify them but are not reduced to them. There is a domain of knowledge of the physical and a domain of knowledge of the living; but there is not in the same sense a real domain of the physical and a real domain of the living separated by a certain (equally real) boundary; the physical and the vital are distinct according to structures and functions without being separate according to the substantial real. There is a certain mode of existence of the physical that should not be confused with the physical after the emergence of the vital; after the emergence of the vital, the physical is an impoverished, uncharged real, a residue of the complete process from which life has emerged by separating. But there is also a physical that can be called the natural and that is both pre-vital and pre-physical; life and non-living matter in a certain sense can be treated as two speeds of the evolution of the real. Perhaps, even here, we shouldn't attempt to recompose totality based on the extreme terms by considering these extreme terms as the substantial bases capable of explaining in their combination the entire relational reality that they omit between them. This intermediate reality, which can be considered after the fact as a mixture engendered by relation, is perhaps that which carries the extreme terms, engenders them, and pushes them outside itself as the extreme boundaries of its existence. The relational appearance perhaps supposes a pre-relational being. The opposition of the inert and the living would be the product of the application of the dualizing schema of hylomorphic origin, with its characteristic zone of central obscurity, which leads one to believe in the existence of a relation where there is in fact the being's consistent center.[6] Seen through the hylomorphic schema, life and inert matter are perhaps the result of two speeds of the individuation of the same pre-vital and pre-physical reality. The study of the individuation through which this differentiation occurs therefore cannot be merely a paradigmatism;

logically, it is a source of paradigms; but it can be a source of paradigms only if it is fundamentally (at least in a hypothetical sense) a grasping of real becoming, based upon which the domains of application of the schemata that it unleashes constitute themselves; here, the paradigm is not an analogical paradigm, like Plato's, but a conceptual and intuitive line that accompanies an absolute genesis of domains with their structure and the operations that characterize them; it is a discovery of the intellectual axiomatic contemporaneous with the study of being, not an initiation to the domain of the knowable difficultly based on a better known domain that is easier to explore (which would suppose an analogical relation between the two domains).

In this sense, it must not be said that the living being appears *after* physical reality and above it by integrating it; on the contrary, the appearance of the living being would have the effect of deferring and delaying physical reality by expanding the initial phase of its constitution; it would necessitate more precise and more complex conditions of initial tension and metastability capable of "neotenizing" physical individuation. Even before the genesis of the individual being in itself, a study of becoming and of the exchanges it involves would allow for the grasping of this possible genesis of the individual being (whether physical or living, vegetal or animal) on a ground of the being's transformations. Since it is a question of the being before any individuation or of the being split after individuation, the method would always consist in attempting to apprehend the being in its center to understand on the basis of this center the extreme aspects and the dimension according to which these opposed aspects constitute themselves: the being would thus be grasped as a tensed unity or as a structured and functional system, but never as an ensemble of terms in relation; becoming and the appearances of relations it involves would consequently be known as dimensions of being and not as a framework within which something happens to being according to a certain order. Becoming is being phase-shifting with respect to itself, passing from the phaseless state of being to the state of being according to the phases that are *its* phases.

Such a conception of the being supposes that the principle of the excluded middle is not used, or that at the very least it is relativized; indeed, the being would first present itself as that which exists in the state of tensed unity, bearing an incompatibility that pushes it toward a structuration and a functionalization that constitutes becoming, with becoming having the capacity to be conceived as the dimension according to which this resolution of the being's first state is possible through a phase-shift. The prime mover thus would not be the simple and singular being, but the being insofar as it is anterior to any appearance of phases, harboring them *energetically,* yet not as *forms* or *structures* that can come forth, in the same way as the position of the problem in a certain sense bears the possible solution as a tension toward a signification that incorporates the data of the problem, albeit without the prior formation of the effective lines of the solution, which would only appear through the real becoming of resolutive invention and which *are this becoming*; thus, the capacity of resolutive becoming is contained in the being before any becoming through the incompatibility that it will be able to make compatible, but not the line of this becoming's existence, which is not already given and cannot be preformed, since the problematic is without phases.[7] The resolutive discovery in its becoming makes structures and functions appear on the one hand, and matter deprived of its tensions on the other, i.e. individual and milieu, information and matter. The resolution makes two complementary aspects appear: the extreme terms on the one hand and the reality that establishes mediation on the other; individual and milieu are two phases of being, the extreme terms of a splitting that intervenes as a resolutive invention, which presupposes a preliminary tension and incompatibility that they transform into an asymmetrical structuration; it can be said that the being phase-shifts into individual and milieu, allowing for a great many modalities depending on whether this phase-shift is total or partial, whether it is capable or incapable of degrees, and whether it admits a continuous progress or proceeds by leaps.

Such a theory doesn't merely seek to explain the genesis of individuated beings and to propose a vision of individuation; it attempts to make of individuation the foundation of an amplifying becoming and therefore places individuation *between* an initial state of the unresolved being and the entrance into the resolutive path of becoming; individuation is not the result of becoming or something produced in becoming, but becoming in itself insofar as becoming is the being's becoming. Individuation cannot be fully known if it is related to its result, i.e. the constituted individual, and if one attempts to give individuation a definition merely seeking to account for the characteristics of the individual in itself; the individual does not make it possible to ascend back to individuation, since the individual is merely one of the aspects of individuation; there is a correlate of the individual that is constituted at the same time as it by individuation: the milieu, which is the being deprived of what the individual has become.[8] Only the milieu-individual couple could allow for the ascent back toward individuation; individuation is what produces the phase-shift of the being into individual and milieu based on a previous being that is capable of becoming individual and milieu. Individual and milieu should be taken only as the extreme, conceptualizable, but not substantializable, terms of the being within which individuation takes place. The center of individuation is not the constituted individual; the individual is lateral relative to individuation. The being taken in its center on the level of individuation must be grasped as splitting into individual and milieu, i.e. undergoing resolution. Eventually, the individuated being can once again be the theater of an individuation, since individuation does not exhaust from the start the potential resources of the being in an initial operation of individuation: the first pre-individual state of the being can continue to exist in association with the result of an initial individuation; in fact, it can be supposed that individuation takes place in a quantum manner through abrupt leaps, each plateau of individuation being capable of once again relating itself to the following as a pre-individual state of the being; a rapport of the successive states of individuation occurs in this way. In particular, this is how the relation between individuated beings can be explained: this relation is only seemingly between beings; it is the collective individuation of a charge of pre-individual reality contained in beings that have received an initial status of individuation. What is defined as an interindividual rapport is in reality the coherence of a systematics of individuation that incorporates the already constituted individuals into a vaster unity. Relation is founded by individuation due to a rapport between successive states of individuation that remain linked by the being's energetic and systematic unity.

A substantialist monism, like that of Spinoza, comes against a great difficulty when it is a question of accounting for the individual being. This difficulty does not arise so much from the unity of substance as from its eternity; this difficulty, moreover, is shared by all substantialist doctrines, even when they fragment substance to the point of identifying substance and individual, thereby composing everything with individuals, as Leibniz does in his acceptance of an infinity of substances. This difficulty is simply more apparent in Spinoza, because, to the end, he accepts the consequences of substantialism and refuses to place a genesis of substance as the constitution of complete individual notions (substantial essences) in the beginning of becoming. It is difficult for the substantial being to effectively become because it is resolved in advance; it is always absolutely monophasic being, since it consists in itself; the fact of being in itself and by itself is also the fact of being coherent with itself, i.e. incapable of being opposed to itself. Substance is *one* because it is *stable*; it is actual, it is not charged with potentials. Despite Spinoza's terminology, what substance lacks is to be nature, or it also lacks the capacity to not be simultaneously and indissolubly natured and naturing. According to the doctrine we are presenting, being is never one: when it is monophasic, pre-individual, it is *more than one*: it is one because it is non-decomposed, but it has enough in it to be more than what it is in its actual structure; the principle of the excluded middle would only apply for a residual being incapable of becoming; being is not several in the sense of realized plurality: it is *richer than its self-coherence.*[9] One being is a being that is limited to itself, a coherent being. However, Our point is that the being's original state is a state that surpasses self-coherence, that exceeds its own limits: the original being is not stable, it is metastable; it is not one, it is capable of expansion starting from itself; the being does not subsist relative to itself; it is constrained, tensed, superposed on itself, and not one. The being is not reduced to what it is; in itself, it is accumulated, potentialized. It exists as being and also as energy; the being is both structure and energy; structure itself is not merely structure, since several orders of dimension are superposed; each structure corresponds to a certain energetic state that can appear in future transformations and belongs to the being's metastability. It seems that all theories of substance, movement and rest, becoming and eternity, essence and accident, rely on a conception of exchanges and modifications that recognize only alteration and stable equilibrium, not metastability. The being (stable, possessing a structure) is conceived as simple. But stable equilibrium is perhaps nothing but a borderline case. Perhaps metastable equilibrium is the general case: the equilibrium of a realized structure is only stable within certain limits and in a single order of magnitude, without any interaction with other orders of magnitude; it conceals potentials that when unleashed can produce an abrupt alteration leading to a new, equally metastable structuration. Thus, being and becoming are no longer opposed notions if it is considered that states are metastable manners of being, plateaus of stability leaping from structure to structure: *becoming is no longer the continuity of an alteration but the linking of metastable states through the unleashing of potential energy whose play and existence are part of the regime of causality that constitute these states*; the energy contained in the metastable system is the same as that which is actualized by the *passage* from one state to another. This structure-energy ensemble is what can be called *being*. In this sense, it cannot be said that being is *one*: it is simultaneous, paired on its own in a system that surpasses unity, which is *more than one*. Unity, particularly that of the individual, can appear within being through a separative simplification that produces the individual and a correlative milieu, which is without unity but homogeneous.

Such a conception could be considered gratuitous and treated as one usually treats the creationist hypothesis: what's the point of pushing the forces meant to account for ontogenesis back into an unknowable state of pre-individual being if this state is only known through what follows it? If this were the case, it could indeed be said that the problem is merely pushed back, just as one does by supposing the prior existence of a creator being: this being is only presupposed as creative to the extent that the notion of creation serves to account for the created, such that the essence of the being invoked as creator is in fact fully known based on the result upon which one must fall back, i.e. being as created. Nevertheless, it seems that the hypothesis according to which a state of pre-individual being exists plays a different role than that of the usual creationist hypothesis. Indeed, this hypothesis concentrates all becoming in its origins, such that every creationism brings with it the problem of theodicy, the ethical aspect of a more general problem: becoming is no longer a veritable becoming: it is fully whole, as though it had already happened in the act of creation, which obliges to contribute after the fact a certain number of local correctives to the creationist theory in order to give a meaning to becoming. Nevertheless, these correctives most generally concern the points that upset the feeling that man has of becoming, for example the problem of moral responsibility. But creationism should be corrected on all points, for it is no more satisfying to annihilate the reality of physical becoming than to diminish that of the becoming of the human being as an ethical subject: this difference of treatment can only be justified by a dualism that is itself contestable. There would be a need to add a veritable physical theodicy to the ethical theodicy. On the contrary, the hypothesis of a pre-individual state of being is not totally gratuitous: it contains more than it seeks to explain, and it is not solely formed based on the examination of the existence of individuals; it is derived from a certain number of schemata of thought borrowed from the domains of physics, biology, and technology. Physics does not reveal the existence of a pre-individual reality, but it shows that there are geneses of individualized realities based on standard states; a photon is a physical individual in a certain sense; however, it is also a quantity of energy that can reveal itself in a transformation. An individual like an electron is in interaction with fields. A structural change of a molecular, atomic, or nuclear edifice produces energy and engenders physical individuals. Physics urges us to think the individual as exchangeable with the structural modification of a system, and thus with a certain definite system state. In the foundation of the ontogenesis of physical beings, there is a general theory of the exchanges and modifications of states that could be called *allagmatics*. This conceptual ensemble supposes that the individual is not an absolute beginning, and that its genesis can be studied based on a certain number of energetic and structural conditions: ontogenesis pertains to the becoming of systems; the appearance of an individual corresponds to a certain system state and presents a meaning relative to this system. Furthermore, the physical individual is relative, it is not substantial; it is relative because it is in relation, quite particularly in energetic relation with fields, and this relation is part of its being. In wave mechanics, an electron has an associated wavelength: in the Davisson-Germer experiment, electrons can be made to interfere; however, electrons are considered as bits of electricity, indivisible charges. This existence of the phenomenon of interference, and generally of all phenomena which are accounted for by defining the associated wavelength, shows that there is a sort of physical collective within which the role of the individual is no longer merely an apportioned role, for which one would want to account by means of the notion of substance; the microphysical individual is as much an energetic reality as a substantial being; it adheres to its genesis and remains present in its becoming, because it is in perpetual relation with fields. The individual is not the entirety of the being; it is only an aspect of the being; what matters is the study of the conditions in which the being manifests as individual, as if this involved not the being but a manner of being or a moment of being. In physics, there is a pre-individual being and a post-individual being; a photon disappears and becomes the structural change of an atomic edifice, or instead it changes wavelength, as if it had become other. Individuality becomes functional in some way; it is not the sole aspect of reality but a certain function of reality.

By generalizing this relativization of the individual and by transporting it into the reflexive domain, the study of individuation can be transformed into a theory of being. Individuation is then situated with respect to being. It appears as a modification of the being based upon which the latter's problematic becomes enriched: it is the appearance of information within the being's system. Instead of treating information as an absolute parameter that is measurable and quantifiable in a limited number of circumstances, it must be linked to individuation: there is information only as an exchange between the parts of a system that involve individuation, because, in order for information to exist, it must have a sense, and it must be received, i.e. it must be able to serve to carry out a certain operation; information is defined by the way in which an individuated system affects itself by conditioning itself: it is that through which there is a certain mode of conditioning of the being by itself, a mode that can be called *internal resonance*: information is individuating and requires a certain degree of individuation in order to be able to be received; it is that through which the operation of individuation progresses, that through which this operation conditions itself. Form-taking, through which individuation is generally represented, presupposes information and serves as a basis for information; there is information exchanged only between already individuated beings and within a systematics of the being that constitutes a new individuation: it could be said that information is always internal; information must not be confused with the signals and signal supports that constitute its mediator. Information must be understood in the veritable conditions of its genesis, which are the very conditions of individuation in which it plays a role: information is a certain aspect of individuation; in order for it to be understood as having a sense (that without which it is not information but merely a weak energy), there must be a certain potential prior to itself; the fact that an information is veritably information is identical to the fact that something individuates; and information is exchange, the modality of internal resonance according to which this individuation effectuates itself. Every information is both informing and informed; it must be grasped in this active transition of the being that is individuating.[10] It is that through which being phase-shifts and becomes. In its separate, recorded, indirectly transmitted aspects, information also expresses a completed individuation and the resurgence of this completion that can extend into other stages of amplification: information is never after individuation alone, for if it expresses a completed individuation, it does so with respect to another individuation that is capable of being completed: as the expression of a completed individuation, information is the seed around which a new individuation will be able to complete itself: it establishes the transductivity of successive individuations, arranging them into series, insofar as it traverses them by carrying what can be taken back up from one individuation to the next. Information is that which overflows from one individuation to the next and from the pre-individual to the individuated, since the schema according to which an individuation completes itself is capable of initiating other individuations: information has an exterior power because it is an interior solution; it is that which passes from one problem to the next, that which can radiate from one domain of individuation to another domain of individuation; information is significative information because it is initially the schema according to which a system has successfully individuated; this is why information can become the schema for another system. This supposes that there is an analogy between the first and the second system. However, in a doctrine that avoids invoking a creationist postulate, in order for there to be an analogy between two systems, these two systems must belong to a vaster system; this means that when information appears in a subset as a schema of resolution of this subset, it is already the resolution not only of this subset but also of that which within it expresses its belonging to the set: it is from the start capable of being transferred to other subsets, it is from the start interior to the original subset and already interior to the set as expressing that which in each subset is its mark of belonging to the set, i.e. the manner in which it is modified by the other subsets that constitute the set with it. It could be said that information is both interior and exterior; it expresses the limits of a subset; it is the mediation between the set and each subset. It is *the internal resonance of the set insofar as it includes subsets*: it realizes the individuation of the set as the progress of solutions between the subsets that constitute it: it is the internal resonance of the structures of subsets within the set: this exchange is interior relative to the set and exterior relative to each of the subsets. Information expresses the immanence of the set in each of the subsets and the existence of the set as a group of subsets, really incorporating the quiddity of each subset, which is the reciprocal of the immanence of the set to each of the subsets. If there is indeed a dependence of each subset relative to the set, there is also a dependence of the set relative to the subsets.[11] This reciprocity between two levels designates what can be called the internal resonance of the set, and it defines the set as a reality undergoing individuation.

Can a theory of individuation provide an ethics through the intermediary of the notion of information? It can at least serve to lay down the bases of an ethics, even if it cannot complete the latter due to the incapacity to present its circumstances. In philosophical systems, ethics is generally divided into two paths that diverge and never rejoin: that of pure ethics and that of applied ethics. This duality stems from the fact that substance is separate from becoming, and because being, which is defined as one and completely given in individuated substance, is achieved: thus, on the level of the essences and outside becoming, there arises a pure ethics that can only manage to preserve the theoretical substantiality of the individuated being and that in fact surrounds the latter with an illusion of substantiality. This first path of ethics, which could be called substantializing ethics (or the ethics of the sage or contemplative ethics), is only valid for a state of exception, which would not itself be stable without its opposition to the state of passion, servitude, vice, and existence in the *here and now*; its substantiality is merely a counter-existence, an anti-becoming, and life must become around it so that it can acquire the impression of substantiality by contrast; contemplative virtue requires merchants and madmen, just as the sober man requires the drunk man in order to be aware of being sober, and the adult needs the child to know what it is to be adult. It is only through an effect of perceptive and affective relativity that this ethics can seem like an ethics of wisdom seeking the immutability of being. The same applies for the other branch of ethics, which is allegedly practical; it is only practical relative to the first type of ethics, and it utilizes the values defined by the first in order to have the ability to be constitute itself with stability; in fact, what has a signification is the pair of the two ethics, not each ethics by itself. Nevertheless, they define norms that provide incompatible directions, i.e. they create divergence; their very pairing is insufficient, in that it merely possesses a common logical axiomatic, not mutually coherent normative directions. The ethics of becoming and of action in the present requires the ethics of wisdom turned toward eternity in order to be aware of itself as an ethics of action; it is in harmony with itself more so in what it refuses than in what it constructs, just like the ethics of wisdom; the internal coherence of each of these ethics forms by way of the negative as a refusal of the path of the other ethics.

The notion of communication as identical to the internal resonance of a system undergoing individuation can, on the contrary, endeavor to grasp being in its becoming without granting a privilege to the immobile essence of being or to becoming qua becoming; there can be a single and complete ethics only to the extent in which the becoming of being is grasped as being itself, i.e. to the extent that becoming is known as the being's becoming. The two opposed ethics, pure theoretical ethics and practical ethics, separate interiority and exteriority relative to the individuated being because, for the ethics of contemplation, individuation is considered anterior to the moment in which becoming-conscious is achieved and, for practical ethics, as always posterior to this moment; theoretical ethics is a perpetual nostalgia for the individuated being in its purity, just as practical ethics is an ever renewed preparation for an ever deferred ontogenesis; neither of the two can grasp and accompany being in its individuation. However, if individuation is considered as conditioned by the internal resonance of a system and can effectuate itself fractionally by way of successive constitutions of metastable equilibria, we can neither accept *an ethics of the being's eternity*—which seeks to consecrate a structure that is discovered once and for all as definitive and eternal (one that is consequently an eminently respectable structure, the first and last term of reference, a structure that translates itself into norms that are absolute like it)—nor accept *a perpetual evolution of the ever-moving being* that becomes and changes continually throughout all the mobile circumstances that condition action and incessantly modify the norms according to which action must develop in order to accompany this ongoing evolution.

The notion of a successive series of metastable equilibria[12] must be substituted for this stability of the unconditional absolute and this perpetual evolution of a fluid relativity. Norms are the lines of internal coherence of each of these equilibria, and values are the lines according to which the structures of a system translate themselves into the structures of the system that replaces the former system; values are that through which the norms of a system can become the norms of another system through a change of structures; values establish and make possible the transductivity of norms, not as a permanent norm that is nobler than the others—for it would be quite difficult to discover a norm that was already truly given—but as a meaning of the axiomatic of becoming conserved from one metastable state to the next. Values are the capacity of amplificative transfer contained in the system of norms, i.e. they are norms led to the state of information: they are what is conserved from one state to another; everything is relative, except the very formula of this relativity, a formula according to which a system of norms can be converted into another system of norms.[13] Surpassing the system in its given form, normativity itself can be considered as value, i.e. as that which passes from one state to another. Taken one by one, the norms of a system are functional and seem to exhaust their meaning in this functionality; but their system is more than functional, and this is why it is value. It could be said that value is the relativity of the system of norms and is known and defined within the system of norms itself. In order for the normativity of a system of norms to be complete, it is necessary that within this very system its own destruction as a system and its possibility of translation into another system must be predicted according to a transductive order. That the system knows its own relativity within itself, that it be formed according to this relativity, that its own metastability be incorporated into its conditions of equilibrium: such is the path according to which the two ethics will have to coincide. The tendency toward eternity then becomes the awareness of the relative, which is no longer a will to halt becoming or to make an origin absolute and to grant a normative privilege to a structure, but the knowledge of the metastability of norms, the awareness of the meaning of transfer that the individual qua individual has. The will to find absolute and immutable norms corresponds to this veridical feeling according to which there is something that must not be lost and which, surpassing adaptation in becoming, must possess the power to guide becoming. But this guiding force that is not lost cannot be a norm; such a search for an absolute norm can lead only to a morality of wisdom as separation, withdrawal, and leisure, which is a way of mimicking eternity and timelessness within the becoming of a life: during this time, vital and social becoming continues, and the sage becomes a sage-figure, he plays the role of a sage in his century as one who watches life pass and the passions dwindle; if he is not of that century, at least his role as a man who is not of the century is indeed in becoming. Wisdom is not universalizable, because it does not assume the whole of becoming, and because it transforms becoming into a mythical representation; like wisdom, sainthood or the other styles of individual life are extreme terms that illustrate the poles of moral life, but not the elements of moral life; on the basis of wisdom, sainthood, or any moral attitude of this type, the moral life cannot be recreated by combination, since there is no preoccupation of universality in these lifestyles that are taken as absolute and are nevertheless not universalizable; they require contemporary life in front of them in order to be what they are: they require a basis of contemporary life that they can negate. A veritable ethics would be one that accounted for contemporary life without becoming numb in the contemporaneity of this life, which should define through norms a meaning that surpasses them. Furthermore, moralities quite generally attempt to fill in this interval between that through which a morality has value and the tendency to fall back (starting from principles of value) onto the norms discovered in contemporary life; but the act of linking between foundations and norms is often arbitrary and poorly formed; it is ethics in its center that is faulty; there is also a central dark zone in this domain between form and matter, between principle and consequences. Values would have to be not above norms but across them as the internal resonance of the network they form and as their amplificative power; norms could be conceived as expressing a definite individuation and consequently as having a structural and functional meaning on the level of individuated beings. On the contrary, values can be conceived as linked to the very birth of norms,[14] which expresses the fact that norms emerge with an individuation and last as long as this individuation exists as an actual state. The plurality of systems of norms can consequently be envisioned otherwise than *as a contradiction.* There is no contradiction arising from the *multiplicity of norms,* except if one makes of the individual an absolute and not *the expression of an individuation* that creates a merely provisional and metastable state as a discontinuous phase of transfer.

Considered as harboring a non-individuated reality within it, the being becomes a moral subject insofar as it is the association of an individuated reality and a non-individuated reality; to want to grant primacy to being insofar as it is individuated or to being insofar as it is not individuated is to oppose norms (which are relative to the individuated being within a system) to values (which are relative to the non-individuated reality associated with the individuated being). Morality is neither in norms nor in values but in their communication grasped *in its real center*. Norms and values are the extreme terms of the being's dynamic, terms which do not consist in themselves and are not sustained in the being by themselves. There is no problem of the relation of values to norms, of the opposition of open morality and closed morality, but a problem of the phase-shift of ethics. A retroactive illusion makes it seem like historical progress progressively opens ethics and replaces closed moralities with open moralities: each new state of a civilization contributes opening and closing based on a single center; opening and closing are the dimension of an indefinite, unidimensional, and bipolar dyad. Every act, every functional structuration, tends to spread out into norms and values according to a correlative couple. Norms and values do not exist prior to the system of being in which they appear; they are becoming, instead of appearing in becoming without being part of becoming; there is a historicity of the emergence of values, just as there is a historicity of the constitution of norms. Ethics cannot be recreated based on norms or based on values, no more than the being can be recreated based on the forms and matters to which abstractive analysis reduces the conditions of ontogenesis. Ethics is the requirement according to which there is a significative correlation of norms and values. To grasp ethics in its unity requires that one accompany ontogenesis: ethics is the meaning of individuation, the meaning of the synergy of successive individuations. It is the meaning of the transductivity of becoming, the meaning according to which in each act there is both movement to go further and the schema that will integrate into other schemata; it is the meaning according to which the interiority of an act has a meaning in exteriority. To postulate that the interior meaning is also an exterior meaning, that there are no deserted islands in becoming, no eternally self-enclosed regions, no absolute autarchy of the instant, is to affirm that each activity has a meaning of information and is symbolic relative to life as a whole and to the totality of lives. There is ethics to the extent that there is information, i.e. signification overcoming a disparation of elements of beings, thus making it such that what is interior is also exterior. The value of an act is not its universalizable nature according to the norm that it implies, but the effective reality of its integration in a network of acts that becoming is.[15] This in fact concerns a network and not a chain of acts; the chain of acts is an abstract simplification of the network; ethical reality is indeed structured in a network because there is a resonance of acts with respect to one another, not by way of their implicit or explicit norms, but directly in the system that they form, i.e. the being's becoming; the reduction to norms is identical to the reduction to forms: it only involves one of the extreme terms of the real. The act is neither matter nor form, it is becoming in the process of becoming, it is being to the extent that this being is, by becoming. The relation between acts does not pass through the abstract level of norms, but it goes from one act to other acts just as one goes from yellow-green to green and yellow by increasing the bandwidth of frequencies. The moral act is one that can spread out, phase-shift into lateral acts and link up with other acts by spreading out from its single active center. Far from being the encounter of a matter and a form, of an impulse and a norm, a desire and a rule, an empirical reality and a transcendental reality, the moral act is this reality that is more than unity and that spreads out from itself on both sides by joining with other realities of the same type; to reprise Malebranche's formula concerning freedom, according to which man is said to have movement to always go further, it could be asserted that the free act, or the moral act, is one that has enough reality to go beyond itself and encounter other acts.[16] There is only a *center* of the act, there are no *limits* of the act. Each act is centered but infinite; the value of an act is its breadth, its capacity of transductive expansiveness. The act is not a unity in the path toward an end, which would imply a concatenation. An act that is only itself is not a moral act. The act that is a unity, that consists in itself, that does not radiate outward and that has no lateral bands, is effectively one, but it is inserted into becoming without belonging to becoming, without completing this phase-shift of being that becoming is. The act that is more than unity, that cannot reside and consist only in itself but also resides and is completed in an infinity of other acts, is an act whose relation to other acts is signification and possesses the value of information. By taking generosity as the foundation of morality, Descartes revealed this power of the act to extend beyond itself. But, since he wanted to found a provisional morality, i.e. a morality that only looks ahead, he did not indicate the retroactive force of the act, which is just as important as its proactive force. Each act takes up the past again and encounters it anew; each moral act resists becoming and does not allow itself to be covered over as past; its proactive force is that through which it will always belong to the system of the present, able to be evoked again in its reality, extended, taken up again by an act, later on according to the date, but contemporaneous with the first act according to the dynamic reality of being's becoming. Acts construct a reciprocal simultaneity, a network that does not allow itself to be reduced by the uni-dimensionality of the successive. An act is moral to the extent that it has, by virtue of its central reality, the power to eventually become simultaneous with respect to another act. The non-moral act is lost within itself, an act that is covered over and covers over a part of the subject's becoming: it is that which achieves a loss of being according to becoming. The non-moral act introduces a rift into the being that will prevent it from becoming simultaneous with respect to itself. If it exists, the immoral act is one that destroys the significations of acts that have existed or that will be able to be called on to exist, and, instead of being localized within itself like the non-moral act, the immoral act is an act that introduces a schema of confusion preventing other acts from structuring into a network. In this sense, the immoral act is not an act properly speaking, but like the inverse of an act, a becoming that absorbs and destroys the relational significations of other acts, that drags them into false paths of transductivity, that misleads the subject with respect to himself: the immoral act is a parasitic act, a false act that draws its semblance of signification from a random encounter. Such is aestheticism as counter-morality, the unification of acts according to a certain shared style and not according to their power of transductivity.[17] Aestheticism is a parasite of moral becoming; it is the creation of abstract forms within the existence of the subject and the illusion of unification according to these abstract forms. Aestheticism, which wants ever new acts, deceives itself in a certain sense and becomes an iteration of novelty according to the extrinsic norm of novelty; in the same way, conformism or perpetual opposition to social norms is a resignation facing the characteristic of the actuality of acts and a flight into a style of iteration according to a positive form of coincidence or a negative form of opposition with respect to a given. Iteration expresses the tendency of an act to dominate all becoming, instead of linking up with other acts; the non-moral or immoral act is one that, because it does not involve a relative inadequacy to itself and attempts to become perfect within its own limits, can only be recommenced and not continued; this act is egoistic in itself relative to other acts; it has a tendency to persevere in its being, which makes it such that it is excised from other acts, is not penetrated by them, and cannot penetrate them but only dominate them; any moral act harbors a certain internal organization that situates it and limits it as an act: it develops according to a certain partially inhibitive regulation that inserts its existence as an act into a network of acts. The act in which there is no longer this index of the totality and possibility of other acts, the act that provides itself with an aseity despite the genetic character of its emergence as a phase of becoming, the act that does not receive this measure (which is both activating and inhibitive and arises from the network of other acts), is the wild or crazed act, which in a certain sense is identical with the perfect act. Such an act is one in which there is no longer the presence of this pre-individual reality that is associated with the individuated being; the wild act is one that tends toward a total individuation and no longer admits anything as real except what is totally individuated. Acts are networked to the extent that they are considered on a ground of nature, the source of becoming via continued individuation. This wild or crazed act remains with only an internal normativity; it consists in itself and sustains itself in the vertigo of its itera-tive existence. It absorbs and concentrates within itself all emotion and all action, makes the different representations of the subject converge toward it, and becomes a unique point of view: every solicitation of the subject calls for the iteration of this act; the subject is reduced to the individual as the result of a single individuation, and the individual is reduced to the singularity of a perpetually recommencing *here and now* and is displaced everywhere like a being detached from the world and from other subjects by abandoning its role of transfer.

Ethics is that through which the subject remains subject, refusing to be-come an absolute individual, a closed domain of reality, or a detached singu-larity; it is that through which the subject remains in an ever-charged internal and external problematic, i.e. in a real present, living on the central zone of being, neither wanting to become either form nor matter. Ethics expresses the meaning of perpetuated individuation, the stability of becoming, that of the being as pre-individuated, individuating, and tending toward the con-tinuous that reconstructs in an organized form of communication a reality as vast as the pre-individual system. Across the individual—understood as the amplificative transfer emerging from Nature—societies become a World.

Notes

FOREWORD

1. On this subject, see J. F. Marquet, "Gilbert Simondon et la pensée de l'individ-uation," in *Actes du Colloque de la Cité des Sciences*, ed. Bibliothèque du Collège international de philosophie (Paris: Albin Michel, 1994).

2. Gilbert Simondon, *On the Mode of Existence of Technical Objects*, trans. Cecile Malaspina and John Rogove (Minneapolis: Univocal Press, 2017).

3. Maurice Merleau-Ponty, *The Visible and the Invisible*, trans. Alphonso Lingis (Evanston, Ill.: Northwestern University Press, 1968), 235. [Translation slightly modified—Trans.]

4. If the original publication date of *The Visible and the Invisible* (1964) seems to indicate that Gilbert Simondon has not read the above cited note such as it was written in this work, we should take care to note that Gilbert Simondon was clearly well aware of the spirit of radical reform of philosophical principles developed by Merleau-Ponty in his courses and conversations and that he could only confirm his own personal undertaking, which arose from a related meditation on the pre-individual order of the world. This would explain the homage of the dedication.

5. This long meditation on the pre-Socratic thinkers was recorded in a text titled "Histoire de la notion d'individu" that was until now unedited and is published here in the complements section (of the French edition). This work of extreme original-ity, whose critical dimension and style of questioning concern our modernity, can-not be measured by an ideal of philological and historical commentary, which wasn't the author's purpose. Instead, it is a matter of an open dialogue that ties this philos-opher to the thinkers that have modeled, since the origin of occidental thought, our categories and our attitudes of thought and that always remain in present conversa-tion with our contemporaneity.

6. See the first paragraph of the Introduction of the present work.

7. Duns Scotus, *The Ordinatio of Blessed John Duns Scotus*, book2, 177.

8. Aristotle, *Metaphysics*, Z, 13: 1038b, 10–11.

9. Werner Heisenberg, *The Physicist's Conception of Nature,* trans. Arnold J. Pomerans (London: Hutchinson & Co., 1958). Werner Heisenberg, *Physics and Beyond,* trans. Arnold J. Pomerans (New York: Harper Collins, 1971). On this subject, also see J. Garelli, *Rythmes et mondes* (Grenoble: Jérôme Millon, 1991).

10. Infra., 4.

11. Infra., 4.

12. "The Ancients only knew stability and instability, rest and movement, but they did not know metastability.... It is therefore possible to define this metastable state of being, which is quite different from stable equilibrium and rest, and which the Ancients couldn't establish in the search for the principle of individuation because they lacked a clear physical paradigm that could clarify its utilization." Infra., 5.

13. Infra., 5–6.

14. Infra., 8.

15. Infra., 15.

16. We have shown elsewhere in numerous poetic and pictorial examples how phenomena of internal resonance are deployed in systems created by images and the play of lines, masses, and colors. See J. Garelli, *Rythmes et mondes,* section IV and J. Garelli, "L'Entrée en Démesure," in *Epokhè,* no. 5 (1995).

17. See our phenomenological description of Pieter Breughel the Elder's painting "Mad Meg" in J. Garelli, "L'Entrée en Démesure."

18. Heisenberg, *The Physicist's Conception of Nature.*

19. Heisenberg, *Physics and Beyond,* 41.

20. Infra., 6.

21. Infra., 6.

22. Infra., 6.

23. Infra., 6.

24. Infra., 6.

25. Infra., 6.

26. Infra., 6.

27. See the titles of the sections, chapters, and paragraphs appearing in the new edition that allow us to immediately situate the methodological stakes of this discussion whose philosophical and epistemological consequences are major.

28. J. Garelli, *Rythmes et mondes.* J. Garelli, "Irréductibilité et Plétérologie," *Epokhè,* no. 3 (1993). J. Garelli, "L'Entrée en Démesure."

29. Martin Heidegger, "Seminar in Zähringen," in *Four Seminars,* trans. Andrew J. Mitchell and François Raffoul (Bloomington: Indiana University Press, 2003).

30. *Being and Time. The Basic Problems of Phenomenology. What Is a Thing? On Time and Being.* We have analyzed these texts at length in J. Garelli, *Rythmes et mondes,* section III.

31. This demonstration was developed at length in J. Garelli, *Rythmes et mondes,* J. Garelli, "L'Entrée en Démesure," and J. Garelli, "Irréductibilité et Hétérologie."

INTRODUCTION

1. [Particularly in the framework of Aristotle's thought, the *súnolon* is the term used to designate the concrete individual insofar as it is a composite of form and matter. —Trans.]

2. Furthermore, the milieu may not be simple, homogeneous, or uniform, but it can be originally suffused by a tension between two extreme orders of magnitude that the individual mediates when it comes to be.

3. And the constitution of a mediating order of magnitude between two extreme terms; ontogenetic becoming itself can in a certain sense be considered as a mediation.

4. [Anterior redaction: "In order to define metastability, we must include the notion of the information of a system based on these notions and particularly on the notion of information that physics and pure modern technology leaves us with (notion of information conceived as negentropy), as well as the notion of potential energy, which takes on a more precise meaning when it is combined with the notion of negentropy."]

5. The ancients had intuitive and normative equivalents of the notion of metastability, but this concept is mostly indebted to the development of the sciences because metastability generally supposes both the presence of two orders of magnitude and the absence of interactive communication between them.

6. [This phrase was removed from the 1964 edition.]

7. Homeostasis and Ashby's homeostat.

8. It is through this introduction that the living being performs informational work, thereby itself becoming a node of interactive communication between an order of reality that is superior to its dimension and an order of reality that is inferior to it and which it organizes.

9. This interior mediation can intervene as a relay with respect to the external mediation that the living individual brings about, which is what allows the living being to make a cosmic order of magnitude (for example, luminous solar energy) and an infra-molecular order of magnitude communicate.

10. In particular, the relation to the milieu shouldn't be considered before and during individuation as the relation to a singular and homogeneous milieu: the milieu itself is a *system,* a synthetic grouping of two or several levels of reality without intercommunication before individuation.

11. By this, we mean to say that the *a priori* and the *a posteriori* are not found in knowledge; they are neither the form of knowledge nor its matter, for they are not knowledge but the extreme terms of a pre-individual and consequently pre-noetic dyad. The illusion of *a priori* forms proceeds from the preexistence of *conditions of totality* within the pre-individual system whose dimension is superior to that of the individual undergoing ontogenesis. Inversely, the illusion of the *a posteriori* stems from the existence of a reality whose order of magnitude, in terms of spatiotemporal modifications, is inferior to that of the individual. A concept is neither *a priori* nor *a posteriori* but *a praesenti,* insofar as it is an informative and interactive communication between that which is greater than the individual and that which is smaller than it.

12. This affirmation does not lead to contesting the validity of the quantitative theories of information and the measures of complexity, but it does suppose a fundamental state (that of pre-individual being) anterior to any duality of emitter and receiver and therefore to any transmitted message. What remains of this fundamental state in the classical case of information transmitted as a message is not the source of information but the primordial condition without which there is no effect of information and therefore no information: this condition is the metastability of the receiver, whether it be a technical being or the living individual. This information can be called "first information."

13. In particular, the plurality of orders of magnitude and the primordial absence of interactive communication among these orders involve such a comprehension of being.

14. On the contrary, the dynamism of the transductive operation expresses the primordial heterogeneity of two scales of reality, one which is greater than the individual (the system of metastable totality) and the other of which is smaller than it, like matter. Between these two primordial orders of magnitude, the individual develops via an amplifying process of communication, the most primitive mode of which is transduction and which already exists in physical individuation.

15. Internal resonance is the most primitive mode of communication between realities of different orders; it contains a twofold process of amplification and condensation.

16. This operation parallels that of vital individuation: a plant institutes a mediation between a cosmic order and an infra-molecular order, storing and distributing the chemical natures contained in the soil and in the atmosphere by means of the luminous energy received in photosynthesis. It is an inter-elementary node, and it develops as the internal resonance of this pre-individual system composed of two layers of reality initially without communication. The inter-elementary node performs an intra-elementary labor.

17. Form therefore appears as active communication, the internal resonance that operates individuation: it appears with the individual.

1. Form and Matter

1. In other words, between the reality of an order of magnitude (which is superior to the future individual and contains the energetic conditions of the molding) and the matter-reality (which is, grain by grain in its availability, of an order of magnitude inferior to that of the future individual, the real brick).

2. Thus, the mold is not just the mold but the end of the inter-elementary technical chain, which consists of vast ensembles that envelop the future individual (worker, workshop, press, clay) and contain potential energy. The mold totalizes and accumulates these inter-elementary relations, just as prepared clay totalizes and accumulates the molecular intra-elementary interactions of the aluminum hydrosilicates.

3. This energy expresses the macroscopic system state that contains the future individual; its origin is inter-elementary; however, it enters into interactive communication with each of the matter's molecules, and it is due to this communication that the form emerges contemporaneously with the individual.

4. Thus, the individual is constituted through this act of communication that occurs within a society of particles in reciprocal interaction, i.e. between all the molecules and the action of molding.

5. Although this energy is a state energy, an energy of the inter-elementary system; the communication between orders of magnitude consists in this interaction between two orders of magnitude on the level of the individual as an encounter of forces; this communication is due to a singularity, which is the principle of form and initiator of individuation. The mediating singularity is the mold here; in other cases, in nature the stone can be the initiator of the dune or gravel can be the germ of an island in a river depositing alluvia: the singularity exists on the intermediate level between the inter-elementary dimension and the intra-elementary dimension.

6. In this instant, matter is no longer pre-individual matter or molecular matter but already individual. The potential energy that is actualized expresses an inter-elementary system state vaster than matter.

7. This reciprocity causes a perpetual energetic availability: in a very limited space a considerable amount of work can be carried out if a singularity primes a transformation in that space.

8. These real singularities, which are the occasion of a shared operation, can be called *information*. Form is a device *[dispositif]* for producing them.

9. It only manifests the singularities of the *here and now* that constitute the conditions of the information of its particular molding, which include the wear and tear of the mold, pebbles, irregularities, etc.

10. The individuality of the brick, that through which this brick expresses a certain operation that has existed *here and now*, envelops the singularities of this *here and now*, prolongs them, and amplifies them; however, technical production seeks to reduce the margin of variability or unpredictability. The real information that modulates an individual seems like a parasite; it is that through which the technical object remains inevitably natural to a certain extent.

11. This implicit form, which is an expression of the old singularities of the growth of the tree (and through them, the expression of all types of singularities: the action of the wind, of animals, etc.), becomes information when it guides a new operation.

12. Implicit forms are information in the operation of form-taking: here, these forms are ones that modulate the activity and partially direct the tool, which is overall controlled by man.

13. The most perfect technical operation (producing the most stable individual) is the one that makes use of singularities as information in form-taking, like wood cut with the grain. This does not require the technical gesture to remain close to the microphysical level of a particular singularity, because when they are utilized as

information, singularities can act on a larger scale by modulating the energy contributed by the technical operation.

14. They are information, the capacity to modulate different operations in a determinate way.

15. The mold is a device *[dispositif]* for producing an information that is always the same for each molding.

16. [This passage was removed from the 1964 edition.]

17. While the system is in a state of metastable equilibrium, it is able to be modulated by singularities and is the theater of processes of amplification, summation, and communication.

18. Neither form nor matter are strictly intrinsic, but the singularity of the allagmatic relation in a state of metastable equilibrium, the individual's associated milieu, is immediately bound to the birth of the individual.

19. [*Conata* translates to "exertion, struggle, desire," and the entire phrase roughly translates: "struggle is in vain" or "without results".—Trans.]

20. On the other hand, this reality consists of orders of magnitude that are different from that of the individual and of the singularity that initiates it, such that the individual plays a mediating role in relation to the different orders of reality.

21. [This passage was removed from the 1964 edition.]

2. FORM AND ENERGY

1. Also, potential energy is therefore linked more generally to the superior order of magnitude of a system considered in its large differentiated, separated, and hierarchized ensembles.

2. These conditions are sufficient by themselves to initiate a transformation: a pendulum that is drawn back from its equilibrium position and tied up cannot oscillate before it is released.

3. Except in the particular ideal case of completely reversible transformations in which entropy remains constant.

4. It could be said that energy has passed from a *formal system* of supports (an order of dimensions superior to that of the theater of transformations, i.e. the bullet) to a *material system,* which involves a dimensional order inferior to that of the theater of transformations, i.e. the different molecules of the bullet.

5. It should be noted that the formation of new crystals within the prismatic crystal occurs on a scale smaller than that of the prismatic crystal, which then plays the role of an initial milieu and of a surrounding system that contains the formal conditions of becoming in its structural state. Here, the form is the macrophysical structure of the system insofar as it energetically conditions future transformations.

6. This gradual propagation constitutes the most primitive and fundamental mode of amplification (amplifying transduction) that borrows its energy from the milieu within which the propagation takes place.

7. The imposed temperature belongs to the formal conditions of each subset of the system and defines in each subset the presence or absence and degree of a potential energy.

8. The substance's nature is what contains the material conditions, particularly by determining the number and type of the different systems of individuation that could develop there. In this sense, the energetic state of a substance is a pairing of formal and material conditions.

9. This is why the individual can play a role of singularity when it enters into a system in a state of metastable equilibrium and initiates an amplifying structuration.

10. [The bracketed text has been removed from the 1964 edition and replaced by the fifteen preceding lines.]

11. As in every operation of modulation, three energies are present: the strong potential energy of the amorphous substance in a metastable state, the slight energy borne by the crystalline germ (modulating energy, information), and finally an energy that pairs the amorphous substance and the crystalline germ, which is confused with the fact that the amorphous substance and the germ form a physical system.

12. This polarizing function, due to which each new layer is also a singularity that plays a role of information for the contiguous amorphous matter, explains amplification through transductive propagation.

13. The relation between the germ and the amorphous substance is an information process of the system.

14. The saturation of a solution perhaps creates a polarity on the microphysical level that renders the amorphous substance sensitive to the action of the crystalline germ. Supersaturation is in fact a physicochemical constraint that creates a metastability.

15. [This bracketed passage has been removed from the 1964 edition and replaced by the two preceding lines.]

16. [This phrase roughly translates to "a third something" in the Platonic dialogues.—Trans.]

17. [*Phthorá* means "corruption" or "passing away" and is terminologically in opposition to genesis.—Trans.]

18. [The *metrion* is that which is well-measured.—Trans.]

19. A relation made possible by the existence of an analogical rapport between the amorphous substance and the structural germ, which amounts to saying that the system constituted by the amorphous substance and the germ contains information.

20. Jean Wyart, *Cours de Cristallographie pour le certificat d'Études Supérieures de Minéralogie* (Paris: Centre de Documentation Universitaire), 10.

21. In nature, these imperfect individuals are often formed by a crystal around which an amorphous substance is deposited under certain conditions (snow, fog). The conditions of formation of these imperfect individuals are comparable to the conditions of supersaturation: the formation of rain or snow can be deposited by distributing crystals into a saturated air.

3. Form and Substance

1. [This chapter, which appeared in the original dissertation (1958), was removed in 1964 for the first publication. Only the pages on "Topology, chronology and order of magnitude of physical individuation" were kept.]

2. [*Sphairos* is Parmenidean Being and mostly designates an undifferentiated amorphous matter that is devoid of all internal differences.—Trans.]

3. ["The tranquil shrines of philosophy," a paraphrase of one of Lucretius's lines of poetry.—Trans.]

4. [This phrase can be found in Plutarch and Pseudo-Plutarch, and roughly refers to the "constructive fire that breaches the whole."—Trans.]

5. [*Autarkos kai apathos* roughly translates to "self-sufficient and dispassionate."—Trans.]

6. [This phrase comes from the *Enchiridion* of Epictetus and designates "that which is not in our power."—Trans.]

7. Text cited by Arthur Haas in *Wave Mechanics and the New Quantum Theory*, trans. L. W. Codd (London: Constable, 1928).

8. [This adjective describes "of sea-purple" and "of true colored dye" and therefore shows the tendency to see the color of the sea as purple, which is on the shortest wavelength end of the visible spectrum, rather than green or blue.—Trans.]

9. [Founded in 1946, this organization served to facilitate the probability of assured communication for the use of short wavelengths at a given time and for a given frequency.—Trans.]

10. Louis de Broglie, *Ondes, corpuscules, mécanique ondulatoire* (Paris: Albin Michel, 1945), 18–19.

11. [*Kainologia* refers to a usage of new or invented language or phraseology.—Trans.]

12. Yves Rocard, *Electricité* (Paris: Masson, 1966), 360.

13. Stéphane Lupasco, *Le Principe d'antagonisme et la logique de l'énergie. Prolégomènes à une science de la contradiction* (Paris: Hermann & Co., 1954), 41–42.

14. Louis de Broglie, *Ondes, corpuscules, mécanique ondulatoire*, 33–34.

15. *Ondes, corpuscules, mécanique ondulatoire*, 35.

16. *Ondes, corpuscules, mécanique ondulatoire*, 39.

17. *Ondes, corpuscules, mécanique ondulatoire*, 73.

18. Louis de Broglie, "Communication faite à la séance de la Société Française de Philosophie" (paper presented at the annual meeting for the Société Française de Philosophie, Paris, France, April 25, 1953).

19. "Communication faite."

20. Louis de Broglie, "La mécanique ondulatoire et la structure atomique de la matière et du rayonnement," *Journal de Physique* 8, no. 4 (1927): 225.

21. Louis de Broglie, "La physique quantique restera-t-Elle indéterministe?" *Société Française de Philosophie, Bulletin* 4 (October–December 1953): 146.

22. "La physique quantique," 147.

23. "La physique quantique,"148.

24. "La physique quantique,"156.

25. "La physique quantique,"156.

26. [Cited in English in the original text.—Trans.]

27. "La physique quantique,"150.

28. Haas, *Wave Mechanics and the New Quantum Theory*, 161.

29. In this case, the communication between orders of magnitude (here each nucleus and the total population of nuclei) is insufficient.

30. In an arrangement like this, it can be said that an individuation is produced the moment when the system can *diverge*, i.e. can receive information.

1. Information and Ontogenesis

1. "Measure" here is taken in the sense of "estimation of levels": it is a matter of evaluating levels, and therefore a question of a quantum measure, not of a continuous quantitative measure.

2. In this way, termites construct the most complex edifices of the animal kingdom, despite the relative simplicity of their nervous organization: they almost act as a single organism by working in a group.

3. This would be true if we considered the physical world as matter and as substance; but this is no longer true if we consider it as containing systems where potential energies and relations exist, which are supports of information. Materialism does not take information into account.

4. This resonance is the active analogy or pairing of non-symmetrical terms that exists in a system undergoing individuation, like between the crystalline germ and the solution.

5. In this sense, it can be said that there is a relation of information between the species and the milieu in the natural system.

6. For example, in polyps.

7. This does not mean that there are beings who merely live and beings who live and also think: it is probable that animals sometimes are in a psychical situation. It just means that these situations that lead to acts of thought are less frequent in animals. Since humans have access to more extensive psychical possibilities particularly due to the resources of symbolism, they call upon the psyche more often; what is exceptional for humans is the purely vital situation, wherein humans feel most helpless. But this does not involve a nature or an essence that provides a foundation for an anthropology; a threshold has simply been crossed: the animal is better equipped to live than to think, and man is better equipped to think than to live. But animals and humans both live and think, either in a typical or exceptional way.

8. This disparation is what is treated as information and what makes the psyche appear.

9. Which supposes three levels of composition: organism, organ, and cell.

10. This relation is amplificative, for a colony can emit several individuals capable of generating a complete colony.

11. [From this point on, we have opted to translate the author's use of *instinct* as "drive" in order to bring it in line with the way in which Freud's concept *Trieb* is generally translated today. The reader should also keep the notion of "drive" in mind when the author uses the adjective "instinctual."—Trans.]

12. Which, in the individual, is the expression of discontinuity, of the original singularity translated into behavior, and which is essentially the instrument of the amplificative capacity through the transductive propagation that characterizes individuation.

13. This expression is often used by Freud, especially after the First World War.

14. From this point of view, it would be interesting to consider superior animal forms as arising from the *neotenization* of the inferior species in which the stage of individual life corresponds to the function of amplificative reproduction, whereas the stage of life *in colonies* corresponds to the continuous, homeostatic aspect. In superior species, individuals are ones that live in society: the two stages and the two manners of being become simultaneous.

15. An approximation can be made between the plurality of stages of the individual's development (larva, nymph, and imago) and the individual-colony alternation.

16. Étienne Rabaud, *Zoologie biologique* (Paris: Gauthiers-Villars, 1934), 4: 475.

17. Perhaps the change of this rapport would have to be seen in the initial expression of the process of amplification that is prolonged in reproduction. (Perhaps the initial expression of the process of amplification that persists in reproduction would have to be seen in the change of this rapport.)

18. Rabaud, *Zoologie biologique*, 4: 486.

19. *Zoologie biologique*, 4: 487.

20. *Zoologie biologique*, 4: 489.

21. *Zoologie biologique*, 4: 491–92.

22. Here, the individual particularly seems like what corresponds to conditions of crisis, discontinuity, transfer, and amplification through remote propagation, which implies risk, mobility, concentration, and provisional independence with respect to nourishment, autonomy, and temporary freedom. This rapport between the individual and the colony is similar to that of the seed to the plant.

23. [The Greek word for heap is "sorites," and this is why in philosophy the paradox of the heap is also known as the sorites paradox.—Trans.]

24. *Zoologie biologique*, 4: 492.

25. This fact, which is very important theoretically, could contribute to supporting the hypothesis presented above of a *neotenization* as the condition of an individuation.

26. *Zoologie biologique*, 4: 510.

27. *Zoologie biologique*, 4: 511.

28. For this reason, a seed must be considered as an individual, since it bears a specific, complete message and is endowed for a time (generally several years) with an absolute autonomy.

29. This expression "information signals" is used to maintain the difference between information properly speaking (which is a system's manner of being that supposes potentiality and heterogeneity) and information signals, which are called information in general, although they are merely an unnecessary instrument of information and particularly develop when the parts that form a system are distanced from one another, as is the case in a macroorganism or in a society.

30. A centripetal information signal is a type of signal that involves the sense organs. A centrifugal signal is one that incites a reaction, a posture, or a gesture.

31. A macroorganism can have localized individualities: reflexes, reaction of the skin's pigmentation to ultraviolet rays, local horripilation, and local defense reactions against a microbial invasion.

32. *Zoologie biologique,* 4: 517.

33. [The terms "homophyseal" and "heterophyseal" *(homophysaire* and *hétero-physaire)* are neologisms for translating these concepts from the French biologists Biard and Rabaud. Homophyseal is an adjective that describes living beings growing together within the same symbiotic complex, while heterophyseal describes living beings growing on their own within the same symbiotic complex.—Trans.]

34. This term is mostly used for plants, but it can be used to designate the morphological regression of the constituents of the heterophyseal complex.

35. Indeed, the more well-adapted and vigorous the parasite is, the more it damages and diminishes its host, since it does not respect the host's functional autonomy. If the parasite develops too much, it winds up destroying its host and can then destroy itself, just as mistletoe kills the tree on which it settles.

36. Green algae carry out the chlorophyllic synthesis and provide nourishment for the fungus by decomposing carbon dioxide in the air. The fungus retains humidity and attaches the lichen on the support; it provides water for the green algae.

37. This is the case of the male crab parasited by the sacculina.

38. This association remains in reproduction (in what can be called the strictly individuated stage of the lichen): in fact, lichens reproduce through the spores of the fungus whose mycelium will surround the green seeds of the algae. This type of reproductive unity, the soredium, is the equivalent of a seed.

39. In the lichen, the fungus is like an exterior milieu for the green algae (which are algae that develop on rocks or humid earth), and the algae give to the fungus the food that it could only find in a vegetal milieu, since it lacks chlorophyll.

40. For example, supercooling.

41. The capacity of the individual to found a colony and thus to transport an effective information is similar to this.

42. See the international colloquium of the National Center for Scientific Research on the polarization of matter, April 1949.

43. This representation also applies fairly well for the continuous functions of a colony; but it does not express the discontinuous characteristic or the characteristic of information and the amplifying role of the individual.

44. This word is borrowed from the psycho-physiological theory of perception; there is disparation when two twin ensembles that are not completely superposable, such as the left retinal image and the right retinal image, are grasped together as a system, allowing for the formation of a single ensemble at a higher degree that integrates all their elements due to a new dimension (for example, in the case of vision, the layering of depths of field).

45. [English in the original.—Trans.]

46. The process of integration and constructive amplification is not necessarily continuous; when the individual founds a colony, when the larva becomes a nymph, when the soredium settles and yields a lichen, the individual transforms, but the amplification remains.

47. Ontogenesis itself can therefore present itself as an amplification; the action of the individual toward itself is the same as toward the exterior: it develops by constituting a colony of subsets within itself via reciprocal interlacing.

48. Through its differential usage, sensation supplies plurality, the non-compatibility of data, the problematic capacity that carries information. Perceptive integration can only be carried out through construction, which generally implies an effective motor response, the amplification of the sensorimotor universe.

49. It could therefore be said that the essential function of the individual is the activity of amplification, whether it exerts this activity within itself or transforms into a colony.

50. In other words, according to this doctrine, the generative pair of disparation is the individual-world rapport, not a duality the individual would bear within itself initially.

51. [This phrase literally means "the mind's fluctuation, vacillation, or hesitation" and can be found specifically in Spinoza's manner of characterizing the psychical tension in a simultaneity of affects. See Spinoza's *Ethics* Part III, Proposition XVII and its corresponding scholium for the direct use of this term.—Trans.]

52. In this sense, growth is a form of amplificative action. It can be the only action possible for certain living beings, like plants.

53. Moreover, the totality of each of these worlds is not that different from the totality of the others due to qualitative and structural differences; the key points are not organized according to exactly superposable networks; similarly, in monocular images, the right image and the left image are grasped from different *points of view*, which in particular creates a difference of perspectives.

54. One of the greatest merits of Lamarck is to have considered evolution as an incorporation into the individual of effects randomly supplied by the milieu (like the nourishment conveyed by currents of water, then integrated due to vibrating cilia), which carries out an amplification of the zone of the living being.

55. Inversely, individuation is not the only vital reality. In the strict sense, individuation is in some manner a provisional, dramatic solution of urgency. And yet, because it is directly linked to a process of neotenization, individuation is the root of evolution.

56. [*Apeiron* can be traced back to the Greek pre-Socratic philosopher Anaximander, and it literally means that which is "without limit" and is chiefly used in a cosmological sense to describe a principle that organizes primordial chaos. Aristotle takes up this conception attributed to Anaximander in his *Physics*.—Trans.]

57. [The word "charge" here should be taken in the multiple senses in which Simondon has used it throughout the work, specifically in the sense of the charge of the pre-individual milieu. The etymological sense of the word "charge" is related to

the words "cargo" and "carry" and relates not only to notions of loads or burdens but also to that of potentials.—Trans.]

58. An analogous phenomenon occurs in the case of the plant: an old tree can continue to grow, but if one if its large branches breaks, the tree does not manage to recover the equilibrium of its structure; however, its foliage continues to grow regularly; a young tree that experiences a break reorients its growth and recovers its verticality, and one of its lateral branches that was previously diageotropic then becomes ortho-geotropic.

59. *World as Will and as Representation,* vol. 1, book II.

60. This applies in the case of species that do not produce a colony. When the individual founds a colony, it is the colony that corresponds to its maturity and its achieved action.

61. [The usage of the word "actual" and its variations should be taken in its double meaning in French, which is that of "current, contemporaneous, present (in time)" and in the more traditional philosophical sense of "actual" as opposed to "potential" or "virtual."—Trans.]

62. The individual is a solution for problems of discontinuity through discontinuity. Continuity is reestablished in the collective.

63. It is because there is no simple unity (substance) that the individual seeks to found a colony or to be amplified in the transindividual. The individual is a problem because it is not the whole of life.

64. [English in the original.—Trans.]

65. There is only information when that which emits signals and that which receives them form a system. Information is between two halves of a system in a relation of disparation. This information does not necessarily pass through signals (for example in crystallization); but it can pass through signals, which allows for realities distant from one another to form a system.

66. [Here the words "come forth" and the following phrase "to come" all relate to the French word *avenir,* which means "future" as a noun and "to come (to)" as a verb.—Trans.]

2. Psychical Individuation

1. Gestalt theory does not establish the essential distinction between an *ensemble,* the unity of which is structural and not energetic, and a *system,* a metastable unity consisting of a plurality of ensembles between which there is a relation of analogy and an energetic potential. The ensemble does not possess information. Its becoming can only be that of a degradation, an augmentation of entropy. On the contrary, the system perseveres in its metastable being due to the activity of information that characterizes its systemic state. Gestalt theory has taken for a quality of totalities, i.e. ensembles, what is in fact a property that only systems possess; yet systems cannot be *totalized,* since the fact of considering them as a sum of their elements ruins the awareness of what makes them systems: the relative separation of the ensembles they contain, analogical structure, disparation, and the relational

activity of information in general. What is at the basis of the nature of a system is the type of information it contains; however, information (relational activity) cannot be quantified abstractly but solely characterized in reference to the structures and schemata of the system within which it exists; information shouldn't be confused with information signals, which can be quantified but which wouldn't be able to exist without a situation of information, i.e. without a system.

2. The 1958 manuscript here included the following specifications: "The spider bothers us because it has no apparent polarity: we do not know where its head is; this also applies to the snake, an animal which coils around itself and reorients at any moment. A simple form like that of the cross bothers us because it proposes several polarities all at once; it is the very image of this plurality of polarities. The circle in certain conditions can produce the same effect, if it is large enough with respect to the subject to not be perceived as a small localized object but as an indefinite plurality of directions: for example, this is the case of a cylindrical tunnel. A square should be a better form than a rectangle; in fact, if a choice is given to subjects between squares and rectangles of different lengths for an invariable width, a preference for rectangles is revealed: this is because the rectangle is oriented: it has a length and a width."

3. In fact, the number of decisions diminishes when contrast is sharper: if there is nothing but an image in black and white, there will only be two possible states for each physical unit of surface; if there are various nuances of grey, there will be a large number of possible states, i.e. decisions.

4. The scrolling of a magnetic tape at high speed is the equivalent of the perception of a photograph from a great distance.

5. Only the degree of probability of the appearance of this form can be taken into account; good forms are finite in number, whereas unspecified assemblages can be indefinitely varied. But it is only through the intermediary of a possible coding that implies a low number of decisions that the good form is easy to transmit. In the case of lines, a very simple coding consists in reducing the number of possible states to two: black and white. It is in this sense that a pencil sketch is easier to transmit than an image in various tones of gray.

6. Already in the reflexes of perception accommodation, one finds both functionings that increase the quantity of signals (convex lens) and others that orient the living being and selectively privilege interesting signals: fixation, the ocular scanning of a moving object.

7. Simple heterogeneity without potentials cannot instigate a becoming. Granite consists of heterogeneous elements (quartz, feldspar, mica), and nevertheless it is not metastable.

8. This word is here taken in the sense that physics gives it, particularly in the theory of energy exchanges between an oscillator and a resonator.

9. Because it was part of a system, it was one of the real symbols existing with respect to another system: an information existed *in the system between the living individual and the milieu,* which is not the case for the physical individual.

10. The heir is indeed also a double of the contemporary, a symbol with which the contemporary is reciprocal. The heir, a symbol in the future, fills in the absence of being that the symbol of the past contains. In certain primitive groups, the last-born receives the name of the last person to have died.

11. [Simondon here is using the English word to correspond with the meaning of "average" in the above sentences. The italics are his.—Trans.]

12. Emotion modulates psychical life, whereas affection intervenes only as a content.

13. We take this word in the Platonic sense of σύμβολα [súmbola] (the two pieces of a broken stone) that reconstitute the original whole object when they are brought back together again to authenticate a relation of hospitality.

14. For example, recall the incomprehensible suicide of Georges Eastman, an American engineer who worked on photographic apparatuses, invented roll film in 1886, and founded the Eastman Kodak company in 1888. See P. Rousseau, *Histoire des techniques et des inventions*, p. 421.

15. In particular, we can recall the recent development in the theory of quarks.

3. COLLECTIVE INDIVIDUATION AND THE FOUNDATIONS OF THE TRANSINDIVIDUAL

1. Cf. *The Two Sources of Morality and Religion*.

CONCLUSION

1. To this extent—for the living being—pre-individual reality is *also* post-individual reality; the individualized phase is a transfer between two types of colony phases.

2. It could even be said that there is a complementarity of the individual phase and the colony phase. With the complex forms of vital organization and due to neotenization, these phases come closer together within the collective.

3. It is only starting from this middle—which is also an optimum—that one can establish measurements (for example that of the coefficients of spectral lucidity) with respect to the minimum of the mechanical equivalent of light, which is measured for the best specific luminous efficacy.

4. Physical individuation is considered here as an individuation that jumps the gun, i.e. that does not sufficiently remain in suspense at its origin; vital individuation would be like a dilation of the inchoate stage that makes possible an organization, a deepening of the extreme beginning.

5. This amounts to saying that there is no possible definition of becoming as amplification if we do not suppose an initial plurality of the orders of magnitude of reality.

6. This center consisting of the being is that of the communication between orders of magnitude—which are molar and molecular, inter-elementary and intra-elementary; starting from this center, a rapid and iterative individuation produces a physical reality; a decelerated, progressively organized individuation produces the living being.

7. Furthermore, it supposes an absence of communication between several orders of magnitude; individuation intervenes as an amplifying mediation through a becoming.

8. And an origin of the individual, a pre-individual situation.

9. It could also be said that the being transfers a problem, that it transports the possibility of an amplifying activity. It tends toward an entelechy that is not limited to its personal reality, for it is a condensed mode of the real and tends toward a phase of amplification.

10. To the same extent, the individual, which emerges from a communication between initially isolated orders of magnitude, carries the message of their duality and then reproduces the ensemble through amplification. Information conserves the pre-individual within the individual.

11. This is the condition of communication, which is found first at the moment of individuation and a second time when the individual amplifies itself into the collective.

12. The individual qua individual, which is distinct from the colony and the collective, emerges from a singularity and has a sense of discontinuity; but this discontinuity is amplifying and *tends* toward the continuous through a change in order of magnitude.

13. A system of norms is problematic, like two images in a state of disparation; it tends to resolve itself within the collective through constructive amplification.

14. Values are the pre-individual of norms; they express the attachment to different orders of magnitude; arising from the pre-individual, they turn toward the post-individual, either in the form of the colony phase or in that of the transindividual for superior species. They come from the continuous and again find the continuous by way of the individual, i.e. discontinuous transfer.

15. In other words, the amplification through which it finds the dimension of the continuous by inserting into the becoming of the colony or the reality of the collective; although according to norms it is an act of the individual, according to values it is an act toward the collective.

16. In other words, one that contains within itself a power of amplification.

17. Aestheticism causes the same loss of information as abstract knowledge. Thus, in order to form the comprehension of the species, it only retains what the individuals have in common between them.

Bibliography

This bibliographical list, which was included in the initial doctoral thesis, was not part of the originally published edition in 1964. It includes only scientific and technical references and not ancient or more recent philosophical texts that have already been included into the history of thought.

de Broglie, Louis. "Communication faite à la séance de la Société Française de Philosophie." Paper presented at the annual meeting for the Société Française de Philosophie, Paris, April 1953.

de Broglie, Louis. *Ondes, corpuscules, mécanique ondulatoire*. Paris: Albin Michel, 1945.

de Broglie, Louis. *Physique et microphysique*. Paris: Albin Michel, 1945.

Réunions d'études et de mises au point tenues sous la Présidence de Louis de Broglie. *La cybernetique. Théorie du signal et de l'information*. Paris: Éditions de la Revue d'optique théorique et instrumentale, 1951.

Dalcq, A. M. "Nouvelles données structurales et cytochimiques sur l'œuf des mammifères." *Revue générale des Sciences* 61, nos. 1–2 (1954).

Doucet, Yves. *Les aspects modernes de la cryométrie*. Mémorial des Sciences Physiques. Paris: Gauthier-Villars, 1954.

Gesell, Arnold. "L'ontogénèse du comportement de l'Enfant," in *Manuel de Psychologie de l'Enfant*, ed. L. Carmichaël. Paris: P.U.F., 1952.

Goldstein, Kurt. *La structure de l'Organisme*. Paris: Gallimard, 1951.

Haas, Arthur. *La mécanique ondulatoire et les nouvelles théories quantiques*. Paris: Gauthier-Villars, 1930.

Heisenberg, Werner. *La physique du noyau atomique*. Paris: Albin Michel, 1954.

Kahan, Theo, and Bernard Kwal. La mécanique ondulatoire. Paris: Colin, 1953.

Kubie, Lawrence S. "The Neurotic Potential and Human Adaptation." Paper presented at the Sixth Cybernetics Conference, New York, March 1949.

Lewin, Kurt. "Le comportement et le développement comme fonction de la Situation totale," in *Manuel de Psychologie de l'Enfant*, ed. L. Carmichaël. Paris: P.U.F., 1952.

Portmann, Adolf. *Animal Forms and Patterns*. London: Faber and Faber, 1952.

Rabaud, Étienne. "Sociétés humaines et sociétés animales." *Année psychologique* (1951).

Rabaud, Étienne. Zoologie biologique. Paris: Gauthiers-Villars, 1934.

Wiener, Norbert. *Cybernetics: Or Control and Communication in the Animal and the Machine*. Paris: Hermann et Cie; Cambridge, Mass.: The Technology Press; New York: John Wiley and Sons; 1948.

Wiener, Norbert. *Cybernétique et Société*. Paris: Deux-Rives, 1952.

Conference on Cybernetics: Transactions of the Sixth Conference, 1949. Ed. Heinz Von Foerster. New York: Josiah Macy, Jr. Foundation, 1950.

Conference on Cybernetics: Transactions of the Seventh Conference, 1950. Ed. Heinz Von Foerster. New York: Josiah Macy, Jr. Foundation, 1951.

Conference on Cybernetics: Transactions of the Eight Conference, 1951. Ed. Heinz Von Foerster. New York: Josiah Macy, Jr. Foundation, 1952.

Colloque International du Centre National de la Recherche Scientifique sur la polarisation de la matière, Paris, April 1949.

GILBERT SIMONDON (1924–1989) was a philosopher of technology and knowledge, of ontology, and even of moral philosophy and ethics. The breadth of his intellectual inquiry spanned a variety of disciplines at the forefront of the fields of technology, cybernetics, and psychology, during the 1960s. His work engages in a radical discussion with that of Karl Marx, Martin Heidegger, Henri Bergson, and Maurice Merleau-Ponty, as well as with ancient philosophy. His principal publications inspired the work of several generations of thinkers including Gilles Deleuze, Herbert Marcuse, and Jean Baudrillard, and continue to find a large readership in contemporary discussions in philosophy of technology, media theory, and aesthetics, among other fields. His works *On the Mode of Existence of Technical Objects* and *Two Lessons on Animal and Man* are available from the University of Minnesota Press.

TAYLOR ADKINS is a translator of contemporary French philosophy. He has translated the work of Gilbert Simondon, Félix Guattari, and François Laruelle, among others.

JACQUES GARELLI (1931–2014) was a French-language poet and philosopher. Among his wide-ranging list of works include *Le poétique de la gravitation* and *Rythmes et mondes: au revers de l'identité et de l'altérité*.